Praise for Cathleen Miller's *Champion of Choice*

"Cathleen Miller's *Champion of Choice* is a rigorous yet eloquent account of Dr. Sadik's inspirational career and a beautiful and long-awaited tribute to one of the greatest women's advocates of the twentieth century. The issues to which Dr. Sadik has so passionately dedicated her life are becoming only more salient as our global community strives to protect both our people and our planet, and Dr. Sadik will certainly remain an invaluable and unequaled leader in this field for years to come."—**TED TURNER,** UN Foundation founder and chairman and founder of CNN

"Nafis Sadik is one of the most courageous women of our time. She has bravely confronted all opponents of women's reproductive rights from Pope John Paul II to Islamic fundamentalists. Her story will inspire human rights defenders worldwide."—**FRANCES KISSLING,** former president of Catholics for a Free Choice

"I think now the things that Nafis stands for, most women would say absolutely right—good woman—but that's to underestimate how brave she had to be starting off thirty years ago when most people weren't saying any such thing."—**CLARE SHORT,** former member of Parliament, United Kingdom

"Nafis has been the scourge of the men in robes."—**NICOLAAS BIEGMAN,** ambassador to the United Nations from the Netherlands

"A strong believer in women's equality, the articulate and forthright Sadik has guided policy on improving the status of women in the developing countries while fighting to contain the population explosion."—**MARY ANN SIEGHART,** political columnist, *London Times*

"Here's a woman who has a very clear sense of what she wants to do. I would not like to be on the other side of the table negotiating with her." —**TIMOTHY E. WIRTH,** president of the UN Foundation

"Nafis Sadik was a remarkable manager who was focused and possessed charm, wit, and strength. Most importantly, she delivered in an area of tremendous difficulty."—**MECHAI VIRAVAIDYA,** former cabinet minister, Thailand

CHAMPION OF CHOICE

CHAMPION
OF CHOICE

THE LIFE AND LEGACY OF
WOMEN'S ADVOCATE NAFIS SADIK

Cathleen Miller

UNIVERSITY OF NEBRASKA PRESS | LINCOLN AND LONDON

Publication of this volume was assisted by the
Virginia Faulkner Fund, established in memory of
Virginia Faulkner, editor in chief of the University
of Nebraska Press.

All photos are courtesy of Nafis Sadik and are
reprinted with her permission.

Library of Congress Cataloging-in-Publication Data
Miller, Cathleen.
Champion of choice : the life and legacy of
women's advocate Nafis Sadik / Cathleen Miller.
pages cm
Includes bibliographical references and index.
ISBN 978-0-8032-1104-9 (cloth: alk. paper)
1. Sadik, Nafis. 2. Women social reformers—
Pakistan—Biography. 3. Women physicians—
Pakistan—Biography. 4. Family planning—Developing countries. 5. Reproductive rights—Developing countries. 6. Women's health services—Developing countries. I. Title.
HQ1745.5.Z75S236 2013
305.42092—dc23 [B]   2012035075

Set in Garamond Premier Pro by Laura Wellington.
Designed by A. Shahan.

This book on courageous and smart women,
a tribute to the power of sisterhood,
is dedicated to my sister, Susan Miller Vollmer.

CONTENTS

ILLUSTRATIONS

INTRODUCTION

The first time I ever saw Nafis Sadik, I had the same reaction countless others have probably had: *who on earth is that woman*? I was in Manhattan working on *Desert Flower* when I noticed this older Pakistani lady, around sixty; she stood at the front of the room at a United Nations reception wearing a colorful blue print sari, its fabric draped gracefully over one shoulder. Diamond pavé earrings the size of dimes peeked from beneath her dark pageboy. I watched her receiving guests, and she seemed to know everyone. When it was my turn to be introduced, I remember being transfixed by her eyes, the likes of which I'd never seen before—enormous black pupils surrounded by a pale blue ring—all the more outstanding for being set in her dark complexion. The eyes stared back at me with a type of unflinching scrutiny that made me squirm.

Never did I dream that within a few years I would be writing about those eyes and scrutinizing every aspect of *her*. When Dr. Sadik retired from the United Nations, I took the opportunity to write her biography, the tale of how she became what the London *Times* calls "one of the most powerful women in the world." The year I embarked on this journey was 2001, and little did I know that yoking myself to Nafis Sadik's life was a bit like handcuffing myself to a racing fire engine.

Throughout the book I have sought to fulfill what I believe are the innate desires of readers of biography: to learn about the lives of others so we may solve the problems of our own lives. By emulating the success of the subject, we hope to skip the painful trial-and-error lessons and jump to the head of the class where we can build on what we have learned from the hero or heroine's path. In the case of Nafis I identified one powerful lesson as her upbringing, and one of the subtexts to this work is what I call "the primer on how to raise your daughter to be a world leader." Also in recounting Nafis's story I've taken special effort to transmit the "how-to," just in case you yourself have aspirations to change history.

Two challenges that emerged as I delved into the project were (1) by virtue of what Dr. Sadik does for a living, her colleagues are scattered throughout the galaxy; and (2) much of the work she and her colleagues do is abstract to most of us. Certainly in the United States we have a blissfully limited knowledge of problems like obstetric fistula. To kill both these birds with a single shotgun blast, I organized a trip around the world to interview Nafis's family, friends and professional associates, an amazing experience that afforded me the opportunity to meet some of the great minds of our time.

During this trip I also sought out women and girls who could speak firsthand about the issues on which Nafis has worked her entire life, and have included brief profiles of them. These accounts are the Vignettes that I have sandwiched between the chapters of Sadik's life. In their design I chose to give the reader a peek into what goes on while getting these stories, to take you into the moment with me so you are able to visit with these women as I did.

A word on some of the other stylistic elements I've used in the writing of this book. The information contained herein is predominantly from interviews I conducted with individuals; in many cases the sources have recounted tales that I have passed along for the reader. I have not created stories, but I have cleaned up the dialogue to make it more palatable for a literary work. The only artistic license

I've taken is in a few instances I have imagined what went on in an individual's mind, and these portions I've rendered in italics. In a few cases I have indicated where I changed an individual's name to protect her privacy.

When I launched into this project, the United Nations was under attack for a variety of reasons: George Bush had just defunded the United Nations Population Fund (UNFPA) for aiding coercive abortions in China, the UN weapons inspectors were vilified as inept for locating no weapons of mass destruction in Iraq, and an assortment of wags were calling the UN irrelevant for being incapable of solving the planet's ills. As these claims mounted, I admit to being quite concerned about what I would find during the course of researching Nafis's career, and if it was horrible, wondering how I would deal with that reality. What would I do if I discovered the agency's work was a sham—or worse yet, UNFPA was involved in eugenics, ethnic cleansing and forced sterilizations as some critics claimed? I decided I would just have to keep an open mind and do the legwork to find out the truth.

As I embarked on this mission and collected stories for the Vignettes, I noticed a pattern, a sort of narrative arc that would begin in the women's victimization, and then they would transform that experience into advocacy. I have let this pattern of transition come through in the book's structure. All but one of these resilient females have soldiered on and have made a decision to rise above their circumstances to better their own lives. Many have chosen to use their energy to benefit the lives of others as well.

Another phenomenon emerged during my travels. I would land in a different country each week, and through the web of connections—UN contacts, Nafis's associates, nongovernmental organizations, the media, and friends of my own—the word would spread about my book and the research I came to do. Then even when I wasn't working—that is, recording interviews—women began to tell me their stories. Whether I was talking to the cream of Karachi society at a cocktail party or chatting with a fellow traveler at my Buenos Aires hotel, when they learned what I was writing about they voluntarily opened up and shared their own tales of violence, rape, incest, abortion. With a growing dread I began to wonder if every female on earth carried a cruel secret of abuse. The profound importance of Nafis Sadik's work came into focus: her insistence that governments address the plight of women and stop accepting their suffering as the inescapable lot of "the weaker sex."

CHAMPION OF CHOICE

1 BIRTH

On a table, in the lantern light, a mother writhed in labor. She was an Indian housewife in her thirties, and she was surrounded by other women, some relatives, some strangers, who tried to assist in the birth of her baby. As she strained, the helpers crushed into the room in the oppressive August heat, sealing off the small servants' quarters that had been turned into a delivery room.

On the other side of the door another type of birth was taking place—but this delivery involved millions. The year was 1947 and the creation of a new republic, Pakistan, was tearing the British Raj in two as the friction raged into a civil war. As the subcontinent was divided into two nations based on religion, the rioting in the Indian capital forced Muslims to flee to the Pakistani High Commissioner's home for safety. This estate, located in a fashionable district of New Delhi, sheltered around five thousand people as the siege outside the garden walls continued.

The baby—oblivious, of course, to the war that had brought his mother into this stranger's home, and to the timing of thousands of people dying outside its protective confines—chose this moment to be born. As he struggled through the birth canal, one of the women called out, "Where is that chit of a girl, the one who's studying to be a doctor?"

They were referring to Nafis Shoaib, the self-appointed bathroom monitor, who had taken it upon herself to stand outside the toilet door and limit how long each woman spent inside. She cut off chunks of soap and parceled them out, rationed the toilet paper, and insisted that each user clean the facilities before her exit. During her introduction to medical school, Nafis had learned some things about creating a sanitary environment; now she seized an opportunity to put this knowledge into practice. Her rationale was that one must impose some order in this time of chaos. Otherwise, conditions in this private home, which was never designed to accommodate thousands of people, would quickly devolve from unpleasant to unsanitary, and shortly they would have an internal health crisis on their hands to accompany the calamity on the streets created by warring factions of politics and religion.

Nafis hailed from an upper-class Indian family; they had arrived in Delhi the week before when her father, Mohammad Shoaib, was summoned from Calcutta to assist in the formation of the fledgling Islamic state. Mohammad had planned to relocate his family to Delhi as he represented Pakistan on the Joint Properties Commission. He would help the commission cleave the subcontinent into two separate nations.

The economist was respected as an intellect and an independent thinker, and yet family members felt there was one area where he required their counsel: they had advised Mohammad not to let his daughter become a doctor. He had ignored this warning, and at eighteen she had already completed one year of medical school. However, Nafis's studies to date had been textbook theories of physiology and anatomy, and her patient examinations had been confined to the dead. Dissecting frogs and memorizing cell structures had not prepared her for the messy reality of delivering a baby in the sweltering confines of this estate-turned-refugee-shelter.

The pregnant woman's sister went to fetch the medical student, and the crowd of attendants parted to let Nafis enter the room. The doctor-to-be was slender, with short wavy black hair combed back from her face and smooth caramel-colored skin. A black mole created a punctuation mark on the right side of her strong nose. But upon meeting Nafis, all these traits receded into the background because the viewer was mesmerized by the cobra-like quality of her hooded eyes. The black pupils were the size of dimes, surrounded by a ring of icy blue—the type of heavy-lidded eyes suggesting mystery and veiled seduction, the type of eyes that had gazed from the images of goddesses in Indian art for millennia. The eyes Radha used to lure the god Krishna. Needless to say, on any given day Nafis was quite sure of herself, but on this particular night she faced a challenge about which even she had misgivings.

When she entered the room, the patient was in the advanced stages of labor, breathing hard. One group of women set about to boil a pot of water, which became its own production; someone brought the liquid in a small container, and to heat it another attendant located wood to build a fire. During this lengthy process Nafis didn't have the heart to ask what the boiled water was for. She knew that in the movies a helpful soul always shouted, "Boil some water!" whenever a woman went into labor, but she had never understood why. However, her attention was drawn away from this quandary by her patient, who lay moaning on the table.

On August 15, 1947, after nearly two hundred years of colonial rule, the British had relinquished their control of the subcontinent. At midnight in New Delhi, the nation's capital, a member of the Constituent Assembly blew a conch shell in the traditional Hindu salute to the dawn, signaling a free India. Later that morning ceremonies took place at the Red Fort, an ancient red sandstone fortress where Lord Mountbatten, King George's cousin and the colony's last viceroy, handed Prime Minister Nehru the reins of government. Outside, the half million citizens jamming the streets of a newly independent India went wild in celebration. The colors of the nation's freshly minted flag—orange, white, and green—painted the city, adorning everything from bullock's horns to tricolored saris to horses' legs.

As part of the process to vacate India, the British had created a separate Muslim nation called Pakistan, hoping this solution would assure order after their departure. In Delhi a provisional government gathered to handle the difficult task of apportioning the land and assets of one of the world's most populous nations into two individual states. A line running north to south through the Punjab would divide the Asian subcontinent: west of the border Muslims would reside; to the east, Hindus and Sikhs. But when independence was trumpeted that August morning, the process of sorting the masses based on religion had just begun.

As millions of people looked at being displaced, tensions between the factions exploded. Feelings were exacerbated by the forced uprooting of millions from ancestral homes and the loss of their livelihoods and entire way of life. Rioting swept through the capital like the summer monsoon rains, as Sikhs, Hindus, and Muslims murdered one another.

Jawaharlal Nehru, the newly appointed Indian prime minister, sequestered the Muslims inside the High Commissioner's walled estate in an attempt to protect them from violence. Armed soldiers guarded the perimeter of the post–art deco house on Harding Avenue, a white boxy structure fronted by mullioned windows that emphasized the rigid angles of the facade. The men slept on the manicured grounds, catnapping under the lush tropical foliage while they prepared to ward off attack. Inside the house every inch of floor space—from the foyer, rising up the grand spiral staircase to the attic—was covered by blankets where the women and children slept, and more Islamic refugees continued to arrive each day. Rumors of impending raids swirled through the frightened island of Muslims trapped in the rioting city.

However, that evening the women in the servants' quarters had other concerns to occupy their attention, as their patient's labor advanced. At age thirty, the woman had already borne several children, and as she pushed, she instructed Nafis on the delivery, calling directions from the table. Soon blood and amniotic fluid flooded the floor of the cramped space. An elder assisted by holding the lantern at the foot of the table so the light shown between the mother's legs, and Nafis could see the baby's crowning head. Within the hour an infant had made his debut into the world, and Nafis held a straight razor in the lantern flame to sterilize the blade. The yellow light glinted off the steel as she sliced the umbilical cord, thereby parting mother and child.

Eighteen years before this night Nafis herself had been born into a privileged family outside Varanasi. At the time her mother, Iffat Shoaib, was still a mere girl, with a waterfall of flowing black hair and sad doe eyes rimmed by thick lashes. She had returned to her husband's ancestral estate at Jaunpur to have her baby—a pattern she would repeat for future deliveries.

The tradition in India was to return to your own *amma*, the Urdu term for "mother," when your due date was near, so that she could act as midwife. But Iffat's mother had died giving birth to her, so the girl was already familiar with the shared pain and joy of childbirth. Instead of returning to her own home in the United Provinces for her delivery, she came to stay with her father-in-law, Mohammed Abdulla, the patriarch of the Shoaibs. He had built an estate where several generations lived together, and this is where his granddaughter Nafis entered a family formerly devoid of girls. And where she immediately became the darling of the entire clan.

Later her father was posted with the Indian Civil Service in Calcutta, and as she matured there, the precocious child knew that she wanted "to do something." This vague notion was unusual for a female of her era, including the Shoaibs' social circle, where it was assumed that all girls would become wives and mothers. Her brother, Kemal, could recall no precedents; in this early stage there were no role models for Nafis's goals. "We didn't know any women who were professionals, let alone doctors."

Nevertheless, in Nafis this fantasy "to do something" gradually solidified into a formidable ambition. "I considered many professions: becoming a tennis pro, a singer, an engineer. This last option prompted me to take advanced math and physics courses, until I decided that this career choice wasn't very exciting. Engineering wasn't going to change the world," she concluded matter-of-factly. "I didn't know what I was going to do. In those times I remember vaguely thinking, 'I'm going to help the poor.'" Then after much consideration, she determined medicine was her true calling.

But when she began to seriously consider becoming a physician, Kemal remembered that their extended family was "amazed that any woman would want to be anything other than a housewife. You grew up, got married, and you had your life through your husband—not any other way. That's the way our family and most families here on the subcontinent were. And when Nafis declared that wasn't her way, it created a real furor." However, while her father thought the plan unusual, he was quite pleased at the news that his daughter had ambitious goals for her education, and he became her strongest supporter.

The nuns at Loretto College, her convent school, became the next obstacle when they advised her father against this career path. "Nafis should study literature," Sister John the Baptist informed Mr. Shoaib. However, once his decision had been made, the sisters acquiesced. And although they had been opposed to the idea of Nafis becoming a physician, they readily set about to prepare her with the requisite science courses, even bringing in a biology professor from outside the school, as they didn't have anyone on staff qualified to prepare Nafis for this challenge.

When the sisters awarded their star pupil a scholarship, Nafis's father in turn gave the money directly to his daughter. "You earned it," he explained. With so much cash in her purse, the girl suddenly felt quite important, and being a sports aficionado, she used her windfall to buy tennis rackets for the entire family.

The young Nafis's energy bubbled up like an artesian well, fueling her academic and athletic prowess, her preternatural curiosity, and her numerous rebellions and intrigues. It seems the girl's desire for experimenting with new things extended beyond the classroom. When Mohammed and Iffat's oldest child announced that she was volunteering to teach English and poetry at the orphanage, her parents readily agreed. They were astounded by her commitment to get up at 5:00 a.m. and report for this duty each morning before school. The plan was that the Shoaibs' chauffeur would drive their daughter to the orphanage, wait for Nafis to finish her work with the children, and then take her on to the convent for her own classes. But what her parents didn't know was that their daughter conducted a daily assignation with their driver.

Once the car was out of sight of the family home, the thirteen-year-old would instruct him to pull over, and she would slide behind the wheel. It was rare for women to drive a car in India, and certainly unheard of for a teenage girl. But Nafis convinced the chauffeur to teach her how to negotiate the early-morning traffic and swore him to secrecy about her plot. Years later these clandestine driving lessons would be put to good use as she maneuvered her Jeep along rutted dirt roads, providing health care to women in remote mountain villages.

As she matured, Nafis formed other schemes beyond learning how to drive. Through her father's role in the creation of Pakistan, his daughter was familiar with the great optimism surrounding the formation of the Islamic state. There was a lot of excitement in the air about the new nation, and so Nafis, ever the instigator, informed her Muslim friends that they must also contribute. How they were going to contribute at the age of fifteen or sixteen remained to be seen. But in order to participate in the action, she evolved a plan: "We must teach all the women first aid in case of emergency." Problem: none of the girls knew any first aid, so they had to learn it themselves before they could impart this wisdom. Admittedly this step slowed down their momentum, but undaunted, Nafis followed with another directive: "And we must do exercise, and become physically fit." This phase lasted for about a month; every morning PT—physical training—was attended by about ten or fifteen women. Some participants were quite obese and out of shape, but during the jumping jacks their ebullient leader shouted to them all the same: "We've got to be fit—fit for Pakistan!"

Familiar with her pattern of fierce yet fleeting passions, Nafis's extended family hoped that one casualty would be her plan to become an obstetrician. They were appalled by the notion of the girl becoming a doctor. "What's this—you expect her to work?!" the aunts and uncles exclaimed to her parents, a degrading consideration for women of their class. "You know in medical school she's going to learn *everything*," they whispered, a reference to what would surely be an encyclopedic knowledge of sexual matters. Friends and relatives also warned that the long years of study would place the girl in a terrible predicament. Tradition held that brides married at sixteen or seventeen, and by the time she finished her training at twenty, who would want her? Her father informed his advisers: "Nafis is not your daughter, and it's not your decision. It's mine." During this time he fielded numerous marriage proposals for his determined teenager, and to all of these offers he replied, "Certainly not."

But in the process of these repeated discussions, Nafis's mother grew concerned. She didn't want her daughter to become an old maid by waiting until twenty to accept a husband, and appealing to the girl's weakness, she cajoled her with a promise: "Now give up this medical school business and I'll buy you lots of clothes and jewelry."

But Nafis still insisted she wanted "to do something," and she was quite unconcerned about her prospects for marriage. "Amma, I'll become a doctor and buy my own clothes and jewelry," she reasoned to her mother.

At fifteen Nafis took the examinations at the convent to graduate from high school. As was the tradition, the nuns sent the tests back to Cambridge University to be graded, and their pupil waited nervously for the results. Several weeks went by and they didn't come, but since the year was 1944 and World War II dominated daily life back in England, some delays were to be expected. Nafis was convinced, however, that there was another explanation: "I felt sure I'd failed and the nuns couldn't bear to break the news to me." Eventually even her father became concerned. When the scores finally arrived, Nafis learned she'd ranked as one of the top students in India, no small feat in a country of its size, and jubilation at the news spread through her parents' social circle.

But unbeknownst to her, while Nafis planned for college, her uncle was busy matchmaking. He had decided her academic triumph provided the perfect opportunity to arrange a marriage for her. When the Shoaibs went to visit Mohammed's brother for the holidays, Nafis overheard her uncle saying that a promising matrimonial prospect was coming from out of town to meet her parents. Furious that after years of effort to achieve her goals, her success was now being used as fuel on the pyre to immolate her dreams, Nafis created such a scene that it left her entire family speechless. Her father announced it would be best for them to leave, much to the shock of his brother and sister-in-law; and with that the family departed and returned to Calcutta. There was no more talk of finding a husband for Nafis.

Her best friend, Shamsa Ahmed, was a fellow student at Loretto College, and her father was an ophthalmologist at the local Muslim hospital, Islamia. There were very few Muslim children in the convent school, and the two girls had become fast friends. Besides their religion, they shared being the eldest sibling in their family.

The two girls graduated from the convent together and took their Cambridge exams. Nafis was fifteen at the time. While she and Shamsa awaited their test results, they embarked on a course of typing and shorthand—skills they calculated would help them at medical school. Two other students joined them, and a fifth young woman, the niece of Mirza Abol Hassan Isphahani, was their teacher. Mr. Isphahani was a great friend of Mohammad Ali Jinnah, a pivotal figure in world history. The two men had become acquainted at law school in London when they became involved in a political party called the Muslim League, a group that advocated the creation of an Islamic nation separate from India. When Jinnah later became the first president of that nation, he would earn the epitaph Quaid-e-Azam, a term that means "great leader." But at this point, a fragile, tubercular Jinnah traveled throughout India to raise support for his plan for an independent Pakistan. Tall, skeletally thin, with a gaunt, alert face, he wore his signature karakul hat fashioned from tightly curled lamb's wool and cut a striking figure as he toured the country in an open white Packard. He arrived in Calcutta to great fanfare and was staying at the home of Isphahani when the determined shorthand/typing crew learned of his arrival. Eager for an introduction to Jinnah, they pestered their teacher until she arranged the meeting at her uncle's home.

The five girls trooped in to meet the leader, and as Shamsa recalled: "So, we went in and Mr. Jinnah said, 'Nice to meet you young ladies. What are you planning to do in the future?' He told us that he had visited an Islamic hospital that morning, but had only found one Muslim doctor. He was unaware that he was referencing my father, who was the superintendent of Islamia. Then Mr. Jinnah asked us, 'If tomorrow we get Pakistan, who will care for our ladies?' You know, he was so dignified, and the way he spoke was so convincing, that when we came out, my sister, Nafis, and myself, all three of us agreed about the importance of going into medicine."

What the political leader knew was that Muslim women would not want to be attended by a male physician. Whatever doubt had remained in the minds of these girls was gone, as they now saw their professional calling linked to the future success of their new Islamic nation.

While the rest of their friends talked of getting married, Nafis and Shamsa talked of becoming doctors. However, the next stumbling block was the exams for admission to get into medical school, particularly the requirement to write an essay for intermediate science in Urdu. While Nafis spoke the language at home, most of her formal schooling had been conducted in English. She worried that her Urdu wasn't sophisticated enough to live up to the family tradition of excelling on exams. She decided plagiarism was the solution, and she found four general essays that could be used to answer a variety of possible test questions. Then she memorized them in Urdu, word for word. This trick won her an honors distinction on her scores.

Armed with these results, Nafis and Shamsa anxiously applied to Calcutta Medical College, a large academy with hundreds of students. "It wasn't easy to get into this school," Nafis remembered. As part of the application process, Mr. Shoaib accompanied his daughter to interviews, to make sure she was treated fairly. Thanks to her glowing exam results, she was readily accepted. Nafis and Shamsa continued to live at home under the watchful eyes of their parents, matriculating together at seventeen.

Shamsa recalled their reaction at visiting the cadaver room for the first time: "We went in and were so—I won't say horrified, but stupefied—that there were these dead bodies lying on the table. They didn't look human, because you know they were shrunken and blackened and they had dye injected into them to make it easy for our dissection classes. Then I got the shock of my life on the first day of our dissection. I found the senior students kept their sandwich boxes on the same table as the cadavers. I just didn't understand how they could dream of eating while they were doing their work."

Being two of ten females enrolled in medical school (versus two hundred men), and the only Muslim women, Shamsa and Nafis stuck together on all things—including their disinterest in a male population that seemed exceedingly interested in examining them.

During that first year at Calcutta Medical College, while Nafis focused on her studies with a laser-like intensity, she learned that not all the other incoming students were equally suited for the rigors of this institution's training. For example, in histology class one of the other female students fainted every time she tried to prick her own finger to provide blood for a lab assignment. Her fingertip never even came into contact with the needle; she just passed out at the mere approach. Some of the boys keeled over during their first time in the operating room. Other students got queasy at the rumors that circulated on the history of the cadavers they dissected. The pranksters concocted macabre stories as they split open an abdomen or poked about a skull. Nafis took it all in stride.

She was simply grateful that her parents had been progressive enough to let her become a doctor. Whenever friends and family asked, "Is Nafis settled?" (a common question in this part of the world meaning "Is she married with children?"), Nafis would think impatiently: "Of course I'm settled. I'm settled at school." This sentiment demonstrates a character trait that would serve the doctor all her life: an ability to bore into the task at hand with a singular diamond-tipped devotion, while she ignored distractions and criticism. The opinions of others bounced off the protective armor of her self-assurance like inconsequential flotsam offered up by an interfering world. She earned the admiration of many and a reputation for hubris among others; however, she scarcely noticed. Nafis was too busy forging ahead to pause and wait for approval.

Back at the Pakistani High Commissioner's crowded home on that hot August night in Delhi, the budding obstetrician's first delivery was a success. Both mother and child were healthy, living to worry about surviving in a city in the throes of a civil war.

Along with their fellow Muslim refugees, Nafis, her parents, and younger siblings remained under siege at the estate. Until they could be safely dispersed, Prime Minister Nehru sent rations into the compound to feed the amassed thousands. Meanwhile, the family's baggage and furniture gathered dust at the airport; although their belongings had arrived safely, it was unsafe for the Shoaibs to collect them.

After two weeks Nafis's father was able to move the family into their own home and attempted to return to his work with the Joint Properties Commission. But throughout August and into September, rioting in the Hindu capital continued to escalate.

As the monsoon clouds gathered overhead, gangs roamed the streets, sprayed machine-gun fire through courtyards, and set buildings ablaze. They worked themselves into such a frenzy that they were soon ripping doors off hinges, then hacking and beating to death the children and old people inside as they ran for their lives.

The violence was not one-sided. Muslims retaliated in kind; having lost their homes, businesses, and loved ones, many had nothing left to live for. While the torrential monsoons flooded the subcontinent, a growing tidal wave of brutality spread outward from Delhi, providing a man-made counterpart to the natural disaster. Within a matter of months, an estimated one million people were murdered during Partition.

By October Nehru felt that the only safe course was for all Muslims to evacuate India; he could no longer guarantee protection, even to the diplomatic corps charged with creating the Pakistani government. Up until this chapter of her life, Nafis's personal history had been one of doting relatives and individual accomplishment. But this period provided the teenager's first exposure to violence and the influence it had on women and children, who became its greatest victims. Muslim refugees reported how Sikhs had stripped and paraded their wives and daughters through the crowds, raped them, and then killed them. The women's naked bodies littered village streets.

At the time Nafis and her younger siblings looked on the siege and their ensuing escape as an adventure, albeit one they were quite happy to survive. As one observer noted, the Shoaibs had a reputation for being level-headed in times of crisis, a type of unemotional practicality. But decades later the memories of the violence in Delhi lingered, as the diplomat struggled to protect women in war-ravaged societies like Bosnia and Somalia from crimes perpetrated by their enemies—and even their own governments and families.

In October of 1947, after two months in the war-torn capital, the Shoaib clan left Delhi, taking the train to Bombay. The ancestral home in Jaunpur that Mohammed Abdulla had built—the place where Iffat had given birth to her children—was lost to them now, as it was on the Hindu side of the border.

The family began a voyage into the great unknown, leaving behind all that was familiar, to set sail for Karachi, where they would land in the newly formed capital of Pakistan, their newly formed republic, and begin a new life.

Zadia Birru | Addis Ababa, Ethiopia

Probably no other rite of passage is capable of changing a woman's life like giving birth—an event that can alternately propel her into the joys of motherhood, provide caretakers for her old age, earn her the respect of a community, ensure her place on a nation's throne, offer undeniable proof of an illicit affair, trap her in a miserable marriage, maim her for life, or kill her.

No group knows this better than the patients lying here in the hospital ward in Addis Ababa, a room that is so clean that upon entry, the viewer has the momentary feeling of being snow-blinded. The whitewashed walls and ceiling gleam, reflecting the sparkling sunshine that flows through polished windows. Two facing rows of hospital beds covered in sky blue blankets line either side of a central divider. This hygienic atmosphere presents a refreshing contrast to the patients lying in those beds, all of whom have dwelled—some for as many as fifty years—in the constant filth of their own bodily waste as a result of giving birth.

I see them recovering in the ward and walking around the lovely parklike grounds, all draped in handknit shawls, the contribution of a ladies' church group from Australia. Most of the patients are mere girls, like Zadia Birru. She doesn't know her age, but she looks

A pseudonym has been used to protect this girl's privacy.

about thirteen or fourteen. If she had been born in different circumstances, this classic beauty could have easily been a model. With her dark wavy hair pulled into a French braid, her face possesses an elfin charm, a gracefully curving jaw line, large expressive dark eyes, a full-lipped heart-shaped mouth and a beauty mark that highlights her café-au-lait colored skin. Her smile sparkles, transforming her face like sun bursting through clouds.

Zadia's tiny frame measures around four foot eight; draped in a pale blue cotton nightgown and a handknit shawl of primary-colored squares, her body hunches with pain. Through the opening of her gown I can see that her breasts have stretch marks, a detail that seems strangely out of place on such a waif-like girl. But when I hear her story, I learn the reason for the telltale puckered lines.

Zadia had never been to school when her parents arranged her marriage to a farmer from their community. She doesn't know how old she was when she wed her husband, but they had been married for three years before she started her period. In the beginning their relationship was good, but during the fourth year—with no access to birth control—she learned she was going to have a baby. This was when her husband began seeing someone else. The couple quarreled constantly, and when Zadia was four months pregnant, he left her.

The child bride returned to live with her parents in the village of Aju. When it came time for her delivery, she was in labor for two days at home with unbearable back pain because the baby was unable to pass through her tiny pelvis. When she started getting weak, her father decided to take her to the hospital. The family loaded her onto a bench and walked two hours, carrying the child to a district health center. Precariously balanced aboard the plank, she thrashed about in labor.

At the health center Zadia finally gave birth to a stillborn son. Later she learned that ironically his death had allowed him to be born. The fetus, which cannot withstand the rigors of days of obstructed labor, detaches from the placenta and dies. At this point the bones soften, and the baby shrinks enough so that it can pass through the birth canal.

Zadia herself nearly died and was unconscious in the hospital for fifteen days. When she came to, she learned that the stressful delivery had ripped a hole between her vagina and bladder, a condition called obstetric fistula, which permits waste to leak uncontrollably into the vagina. Like an infant herself, she was constantly soiled and reeked with the stench of urine. At this point her doctor referred her to the Fistula Hospital.

Unfortunately Zadia's experience is not a rare occurrence in Africa, where one in twelve births results in the mother's death. Although the choice to marry has been enshrined as a human right since 1948, in much of Africa half-starved girls as young as six are married off by their families. The poverty-stricken parents look at them as a commodity to be traded for livestock or other goods. In most cases they feel they're doing their daughters a favor to try and place them in stable homes where they'll be provided for. And when these girls become pregnant—as they immediately do without birth control—their young bodies are too small and frail to withstand the rigors of childbirth.

This combination of events results in an untold number of cases of obstetric fistula per year, but thousands and thousands of victims have come forward for treatment. The force of delivery on these slight, malnourished bodies can rip the fragile birth canal and tear holes between the girls' rectum or bladder, allowing feces and urine to flow uncontrollably into their vagina. In the vast majority of cases the husband divorces the girl because she is unclean and unfit for sex. Zadia was one of the lucky ones whose family was willing to take her back. In many instances the family refuses, and the girl—whose only crime was obeying her parents and then her husband—is turned out into the street with no home, left to live in daily humiliation as a social outcast who scavenges for food like an animal.

I hear similar stories to Zadia's from the other patients: a childhood marriage, an early pregnancy that results in a fistula and stillborn delivery, followed by divorce. One patient breaks into tears when she tells me about her happy marriage, a union that ended with the fistula she received after five days of being in labor. Another young woman was single and living at home with her family; disabled by a club foot, she was unable to walk to church with them, and while they attended services, she was raped by a neighbor and became pregnant. Her obstructed delivery nearly killed her, and she developed a fistula that left her leaking urine constantly. She worked for two years to save the money to travel from her village to Addis Ababa for the free surgery the hospital provides to women with the condition.

Fortunately the operation to repair the condition is a relatively simple procedure, and if the girls can make it to the Fistula Hospital, they have a 93 percent chance for a full recovery. This center was the creation of a couple of idealistic Australian gynecologists who saw an ad in the *Lancet* medical journal asking for doctors to come to Ethiopia. Catherine and Reginald Hamlin ventured to Addis, planning to stay for three years. When they arrived, one of their colleagues told them that "the fistula patients will break your heart." The Australian pair soon learned the full meaning of these words as the girls came in from the countryside for treatment.

In 1974 they decided to build a hospital devoted to repairing fistulas. The Hamlins obtained special permission from the Ethiopian government to buy the land, and the Kellogg Foundation in the United States donated money to build the structure. The project has grown since those early days, with more buildings and expanded offerings, like training programs that teach literacy and trade skills to the patients and legal counseling that apprises them of their rights. Recently Catherine Hamlin approached the mayor of Addis, who donated adjacent city public land to the hospital at her request.

There is a small group of women who cannot be cured by the operation; they will be forced to live with their incontinence for life. For them the hospital has provided a special opportunity. Around fifty have stayed on and have become nurses' aides; they do everything from office work to assisting in surgery. Who better to understand what the patients are going through?

The Fistula Hospital is a marvel of self-sufficiency; even the bloodied gauze is bleached, dried, rolled, and reused. The center has also created a village where other incurable fistula patients stay together in a communal living situation. Here they can receive ongoing medical attention, and this environment provides them an alternative to returning as outcasts to their villages.

Reginald Hamlin passed away in 1993, but at eighty-three Catherine still performs surgery on patients and helps to train doctors who come here from all over the world. They operate on about 1,200 girls and women a year, and all services of the hospital are free of charge to patients. This facility receives support from a variety of organizations, from the UN Population Fund to the women's church group that knits shawls to keep these patients warm—and ships them seven thousand miles from Australia to Ethiopia.

Zadia is nervous as she awaits her surgery, but she's looking forward to being clean again. After her recovery, she'll don the new dress the staff provides all patients upon leaving the hospital—a symbol of her new life. Then she'll return to her parents' home, where she'll help with the chores: cleaning, cooking, carrying water and firewood. But after her disappointing experience, she doesn't plan to marry again.

When she stands up to leave, I watch the nurse wipe the girl's urine off the plastic chair.

Nafis in 1949.

(*top*) Polishing silver at home in Karachi. (*From left*) Cousin Aziz, mother Iffat, Nafis, brothers Hassan and Kemal, and sister Chicky, 1949.

(*bottom*) Nafis and Azhar leaning on a car in Karachi, 1949.

Nafis and friends at the beach in Karachi, 1949.

The Shoaib family, 1953. From left: Tariq, Chicky (*top*), Iffat (*bottom*), Nafis.

Nafis in 1953.

2　WELCOMING THE GIRLS

We have all questioned the luck of the draw that shapes our destiny, examining how fate favors one girl born into a wealthy family that gives her every opportunity versus another girl who comes into this world as chattel to be traded for cattle. Although there are as many theories for shaping personality as there are philosophies and religions—from karma to reincarnation to environment to genes—for those who believe in the influence of the stars, we must consider what it means to be born a Leo, the lioness of the zodiac.

On the eighteenth of August, 1929, Iffat Shoaib gave birth to the couple's first child. The baby was a girl, a situation that normally would have prompted grief and condolences in most traditional Indian households, but not in this one. After the Shoaibs christened the newborn "Iffat," like her mother, they always called their daughter "Nafis," meaning "precious or extraordinary."

Following the child's birth, acquaintances all asked the proud parents: "Does the baby have light skin?" referring to a desirable trait in Indian culture. No, she did not. The infant's gender and complexion had both failed to pass the mark, because Nafis had dark skin and a temperament to match. However, her family—particularly her grandfather—adored the child all the same.

The patriarch of Nafis's family, Mohammed Abdulla, had left his village in the United Provinces in eastern India and moved to Jaunpur, located about two hundred miles west of Calcutta, to practice law. There he built an impressive estate surrounded by gardens and fields, which would serve as the home of three generations and dozens of extended family members. He ran an open household where a constantly changing diorama of characters came and went: servants, sons, their wives, grandchildren, cousins, second cousins, and relatives with such a tenuous thread to the family fabric that no one could quite remember how they were woven in. The visitors arrived with their baggage and bunked in spare rooms, the children's rooms, wherever there was room. They stayed for weeks, months—sometimes long enough to get a college education. It was the patriarch's concept of noblesse oblige that prompted his generosity, a concept his son would later emulate.

A private inner courtyard served as the heart of Mohammed Abdulla's whitewashed brick house. It was surrounded by the numerous rooms of the family's private residence, which included separate quarters for his sons and their wives and children. A broad, shady veranda rimmed the second story.

As his legal practice thrived, Mohammed became such a respected member of the community that he designed a special room to receive guests who came seeking advice and favors. He made his headquarters a study that had an outside courtyard, and on the door to these chambers the gentleman placed an enormous photographic portrait. The subject was an unlikely representation for such a grand work: a one-year-old baby Nafis, with a couple of teeth and a shaved head— the shearing a practice that was thought to encourage a lush, full head of hair upon regrowth.

Nafis's grandfather died when she was just seven years old, struck down by kidney failure. As was the custom of his generation, Mohammed Abdulla had not kept track of his age, but his family believed him to be in his sixties. Nafis remembered that "he always had his arms outstretched for me to run to him." He doted on his granddaughter, bragging about how clever she was and prompting her to recite for guests. Perhaps this was because his two female babies had died in infancy and a third daughter had succumbed to tuberculosis in her twenties. Nafis's grandmother had wailed, "There are no girls in our family!" Thus when her son Mohammed produced a daughter, the baby was joyously welcomed into the family. This fact was unusual in a society where the news of a girl's birth was frequently greeted with pity: "Maybe you'll have better luck next time." Instead of being treated as a second-class citizen, Nafis was celebrated for her gender; as she grew up and went about the world, she found the absence of this fact in other households as unnatural as she did intolerable. On the global stage she would spend the rest of her life promoting her family's vision of the fundamental worth of girls.

The attorney from Jaunpur had three sons and a daughter and was noted for emphasizing education for all his children, pushing them to excel, especially Nafis's father, Mohammed. Confident of their son's intellectual abilities, his parents had lied about his age to permit him to enter school early. The boy lived up to his parents' academic expectations, except for once when he was young he came in second in his class. Disgusted, his normally placid father rapped him on the hand, so startling the child that he lurched and cut his chin on a cup. The scar his son carried from that incident always reminded him that it was wise to excel at his studies.

The younger Mohammed was known as a refined lad, so fair-skinned and handsome that he was called Sahib by his friends, a respectful form of address on the subcontinent normally reserved for the Brits during the colonial period. In photographs from the 1950s—with his self-assured elegance, dark hair slicked back, tailored suits, and hand poised with a cigarette as he escorted his daughter past photographers—he resembled a continental film star.

He made his father proud of him by attending Allahabad University and writing an award-winning master's thesis on economics. He went on to receive a law degree as well and then started his career working in the Indian Civil Service. In 1934, when Nafis was five years old, Mohammed was posted to Calcutta, and he and his young family left his father's home, relocating so that he could climb the next rung in the career ladder.

When Mohammed Shoaib was twenty-two and settled, his parents arranged for his marriage to Iffatara, a fifteen-year-old girl whom he had never met. Her name divided in half represented her two different personas: in the formal, public arena she was known as "Iffat," but her loved ones called her "Tara." Iffat's and Mohammed's families hailed from the same area in the United Provinces, and the young lady's father was also an attorney. With similar socioeconomic status, temperaments, and interests—the factors matchmakers considered in pairing newlyweds—their parents felt Mohammed and Iffat were well suited for each other. The prospective bride's father examined the groom to see if he was stable and would make a good provider; the prospective groom's people investigated the woman (or more aptly in most cases, the girl) to see if she could cook and sew and if she had the qualities of a capable mother. According to the rules of Islam, the couple's fathers agreed on a sum that the groom's family would place into a bank account in the bride's name; if she ever wanted a divorce, the money would give her the means to start a new life.

However, there was one way in which Iffat and Mohammed were not compatible. At the time of their marriage Iffat could read and write Urdu, but not English, and her new husband felt that this was a critical skill one needed to get on in this world. Mohammed offered to hire a tutor for his young wife; she so wished to please him that she agreed to this suggestion and began meeting with her teacher every day, from 9:00 a.m. until 3:00 p.m. Even after Iffat had three children, she continued working with her instructor—the result being that at the end of six years she spoke English fluently and possessed a commanding knowledge of history, art, and literature. She had transformed from a village child bride to an educated, worldly woman, an appropriate wife for a man of Mohammed's ambitions, and this goal, as her daughter noted, was the root of her mother's studies. She simply wanted to please Mohammed because "she adored my father and he adored her." This was lucky for Iffat because the mindset of her culture was that even if her married life had been miserable, she would have been expected to make a go of it. Only the direst circumstances would have been grounds to withdraw that money from her bank account and divorce.

For the rest of her short life Iffat would be a satellite, orbiting her family's dynamic nucleus, her own interests revolving around her husband and children, her only aspiration to live through their accomplishments. Her children watched relatives, neighbors, and even their young friends drawn to the Shoaib household by Iffat's loving kindness. One contemporary of Nafis's admitted many years later: "I came to your house every day, not for either of you sisters, but because your mother was such a wonderful, warm person, and you had such a happy family life."

The Shoaibs were Sunni Muslims, and Iffat's other driving passion was her devotion to this faith. If Mohammed went away, she would be on her knees on the *janamaz*, her prayer rug, asking Allah for her husband's safe return. She instilled this respect for Islam in her children, and they observed all the rituals of the religion when they were growing up, praying five times a day like their mother and observing the high holidays of Islam during the month of Ramadan.

This respect for the traditions of Islam was a legacy from Mrs. Shoaib's childhood. Nafis remembered traveling over a thousand miles from Calcutta by rail each summer, returning with her mother to visit relatives in her ancestral village of Bangawan, in the eastern United Provinces. After Iffat's mother had died giving birth, the aunts and a large, loving, extended family had raised the infant. (Perhaps knowledge of her mother's history was another influence on the young Nafis's career choice, the awareness that her own grandmother had not survived the process of childbirth.)

On those summer journeys back to Bangawan, after days of being cooped up in stifling train cars, Nafis and her siblings rushed out onto the platform while their mother donned a burqua. Their excitement was fueled by more than just reuniting with kinfolk; the children anxiously awaited the opportunity to ride an old elephant the family kept as a pet. When they left the station, Iffat and her brood climbed into a *palki*, a throne-like chair positioned atop two long horizontal poles, which was carried on the shoulders of four men. Thus they were grandly delivered to the family home. "How much shouting and affection when our mother arrived at the house!" Nafis remembered. "They just loved her so much. And then when she left, with the amount of screaming and crying, you really felt as if someone had died."

After Nafis's birth, her mother returned to Mohammed Abdulla's estate in Jaunpur for two more deliveries. In short order she gave birth to a son, Iqbal, and then another girl, Nighat. These three children would form a tight-knit group of siblings, with Nafis playing the role frequently assumed by the eldest child. Her personality would evolve as a textbook example of firstborns: serious, conscientious, take-charge, goal-oriented, aggressive, exacting, organized, responsible, and a natural leader. She was the fierce protector of her younger brother and sister, the instigator of their offerings, and the brains behind many of their crimes.

The second sibling in the family was brother Iqbal, only nineteen months younger than Nafis, and their closeness in age provided a healthy rivalry. Their play consisted of soccer games and frequent fights. During these battles Nafis never cried; the sparring matches continued until Iqbal went away to boarding school at Dehra Dun and studied boxing. After their next round of fighting, the big sister swore she'd never hit him again. However, while he may have excelled at boxing, he ran so slowly that he could never catch Nafis; in the option of fight or flight, she quickly learned she could win at the latter. And the situation earned Iqbal the title "Slow Coach," which infuriated him even more.

With her baby sister she took a gentler approach. Nighat remembered that whenever Nafis went to visit her friends, she'd always take the toddler along. "I didn't have to say anything because she's such an extrovert. She did all the talking while I sat quietly." People began to inquire if Nighat could speak.

As the girls grew, their differences in personality became even more marked. When Nafis and her brother played rousing soccer matches with the neighborhood children—a practice her mother frowned upon for a girl—her elder daughter came home with torn and dirty clothes. Meanwhile the dainty Nighat remained clean and proper. As Nafis remembered, "When we were younger, my brother and I protected Nighat, but we also used to think she was our parents' pet. She was such a goody-goody. She never dirtied her clothes and all that like we did." Little Nighat was also considered a cry baby; unlike Nafis, she always ran to her parents, who would demand to know what the older children had done to her. "But on the other hand, we always loved her and watched out for her because she was so helpless."

When the two young sisters were ten and seven, they journeyed to visit their uncle in Orissa, a resort area on the eastern coast of India, for summer holidays. As they strolled along some rocks next to the river, Nighat slipped and fell into deep water, and immediately the current began to tow her toward a waterfall. Nafis reached down and tried to pull her little sister out, but she slipped in as well. Neither girl could swim, and out of sight of their uncle, they swept along underwater toward the falls, with Nighat thinking, "Oh my God, this is it. We're going to die . . ." They were spotted by a man next to the river who jumped in—still wearing his boots, his pockets stuffed full of important documents—and dragged them both to safety. After that experience, the sisters maintained a lifelong suspicion of the water, causing Nafis to never conquer swimming, which she considered a great shortcoming in a sportswoman.

While the Shoaibs' oldest child may not have mastered swimming, her academic studies thrived, thanks to her father's encouragement—a notion he inherited from *his* father. Mohammed Abdulla had provided the same opportunities for both his male and female offspring—an extraordinary notion at the time. The younger Mohammed held similar ideals for his children, just as he had for his wife. He saw to it that the school uniforms were made. He accompanied his children on the first day of classes, just as he would later escort Nafis to her medical school interviews. He became acquainted with each of their instructors. All this attention grew out of Mohammed Shoaib's belief that the most important legacy he could bequeath his sons and daughters was a proper education.

As a result, in his household the library was considered a sacred place; although guests might be stacked up like cordwood—bunking in every corner of the home—no one was ever permitted to sleep in this room. The library was reserved so that all members of the family had a quiet place to study.

One of Nafis's earliest memories was of having wandered into this haven in their family home, where she proceeded to take down volumes one by one to look at the pictures and scatter them about the room. When her parents finally discovered the toddler, she had emptied most of the lower shelves onto the floor. Her mother began to scold the child, but her father placed a hand on his wife's arm and said gently, "No, it's okay . . . she loves books." To Mohammed this was a positive sign for his daughter's future.

At age six the girl who loved books was packed off to boarding school at Loretto College because she was so naughty and unmanageable that her mother could no longer cope. When the child enrolled in school, she learned a most distressing fact about her past: she was legally named "Iffat," like her mother—a name she promptly announced she detested. Little Iffat naturally informed everyone at school that they must continue to refer to her as "Nafis"—her nickname meaning "precious."

She adapted quickly to life at the convent. "All the children went to communion. I didn't know I wasn't supposed to go, so I went, too. You had to have confession, but I didn't know what confession was. So I just received Holy Communion then walked out. All the Catholics said, 'What are you doing? You aren't supposed to go up there.' I said, well, nobody told me. So that was my first and last Holy Communion."

When Nafis caught measles at school, her mother relented and brought her naughty daughter home to live, but Nafis continued to attend the day school at Loretto College, where she was later joined by her little sister, Nighat. Even before the children were sent to the best private schools in the area, they had been working at home with their own tutor. In daily life the family spoke Urdu, but with the same logic he had used for Iffat's study of English—that one must speak it to get on in this world—Mohammed Shoaib hired an Anglo-Indian woman to work with the children on their language skills. The new instructor came to the house in Calcutta each day to polish Nafis, Iqbal, and Nighat's English and help them with their other subjects as well. Her name was Mrs. Newman, but for the next ten years she would simply be known as "Teacher."

As the three siblings studied English, Nafis decided they needed appropriately British nicknames. Technically, the girls already had pet names, Nafis's being in use since she was born, and Nighat being called "Chammo," which meant "endearment," a name her mother borrowed from one of her best friends and bestowed upon her second daughter. But the study of English prompted new ideas in address, so Nafis donned Queen Elizabeth I's sobriquet, Gloriana, a label befitting her position as household royalty. Her brother and sister also experimented with various handles until the logical solution emerged: adopting the first letter of each of their names, they would add "icky." Thus Nafis became "Nicky," the hapless Iqbal became "Icky," and from Chammo emerged a moniker by which the elegant Nighat would be known for the rest of her life: "Chicky."

After a gap of six years, Iffat gave birth to two more boys, Hassan and then a year later, Kemal. These two brothers formed another unit in the Shoaib household, with their own sibling rivalries and traditions. Fortunately Hassan and Kemal did not become "Hicky" and "Kicky." Rather Hassan, whose striking eyes resembled Nafis's— enormous black pupils surrounded by a ring of icy blue—became "Sheikhoo," the nickname of one of the Mongol emperors, echoing his big sister's desire for the trappings of royalty. But oddly Kemal was always just "Kemal."

The two boys became competitive in sports and academics and were evenly matched until Kemal began to shoot up, growing taller than his older brother. He developed into an excellent table tennis player who went on to win several championships.

Their verbal attitudes also echoed the older sisters' divergence; Kemal was outgoing and talkative. Hassan was reticent and hated to be queried about anything. Once the brothers returned home from boarding school together, and Kemal was inside the house chatting with the family when someone inquired after Hassan. It turned out he was still sequestered in the car, waiting for the family to disburse, because he feared they would all start asking him questions. When someone went to fetch him he said, "No, no, I'm not coming in until everyone's gone."

While the family lived in Calcutta, the boys were sent away to private school at age eleven. They attended Doon School in Dehra Dun, located in the foothills of the Himalayas. The academy was patterned after British schools, including a headmaster from England, Mr. Foote. The future leaders of commerce and government for both Pakistan and India were the Shoaib boys' classmates.

Iffat's last child, Tariq, was born in 1948, eighteen years after she had given birth to Nafis. Ironically her oldest daughter was already delivering babies when Iffat's youngest was born. Tariq's next oldest sibling was Kemal, twelve years his senior, and throughout his life, all his brothers and sisters treated him as a pet. By all accounts he had an angelic disposition, so his pampering was well deserved, which made his early death all the more tragic.

As the children grew up, Chicky and Nicky continued their education at Loretto College. They went to the convent each day wearing traditional Catholic school girls' uniforms: white blouses with white pleated skirts in the summer, traded for navy skirts in the winter.

Though the students' outfits were identical, at this institution a young Nafis was exposed to a veritable UN of nationalities, as well as an array of religions; the non-Catholics were led in nondenominational prayer and were not required to observe the order's traditions, like making the sign of the cross. However, the students did take a class called "moral science" outlining the church's views, a course that got Nafis into hot water. When one of the nuns stated that marriages were made in heaven, Miss Shoaib begged to differ. "Marriages are not religion, Mother. They are *not* made in heaven. In my religion, divorce is allowed." This argument was not well received. The nuns wondered aloud how little Nighat could excel in moral science while her big sister was so difficult.

Besides Catholics at the convent, there were Jews, Protestants, many Hindus, and a few other Muslims. Two of these students were women Nafis would still be friends with seventy years later: Shamsa, who went on to attend medical school with her, and Hashmat Shahabuddin, the niece of Khwaja Nazimuddin, who took over as president of Pakistan following the death of Jinnah.

Hashmat, by her own account, was "the quiet fat girl at school." Nafis was a year senior to Hashmat, a distinction that can seem enormous at that age. At first Hashmat observed the "vivacious" Nafis from afar, whom she recalled as "a tomboyish pretty girl that all the boys were crazy about."

When Calcutta was being bombed during World War II, Hashmat's father sent her away to Aligarh in the countryside, out of harm's way. When she returned to Loretto College, one of the male professors brought the girl in to introduce her. "Class, this is Hashmat Shaha—"

"Oh, Lord, she's as fat as ever!" exclaimed Nafis, and the only person who blushed harder than Hashmat was her teacher.

However, through their families the two girls became acquainted, and eventually they became friends. As the excitement of the new Islamic nation was being discussed, they joined with Shamsa and some of the others to create the Muslim Girls Association, the group that visited Jinnah and taught first aid. And, much to Hashmat's chagrin, physical training.

Nafis was not about to be left out of anything at school and thus pursued her interest in the performing arts. She sang in the choir and developed a strong alto voice. She was also in theatrical productions. When one of the leads cancelled sick at the last moment, the nuns asked, "Oh, who has a good memory?" and Nafis wound up performing in *The Robe*, not even knowing what her part was about.

On top of all this the young athlete played several sports in school. She was on the net ball team, a game similar to basketball, and outside of school Nafis's home life was also full of sports. Her father took the Shoaib clan to watch professional cricket and tennis matches.

At any given moment the Shoaib residence housed so many people that one could easily organize a game of most anything, and the siblings became quite competitive. First off, there were the rousing soccer matches with Nicky, Icky, and the neighborhood boys. Also, their home possessed courts where all the family learned to play tennis and badminton. Chicky remembered that at one point playing badminton became a major part of their daily ritual: school, homework, badminton for several hours, more homework, dinner, then bed. As a result, Nafis became a championship player, later representing her university and eventually Pakistan in international badminton competition.

One instance where her skill at this sport roused the ire of her father occurred when she was around thirteen and already very proficient. Nafis was playing doubles with someone who was older than she; however, her partner was not up to par with her skill. And unfortunately for him, he missed so many shots their team was losing. She became mortified that all her friends were watching this debacle, so she decided to just throw the game and get it over with. Unfortunately for *her*, Mr. Shoaib was also watching; he became furious, giving his daughter a lecture on the importance of being upright and determined in all one's endeavors.

Kite fighting was another passion that the children shared, a competition that was popular in Calcutta. Although they purchased the kites ready-made, doctoring the string was considered one of the primary secrets to success, and a pastime that occupied much of their time and energy. The goal was to slice the string of your opponents and bring down their kites. The Shoaib children starched their twine and ground up glass bottles to coat it, making the line razor sharp. Then delicately—so as to avoid slicing their young fingers—they wound the string around a *charak*, a wooden spool designed to hold it. One member of the team headed up to their rooftop, holding onto the *charak*, and another ran out into the neighborhood to release the kite and catch the wind—a practice that required great skill. Around the city other children would be sending their own kites out to do battle. Against Calcutta's blue skies you could see red and yellow diamonds, their tails fluttering in the wind as they circled each other until the victorious kiter sliced the line of his opponent, to bring the coveted object spiraling down. The winner was now the proud owner of two kites, and members of the team ran to fetch the spoils.

One of the facets of childhood that all the Shoaib siblings remember is never having a room to oneself in their Calcutta house. Carrying on the traditions of his father, Mohammed strongly believed in the concept of noblesse oblige, educating and shaping the careers of many who sought his help. Since both he and Iffat hailed from rural areas, their relatives from back home would come to live with them in the city so that they could further their ambitions. As a result their home was always full of guests, and Mohammed funded the college education for several of them. He would then advise them on their professional path and help them with connections.

Nafis remembered that houseguests would come and stay for two or three months. "My vision of my mother in Calcutta is that it seemed like she never got off the dining table. She had one shift for breakfast, then a second one, then it was time for lunch, then the second lunch seating, and so on." What Nafis learned from watching her parents and grandparents help others shaped her own concept of noblesse oblige. With her career she would become the next generation to take seriously the opportunity to use her social position for good, and instead of resorting to the decadence that was common in her circle—the well-to-do who spent their days moving from the track to tea to bridge to cocktails to dinner—she learned from her father's example to use her privilege to help others less fortunate.

During this time the siblings enjoyed staging their own Judy Garland/Mickey Rooney–type productions of magic shows, circuses, and plays, which they performed for relatives, their parents' friends, and hapless houseguests—for a fee. Nafis was the ringleader of their own five-person circus, starring the Amazing Nicky, Icky, Chicky, Sheikhoo, and Kemal, and featuring such death-defying feats as walking a high wire suspended above two stacked tins. They staged other notable offerings, such as *A Midsummer Night's Dream*. Displaying early a management style that allowed no room for slipshod performance, Director Nicky became livid when her little sister forgot her part; Nafis pasted Chicky's lines on the garage wall, and then when the younger girl fumbled her lines, Nafis shoved her aside to deliver them properly.

Her lust for the limelight was aided by the fact that Nafis could sing like a nightingale, and she worked with a respected voice coach who taught her classical Indian music. Without any coaxing the budding star would perform at parties and picnics, later even singing on Radio Pakistan. At thirteen she was so serious about her singing that she considered life on the stage as one of her potential careers. Yet her desire to "change the world" caused her chanteuse fantasy to evaporate along with other options for her future—like becoming an engineer, tennis champion, or teenage bride.

During the early 1940s, India was still highly influenced by Victorian England, especially in the structure of daily life among the country's elite, since for a couple of centuries the two cultures had intermingled. And after all, Queen Victoria had reigned for sixty-three years over the empire upon which the sun never set, the crown jewel of which was India. Passions for tea, paisley prints, and polo sprang from the subcontinent and traveled back to the British Isles. They were exchanged with a taste for bridge, English literature, and an "Oxbridge" education. Also handed down from the British aristocracy was an attitude about child rearing, that one really should leave this messy matter to servants, a predilection most famously practiced by the queen herself.

Another view shared with the Commonwealth was the importance of a girl's refinement in the domestic arts—no matter the likelihood that she would actually be pressed upon to use them on a daily basis. In this vein, the young Shoaib girls learned cooking and sewing. Nafis started baking pizzas, but she soon lost interest in this enterprise. Next the sisters were taught the basics of embroidery, mastering cross-stitch and French knots, but naturally our over-achieving heroine could not be content with such a mediocre accomplishment.

In her early teens Nafis took up tailoring, generously stitching up pants for her younger brothers. They universally refused to wear any of her creations, and this was the source of no small resentment in the family. "I got very angry, but obviously these clothes were terrible. Then I lost my interest in the sewing business, because, you know, it was not that rewarding." However, not to be deterred, she learned to knit, an activity that brought her greater appreciation. At this point Nafis began to fashion sweaters, vests, and scarves for the entire family, with her father coming to the elder daughter with special requests for garments, a distinction that made her feel important.

Mohammed's influence continued to be a guiding force for the tastes and avocations of the entire family. Because he was an avid bridge enthusiast, his wife and children all mastered the game. In the evening he would sit down and play a few hands with them. No one liked playing against him, because by all accounts he had a photographic mind and could remember the cards that had been played. Nafis, ever the disciple of her dad, also became an avid player, and even as a child, if the fourth player failed to show up, she would become her father's partner. "Okay, sit across—I'll carry you."

Mohammed liked to challenge his children intellectually and provided them with mathematical puzzles. "Now if you can't figure it out," he'd advise, "then sleep on it. Sleep, let your mind rest, then in the morning you'll have the answer." Strangely, Nafis remembered that this strategy did work for her. "We would believe it, you see, and in the morning, I *would* have the answer."

Nafis cut the teeth of her diplomatic career by negotiating with her father. She was always the go-between, bargaining with her parents for the benefit of her younger siblings. When there were misdemeanors, and Nafis denied responsibility, her parents would say, "But we're sure you arranged for them to do it." Her punishment was to stand in the corner and be denied dessert, a treat she dearly loved.

Yet due to the support of her family, particularly her father, Nafis was able to take risks and to experiment with the types of options that are available to a girl who knows she is loved and supported, one who can go back to the flock if she fails. In this patriarchal society, having a father who championed and protected his daughter gave her access to her dreams.

And this support included the nuclear family. Having each other, this unit of eight people really didn't need anyone else—although they never wanted for friends outside their household. This solidity enabled them to sail off for Karachi and start a new life, without the withering trauma that might have marred others.

Instead of becoming a fading star in this new country, Nafis would shine ever brighter—as befitted any self-respecting Leo given a new galaxy of potential admirers. In Pakistan she would forge the next steps that would determine her future, and she would meet Azhar, the man who would become her mate for life.

Nargis Ansari | Bhanwargarh, India

"I have never really told anyone about myself . . . until now," Nargis Ansari says with a somewhat defiant look on her face. "I lost my father when I was very small; I don't even know what he looked like." I note by the fact that she begins her personal story with his, that she must have considered his loss a defining moment in her life.

Nargis and I are talking with fourteen other young women at the Doosra Dashak project, a residential school funded by UNFPA that provides education to adolescents in a remote region of Rajasthan in western India. We are seated on maroon and saffron striped mats on the floor of the main classroom building while the school's guru, clinical psychologist Charu Mitra, translates. The room sizzles as the temperature approaches ninety degrees Fahrenheit; four ceiling fans overhead sit idle as the solar power has not recharged enough to turn their blades. The small grouping of rustic buildings provides a completely self-contained unit where the youth who missed out on proper education can return to school. They live in a communal environment that alleviates the need for transportation in this region where potholes could swallow a brahma bull, and automobiles share the road with camel carts and goat herds. Instead of onerous commuting, students are able to concentrate on their studies, creating a community that helps each other with tutoring, cooking, and cleaning.

I marvel at these women's sparkling, fashionable appearance, especially considering their poverty, the region's soupy climate, and the fact that their homes contain precious little indoor plumbing or electricity. Later Charu Mitra explains that people donate used clothing for her students.

Today Nargis has volunteered to tell me her story, and as she speaks confidently, I notice a disconnect between the northern and southern hemispheres of her face. Her mouth stretches in a slight smile, while her luminous black eyes maintain an intense, unsmiling glint. They focus beyond me on a world I cannot see: her childhood. She has an oval face, with a wide, slightly flattened nose sporting a diamond stud. Her thick black hair smoothly braids into a rope that looks heavy enough to anchor a freighter.

"I am from Baran district, from a Muslim community, and my age is about twenty-four years old," she continues. "My parents had moved to Baran to care for my grandmother. Shortly after they arrived, my mother tells me that there was a fight between herself and my father. He left the house and walked to another village. In his anger he had a clash with some other person, and so he left that place and continued walking. It was extremely hot and he suffered a heat stroke and died."

Now lacking the support of her father, Nargis, her mother, elder sister, and brother were all dependent on her grandmother for survival. Unfortunately, the grandmother was very conservative and didn't believe in the education of girls.

"My grandmother was very, very, very domineering, so that even my grandfather was scared of her. It was always my grandmother who determined who will go where, who will get married and at what age—so it was Grandmother who decided that my elder sister should get married at the age of fourteen. When my sister was in sixth standard she could read the Koran, so that was the measurement. Grandmother said to my mother, 'Now she can read Koran, you should see that she stops her studies.' And my sister went along with it. She never retaliated like I did."

The matriarch had strict ideas on how the family should behave. Her widowed daughter, Nargis's mother, should stay in the house and let no one see her face in the morning. However, she believed the male child, Nargis's brother, should continue his studies. And like her sister, Nargis should drop out of school and marry; but when she refused, her frustrated mother was trapped between two headstrong females and became abusive to her daughter, beating Nargis daily. In spite of this the girl scored honors while her brother flunked out of the *madrasa*, the Islamic parochial school.

The friction at home continued and forced Nargis and her mother to move out. They struggled to support themselves by taking in boarders and by hand-rolling beedies, Indian cigarettes.

Stories similar to Nargis's scenario would be repeated over and over by the other students during my visit. Their education ceased when family members thought they should be married at fourteen . . . thirteen . . . twelve—or they were pulled out of school at an equally young age to make beedies because their families needed the income to survive. To free themselves from this predicament, the girls are forced to make painful choices. As one teenager in our discussion laments, "We have to struggle against the people we love, the people who have taken care of us."

Luckily Nargis's mother agreed to let her daughter continue her studies while she worked. When the girl went on to college, people in the community joined her grandmother in the chorus that she should be married now. And yet both the mother and child resisted this pressure; in spite of their financial predicament, once the two women were living on their own, the mother was able to consider her daughter's future with a more open mind.

Finally Nargis agreed that a marriage could be arranged while she finished her degree. "My grandmother and mother selected the boy for me and within a month's time I was supposed to marry him. Although he was educated, he was from a very remote village that had neither lights nor water connections, no toilets in the house, and there were just two rooms in which the whole family was living. So I told my mother that I don't want to marry this boy unless he is ready to come to Baran and settle here." This pronouncement created even more friction within her family and so enraged Nargis's brother that he slapped her. Negotiations for the marriage unraveled, and the wedding was called off.

However, Nargis continued with her studies, graduating with a bachelor's degree in science and going on to receive a master's degree in pubic administration, which she puts to good use as a counselor at Doosra Dashak. Currently Nargis is engaged again, this time to a man of her own choosing; he is taking a computer course, and they will wed when he is settled financially. She has negotiated with him the terms of their marriage: that she may continue her work, and that he will let her study English and computer science. And she will not be forced to wear a burqua.

Today the determined young woman advises others on how to persevere and make their education a priority, and she advises their parents as well. As Charu Mitra says, "If you are working with youth, and you are not working with the community, then how are you going to empower them? Because the community needs to think the same way as their children. To get the youth out of that community you have to do the counseling for the parents as well. This is a cycle that goes on, and when you start off with any one thing, it encircles everything."

Nargis considers the situation and sums it up: "Since I had a traditional ritualistic background, I accepted whatever people said—even though I didn't believe it or like it. Since I've joined Doosra Dashak it's given me the opportunity to *think*, to decide if these rituals are right or wrong. And think about what is right or wrong *for me*."

3   AZHAR

One theory of soul mates says that at some point in their lives they will both be in the same place at the same time—before they meet. And so it was with Nafis and her future husband, Azhar Sadik. He grew up in Lahore, and she in Calcutta, a thousand miles apart. But during the summer that the medical student and the multitude of Muslims took refuge in the High Commissioner's home in Delhi, her future husband was also wandering around that city on patrol.

Because Azhar was captain of the cricket team he had been selected to accompany Major James Wilson, an Englishman who was adjutant of the Indian Military Academy, on a mission. Wilson had an appointment to meet British Field Marshall Claude Auchinleck, the commander-in-chief of the Indian Army, to discuss the division of the military academy's assets in order to provide Pakistan with the means to launch their own institute after Partitioning. The fighting in Delhi had now spread throughout the Punjab, becoming a full-scale civil war; as a precaution every vehicle leaving the academy's grounds took armed escorts. Thus the entourage shaped up that would head from Dehra Dun to their appointment in Delhi: a Hindu cadet, a massive Sikh driver, and, since the school's leader was very keen on cricket—another British import to the subcontinent—the team's captain, Azhar.

Delhi was a city under siege at this point, and as the armed delegation in battledress marched across the polished lobby of Maiden's, a five-star colonial hotel built to house the British aristocracy, they attracted much scrutiny. They stayed in Delhi for a few days, and after the major had finished his discussion with Auchinleck, the group headed back to Dehra Dun. However, when they tried to take the bridge across the Jamuna River, they learned that the river was in flood, preventing their passing. The monsoon had stranded them on the west side of the waterway, and they were told they would have to drive south to Agra to cross.

This deviation proved a gift, because for the first time the young Azhar, peering across the swollen, mauve river, laid eyes on the Taj Mahal, its white domes incandescent through the moisture-laden haze of twilight. He had longed to see the marble mausoleum, a jewel of Muslim art created by a grieving shah to commemorate his wife who had died in childbirth.

The soldiers continued searching for a place to cross the river until darkness fell and the famished group stopped to make camp. Upon orders from his commanding officer, Azhar strode into the village to buy something to eat. The future British Army general should have thought better than to send the Muslim into the Hindu village that night, but at the academy he hadn't been concerned with his pupils' religious affiliation. Azhar was known to him as only a fellow cricketer. The handsome young cadet was of medium build, but his classic good looks, cleft chin, dark moustache, and luminous eyes set him apart from the crowd. On this night he wore the Indian military's traditional field uniform: khaki pants and shirt, trousers tucked into his gun boots, an ammo belt slung across his chest, and a light blue beret, signifying his status as a cadet, pulled over his thick black hair.

Unfortunately, although he was traveling with a fully loaded rifle, he did not think to carry the weapon when he approached the shopkeeper in search of food.

Azhar had joined the Indian Military Academy two years prior in Dehra Dun, but a couple of months before graduation, the army had emptied the classrooms and sent the cadets on patrol. Partitioning forced these students into the real world, a bloody civil war. Theory suddenly became reality as the cadets were mobilized to guard the fifteen million people traversing the subcontinent as they relocated. The exodus consisted of Hindus and Sikhs headed east into India; they passed Muslims traveling westward into Pakistan, their new nation. Of the émigrés, a fortunate few journeyed by automobile while others carried their possessions in bullocks' carts. But the vast majority walked hundreds of miles on foot, grouped into caravans comprising tens of thousands of people, multilimbed organisms several miles long that snaked across the Punjab with their belongings balanced on their heads, plows and babies in their arms. As in the old wagon train days of the American West, the route was littered with precious items that had become too cumbersome to carry any further. The weary pilgrims walked on toward the future on the horizon, many with nothing but the clothes on their increasingly frail limbs. As the violence escalated, the slaughter of these individuals became an epidemic; even with armed troops and tanks present, mobs in a suicidal rage would attack the caravans, swooping in to massacre hundreds, wiping out entire families within a matter of minutes.

But as Azhar witnessed, the wayfarers who boarded refugee trains bound for their new homes were not always luckier than those traveling on foot. Mobs yanked passengers from the cars and murdered them. At Wazirabad Station in Pakistan, one train had even arrived bearing nothing but corpses, after the cars were swarmed by rebels who slit the throats of every man, woman, and child aboard. He saw lifeless bodies heaped in piles on railway platforms, rotting in the summer heat. "It struck me as very strange, how small a human being looks when they're dead."

The nineteen-year-old cadet saw scenes that would never leave his mind: Infants torn from their parents' arms. Children watching their mothers raped, their fathers murdered. Both sides were equally guilty, and as Azhar noted, "We were two nations bereft of any human feeling whatsoever." Perhaps the memories of these atrocities guided him in one of the most difficult decisions he would ever make, thirty years later.

Back in the Punjab, Azhar set out as ordered by Major Wilson to find food for his comrades. He strode into the village alone, about a hundred yards from the road. The community consisted of no more than a few ramshackle structures thrown together out of matting, scrap lumber, and corrugated tin, and in the late evening, the clearing was lit by a single kerosene lamp. Azhar found a market open with a shopkeeper shelling peanuts. While the young soldier bargained for some sweetmeats and graham, villagers began to gather, as they always did to inspect any stranger in their midst. They circled Azhar, studying him curiously, as the shopkeeper casually wrapped the purchases. "By the way," he inquired, eyeing his customer, "*who are you?*"

"I am a cadet of the Indian Military Academy."

"No, no, that's not what I'm asking. What is your religion?" Now Azhar sensed that he was in serious trouble, because this was clearly a Hindu region.

"My religion's immaterial. I am from the Indian Military Academy at Dehra Dun." At this point Azhar peered into the shadows, where about sixty people had gathered, pushing in around him, impatiently awaiting an answer.

Meanwhile, back at the car, Major Wilson realized that it was taking too long for Azhar to return and sent the Sikh driver to investigate. After his initial error of sending the Muslim soldier into the Hindu village, he did not want to make a second mistake. If he sent the Hindu guard he realized his religion would not be instantly recognizable to the villagers, and so it was better to send the gargantuan Sikh, whose beard and white turban would immediately designate his faith.

Azhar recalled the situation: "The driver walked into the gathering and hailed me. By this point the men had pressed up against me, and the Sikh announced, 'I am taking this chap,' and we took to our heels and ran for the car."

As Azhar's experience exemplified, the British Army was feeling the enormous strain of trying to maintain peace during this civil war—at the same time they were looking at pulling out of India and helping Pakistan to create its own military. The troops were also affected by the upheaval, which made it very difficult for them to function as a unit, especially as their own lives were marred by the violence and destruction. One of the Hindu cadets at Dehra Dun had just received a telegram that his entire family had been massacred in Pakistan, and Azhar remembered having a conversation about this situation with another Hindu, who had been giving anti-Muslim speeches. "I said, 'I am really surprised to hear you say these things. We are all armed to the teeth here, and do you believe that when we go out on patrol tonight that this Hindu chap who just lost his family, he would be justified in putting his bayonet through me?'"

"Absolutely."

Azhar had been shocked to hear his educated compatriot promoting violence. "At this point I felt this madness might not ever end. Somebody killed this Hindu's family, and so he kills me, and to avenge my death, my relatives would go and kill some other poor chap. I realized that feelings, even amongst the more liberal-minded people, had become so enflamed that we'd lost all reason."

Azhar Sadik lost a few distant relations from his own family during Partition; but luckily most of his clan were safe, as they lived in Lahore, a major city in the western Punjab that would remain part of Pakistan. But while his family was free from harm, his father was forced to abandon the house where Azhar had been raised in the princely state of Patiala.

The princely states of India were independent from the national government, ruled by either a maharaja or nawab, and these individuals were dictators with total autonomy over their domain. They enjoyed a peculiar relationship with the British, who basically looked the other way so long as the Indian royalty behaved properly toward the Crown, leaving these rulers to treat their subjects as they saw fit. And some of them saw fit to treat their people admirably, and others treated them miserably.

Into one such princely state, Patiala, Asghar Sadik had moved his wife and children when he took a job as the monarchy's director of agriculture, working for the maharaja, Bhupinber Singh. The region was a dust bowl unless properly irrigated; yet with water the crops of cotton and winter wheat flourished.

Azhar was six when they arrived, and he remembered his childhood in Patiala as "an era that will never come again—a time of opulence, of everything done on a grand scale, of growing up with a wonderful couldn't-care-less attitude." In short, it was a terrific time to be a boy. Maharajah Singh, a Sikh, organized a big parade once a year, an opportunity for him to survey his kingdom from atop an elephant as he rode in the pageant. He was a colorful, flamboyant character, obsessed with hunting, or as the British call it, shooting. And to this end he owned a huge kennel housing several hundred gun dogs.

He was also mad about cricket and aimed to build a team that could win. He lured cricketers from all over the world, including some of England's top players, and paid them handsomely to be the lords of his sportsman's utopia.

Because his director of agriculture, Azhar's father, also enjoyed shooting, he and the maharajah got along famously. In the afternoons Mr. Sadik's sons, accompanied by a domestic, would hunt for partridges and ducks or fish in the local lakes. The prince gave the Sadiks a large, comfortable home, where they kept their own kennel of gun dogs, allowing only the great favorites into the house.

The surname "Sadik" means "truthful." The clan had originally hailed from Kashmir—a region known for natives both handsome and very proud of their heritage. Azhar's family had lived there for hundreds of years before migrating south to Amritsar in the Punjab, just east of the demarcation line that would eventually divide Pakistan from India. There Azhar was born in 1928, and he would continue to visit his grandparents' home in Amritsar after he moved to the maharajah's estate in Patiala.

His ancestors had been wealthy merchants, trading mainly in carpets. They had evolved a family tradition of alternating attendance at the prime British universities, beginning with Azhar's great-grandfather, who matriculated to Oxford. After that his son, Azhar's grandfather, went to Cambridge, and his son, Azhar's father, returned to Oxford, where he rowed for his college and received a degree in agriculture.

When Azhar's father returned to India, he joined the army reserve and received a King's Commission from the British before landing his position managing the farmlands of Bhupinber Singh. While studying in England, he had married an Irish woman named Doreen, and they had three children: a daughter, Ilmas, and two sons, Azhar and Younis.

Doreen Sadik loved life on the princely estate, socializing with the maharanis and the upper rungs of society. A bevy of servants looked after her family's needs—a luxury she was well aware she would not have enjoyed in her homeland.

Even though the Sadiks' nuclear household of three children was relatively small for this era, Azhar's family, much like Nafis's family, kept in contact with a large contingent of first, second, and third cousins, an extended clan numbering around four hundred people.

Unfortunately this era of domestic content ended in 1947 with the division of the subcontinent. Azhar's father, an army reservist, had already been called up for active duty during World War II and stayed on during Partitioning. Marriage to his Irish wife ended in divorce. His three children were grown, and his sons were also mobilized, Azhar in the military and Younis in the Indian Airlines. During this period of national upheaval, while Azhar escorted émigrés in their migration, his own childhood home slipped away. Like millions of others, the house in which he was raised became off-limits to him, as it rested on the other side of the border separating two religions.

When the British still ruled India, when Pakistan was a mere philosophical notion, they had imported another tradition from Mother England: sending the children off to boarding school for a solid education. After kindergarten Azhar's sister, Ilmas, had been sent to a Catholic school for girls, Queen Mary College in Lahore, and at ages seven and eight the boys went to Aitchison College in that same city. Aitchison College was exalted as one of the region's top five schools; a child's family had to be mentioned among the chiefs of India to even have a prayer of admittance.

Even though it was a shocking transition to be uprooted from his happy family life at such a young age, Azhar remembered his days at boarding school with affection—the camaraderie of fifty other lads, the caring teachers, the five hundred acres of parklike grounds—all this made the experience more like living in a luxurious private home than an institution.

At the end of his regular term at Aitchison, Azhar stayed on for the newly created junior college program; these older boys held a place of esteem on campus, maintaining a separate house for themselves. Best of all this extended education offered him an opportunity to prepare for university.

In the family tradition it was Azhar's turn to attend Cambridge, a duty he was eager to fulfill, as many in his class were heading off to one of its colleges upon graduation. An Oxbridge education was considered the passport to success in the business world on the subcontinent, a universe dominated by a small number of British and American corporations; when hiring they would be interviewing graduates from their own institutions of higher learning.

But it was not meant to be. Azhar's father took him aside and informed him that over the years the family finances had dwindled, and Mr. Sadik did not have the money to send Azhar to join his friends at Cambridge. His father advised that the army was the boy's best bet—a fate that his sensitive son would regret all his life.

Heartbroken, but realizing he had no other viable opportunity, Azhar followed his father's advice and enrolled in the Indian Military Academy at Dehra Dun, in the foothills of the Himalayas, "because it seemed to be the only way to get on with life."

The cadets received the equivalent of a bachelor's degree while being run through the paces to prepare them for a career in the army. "We were worked to the bone. At the end of the day, you just fell flat on your bed and passed out. It's a tough life. They make it that way. They make it that way to get their discipline into you."

The apprentice had two more months of training until graduation; but when Partition took place, the decision was made by his superior officers to grant the cadets' commission early. After his missions to keep the peace in the Punjab, Azhar and some of his newly appointed fellow officers became the last Muslims out of India. They boarded a plane just past midnight on the eve of the deadline, October 15, 1947, and were told to report to General Headquarters upon arrival in Pakistan.

When they touched down in Rawalpindi the next morning, they landed in the setting of a political theory that had become a reality, entering a realm in total chaos. The new nation didn't even have a monetary system because the Indian rupee was no longer common currency, and the fledgling government had yet to iron out all the wrinkles in issuing the Pakistani rupee. "It was weird and wonderful," Azhar remembered.

The army was no more organized. When the new officers arrived, no one knew what to do with them. "If you wanted to furnish your office, and you saw a table on the street, you grabbed it. One officers' commissioning ceremony was held on a tennis court outside headquarters for lack of a better location."

Azhar had ranked at the top of his class at the academy, and so he received his first choice of regiments: Probyn's Horse. This was a historic unit founded by Sir Dighton Probyn, an Englishman and winner of the Victoria Cross, and it had been granted to Pakistan upon Partition. The regiment had originally been a horse cavalry, but by the 1940s tanks had replaced the soldiers' steeds.

Even though these troops were now part of the Pakistani army, many formal British traditions remained, and each evening—no matter how hot the temperature—the regiment's fifteen officers would dress for dinner in their formal uniforms, called blue patros, looking sharp in their fitted royal blue jackets with gold epaulets and tailored trousers. They sat rigidly at attention while dining until the senior officer got up. As a bachelor, Azhar was given quarters in the officers' mess while millions not so fortunate milled around the countryside looking for a home.

In this political incubator the second lieutenant was quickly promoted to captain, and then he applied for the position as aide-de-camp to Pakistan's president, Khwaja Nazimuddin—the uncle of Hashmat, Nafis's chubby friend from Calcutta. His new post took Azhar away from his regiment and to Karachi, which at the time was serving as the republic's capital—a move that proved to be an important turning point in his life.

In 1951, fleeing the heat of the sweltering city, President Nazimuddin went on a holiday to the cooler climes of the hill country, and it was there that his wife fell ill. He sent his aide on a mission to neighboring Rawalpindi to fetch some medicine from the prime minister, Liaquat Ali Khan. When Azhar arrived at the prime minister's home, Khan was at a public meeting, and none of his retinue could find the medicine. They suggested the young officer should head over to the event and speak to Khan on the dais. However, just as Azhar was leaving, someone located the drugs, saving him a trip.

On his way back to the president, Azhar stopped for tea with an old friend, and as they chatted, they noticed crowds frantically running past. They rushed out, stopping a man on the street who told them: "Don't you know what's happened? The prime minister has just been assassinated. Someone shot Liaquat Ali Khan on the dais at a public meeting." Azhar had narrowly avoided being on stage with Khan when he was shot, but within hours he had received a new duty: accompanying the prime minister's body back home for the funeral.

Karachi, formerly an inconsequential port on the Arabian Sea, had suddenly exploded into a place of importance with the city's status as capital of the new republic. While Captain Sadik assisted the president there, Nafis was also in Karachi because her father was working at the new Ministry of Finance, an institution in charge of creating—among other things—Pakistan's monetary system.

Azhar was considered a very eligible bachelor, well connected and dashing in his military uniform. At the same time Nafis was part of a group one friend called "a roving pack of debutantes," elite young ladies whose names wound up on a list of invitees for garden parties and soirees in the nation's new capital. As they had done in Delhi the year before, the couple traveled in a parallel universe—except this time their universes would collide.

Chanti Prattipati | Berkeley, United States

The universes of a rather unlikely group collided on a Berkeley side-walk in November of 1999: three teenage girls from a poor village in India, a Berkeley graphic designer, and a multimillionaire real estate tycoon. Designer Marcia Poole was driving west down Bancroft Way in Berkeley, running errands in preparation for Thanksgiving the following day, when she noticed something unusual. The setting looked benign enough on that autumn afternoon: a tree-lined residential street only two blocks from the UC Berkeley campus. She passed a white apartment building, the type of nondescript 1970s architecture thrown up hastily to house students. But for some reason Marcia paused when she saw a group of Indian men carrying a rolled-up carpet toward a van marked Reddy Real Estate. As she stared from her car window, much to her amazement, she saw a girl's leg drop from the bundle.

"I realized that something was terribly wrong, and then I saw another group of Indian men and a woman trying to drag a hysterical teenager into the van. But this girl was resisting with all her might." Years later, as I stand here at the scene interviewing the witness, the hair is standing up on her arms as she remembers her shock and feeling of danger on that November day.

As the group pushed and pulled the girl toward the van, Poole

53

jumped out of her car and demanded to know what was happening. "There was a portly, balding man in his sixties, all dressed in white, standing off to one side. He comes over and says to me, very authoritatively, 'Go away! This is a family affair. This is none of your business.'" However, she did not go away; instead she hailed a passing motorist and asked him to call 911. Everyone froze into a type of standoff, with the Indians holding their captive and watching Poole, who blocked their way to the van. No one spoke, but after what seemed an eternity, they all heard sirens; the would-be kidnappers disappeared, leaving only the terrified girl and the Berkeley artist standing at the curb.

When Poole looked into the van she saw the bundle was moving, and instructed the paramedics and police to rescue the body inside. The portly gentleman reappeared, and as police tried to question the teenager, Laxmi Patati, who spoke no English, he offered to translate her language, Telugu, for the officers. Lakireddy Bali Reddy, the helpful translator, turned out to be the largest private landowner in Berkeley, the owner of a thousand rental units. Other members of his previous entourage also reappeared, and he introduced the parents of the girl wrapped in the carpet to police, explaining they had been taking the girl to the emergency room when Poole stopped.

Law enforcement took Laxmi into custody, and the ambulance took the unconscious girl, Lalitha Prattipati, to the hospital, where she was treated for carbon monoxide poisoning and released on Thanksgiving day with her life to be thankful for. However her sister, Chanti, was not so lucky.

Chanti Prattipati, her sister Lalitha, and Laxmi all grew up on the other side of the world in Velvadam, a village of eight thousand people in southern India. They were Dalits, "untouchables," part of the 250 million people on the subcontinent ranked so low that they are beneath the bottom rung of the caste system. As Dalits they were considered subhuman, and this designation, which they inherited on the day they were born, played a part in the convergence of events that ended on Bancroft Way on Thanksgiving eve.

Chanti's father worked as a laborer carrying cement for a construction crew, and the family lived in a mud-walled hut with no electricity or running water. He did not have the funds to educate his daughters or pay their dowry for marriage. When a local millionaire philanthropist took Chanti to work as a maid in his mansion, the father thought this solution a godsend. She was fourteen, and her benefactor, Lakireddy Bali Reddy, began having sex with her shortly after she moved into his home.

This fate would also befall her younger sister, Lalitha, who went to work for Reddy when she was twelve, and he immediately began abusing her. Three years later, when he offered to bring the girls to America to work for him at the princely sum of $10 an hour, no one questioned his motives. The mogul, who had received a chemical engineering degree from UC Berkeley and then built a business empire in the Bay Area worth $70 million dollars, returned to Velvadam each year; in his home village he built hospitals, schools, an eponymous engineering university, and provided an endless stream of charity. The villagers called him "our Mother Teresa."

His good deeds extended to helping Venkateswara Vemireddy, a man for whom Reddy had settled debts back in Velvadam. In return Vemireddy agreed to pose as the Prattipati girls' father, and his sister would pose as their mother; the four would emigrate to the United States under an H1-B visa, claiming the nearly illiterate Vemireddy was a computer analyst. The conspirators obtained passports for Chanti and Lalitha under fake names, and when they flew into San Francisco International Airport, Reddy was waiting for them. He set the imposter parents up in one of the apartment buildings he owned and installed the sisters in another, a one-bedroom pad on Bancroft Way that they would share with one of his other sex slaves, Laxmi Patati. She remembered that he welcomed the sisters to America, the land of the free, by having sex with both teenage girls on the night of their arrival.

This pattern of abuse, which included group sex with Laxmi, would continue for the next three months, along with claims of beatings and being forced to work in Reddy's Pasand Madras Cuisine restaurant, where the boss, Reddy's son, kept the girls' tips. Chanti and Lalitha, just seventeen and fifteen years old, also did maintenance on the landlord's fleet of properties. Residents recalled seeing them atop bamboo scaffolding tied together with twine, painting the millionaire's apartment buildings in their saris. Not coincidentally his name topped the list of frequent tenant complaints brought before the rent board in liberal Berkeley.

However, in spite of the terrible reality of their daily lives, the three teenagers did not see a way out. As is frequently the case with victims of human trafficking, they were kept with no money, spoke no English, had no education, and in this strange country knew no one other than their captors. Ignorant of U.S. law, they could not imagine that there were legal entities willing to help them.

Another tactic these slavelords use is warning their immigrant victims that if they go to authorities *they* will land in jail for entering the country illegally; and if they are deported, they will face retribution back home. Either way, their families, whom the traffickers know, are in danger of being tortured or murdered. This threat alone becomes one of the most successful tools to keep the captives from escaping.

But one day Chanti's suffering was over. On the day before Thanksgiving Laxmi left the apartment, and when she returned she found the Prattipati sisters unconscious, having passed out from carbon monoxide fumes produced by a blocked heating vent. On a bedside table was Reddy's prescription medication—a bottle of Viagra.

Laxmi called Reddy's Pasand restaurant, which was only a half block from the apartment; Reddy and some of his co-conspirators, including the imposter parents, rushed to the scene. From the second floor they lugged the unconscious Lalitha down to the van, but when police arrived at 2020 Bancroft Way they also found "a slim girl with wavy black hair gathered in an eighteen-inch braid, and she wore cheap yellow earrings and bracelets on each wrist." She was lying in a heap at the foot of a flight of concrete stairs. Chanti was pronounced dead on arrival at Alta Bates Medical Center. An autopsy later revealed she had been pregnant.

Thanks to the fabricated information Reddy initially gave officers on the scene, while pretending to translate for Laxmi, it took several weeks for the real story to unravel. He kept up the subterfuge, identifying the deceased as "Seetha Vemireddy," opining that she was "not at all lazy," and remembering her as "very pretty, tall, about five feet, six inches, and very charming." Her parents also spoke to police and the press, but Marcia Poole, the only eye witness, told authorities it seemed odd to her that the family of a dead girl displayed no emotion. However Chanti's father explained his feelings on the loss of his daughter to a reporter: "It is karma. What else can I say? We have to accept it." And then he sighed.

But while Bay Area papers were still treating news of the death as no more than an unfortunate accident, two local student journalists, Megan Greenwell and Iliana Montauk, wrote a piece for their high school paper that led off with a profound observation: "The recent death of a young Indian girl in a Berkeley apartment has brought up deep issues about the exploitation of young workers." They also questioned why the two teenagers were not enrolled in school. Around this time law enforcement agencies from Delhi to Berkeley began to receive anonymous letters tipping them to the ongoing criminal activity, and the feds pressed charges against Reddy and his sons.

When they were arrested, all vehemently proclaimed their innocence, and the Indian community both in the Bay Area and back in Velvadam rallied to their defense. But as the date for the trial approached, the five defendants—Reddy, his two sons Vijay and Prasad, and the imposter parents—all pleaded guilty to various parts in the smuggling, abuse, forced labor, and fraud involved in bringing the girls to the United States. Lakireddy Bali Reddy confessed to fourteen years of such crimes, involving the illegal importation of at least twenty-five individuals. But back in Velvadam locals had a much higher estimate of the number of persons their benefactor had helped by taking them to America. As George Iype reported from Andhra Pradesh, "rough estimates say at least 500—nearly half of them young girls—have gone over from Krishna district, thanks to Bali Reddy."

Today, however, following Reddy's guilty plea, the scandal has created a reputation for his hometown that makes Velvadam on equal footing with Bhopal. But no one will ever know the truth of how many nameless girls came here searching for the American dream and then disappeared.

Reddy stood to serve a maximum thirty-eight-year sentence, but after negotiations between the defense and prosecution, they struck a plea bargain deal that sent him to prison for eight years. His son Vijay in 1991 had had a previous brush with the law when he pleaded guilty to felony possession of crack cocaine and received a suspended prison sentence. During the Prattipati trial, this married father of twins also confessed to having sex with other teenage girls smuggled into Berkeley for this very purpose. In the end Vijay served two years in prison. None of the other defendants involved in the case served any jail time whatsoever.

Later, though, ten victims brought a class-action civil suit against the Reddys, and ironically the Prattipati sisters' impoverished parents—the people who had given their daughters away because they couldn't afford to feed them—were awarded 8.9 million dollars.

Unfortunately politicos have their work cut out for them to end these scenarios. The CIA reports that as many as fifty thousand women and children are brought into the United States under false pretenses each year and are forced to work as prostitutes, abused laborers, or servants. The global nature of the offense makes it nearly impossible for municipal governments to cope alone, and this trafficking is growing at epidemic proportions, threatening to overtake the drug trade as the top illegal activity of organized crime—and for good reason. Thanks to the brutal intimidation tactics of the traffickers, the victims are usually too terrified to take the witness stand, and without their testimony there's no evidence to convict the criminals.

Worldwide the UN Population Fund estimates as many as four million people are trafficked each year. UNFPA is one of several United Nations agencies working on the problem by training governments and facilitating cooperation between countries that are receivers and senders of trafficked individuals. They understand the international nature of the dilemma and how it's related to poverty and migration—the exact components that allowed Reddy to lure the Prattipati sisters to the United States. In reality, when women and children leave the protection of their communities, they're particularly vulnerable for abuse. California—a place built by immigrants—becomes the natural locus of such dangers, here in a land where nameless people come and go in their search for a better life and too frequently their history is washed away by the tide.

4 KARACHI

Even the bureaucrats charged with locating lodging had none. A tent village housed six hundred government clerks and messenger boys, who shared their camp with meandering livestock, the animals' pungent fragrance hanging in the sultry heat like a suffocating cloud. Pakistan was now home to six million impoverished Muslim refugees who had emigrated during Partition, and as they struggled to right themselves in this topsy-turvy world, many of them rolled into Karachi, the eye of the storm, looking for shelter.

In October 1947 the Shoaibs fled the dangers of unrest in Delhi, taking a train to Bombay, then boarding a ship that sailed across the Arabian Sea, docking in Karachi Harbor. They strolled down the gangplank to find Pakistan's freshly starched green flags, emblazoned with a white star and crescent, snapping in the breeze above a city in pandemonium. Foreign observers noted that the new seat of government "was not much of a capital."

At age eighteen Nafis saw the city that would be her new home as "a beautiful place—the beaches beautiful, the sand beautiful. And the streets were so clean, the air clean. The city had only about 400,000 people then—as opposed to eight million today. We'd really not lived in a place with a beach like that, and even then Calcutta was very, very crowded. So in contrast to Calcutta, Karachi was this clean, beautiful spot we'd come to."

Another observer, Pakistan's first president, Mohammad Ali Jinnah, peered through a monocle to watch his birthplace become the epicenter of his political creation—the world's largest Muslim nation. There was even talk of renaming Karachi Jinnahabad. When his health permitted, he toured the city to shouts of "*Quaid-e-Azam Zindabad*," meaning "long live the great leader"—a command he would disobey within the year.

And still other observers labeled the capital of Jinnah's realm a "one-camel town," a reference in *Life* magazine to the beasts of burden used for hauling goods along Karachi's roads—many of them unpaved, yet grooved with streetcar tracks that ran crosstown until they ended in the desert. Karachi bore the birthing pains of statehood more visibly than the rest of the union. As one historian noted, "Within a year its 400,000 population had more than doubled and the metropolis was blighted by incredibly sordid refugee hovels."

In spite of the chaos, the newly created Pakistani citizens worked alongside their leaders; they built the dream as their officials drafted it, balancing the documents on top of packing crates in lieu of desks. The populace was infused with a contagious enthusiasm that extended from the president down to the youngest schoolchild. Pakistanis had been given an opportunity to create the homeland they wanted, and the upper classes—shielded from the all-consuming burden of daily survival—realized that few people in the annals of history could say they had taken part in anything like this.

And in this respect, Nafis's father, Mohammed Shoaib, was very much a man of his time. As the joint secretary of finance, he was helping to form the government of the new Islamic state. This was no small feat, under the circumstances. The Hindus who had vacated the western subcontinent during Partition used to own most of the businesses in the region. The Muslims who flooded in to take their place were largely farmers—without farms or implements—and bitter battles ensued between them and the fabulously wealthy feudal landowners of the region. The Soviets were working to interest the poor and disenfranchised, including younger, more liberal members of the Muslim League, into adopting Communism, a step the new Pakistani regime worked feverishly to quell. As part of this strategy they knew they needed to develop the republic's economy at light speed, and that meant attracting foreign investment—an enormous challenge considering the instability of the world's newest country, and the fact that the West was still recovering from the ravages of World War II. In 1948 Pakistan's income was estimated at 450 million rupees and its expenditures at 800 million. A general acrimony toward their Indian neighbors continued with the dispute over Kashmir and the feeling that Pakistan had been severely shortchanged in the division of assets during Partition. Only 4 percent of the population could read, and even fewer could speak English, which was Pakistan's current official language.

Mohammed's position meant that the Shoaib family saw little of him. His days were consumed by the infant government even though he had an infant son, Tariq, at home. The holiday outings, the bridge games, and the tennis matches were all just fond memories now. Nonetheless, his contributions as a father remained vital to Nafis's development; as an impressionable young woman, she watched the process of nation-building, observing firsthand the skills it takes to create an administration. As Mohammed's work gobbled up his free time, the staunch Shoaib clan took all the changes in stride. Perhaps timing was actually a blessing, as the older children sought to spend more of their lives outside the home. The family moved into a house built by the British, a residence they received from the government in exchange for the home they had been forced to abandon in Calcutta. Their personal possessions consisted merely of the belongings in their suitcases, what they had brought along on the ship from Bombay. "And yet," Nafis recalled, "somehow we didn't miss anything very much." Their only real yearning was for the people they had left behind, but this wouldn't be a problem for long as the Shoaib sisters quickly made friends.

One new chum, Zeenat Haroon, was symbolic of an emerging Pakistani woman. *Life* magazine featured a full-page photo of this stunning member of the Women's National Guard wearing white baggy trousers and tunic, similar to a karate gi, or training uniform; the camera captured her black mane flying with the violent motion of swinging a bamboo pole. And luckily for Nafis's sister Chicky, Zeenat had a little sister, Laila.

Their father was Sir Abdullah Haroon, a leading politico, newspaper publisher, and supporter of independence for Muslims on the subcontinent. In 1949 their mother, Lady Nusrat Abdullah Haroon, joined with Begum Ra'ana Liaquat Ali Khan, the prime minister's wife, to create an organization called the All Pakistan Women's Association, an important group that focused on the education of young women. Their philosophy was "the role of women is no less important than that of men," and the organization had a girls' auxiliary, which Nafis joined. This environment amounted to a petri dish to nurture her development as a feminist and proponent of women's rights. Contradicting the stereotype of the repressed Muslim female, she was surrounded by female leadership.

In 1947 the *Nation* described the antagonism already developing for these females choosing to live outside the veil of tradition: "Moslem religious leaders are attacking young, modern-minded progressives as 'anti-Islamic,' and telling the women to forget about politics and go back into *purdah*," meaning the practice of keeping men from seeing women by segregating them or hiding them under burquas. The article ended with the words of a Lahore housewife: "it is not easy to turn back the clock. We have learned that even women have power, and they can't make us forget it."

While their parents struggled to organize the new regime, the younger generation sallied forth, transporting some of their old pastimes from Calcutta and creating new activities to fit their adopted home. Their clique consisted of Nafis and Chicky, the sisters Zeenat and

Laila Haroon, and two old friends from Calcutta: Hashmat, and later Shamsa, Nafis's medical school colleague.

The ingénues liked to visit the president's estate, where his guards were accomplished equestrians. Their horses, used mainly for ceremonial functions, were well trained, and Nafis and her troop put them through their paces as they trotted, cantered, pirouetted, and galloped across the grounds.

Other days they'd go for bike rides, rising at 6:00 a.m. while the day was still cool and the traffic manageable. The ladylike Chicky, an aggressive cyclist, screamed "fool" or "idiot" at pedestrians who faltered into her path. Once, when she crashed into an innocent gentleman, she jumped up in a fury and accused: "Look at what you made me do! Why were you in my way? You dropped me from my cycle!" Nafis and company threatened to leave her on the spot.

This devotion to sports had other rewards. In order to help her daughter slim down, Hashmat's mother asked her to join the athletic Nafis for morning walks, and years later she fondly remembered their routine: "I was always very skinny, because I used to walk two or three miles every day. But the incentive for me to take Hashmat was that her mother had all this cream and used to make me some lovely things for my breakfast. When I arrived at their house, her mother would give me this plate of *namash*." She was describing a dish that, like the food of the fairies, is made by leaving milk out overnight under the stars to collect the dew. Then before sunrise, it's taken in and whipped up in the cold predawn air till the milk is frothy, and the froth is served in bowls to the lucky individuals. Another even more decadent treat was *malai*, a type of clotted cream made by slowly boiling fresh milk. "So that was my incentive, and Hashmat later admitted: 'I hated Nafis because she could just sit there and eat all this stuff, and *I* wanted to eat it.'"

In spite of this jealousy the two young women remained close friends, savoring their shared Calcutta past—a link that had become even more precious now that both were in this strange city.

One interesting by-product of the migration to create Pakistan was that most everyone needed to make new friends. Suddenly millions of people found themselves in unfamiliar surroundings, and this upheaval stirred the pot of the rigid social strata of the subcontinent's upper classes, adding much spice to the social curry. Families who had prospered in a region for centuries, distilling their traditions down to a recipe for future generations, were now forced to experiment—whether they liked it or not—and this produced some interesting results.

These experiments formed the social milieu of the New Karachi, which revolved around parties—garden parties, tea parties, diplomatic functions, luncheons, dances, and dinners—where Nafis found herself on the guest list along with the Roving Pack of Debutantes. That they should be attending parties at all was a point of contention, as in traditional conservative Indian households, young ladies were forbidden to mingle with strangers and were sequestered at home where they could be supervised and protected. Thus Iffat informed her daughters that they could not be seen at these functions.

But as a willful young woman, Nafis was ready to experience this *société nouvelle*, and so in her role as the eldest she tested her diplomatic mettle against no less a formidable opponent than her father. She lobbied that she and her sister should be allowed to attend "mixed" parties—events where both men and women were present, occasions for her to dance, or even sing. When Nafis pouted, her father scolded his petulant daughter: "Don't just sit in your room and sulk. You've got to make your case if you want something, because if you don't make your case, you've lost it." Even in the midst of their competition, her father was teaching her how to win.

Taking full advantage of Mr. Shoaib's strategy, Nafis did win her case, and soon she and Chicky were the toast of Karachi. As their friend Jamsheed (Jammy) Rahim remembered: "Everybody invited Nafis to their parties, because she was always ebullient, full of beans, and at the end of every evening—you know how it is—you've finished eating, you go into the drawing room, you sit down, and you say, 'come on Nafis how about a song?' And she invariably—without any further persuasion—got up and sang. I would say my main adjective for Nafis back then was that she was a great sport. She was quite unusual in that kind of society in those days, you know. You had these wallflowers, who were barely allowed to come out by their parents, and then they must go back soon after dinner. Not so in this case. The sisters came out together, and they were extremely good fun and enormously popular as a consequence."

While they may have bucked tradition to attend parties, Nafis and Chicky always appeared at these functions outfitted in silk saris and *shalwar kameezes*, floor-length garments cut to preserve their modesty. However, like the rest of their social circle, the Shoaib women did not cover their heads, contrary to the practice in more conservative Muslim households.

Jammy commented further on the sisters' party personas: "Nafis was becoming a doctor. So she was much more serious, if you know what I mean. She went to all the gatherings, surely, but Chicky, on the other hand, most definitely was a person to have around a party. She was considered to be very attractive."

Their social profiles became a harbinger of other things to come, as their brother Hassan noted: "Even as a youngster, Nafis wasn't concerned about girls' things—in gossiping and talking about clothes and shopping and servants—this problem with such and such servant. I don't think Nafis was ever interested in that. She was never much into being a housewife. She was more attracted to what we consider male topics: politics, and what's going on in the world, or business and finance. And I used to see her often times at parties as the only woman in a group of men, holding her own in these discussions."

Not that sister Chicky was any dummy just because she didn't want to talk about international affairs. She studied English literature at college, and as her father would later say, "You are the only one in the family who is truly educated," a reference to the fact that the other siblings' schooling had centered on a trade. But the two sisters clearly had very different personalities.

Since their childhood, the extended family had always compared the two. As the girls matured, relatives continued to note the sharp contrast between them. Later they would frequently comment on these differences in unflattering ways, complementing the children's parents on their pretty daughter, then pointing to Nafis, and saying: "But who is ever going to want to marry *her*? She looks so unfeminine—so terrible—and she's so naughty!" At this point Iffat would pipe up and say, "Yes, but Nafis has brains, and brains are just as important for girls."

Finally one day Nafis accused her mother, "You say I've got brains, but you think I'm ugly!"

"No, I never said that!"

"Then you should say to them, 'she's not only pretty, she's got brains!'"

Nafis's looks and grooming improved dramatically as she got older, but she remained the headstrong one, the intimidating one among the children. Even though she could no longer thrash her brother in boxing matches, she learned to use those brains to get her way.

One activity fit in nicely with Nafis's desire to expand her brain *and* to join her sister as one of the belles of Karachi. Nicky and Chicky joined an "intellectual society," a group of about twenty young adults who met weekly to research and discuss matters of the day: politics, science, the arts, and their travels abroad. At each meeting one member would present a topic for discussion. Nafis, brandishing her knowledge from medical school, presented on Mendel's genetic theory and the inheritance of traits. In remembering this activity today, she noted wryly that in this era before television, computers, and mass entertainment, "You know, we didn't have that much else to do, so our energy went into socializing with each other."

The group's roster included Nafis, Chicky, and their friend Zeenat. Interestingly enough, the Intellectual Society was a "mixed" society, with equal numbers of male and female intellectuals present, one of the few opportunities for the two genders to mix unchaperoned. Also present were Iqbal, the Shoaib sisters' eldest brother, and their friend Jammy Rahim. Other peripheral members dropped by when they were free, such as Jammy's cousin Safda, who happened to be in an exclusive army regiment called Probyn's Horse. He frequently brought along his good friend, Captain Azhar Sadik.

And it should come as no surprise that three marriages took place out of this group. As Jammy noted: "We all knew each other very well, and marriages took place between people who knew each other. Otherwise, you see, most of us were new in Karachi and there was literally a sort of divide between the people who originally belonged to Karachi and the enforced, like all of us, who came from other parts of India. It was a very interesting time. And I must say, much fun was had by all."

Even though Azhar, the dashing aide-de-camp to Pakistan's president, was swamped with responsibility, he made time for "much fun," including hunting partridges early in the morning. He had retained his affection for shooting from his boyhood days in Patiala on the maharajah's estate and eagerly joined Jammy in this diversion. In fact, there were many similarities between Captain Sadik's upbringing and his current position as ADC to Khwaja Nazimuddin. Although his family's affluence had evaporated by the time Azhar was ready for college, he still managed to share the lifestyle of his more well-to-do colleagues who had headed off to Cambridge. When his name was added to a list of possible candidates to fill the ADC position, the deciding factor had nothing to do with his résumé. Rather, he met Nazimuddin, and based on the applicant's looks and manners, the president decided whether he would like to have this gentleman living in his household, interacting with his wife and children, and socializing with him on a daily basis. Azhar, having grown up in the company of Indian royalty, was well trained in the social graces. In service to his country the army officer sacrificed camping in tents and eating rations on maneuvers for quarters in the presidential palace.

His professional obligation to attend social functions included dances where the Pack of Roving Debutantes practiced their considerable ballroom skills. Nafis, particularly, floated across the floor, displaying her command of the waltz, foxtrot, tango, and rumba. However, one friend remembered, "Azhar wasn't keen on the floor." Perhaps he preferred gatherings of the Intellectual Society, where he got to stare into the smoldering, heavy-lidded eyes of an intriguing young woman named Nafis Shoaib, who stared back at him with all the mystical sexuality of Radha while they discussed subjects on a deep philosophical level.

Nafis was the only female in this group with her own professional goals. She attended Dow Medical College, Pakistan's newly created campus consisting of three-story stone-block buildings rimmed with verandas. Dow was a much smaller school than the university in Calcutta, but her gender still put her in a distinct minority. She no longer had the support of her colleague Shamsa, who had moved to Dhaka after Partition, where her father had taken a position. However, the smaller school meant that the pupils received more individual attention from the faculty, and Nafis was pleased that the professors treated the men and women as equals.

Some of the male students kept a watchful eye on her, worried that she would flunk out because she spent so much time on extracurricular activities. "Some boys in my class used to always be very concerned because I was doing so many things like playing sports and attending parties. They used to say to me: 'You are going to fail—you know that, don't you?' And I used to reply: 'You keep saying that as if you *want* me to fail. Why do you keep bothering about me?' No, they assured me, 'We want you to pass because we like you, so we want to help you!" With that, Nafis's concerned colleagues convinced her that she should join a study group in order to succeed.

Much like the Intellectual Society, the system was that one member of the study group learned a chapter and then presented the findings to the assembled. "I found this so tedious, I never did my chapter. One of the men was quite concerned—he had a little bit of a crush on me—and he decided he was going to do my chapter—and teach it also. And I said, 'that's wonderful.'" At this point the coed was already learning the powers of delegation that would make her prime management material.

Another educational challenge involved the rendering of microscopic slides for physiology class; all her male cohorts used to turn in handsome representations. "I was terrible at art, I couldn't even make a circle. It happens I had just mentioned to one of my brother's friends, 'Oh, this drawing thing! All these boys spending so much time on it. They'll get ahead of me—even though they know less than me—just because of this silly drawing.' So this friend said, 'I'll do it for you.' He made these perfect diagrams—beautifully done, with all these different colors. The whole book was complete in about four or five days, and I presented it to the study group first before handing it in. They were stunned and said, 'But you can't draw!' I said, 'Well, I just spent some time on it, got some help, and did it.'" Nafis laughs as she recounts this story fifty years later, clearly amused at her own brazen behavior. She had already learned to let the roosters do the hen's work.

While Nafis may not have been a Rembrandt, what she did extremely well was focus on lectures in class. She took notes, which she never read, but the act of writing helped her to memorize the material. Still, before each test she would fret to her parents that she couldn't possibly pass this exam. And each time they assured her that she would be fine. "No, no, this time, I am definitely going to fail." Instead, she learned to write very quickly for exams; she prioritized the information she recounted, in order to give the most complete answer in the time allotted. She became one of the top students in her class, receiving high marks throughout the second year.

In 1949, during her third year of medical school, Nafis was ready to take on a leadership role at Dow. She decided that the college should have an all-female student council, and she organized the women, including herself, to run. Naturally the Leo loved speaking in the halls during the campaign. Even though the men made up 80 percent of the student body, many of them voted for their female colleagues, which brought them to victory. However, the professor in charge of student affairs declared the election "irregular, null, and void." Nafis informed him that the students could choose their own slate, and that there was nothing in the guidelines saying the candidates should be of a certain gender. As an adviser, she declared, he could change the rules before the election, but not afterward. When he refused to let the all-female council take their posts, Nafis organized a strike of the student body, and it was during this time that her gynecology professor forever earned her respect.

When some of the male students went into his class soon after the strike had begun, he asked, "Where are the others?"

"They are on strike to protest this election business."

"Then what are you doing here? Get out of my class! You don't earn marks by not being in strong solidarity with them."

When their boycott of classes failed to produce results, Nafis organized a protest march to the health minister. As she paraded down the boulevard with the other students, waving a huge banner, she passed a car in which her father rode with one of his colleagues from the Finance Ministry. "Isn't that your daughter Nafis?" the fellow said with a nudge.

Mr. Shoaib pretended not to recognize her. "No, no, that's not her—she's in college." Nafis didn't even realize she'd been spotted until that evening when her father demanded to know why she was cutting class instead of cutting up cadavers. When she explained that she was protesting an injustice, he said: "Well, maybe the cause was right, but I don't think that was the correct way to do it—to take all the students out of school and march. But still, as long as they followed you. . . ."

After a month with no results, his ever-pragmatic daughter decided they were just wasting their time and missing their studies. She called off the strike and ordered everyone back to class.

In 1950 her colleague Shamsa, who had been sickly since their move to Dhaka, came with her father on a business trip to Karachi. After a week of visiting with Nafis, the doctor noticed his daughter had regained her color and seemed like her old self, so he decided to let Shamsa transfer to Dow. Reminiscent of the Shoaib family tradition, she stayed with Nafis for the term and joined her friend in the antics of the city's social elite. The two young women resumed their camaraderie from Calcutta days, attending their medical classes together, this time as seasoned veterans.

Many classes later, the twenty-two-year-old Nafis qualified as a doctor and began her internship at Jinnah Hospital in Karachi. And it was during this experience, her first opportunity at working with real patients for any length of time, that the philosophy began to germinate that would shape her future career. "I interned in obstetrics, and that's where I saw these very poor people with all kinds of complications. Many of them used to die of hemorrhage. And you started to see the connections between poverty, lack of autonomy of women, and all that. You could see that many of these deaths could have been prevented if they had either spaced the pregnancies or if they'd been looked after better and not brought to the hospital so late. Even though this was a big city hospital, people often brought their pregnant women in very late in their labor. They did this because of ignorance, lack of attention to women's health, women themselves not knowing how to care for their own bodies, and lacking the authority to make decisions. The common attitude was: 'Pregnancy is a normal thing, so what's all this big fuss about? My mother had many children. It's part of a woman's lot. When they get pregnant, some of them will die.'"

Nafis's internship may have been just the beginning of her sixty-year influence on women's health, but it was the culmination of her quest to become a doctor. Her brother Kemal remembered what happened when his sister received her first earnings as an intern—the princely sum of three hundred rupees. She went to their mother and placed the money in Iffat's palm, closing the older woman's fingers around the bills. "This is for you, Amma," Nafis explained, "because all I am, I owe to you."

Following the tantrum Nafis threw when her uncle planned a meeting with a prospective suitor, no one had dared broach the subject of arranging a marriage for her. She had never stopped her frenzied activity long enough to worry about finding a husband, and yet fate steered a candidate into her orbit.

After meeting President Nazimuddin's aide-de-camp, she informed her girlfriends simply, "I like this chap." She continued to run into Azhar at social functions, but their most significant encounters were the Intellectual Society meetings, where the couple talked about important topics of the day. There the future doctor was able to analyze the captain's psyche under a microscope. "Actually, we were very different from each other. I like people, and he's quite shy and retiring—not outgoing. But I think he just liked my personality, and I liked his personality. And we talked a lot about books, and that kind of thing." She found one of Azhar's more unique traits particularly endearing: "I remember he was interested in my work and my career, which was very unusual for a man in our part of the world. So I think we had an affinity for each other."

After several months of circling past Nafis in Karachi's social whirl, Azhar cut his leg in an accident. When the medical student called him at home to inquire about his health, he confessed: "Oh, well . . . I wanted to ring you up, also, but. . . . " The man who had warded off murderous raids during Partition had been too shy and afraid to phone a woman. After Nafis's call, they became a couple, and Azhar began to visit her at home. Next they began playing tennis together on the president's courts, with both of them dressed in the gentle-man's traditional tennis whites to hide Nafis's shapely legs beneath long trousers.

While the other members of the Pack of Roving Debutantes were quietly pairing up, Hashmat fretted: "They all had admirers. I was the only outcast, and I cried, 'Nobody likes me! I'm not going to get married—I'm going to become a scientist.' To which the girls all used to say, 'Oh, for God's sake, shut up and fall in love—you get on our nerves.'"

And then, to her surprise, an opportunity to do just that appeared from within their midst. In this tightly knit society, the stitches continued to be closely intertwined. Azhar had taken over the reins of his position as aide to President Nazimuddin, Hashmat's uncle, from another army officer, Captain Noor Husain. This officer met Hashmat in the endless round of Karachi parties, and the nervous girl confided to Nafis that she thought he liked her. Nafis worked to facilitate the romance, encouraging Captain Husain to pursue her friend, and craftily trading places at dinner parties so the two could get to know each other. Soon he was calling Hashmat at home; one day they were chatting on the phone, when she saw the prime minister's secretary mounting the stairs. "Liaquat Ali sahib has been trying and trying to ring your father, but the line's busy. There has been a riot and he needs to speak with him immediately!"

Before long Hashmat's admirer was not satisfied with phone calls and chance dinner conversations; he brought a marriage proposal to her family, and even her uncle—Noor's former boss—was shocked. "My father told Uncle Khwaja, 'Captain Husain has proposed,' and he responded, 'Well, well, silent waters run deep.'"

Nafis, now nearly finished with medical school, helped the betrothed prepare for her wedding in more ways than one. She realized that her old friend, a very innocent girl, knew nothing about sex, or what would be expected of her as a wife, since these topics were verboten at the Shahabuddin's home. So on one of their daily walks to help the future bride slim down, the two young ladies marched down to the bookshops on Elphinston Street. As her relatives had feared, Nafis had lost all inhibitions as she learned *everything* about sex through studying obstetrics and gynecology. In front of the mortified Hashmat, she bought a book explaining marital relations. "Go and read this," were the doctor's orders.

The wedding of this nineteen-year-old girl from one of Pakistan's most prominent political families became the apex of Karachi's social scene. And fortunately, the revelry surrounding the nuptials provided numerous opportunities for the other young lovers to meet. Even though Nafis was taking her final exams for medical school, she was loathe to miss a single get-together, knowing the bride would soon be departing for a frontier army outpost with her new husband. On Hashmat's wedding night, as she prepared to leave for her honeymoon after the reception, President Nazimuddin bid farewell to the guests and slipped up the back steps to say good-bye to his niece. He found her sitting among a group of friends, and when Nafis started to howl at the reality of losing her bosom pal, he offered cheerfully: "Don't worry, dear, you'll be getting married soon enough," and everyone started to laugh.

The two women corresponded after Hashmat left town. The young bride eagerly awaited her chum's letters outlining the social happenings in Karachi—a life that she already desperately missed as she sat home alone in an unfamiliar, primitive corner of Pakistan.

When the Roving Pack of Debutantes were in circulation, they knew that even though their parents were progressive enough to let their daughters attend social functions in groups, there was a limit to their access to the opposite sex. There was no dating in their culture. The timid Hashmat never broke this stricture; even though Noor wanted to take her out, she refused. But the rebellious Nafis was different, as Hashmat remembered: "She wrote me, 'I am not like you—I went out with Azhar.' I was shocked, frankly, because in those days, this was very unusual. All courting was hide-and-seek."

Miss Shoaib's parents would not have approved of their daughter secretly dating the handsome army officer, but in spite of his poverty, they did approve of him. In fact, Iffat was so fond of Azhar that Nafis used to chide her mother, "I think he is your child—not me."

The couple were in love, and in their era, it was assumed they would marry. It was also assumed that sex before marriage was out of the question—which for the passionate young pair added an urgency to set a wedding date. However, as Captain Sadik planned his official proposal to Nafis's parents, he didn't bargain on one thing: Mohammed Shoaib was about to accept a position with the World Bank and take his unmarried twenty-three-year-old daughter—the light of Azhar's life—half way around the world to America.

Dora Chemenu | Manhea, Ghana

In another century and another continent, abstinence is still being preached to young lovers. The admonishment to ignore biology, the drive that has kept the species alive, is promoted as the chief method of birth control here in Ghana, as I learn visiting one community outside Accra.

I am attending services at the Manhean Presbyterian Church, where I cannot help but compare the modest house of worship to ones in my city, San Francisco. The plaster walls do not go all the way to the corrugated tin roof; the windows have wooden shutters, but no glass. The ceiling fans, hanging from the rafters, occasionally whir to life with a surge of power, as does the public address system. Luckily the forceful young minister delivering the sermon in Ga, the local tribal language, doesn't need the mike.

The parishioners are divided by gender; on the left side of the aisle women wear brightly colored cotton dresses in an array of frenzied patterns: geometrics, chevrons, spider webs, florals. Their outfits are completed by "headgear" matching their dresses, a sort of fabric turban that ties at the nape of the neck. The men wear equally vivid patterned dashikis, except for a lone gentleman wearing a flowing robe like Cato the Elder. A trait that the sexes share in common is that they do not even pretend to be awake and listening to the sermon.

Despite the riot of color and the reverend's impassioned delivery, the congregation seems to be suffering from an epidemic of narcolepsy; matriarchs have their heads thrown back onto the chair, white-haired elders, many with scars like slash marks on their cheeks, are hunched over with those scars buried in their hands, and children snore, their shiny faces lying on their shoulders. I am one of the few people awake, and I note wryly that this much they share with their brethren at church services back in my country. In the distance beyond the open windows some of their neighbors are shrieking and hammering rhythmically on jungle drums, causing me to ponder the long-standing dichotomy between missionary and tribal practices on this continent.

Suddenly an explosion of music changes everything inside the house of worship as the choir begins a song dominated by a preponderance of high soprano voices. A Mama Africa sweetness pours out into the room as if the angels themselves are serenading us. The sleeping congregation leap to their feet and form a gyrating conga line up to the collection box, swaying, clapping, playing tambourines and African drums, and chanting along with the gospel group.

Like many Christian churches in Ghana, this one serves as a community base for peer educators who are working to inform their neighbors about sex education and the dangers of HIV. Because of their religious foundation and high pressure from the Bush administration, the primary building block of this program is to preach abstinence, counseling teenagers and adults alike that they should remain celibate outside marriage, much as the original African missionaries would have done one hundred years ago—before IUDs, injectibles, or condoms were readily available.

As with most poor nations, the influence of funding from donor organizations cannot be overestimated. And this fact has been the source of outrage for many authorities in the field of reproductive health.

One of these is Dr. Andrew Arkutu, Pathfinder International's medical director for Africa. He is considered one of the leading experts in the field of reproductive health on the continent, having formerly worked here for the World Health Organization. He also served as head of UNFPA's mission to Swaziland, Zimbabwe, Tanzania, and Nigeria. His on-the-ground experience provides him with little patience for the promotion of abstinence as a tool for dealing with Africa's life-and-death battle against AIDS, especially considering when the policy launched, countries like Uganda had an HIV infection rate of 33 percent of the population. He has publicly rejected Bush's ABC program, which espouses three components: abstinence, be faithful, and use a condom. "Abstinence" asks young adults to refrain from sex until marriage and views abstinence as the most effective way to avoid HIV infection. "Be faithful" asks people in relationships to be true to their partners and claims that fidelity in relationships reduces exposure to HIV. The last component teaches the participants how to use a condom.

Bush's ABC plan promotes the first two options, "abstinence" and "be faithful," over the last one, with a stipulation that one-third of the total funds allocated for HIV prevention ($15 billion) must be reserved for programs that promote abstinence. However, in interviews with the Manhean peer educators, they admit that their clients prefer and request condoms; very few choose abstinence as their preferred method of birth control.

Bush's plan "shows a complete lack of understanding of our culture," Dr. Arkutu notes. "Most of our women are physically or sexually abused. It's not as simple as ABC. It may be possible for Laura Bush and her ilk to say no, but for a woman who is being abused or raped, she does not have these options. These women who are getting HIV from coerced sex don't have the power to negotiate. ABC is an escape into rhetoric, but it has no sense behind it. It has no understanding of the *realities* of the life of women in Africa."

One of the peer educators who dispenses the ABC formula is fifty-three-year-old Dora Chemenu. She is a plump woman with shiny skin the color of dark chocolate, which contrasts against the sparkling white cotton she wears. Her dress is conservatively cut, floor length but short-sleeved, and decorated with blue circles and zig-zagged lines. Dora's face radiates warmth, dominated by a dazzling smile that reduces her narrow eyes to slits. Her skull is decorated by precise cornrows of golden bleached hair that spiral into a bun at her neck.

She has been working as a peer educator for the past three years, a task she performs on Saturdays when she is not teaching nursery school. She is pleased to see the result of her efforts in family planning, that fewer babies are being born in the community, mainly as a result of condom use and injectibles. Dora travels door to door, sitting down with her neighbors to train them on reproductive health. She doesn't have a problem going into their homes and instructing them on these sensitive topics, only frustration when she shows up and they don't give her time. Sometimes her clients complain that the only reason Dora is delivering her spiel is for the money, but she reminds them that she is not getting paid anything for her work. She volunteers her services for their benefit.

The teacher is used to visiting people at their homes from her other volunteer activity: witnessing for her religion. Her lectures on family planning and HIV prevention are merely an extension of this practice. She tells her neighbors: "This is a very, very fearful disease. I see from their faces that they are afraid of that. I say if you don't take care and you go about—maybe you see a fine girl, but maybe she is having the disease, but you don't know it then. You will get it, and it will finish your life. There is no cure."

Unfortunately the peer educators do not have condoms to dispense; they only carry one for demonstration purposes, and then it is up to their clients to procure their own. They also discuss the benefits of abstinence, of waiting until marriage to begin having sex. Married couples who do not want to use condoms are also advised that they should stop having sex. And as far as Option B, "be faithful," I ask, "What if the wife is faithful but not her husband?"

Charity Gyamera, another volunteer, advises, "We should continue to pray to God for our husbands to be changed." However, she admits that her clients request condoms; very few choose abstinence as their preferred method of birth control, and this includes teenage girls, who wisecrack, "I should stay out a hundred years if some man doesn't come and marry me?"

Dora began her own family when she was a teenager, so her advice to young women is the voice of experience from one who knows the struggles of trying to raise a hoard of children in poverty. Her life to date has personified the quality of life trilogy that aid organizations like UNFPA have pinpointed, the combination of child poverty, teen pregnancy, and high school dropout rate.

As she tells her tale in her deep, lilting voice, Dora explains she didn't attend the university to become a teacher; at first she worked as a farm laborer but accepted an offer to take a course training her to teach the youngsters in her village. When the organization that employed her ran out of money, she traveled for four years until she found another opportunity to teach. Today she works with preschool children, using plays and poems as a storytelling device for instruction.

The teacher herself has learned many lessons the hard way. She first married a man at eighteen, but he left her after they had a child. Later she met her second husband, and they had four children together, but then that marriage also ended in divorce. During the years that followed she traveled doing itinerant farm work, moving from village to village with her young family to look for work. At one point she met a teacher, and they had a little girl, but he also abandoned her. With few options left and six children in tow, she went back home to her parents. Then amazingly, after thirty years apart, she reunited with her first husband.

In spite of the vagaries of marriage in Dora's life, she has persevered and today helps others to make more informed choices, with knowledge that was not available to her when she was a girl. One thing is clear, however: even though Dora followed the tradition of her community by marrying before she had sex and a family, the relationships did not last, and in the end, it was this woman alone who was responsible for her children's survival.

(*top*) Nafis (*left*) and Chicky (*fourth from Nafis*) at a family party.

(*bottom*) Nafis with guests at her wedding.

Nafis and Azhar's wedding festivities, May 1954.
The bride posing at her Georgetown home.

Nafis and Azhar's wedding festivities. (*From left*) Nafis, her brother Tariq, Azhar.

Iffat, mother of the bride, putting muhndi (henna) on Nafis the
day before her wedding; Bushra Qureshi looking on.

(*top*) Nafis with the Sadik brothers in 1954, Azhar (*left*) and Younis (*right*).

(*bottom*) Azhar and Nafis at Le Lido in Paris.

5 THE WEDDING

While Captain Azhar Sadik was conspiring with his relatives to present a marriage proposal, he had no idea if Nafis would accept it. They had never discussed the topic because matrimonial agreements in their culture were made from family to family; for a man to propose to his beloved and then later inform her parents of the couple's decision would be unheard of. She might have been a wild card in many areas, but at least in this regard Nafis conformed to tradition.

Since Azhar's father was divorced, living as a bachelor in Iran where he was now working, he decided that the family's envoy would be his sister and her daughter. The hopeful groom's aunt and cousin wrote the formal proposal and took it to the Shoaibs' home, along with gifts for Nafis.

Mohammed was relatively fond of his prospective son-in-law, and Iffat adored him as if he were her own child, spoiling him and cooking up his favorite things to eat. However, before they agreed to hand over their daughter, they had to deal with a practical matter. In their former lives the bride's family usually knew the groom's; but with all the geographical upheaval that had taken place on the subcontinent since Partition, they were dealing with a new paradigm. Before he would commit, Mr. Shoaib insisted on making inquiries into the Sadik clan. He learned that they were very well regarded in the Punjab, but he was concerned that in some portion of the family there had been many divorces, including Azhar's parents. This was not the case with his and Iffat's kin—who tended to stick together in spite of their problems—and this difference worried Nafis's father.

He discussed his concerns with Azhar, along with an even more critical topic: "You know she expects to work . . ."

"Exactly—don't I know it!"

After satisfying their doubts, Mohammed and Iffat granted their blessing, with one minor stipulation. The wedding would take place when the Shoaibs returned from the United States for their holiday, and Azhar agreed that he would wait.

To cement the deal he ordered an exquisite ring made for his fiancée: gold, encrusted with diamonds and rubies. Their families celebrated the couple's engagement, and then the Shoaibs left Karachi for a new life in America.

Anchored at England's Southampton Harbor lay the *Queen Mary*, the Cunard ocean liner spit-shined from her dark hull to the three smokestacks rising several stories high. Two thousand passengers milled about the deck, celebrating amid bon voyage parties and gaping at the luxurious staterooms, until the midmorning call came over the loudspeakers, "All ashore who are going ashore." With a frenzy the envious bade farewell to those bound for sea and exited dockside. The visitors stood waving from the shore as the gangplanks were raised and the tugboats moved into position. At last the crew cast off the moorings, and with one long blast from her deep-throated whistle, the *Queen Mary* eased out of the slip, headed toward the Atlantic.

As the ship sailed out of the harbor, on board were Mohammed, Iffat, sisters Nafis and Chicky, four-year-old Tariq, and their loyal chauffeur, the one who had clandestinely taught Nafis how to drive back in Calcutta. Still in England were the three older brothers who were attending boarding school.

The Shoaibs' staterooms were in first-class, expansive cabins with antique mahogany furniture, where the clientele could order any-thing they wanted from the room service menu. Nafis, who loved to eat, had been looking forward to this opportunity to try all sorts of foods. What she hadn't predicted was becoming seasick riding the wild waves of the Atlantic, an unfortunate illness that made even the most delectable dish appear putrid. She and Chicky also discovered that privilege has its price; their neighbors were mostly sedate older people, and all the dancing and parties were in the other classes. Hap-pily their appetites improved as the voyage continued, and in the end they considered their crossing a marvelous adventure.

When the Shoaibs sailed into New York Harbor in style, the year was 1952. As so many immigrants arriving before them had done, they gathered on deck to witness the Statue of Liberty—that symbol of American emancipation—glide past. This was their first visit to the United States, and naturally they had many preconceptions about life there, visions they'd pasted together like scrapbooks created from history texts, newspapers, novels, and films. By comparison, though, one reality came as a shock: they were not prepared for the pall of segregation that shrouded the land of the free.

When the dark-skinned family entered a posh restaurant in Man-hattan, they unwittingly created alarm. But when Mohammed removed his hat, and the maître d' saw his hair was straight, he was told, "Yes, sir, please come in." Iffat always wore a sari, and when they were identified as foreigners—as opposed to domestic blacks—they were welcomed.

Mohammed had landed a plum position as an executive director at the World Bank, representing Pakistan and the Middle Eastern coun-tries, and the family, except for Nafis, settled in Washington DC. The freshly minted doctor would be starting as an intern at City Hospital in nearby Baltimore and was stunned that as she migrated south from New York, the segregation restrictions only worsened. She boarded a bus to discover signs reading "Negroes to the back" and learned that

"No Negroes Allowed" was the norm in public restrooms. When she went swimming with friends from the medical staff, they would instruct their Pakistani colleague to stay behind them. "She's been in Florida and has a dark tan," they would explain lightheartedly as they hustled her past the gatekeepers.

Even in a cosmopolitan center like the nation's capital, there was much curiosity and confusion over this clan of Pakistanis. Once on a city bus in Washington DC, when the sisters were headed out for the evening, a helpful soul picked up the hem of Chicky's garment, trailing along the floorboards. "Leave my clothes alone!" she snapped in frustration at this ignoramus who had never seen a sari before.

Chicky was unimpressed with life in the States. Not surprisingly—considering the attention the Shoaib girls had generated in Karachi—Nafis wasn't the only one to leave a beau behind. At twenty, Nighat had been engaged before she left home. Unlike her big sister, she had always wanted to be married by the time she was nineteen. Initially her father's appointment was only supposed to last two or three months, and reluctantly she agreed to the transcontinental move. As time dragged on, though, she became increasingly unhappy in Washington. "I kept begging them, 'Please let me go back to Karachi. I don't want to be here.' I know it didn't make my parents happy, but that's how I felt." Eventually the distance frayed the heart strings of her romance until it disintegrated. Iffat was also homesick for the warm circle of community they had left behind, yet true to her nature, she would support her husband's wishes, living out the last few years of her short life in a foreign land.

Nafis had brought along her signature laser-like focus on the matter at hand, which was to further her medical career, and she looked forward to training in the United States. While she wasn't homesick, she struggled with other irritations in this new land. For one thing, she couldn't understand why information she'd taken for granted as the purview of educated people—like a knowledge of global geography, of countries, capitals, and oceans—was not taught in the center of industrialized civilization. "In the U.S., I found 'history' was not 'world history'—ever. Obviously every country teaches the history relevant to them, but we also learnt world history including something about the American Revolutionary War. Not that we knew that much in detail, but we knew that the Americans were under the British and then got their independence. But in the U.S. people didn't know anything about the subcontinent—or Partition—which was quite a shock to me, because it was such a huge event with a million people dying. It had been on the world's news everywhere just a few years prior! And when I came to intern here, people didn't know anything about Pakistan, even though the U.S. was so involved with our country and we were a strong ally during World War II. They didn't even know where Pakistan was located. 'It's somewhere there . . . ' they'd say with a wave of their hand. And they used to ask, 'Oh, how did you go to school?' 'Well, I went in a car.' 'Oh, a car . . .' I said, 'What did you think, we went on elephants?' Yeah, they had pictures of us going to school on elephants. I mean, really . . ."

Another fact that surprised her was the complete absence of women practicing gynecology or obstetrics in the United States, unlike the subcontinent, where these had actually been considered prime fields for women entering medicine. Nafis found no American female doctors in the obstetrics ward, only a handful of foreign transplants like herself.

She fell into the rhythm of hospital duty, working thirty-six-hour shifts, with twelve hours off, punctuated by a couple of free weekends per month. Befitting this monastic life, her position included uniforms, meals, dormitory housing, and a whopping salary of twenty-five dollars per month. And yet, amazingly, she felt grateful for the opportunity to work in an American hospital.

However, being a foreigner practicing medicine presented some difficulties in the field of communication. Words were pronounced differently than Nafis was used to, and acronyms introduced an entirely new language into the equation. For instance, her colleagues kept referring to SOBs. In Nafis's country SOB stood for "son of a bitch," and she couldn't figure out why the staff kept cursing these patients. "I would sit and ponder over this, and I didn't know whether I should ask. Or I worried that maybe these were terms in medical books that I didn't know about. So I was quite nervous, and finally I questioned a nurse. At first she looked at me very curiously. I said, 'Really, I'm scared to ask anyone else in case they think I don't know anything.' So she said, 'But you know this. This is not knowledge. It's just a way of writing.' And she explained to me that SOB stands for 'shortness of breath.'"

Cultural differences between Pakistan and the United States presented more serious problems than consternation over SOBs. Dr. Shoaib prescribed a sedative for a man in the hospital who was acting strangely, and the medication caused him to become quite violent, racing around the ward until he injured his leg. When her colleagues asked why she'd given this drug to a drunk, Nafis explained that she had never seen a drunk person before and had no idea the gentleman was intoxicated.

She was further mystified by the hospital's philosophy toward patients—an attitude she had not encountered elsewhere. As an intern she sometimes worked in the Chronic Disease Hospital and was expected to do anything to prolong the life of someone who would be dying shortly. "This man's heart had stopped and I was ordered to inject adrenaline into it—all these heroic measures to revive him—in order for him to suffer so he could die again. I didn't argue because I didn't want them to think I was some barbarian who didn't value life, but I thought to myself, I never want to become ill here because I don't want to be treated like this. I'd like to be allowed to just die when I'm ready."

City Hospital was a teaching institute affiliated with Johns Hopkins and the University of Maryland. As a result, Nafis was required to ask the bereaved family members for permission to perform an autopsy on their relative who had just died moments before, so the students could examine the cause of death. "I'd have to say, 'Please sign this form so we can perform an autopsy on your husband.' The first time I did this the family started weeping, and then I started weeping, which was a real trauma."

In spite of the various challenges, she remembered the staff as friendly and helpful, an asset in her medical education. And it was here that she met Isadore Rosenfeld, who would remain a colleague for the rest of her life.

Dr. Shoaib also became close with several of the poor black women who came into the maternity ward to deliver their babies. Again, in Pakistan she had never encountered many of their situations, and she asked them questions about their lives as much out of curiosity as she did out of concern.

"First of all, in Karachi you never even thought of asking a woman who was having a baby if she was married." She soon learned, much to her astonishment, that many of her patients were single. Not only that, but one patient explained that she had three children by three different fathers. "When I asked her why she did that she admitted that she gets maintenance from all of the fathers and maintenance from the state, so that was her income."

On emergency room duty Nafis treated a woman who had been stabbed by her live-in lover. "Well, what will you do now?"

"I'm going back to him."

"How can you go back to this horrible man?"

"Well, first of all, darling, I'm going to beat him up." Nafis had come to City Hospital to get an education, and she was getting more than she bargained for.

She and an Indian woman both volunteered to do docility obstetrical service in Baltimore, where they went into patients' homes to provide follow-up care. They both thought this experience would help them when they returned to their respective countries. What neither expected was that living situations for these patients was no better than that of the poor people on their continent—with a couple of notable twists. "These were mainly black families that lived in one room, and conditions were really bad, with a shower curtain strung up to separate two beds. The children—maybe six or seven—all slept in one bed and the woman in another. Mostly there was no husband around. But what surprised me was some of them had a large television set and a Buick outside—for some reason it was always a Buick—and inside was so much poverty." At this time abortion was not legal in the States, and so Nafis also saw women coming in hemorrhaging from coat hanger wounds, or feverish with infections, after trying in desperation to end their own pregnancy.

Most babies, however, were carried to full term, and the young obstetrician was gaining experience with delivering them—sometimes as many as thirty a day in the 1950s when the baby boom was at full throttle. In this one hospital alone, six thousand infants came into the world in 1952, at a time before family planning became popular in the United States. The *Baltimore Sun* reported on a trend with these births: "There's a new name going around. An intern at City Hospital is obviously well-liked by many people, so they name their babies Nafis."

The rigors of her new life had an effect on Dr. Shoaib. To survive the thirty-six-hour shifts, she added a cigarette to her coffee break in an attempt to stay awake. "All the data on smoking was just starting to come out—smoking and emphysema, smoking and cancer—it was just starting to emerge. Yet at Christmas the tobacco companies sent cartons and cartons of cigarettes to the doctors."

The benefit of the long hours was that she had little free time to pine for her sweetheart. As their separation stretched, the space between them filled with sheaves of love letters, fluttering pages inked with words that flew back and forth across the oceans when the lovers could not. During this time Nafis and Azhar did not dance at garden parties or discuss genetic theory or slip into tennis whites to meet on the president's court. And certainly they did not slip into a stolen embrace. In fact, they did not lay eyes on one another or hear that oh-so-familiar voice for two years. Azhar's term as aide-de-camp had ended, and while he commanded a tank squadron in Rawalpindi, his fiancée was walking her late-night rounds in Baltimore, fourteen thousand miles away.

Sometimes in the evening Nafis would dust off her bridge skills, but it was tough to find available hands that weren't holding a stethoscope or syringe; the only opportunity was when everyone was on duty, and then if a player received a call, the game broke up. In the few moments she had to herself, the young woman with the bewitching eyes dreamed of returning to Pakistan for her wedding, unaware that this would never happen.

In Pakistan marriage was not regarded as the final outcome of a frenzied love affair between two hot-blooded strangers. Rather, it was deemed a very serious contractual agreement between two families; each member of the bride's clan also became a member of the groom's, and it was commonplace for several marriages to take place between the relatives of in-laws, a chance to strengthen their bonds. Before they became husband and wife, Mr. and Mrs. Shoaib were each part of a large extended family, and later one of Iffat's cousins married Mohammed's brother. But when it came time for the couple to arrange the first daughter's wedding, the old playbook went into the trash.

They had betrothed their daughter to a young army officer from the Punjab who lived on the other side of the globe. And in April of 1954 the Shoaibs were living in Washington DC, with no plans on the immediate horizon to return to Pakistan for a holiday, as they had promised Azhar they would . . . two long years ago. Nonetheless, he had been ticking off the days, and when 730 had passed, he insisted that the couple get married. Nafis's relatives had asked the question years ago, "Who is ever going to want to marry *her*?" and now there was a definitive answer. Mr. Shoaib agreed that he had made a deal, but he informed the impatient bridegroom that if he wanted to wed post haste, he would have to do so in America.

Captain Sadik had never been to the States, but his father was friends with the Pakistani ambassador, Syed Amjad Ali, who resided in Washington. The groom's father wrote to the ambassador, asking him to serve as proxy, and Ali generously agreed to assume the elder Sadik's responsibilities.

During the last week of April a nervous Azhar boarded a ship headed for the United States, and like his fiancée had two years before, he sailed into New York Harbor. The Pakistanis sent a driver down to the seaport to fetch him, and rushing to arrive on time, the chauffeur had some difficulty finding parking. When they returned to the car, Azhar was astonished to watch the driver, a man of the world, a man who knew how to work the system, tip a New York City police officer so that he would not ticket the vehicle. To the twenty-six-year-old army captain, the United States was the epitome of all that was virtuous and fair in the world, the epicenter of democracy, and while he was still swaying on his sea legs, this image washed out with the tide.

Azhar boarded a train for Washington DC and, as planned, stayed at the ambassador's house until the wedding. He would be there for the next few days, because according to tradition, the long-suffering lovers still could not see one another until *after* their wedding ceremony.

The Shoaibs had rented a fabulous old house at 1224 Thirtieth Street in Georgetown, where they planned to put on the grand spectacle of entertaining that was expected of a high-society wedding back in their homeland. Decorated in period style with antiques, the estate even boasted a suite where Andrew Jackson had slept. When Azhar first visited his future in-laws' home, he watched in astonishment the preparations taking place for his wedding. He remembered thinking that the house was impressive except for the rundown garden. But lo and behold, one day when he arrived the entire grounds had been redone; scrappy crabgrass had been replaced by fresh green sod and a crimson sea of azaleas. The visitor marveled at life in this strange land, where a veritable Eden could spring up overnight.

The Washington press corps became exceedingly curious about the whole process of this Pakistani wedding. The fascination could be explained by Mohammed's position at the World Bank and rumors that the event would be attended by high-ranking officials, including the ambassadors of several nations and Vice President Richard Nixon. Another titillation was the fact that in 1954 Pakistan was still a relatively new country, at this time only seven years old. The scribes heard mention of exotic nuptial rituals, and this ignited the imagination of every gossip columnist in the District. Azhar explained, "Paomic Ramala, who was married to the foreign secretary, had written a book on weddings in our part of the world—Muslim weddings—and some of these press people went through this thing religiously."

Nafis recalled the badgering her mother took from the society pages: "There were not many Pakistani marriages at that time. So my mother was getting crazy because the press used to ring her up and ask: 'What ceremonies are you going to have?' And she said, 'What's happening? Why are they calling me up? It's none of their business!'

"She had no intention of showing my trousseau, but then somehow the press had to see the trousseau. So the public relations officer at the Pakistani embassy said, 'You have to show it.' Suddenly there we were emerging, and while I'm being made up for the wedding, my clothes are all on display. The press kept coming in to take my picture, and hollering 'hold it, hold it.'"

In these photos we see a stunning twenty-five-year-old Nafis, who is not a scruffy tomboy any longer. Her black wavy hair is combed back from her face and styled into the short bob that was stylish in the 1950s, popular on the silver screen with everyone from Elizabeth Taylor to Ava Gardner. The bride's kohl-rimmed Radha eyes are burning into the camera, their expression intense and triumphant, while a mere suggestion of a smile tugs at one corner of her pouty lips. She is perched on a loveseat in an elegant drawing room of her family's home, her back ramrod straight, holding out to the viewer a silk gown stretched across her arms. Behind her is an ornate Georgian mantle and bookcases, and fanning out around her feet are a dark leather train case and matching suitcases, several trunks, and countless department store boxes, their lids off, tissue paper frothing out their tops, and open to display nine handbags, fifteen pairs of new shoes, and one hundred saris, many of which her father had purchased for the bride during his travels from Pakistan to Paris. Daddy's little girl might have been leaving home, but she certainly would not go naked.

In the end, publications ranging from the *Times of Karachi* to the *Daily Express* of London to *Newsweek* in the States covered the week of celebrations. The front-page story from Baltimore's *Sun Magazine*, "Muslim Wedding," shows the groom with a veil of flowers covering his face—a tradition that prevents the bride from seeing him. Azhar's head is wrapped in a gold turban, the ends flaring out, and a long silver necklace hangs to his waist. He is wearing tight leggings covered by a knee-length white coat with a stand-up color—a style that would later infamously become known as the "Nehru jacket." His shoes, like a vision from the *Arabian Nights*, are upturned at the toes. The bridegroom is seated next to an empty chair, a symbol of the fact that in the traditional Muslim ceremony, he will not see the bride until after they are pronounced man and wife.

Inside the newspaper the feature is oddly titled, "A Woman Doctor from Baltimore Becomes the Bride of a Pakistan Army Officer in Oriental Splendor." The society columnist writes:

> The festivities actually lasted three days. They began with the arrival of the bride's wedding gown and Dupatta—the Pakistan veil—which,

following the Muslim tradition, was provided by the bridegroom—who brought it with him from Karachi where it was made—and was sent on a large silver tray by a servant to the bride's home.

As truly royal as raiment can be, the gown of the finest French brocade is a soft, shell pink heavily embroidered by hand with gold thread and gold sequins in what is known as salma-sitara work. The divided skirt is flounced to the knees with ruffles completely covered with this embroidery, and so full that the division cannot be seen when it is worn. The upper part of the skirt is concealed by a knee-length, tight-fitting tunic, flared below the waist and touched with gold embroidery which also embellishes the filmy Dupatta.

Just as Azhar's cousin had supervised the tailoring of the groom's marriage garments, she had supervised the creation of the exquisite shell pink gown in Pakistan. Nafis had no idea what her wedding dress would look like until it arrived on the silver tray.

The press even reported the extensive toilette that took place before she donned her dress: "The bride had been redressed like a fairy queen; her hair elaborately arranged and sprinkled with gold-dust, 'Afshan'; her lips reddened with 'Pan'; nails tinted with 'Mendhi.'" This last item referred to the bridal ritual where seven happily married women decorated Nafis's hands in ornate patterns with henna. This happens on the night before her marriage as she is surrounded by friends who serenade her with songs. While this was happening, Captain Sadik was enjoying a stag party with the men. But before these rites, the singing and dancing had already been going on for several days, with between one and two hundred people gathering every night.

The actual ceremony took place on May 6 at the Pakistani Embassy so the couple could be married on their native soil. Unlike a Western wedding, this one was strictly business, with representatives of the bride and groom receiving the rites in separate rooms, performed by Dr. Mahmoud Hoballah, head of the Islamic Center.

After the ceremony, the Shoaibs hosted 250 guests for the lavish reception. The evening began with another Muslim wedding tradition, the *arsi-mushaf*. Nafis was seated alone on a sofa, waiting to see Azhar for the first time since the couple had parted two years prior. But before he could enter the room, Chicky, the maid of honor, blocked his way, and he had to pay a ransom for his bride. Then he sat on the sofa next to Nafis, still not looking at her. Friends stretched a gossamer rose-colored scarf over their heads, read a couple of verses from the Koran, and offered Azhar an embossed silver hand mirror. Finally the pair gazed into its reflection for their first glimpse of each other. Iffat placed a candy into the mouths of both newlyweds, a symbol of the sweetness their married lives would bring. While all this is taking place, Chicky steals Azhar's shoe, another custom; she refuses to return it until he promises to look after her sister—oh, and hand over the tidy sum of $50.

The tradition is for the bridegroom's family to host a second feast called *walima* on the evening following the wedding. Since the ambassador was standing in for Azhar's parents, he hosted the *walima* at the embassy, an affair that featured two hundred guests pelting each other with fruits and flowers.

The *Washington Post*, which featured stories for several days including a major photo spread, called Nafis and Azhar's wedding a "storybook Moslem marriage." One full-length shot of the sisters portrays two traffic-stopping beauties with looks that any Bollywood star would envy. Nafis is resplendent, "with all the glitter of a fairybook princess," swathed in yards of pink fabric, the scarf that serves as her veil draped loosely around her head. In the center of her forehead the *jhumka*, a golden ornament, hangs just above her eyes; her eyelids are varnished with dark shadow, her black beauty mark a startling accent on the right side of her nose, her full lips like ripe plums. The look is a tempting mixture of demure bride and exotic oriental dancing girl—ready for the wedding ceremony and definitely ready for the honeymoon.

Not to be upstaged, Chicky stands next to her sister with a protective hand on Nafis's arm. At twenty-two, she is every inch the ingénue in a sari, adorned in elegant blue silk. They share the same smoldering sensuality, but in Chicky's version everything is several shades lighter—almond-shaped tiger eyes and a honey-brown bob that reveals diamonds dangling from her earlobes.

By comparison, in every photo the mother of the bride looks as if she might collapse from exhaustion at any moment. And Mohammed appears to be straight from central casting, the dark handsome foreigner with a cleft chin, slicked-back hair, and the same large expressive eyes as his daughters. The caption under his picture reads: "Pity the father of the bride. Just like an American dad, M. Shoaib, World Bank executive director, totes up the cost. But he's still smiling." In another shot the father of the bride is shepherding his daughter past photographers; he is dapper in a gray single-breasted suit, a cigarette elegantly poised between his fingers. In a rare pose of humility, Nafis's face is downcast away from the glare of the flashbulbs.

Evidently Iffat was not the only one exhausted by the marathon nuptials. The press had begged for the story, but clearly were worn out from their assignment. Evelyn Peyton Gordon summed up the sentiment in the *Washington Daily News*: "Everybody who has taken part in the orthodox Muslim ceremony will heave a sigh of relief tomorrow when the last of the singing, eating, flower-pelting, costume-changing has ended, and the newlywed couple is on its way!"

As newsreel footage of their wedding entertained audiences in eighteen countries around the world, the newlyweds were on their way, traveling for the next two months. Driving south from DC to Key West, Florida, they flew down the highway, unwittingly running through a speed trap in a small Georgia town. Azhar was driving, and he suddenly saw flashing red lights and heard the screech of a siren as the sheriff pulled their car over. The officer had begun to lecture Azhar on his excessive speed when Nafis decided she would interject with the creative excuse that her new husband didn't speak English so he couldn't read the signs. When she piped up the cop said, "Lady, be quiet—I'm not talking to you! I'm talking to the chauffeur."

One can only wonder at the joy of the two lovers being reunited after years, at long last husband and wife. No more religious strictures keeping them apart, no watchful parents, no continents, oceans, or time zones separating them. At last they were finished with the wedding marathon, done with hosting the entertainment of family, friends, diplomats, bankers, and the press. With the veils of flowers and pink silk scarves stripped away, their eyes were finally free to devour each other, uncensored.

As the couple drove through the South they became reacquainted, sharing the events of the last two years and discussing the future. Azhar was surprised to learn that the recently named Mrs. Sadik now smoked cigarettes, a detail that had somehow escaped the love letters.

Nafis had convinced City Hospital to give her credit for the full term, even though she was leaving a month early to wed, and then she would be returning to Pakistan with her husband. After their Florida visit, they drove back to Washington and then headed north to the traditional honeymoon spot of Niagara Falls.

The newlyweds left the States the same way they had arrived: by ship. They sailed out of New York Harbor aboard the *Ile de France*, bound for Southampton. Perhaps Allah was smiling on them, because neither was seasick on the return crossing. When they docked in Europe, they visited London and then headed to the continent— Paris, Lucerne, and Geneva—where Nafis showed off for Azhar, pretending she could speak French. Finally the couple boarded a ship in Genoa and sailed back into Karachi, where they would spend a week being feted by his relatives and her long-lost friends.

But typical of Nafis, within a few months of becoming a wife herself, she would be telling other women how to run their married lives.

Angela Karogo | Narok, Kenya

Angela tells me the story of the events preceding her wedding: "My dad said, 'You are grown up now, so it's time to circumcise you,'" she remembers. "I was ten years old at the time."

At thirteen she resembles a boyish waif, so I can only imagine what she looked like three years ago when her father deemed her "grown up." In fact, if she wasn't wearing the navy blue jumper of a girl's school uniform, I would assume she was a boy. Angela is a member of the Masai tribe, and following their tradition, she shaved her head when she came of age. The blotchy acne of puberty mars her dark skin, and her narrow, elongated brown eyes carry a wary, wounded sorrow that mirrors her history.

Although Angela's native tongue is Masai, we are conversing in English, a language she is learning at boarding school. She speaks in a soft, shy voice, a look of panic occasionally alerting me that she has not understood me. When I ask about her studies her face breaks into a rare grin; otherwise when she is telling me about her family life prior to rescue, her expression is one of detached grief, as if she were talking about some other girl. As if she must remove herself from the reality of her history to survive.

A pseudonym has been used to protect this girl's privacy.

We are seated at the Tasaru Girls' Rescue Centre in Narok, located in Kenya's Rift Valley, some sixty kilometers east of the Masai Mara preserve. On my journey from Nairobi to reach her that morning I witnessed a landscape of tranquil beauty. I saw tribesmen wandering with their flocks of sheep. One young man stood sentinel amidst harvested wheat and corn stalks drying in the morning sun; he was draped in red tartan robes, his outstretched hand holding a staff. Beside him a herd of antelope arced the crest and then disappeared on the other side of the ridge. Zebras grazed alongside the road; a black ostrich paused under the shade of a feathery, flat-topped acacia tree, the bird's unlikely shape silhouetted against the golden light. Miles from nowhere a lone girl swatted her small menagerie of goats with a switch as she shepherded them down the road in the direction of the rescue center.

Much like this young shepherdess, Angela grew up working at her father's house, her mother having passed away when she was a baby. She attended school until she was nine, at which time her father announced he could no longer afford to pay her fees. It was shortly after this that he told Angela it was time for her to be circumcised.

Circumcision is an important rite of passage into adulthood for boys and girls in African tribes, and for none more so than the Masai. For a girl the ritual involves five days of training by elder women on how to be a proper wife and mother; at the end there is a feast attended by the community to mark the successful transition. Then in the morning the girl is seated on a goat skin, and her clitoris, and in many cases the surrounding vulva, are hacked off with a razor blade without any kind of anesthetic. The initiate is merely held down by the guests who have attended her party. Then her wound is sewn up with a needle and thread, or in some cases the skin is knit shut with thorns. Because of the unsanitary conditions and resulting complications of hemorrhaging and infection, the World Health Organization estimates that one in four girls die as a result of this procedure. A survivor loses her ability to enjoy sex and copes with myriad health problems for the rest of her life, especially when she tries to give birth. If she is not cut open so that the baby can come out, she risks being torn to bits and bleeding to death.

Angela had learned about these problems from Agnes Pareyio, who had visited her school to speak to the students about the dangers of female genital cutting. After hearing Agnes speak, the girl knew she didn't want to go through this suffering and told her father so. His response was to slap her and proceed to organize the ceremony anyway.

On the day of Angela's circumcision her dad went off drinking while at his house arrived a bevy of individuals to organize the ceremony—a dozen women including the child's grandmothers. The cooks slaughtered a goat and happily prepared the traditional feast. In the evening, as her home was packed with merry-making guests, the women laughing, the men drinking wine, Angela ate nothing. Instead, as her celebration progressed, she spent the time wondering how she could escape. But the elders had prepared for this scenario as well; ten people surrounded her bed that night, watching her as she pretended to sleep. In the morning her grandmothers and the other females held her down for the ceremonial cutting.

Afterward the girl became so ill from infection that after a week with no improvement, her family sent for the doctor. He gave her a mysterious liquid to drink, and she recovered. In the meantime Angela's father planned her marriage to a forty-five-year-old man who already had two wives. The patriarch struck a good deal, though; in exchange for his daughter he would receive some blankets, tools, and cattle.

Again Angela protested. "I told him I don't want to get married, I want to go to school. He just kept on hitting me and said, 'I am your father and I must direct you. And if you don't obey me I'll kill you.'" The tribesman took her to the household of her new husband's mother, where the wedding ceremony took place amidst more feasting and merriment to celebrate the union between the groom and the ten-year-old bride. By this point Angela had stopped eating at all, concentrating on how she could escape before she was expected to perform her wifely duties—duties that would rip open the wound from her recent circumcision.

The night of the wedding she seized this opportunity, went outside, and ran into the bush. Considering she was now in a remote and unfamiliar place, she had no idea where to go and wound up hiding behind a tree. Meanwhile, her husband and father gathered a posse of villagers to hunt her down; the men found her hiding place, punched and kicked the girl, then carried her back into the house as she struggled and screamed. Luckily the new mother-in-law advised the bridegroom to leave the girl alone until she could adjust to her new role.

A couple of nights later Angela quietly opened the door and slipped outside, running into the bush again. She headed toward her grandmother's house, where she planned to beg for help; but her footsteps awakened the dogs, and their barking alerted her husband. The girl sprinted through the darkness until she spotted a leopard; then she grabbed a tree and clung to it until the animal passed. This is where her husband and father found her. They thrashed her again and returned her to the house.

After this second escape attempt, her husband complained that his new wife kept running away. "The deal is off," he announced to Angela's father; he wanted his goods back and would return the girl. Now she was really desperate because she knew what fate would be awaiting her when she arrived back home.

The next morning, when Angela's husband went off to work in the fields, she decided to take a new approach. She promised her mother-in-law that she would not attempt to run away anymore. Instead, she vowed sweetly to become a good wife and headed outside to wash the dishes at the river. Once out of sight, the young bride ran as fast as she could through the forest until she came upon a road and flagged down a car. The driver took her to the children's center in Narok, and upon hearing her story, staff there brought her to the Tasaru Girls' Rescue Centre, a move that undoubtedly saved her life.

Here she was greeted by Agnes, who, although female, is a true Masai warrior. She's an imposing figure with the regal bearing of her large form draped in traditional tribal finery—red-plaid tartan robes accentuated by stings of brightly colored beads. Agnes, a community leader, founded the center in 2002; today an expansion features a wing funded by Eve Ensler, author of *The Vagina Monologues*. As part of her mission here, Agnes works with other elders to create an alternative rite of passage for the girls, one that keeps all the important parts of their culture but skips the cutting. When Angela's father arrived at the gates demanding his daughter back, Agnes called the police.

Today the thirteen-year-old lives at the shelter with Agnes and other girls with similar histories. UNFPA pays for her boarding school tuition. Angela, a top student, plans to become a doctor. "Then I'll come back to Narok so I can help Agnes and my people."

6 DOCTOR'S ORDERS

When she was a girl, Nafis had dreamed of becoming a doctor, of do-ing something "to help the poor." But like most childhood dreams, while hers provided a beacon on the horizon, the details were fuzzy. Now, after years of preparation, she had indeed returned home to help her people.

After the final hurrah of matrimonial celebrations died down in Karachi, the newlyweds boarded a train heading north, alighting in Rawalpindi, where they would make their first home together, in a city strung along the Grand Trunk Road, a route that had for centu-ries connected Lahore with the Khyber Pass into Afghanistan. Fur-ther north was the Hindukush and the Karakoram Range of the Himalayas, home to some of the tallest peaks in the world.

Pindi, as the locals called it, had been built upon the site of an ancient Buddhist civilization, then had been home to the Sikhs before Partition. Since 1947 it had been designated as the headquarters of the Pakistani Army, sixty miles from the Pakistani/Indian border. This was the spot where a young lieutenant named Azhar Sadik had first landed when he was one of the last Muslims out of India. Pindi was the place he remembered as "weird and wonderful" because the new govern-ment's branches lay in chaos—with the army at the top of the heap.

Now, seven years later, Azhar's post might have been new, but he was back on familiar turf in the Punjab. Captain Sadik was reacquainting himself with the region where he was raised, but the locale was foreign to his bride. She busied herself constructing a new life here—one that would be a radical departure from her recent role as society belle living in a Georgetown mansion.

The couple's first home together was an apartment building that had been built as a barracks during the war. The structure had no air conditioning and was topped by a tin roof, a feature that—in a region where the muggy monsoon temperatures regularly topped one hundred degrees—generated the heat of a solar oven. Nafis conquered the water fear she'd carried since her near-drowning mishap in Orissa, and she and Azhar fled to the swimming pool daily to keep cool. But in the way of newlyweds, they had fun with the novelty of married life, starting from scratch to acquire china and carpets, silver and linens—spinning their humble surroundings into an inviting nest.

Fortunately they lived in this bivouac for only a few months; then they moved to a nicer apartment building, the Mary Green House, which had a large living room, dining room, kitchen, three bedrooms, and—because it was Pakistan—servants' quarters. There was one maidservant to cook, another to wash the clothes, and another to care for the shared garden outside where the neighbors congregated.

The Sadiks fell into a comfortable daily rhythm, adopting a style imposed by the exigencies of life in a hot climate. They rose early and began the work day at 7:00, finishing at 2:00 in the afternoon and returning home for lunch, their main meal of the day. Because many women didn't venture outside their quarters, most of the shopping was done by the men. It was best to take care of these duties before the sun scorched the markets, wilting produce and patrons alike.

In the afternoon the high temperatures forced everyone back indoors, into the shade of darkened rooms where the fans whirred. And here, behind the closed drapes, the couple embraced their addiction: bridge. They began after lunch and would play seven, eight, sometimes nine hours a day. *And they had to play every day.* Nafis had learned from her father, so she was already a force to be reckoned with, and the small stakes betting added more competitive fuel to the fire. By the time the Sadiks had finished their stint in Pindi they had honed considerably their bridge skills—a mixture of information exchange, evaluation, deduction, and tactics—all fine pursuits for a diplomat in training.

Following the traditions with which they were raised, the newly married couple welcomed their relatives, a massive collection when combined. Nafis hadn't met many of Azhar's extended family, and now that the pair were living back in the Punjab where he was raised, the cousins came calling. Nafis remembered the social practice: "They don't telephone and say, 'I'm coming.' They just come. It was normal. When you visit a town you go and call on people. When you live in a town you make sure that you call on various people periodically. So during the visit you spent ten or twenty minutes, you had a cup of tea to find out how everyone was. The calls were then returned. It was not like you had to go to a meal. You just go there to see somebody." Nafis learned her etiquette lesson well, and she would later use this same practice of making social calls to her advantage, both personally and professionally, all over the world.

When Nafis and Azhar married in DC, her brothers had been studying in London and were unable to attend the wedding. But when the boys, now in their late teens, wanted to visit their sister and brother-in-law, Nafis sent them money to cover their travel expenses. Kemal and Hassan arrived in Karachi by ship and boarded the train for Rawalpindi. Nafis had calculated the cost of second-class tickets, but when she arrived at the station to greet them, she was alarmed that their smiling faces did not exit this car. As she looked frantically around the platform, she finally found them, filthy and worse for wear, standing outside the cattle car where they had traveled the day and a half journey from the capital, choosing this more economical mode of transport so they could pocket the extra cash.

Several years earlier when Mohammed Shoaib had stated matter-of-factly to his prospective son-in-law, "You know she expects to work," he was testing Azhar's reaction—one that would demonstrate his suitability as a husband for the headstrong Nafis.

Azhar had replied, "Exactly—don't I know it!" Of course, this was easy to say before the wedding, and before he had taken his bride halfway around the globe, out from under the protective arm of her father. The truth was that it was not unusual for girls to head off to medical school and then readily abandon their careers when they married. And now here was the newlywed Nafis, with her basic creature comforts supplied. After years of working like a galley slave chained to an oar, she could have taken a well-deserved rest. She could have slept in, gossiped over tea with her neighbors, read the classics, and stayed up late nursing her bridge addiction.

But what propelled Nafis was not the desire for a life of leisure, and as a result, within her first few days of arriving in Pindi she was down at the army hospital securing a position for herself treating the officers' wives. She was hired as a civilian doctor to practice in the military facility and started to work immediately.

Nafis rose early each morning and donned her sari. She studied herself in the mirror and, as a friend recalled, "added all the jewelry she could possibly hang on herself." Then at 7:00 she reported for duty at the hospital. Dr. Sadik then made her rounds and returned to the house at 2:00 for the lunch her servants had prepared; afterward she sat down with whatever guests had appeared and shuffled the cards. But if a call came and a patient had a crisis, she put her hand on the table and went back to the hospital, all of which her husband supported.

When Nafis took her job at the hospital in Pindi, she could have officially joined the military. She chose not to because she knew that they could post her to a different region, and then she would be separated from Azhar. This choice to remain a civilian meant she earned a third of the wages she would have earned on the army payroll, but that was her concession. She wanted to work, but her marriage was still her top priority. She also knew that if she had not been fortunate enough to have the support of the men in her life, her career would never have happened.

When Dr. Sadik began walking the wards and treating the officers' wives, she realized just how privileged she was, because many of these women were not valued by their spouses. And they were dying because of it.

What the ob-gyn didn't know when she applied for her job at the army hospital was that on her honeymoon she had gotten pregnant. In March 1955 the couple's first child was born, a beautiful baby girl. They called her Mehreen, a name that means "like the sun" in Persian.

Nafis went to Karachi for her delivery, and her mother came from Washington to attend her. However, immediately after the baby was born Nafis had to return to Pindi because she couldn't obtain leave from her job. "My mother said, 'But I've come all this way to see you!' I said, 'Well, then you'll just have to come home with me.'"

They took little Mehreen back to Pindi aboard the train, and Nafis resumed her work at the hospital. Fortunately she lived close by and so she would come home when it was time to nurse. While she was gone the maidservant cared for the infant. If they were in a jam, there was always a relative or neighbor to pitch in and look after her. Azhar's fellow soldiers came to visit the proud parents and pay their respects, offering comments like, "Sorry you had a daughter. Maybe you'll have a son next time," remarks that infuriated the baby's father.

Seven years after Azhar had landed as a newly commissioned officer in the weird and wonderful Pindi, the army promoted him to major and assigned him as an instructor at the Pakistan Military Academy, which was outside the city in Abbottabad. Just as he had learned soldiering at prestigious Dehra Dun, he would now be training cadets to become leaders.

Luckily Nafis had saved all the moving boxes, and when the news of Azhar's promotion came, she started packing again—a skill she would perfect during her tenure as an army wife. "I would just place everything back into the same cartons. Really, nothing broke. These things were made like battleships, and the crockery and all used to be put into them. We used them for many, many moves."

Located nearly a mile above sea level, the Sadiks' new hometown was in a cooler clime, close to the hill stations where Pakistanis from Karachi escaped the summer heat to relax in the mountains. Abbottabad itself was founded as a British garrison and retained its colonial architecture, all constructed around shady gardens and wide thoroughfares. Nafis and Azhar moved into a house with a lovely yard conveniently located near the military academy and the hospital.

The cadets from Azhar's new post at the academy mixed into the social melee at the Sadiks' residence, as their instructor frequently invited his students home. In many cases he and Nafis either knew the young men's parents or knew of them, so the couple became a surrogate family to the cadets, who ranged in ages from seventeen to twenty. They called Azhar "Major Sadik," of course, but the trouble was what to call his spouse? In their part of the world the practice was to address any woman older than yourself as "auntie" as a term of respect, and certainly there was never a greater test for respect than when dealing with your commanding officer's knockout twenty-six-year-old wife. The first crop of visitors tried the auntie route, but Nafis stopped them cold: "Listen, I'm not your auntie, so please don't call me that."

"Oh . . . then what should we call you?"

"Well, you can call me Mrs. Sadik, or Dr. Sadik, or call me Nafis because that's my name."

"Oh no, no. Then should we call you mom, because you're like our mother?"

"Certainly not. I'm not your mommy." In the end they settled on the very formal Dr. Sadik, which Nafis found hilarious.

Soon Nafis would put to good use her clandestine driving lessons from her youth in Calcutta. In a time and place where no women drove, she tooled around town. The local people had never seen a woman drive before, and so they regarded her in amazement. The first time she arrived at the bazaar, everyone poured out to look at this brazen creature. *Who was she? And where did she come from?*

Nafis clearly was a breed apart and therefore was a source of endless curiosity. One day she was out horseback riding around the academy grounds when she received word that she was needed at the hospital. So she decided to show off and just gallop up to the front door of the hospital and visit her patient in her riding habit, crop in hand.

But normally Nafis made her rounds aboard an army jeep—this in the days when these vehicles were little more than a steel box on wheels and steered like a tank. She tossed her medical bag in the back and chugged up dirt-track mountain roads outside of town, winding through the cool piney forests. Upon relocating to Abbottabad, she opted to do pro bono work that required her to venture into the villages where many of the soldiers lived. To treat their wives she set off alone, never questioning whether this was smart or proper. "I'm sure that someone else might have thought about it, but whatever I wanted to do, I decided that it was the appropriate thing for me to do, and just did it."

Initially she began by treating the army spouses, but in these remote regions with no access to health care, the diabetic grandmother would emerge, carrying a colicky infant in her arms, and Dr. Sadik would examine them all. But what concerned her most was a repeated hazardous pattern—one that flew in the face of her obstetrics training—of women giving birth every year. Many mothers had not spaced their pregnancies the recommended two years and as a result had become dangerously anemic. She knew this anemia could become life threatening, causing a host of complications including hemorrhaging to death during childbirth.

So she ordered these women to stop having babies for a few years.

At this pronouncement, her patients' mouths opened, their eyes widened, and they regarded their physician as if she had just landed from Venus. "I cannot make that decision—that's my *husband's* choice. Besides, I've only got daughters, and my mother-in-law will be very angry if I don't have a son."

"But you're not in good health."

"I know, I know. . . ."

These conversations took Nafis back to her childhood in India, and that attitude she could never fathom: that boys are fundamentally worth more than girls. Here was a patient, a woman who already had many children, willing to risk her life to produce a son; in fact, for many women the only value they had was being the mother of a son. One woman had nine daughters, but so wanted a boy that she gave birth for the tenth time; Dr. Sadik attended her, and when she announced the baby was a girl, the mother burst into tears. In many cases the doctor saw how little the family actually cared for the mother's welfare—that even if they knew the danger, they would say it was worthwhile for the chance to have a boy to spoil rotten.

Realizing her patients' decisions were largely in the hands of the husbands, Dr. Sadik asked to speak with them directly. In effect, she called a meeting of the troops. Since she was a medical officer, she demanded their respect, because if there was anything these men understood, it was the protocol of the military. However, what jarred their notion of protocol was that *this soldier was wearing a sari.* Before them was a petite woman, five foot three, who looked much younger than her twenty-six years. She stood there telling them that they could not impregnate their own wives—and this was a first in the army, a first in Abbottabad—maybe a first in the history of Pakistan. She looked fiercely around the room, her Radha eyes unsettling even the most courageous officer with their unflinching ability to bore through armor. She was sexy and smart and domineering—a walking contradiction draped in diamonds and silk. It was like a bizarre dream—their commanding officer is fused with a doctor who can save their family, and yet it's a woman disguised as the type of teenager who could make a man forget his faith. And she's telling him he can no longer have sex.

Nafis had already been to visit the head of the army hospital to tell him he needed to provide her with contraceptives, which in 1954 meant condoms. She recalled, "He was quite shocked. He said, 'We don't need those things. You know, this is an army hospital.' And I said, 'But we're looking after wives, and wives get pregnant. And if you do maternal health, you have to have contraceptives.' It took several sittings with him, but I pestered him a few times. Finally he said, 'I don't want to see you again. Here's some money for the condoms, and that's it. If you get into trouble—and I know you will!—it has nothing to do with me.'"

Nafis's victory created a strategy she would use for the next fifty-five years. "That's one lesson I learned in life, that you should never give up on anything that you really strongly believe is right. And because you might not get it once—the first time, the second time— eventually you will get it if you persist. And from that incident on, I never worried about having lost something. I just made my point, then went on. I waited and found another opportunity to say the same thing or do the same thing or bring it up again—and again."

While she lectured, the army husbands sat silently—horrified by their choice between giving up sex or killing their wives—which is what this young doctor was saying as she stood there before them: *My wife could die if I get her pregnant again because she is in poor health—when she tries to give birth, she could bleed to death. Not only that, the baby could die, too. So now not only is my wife gone, but so is my child . . . and that could be the end of the son I've been waiting for all these years.* In a few moments the husband has gone from an ordinary man, a religious man, a family man, to a man who must make a choice between murdering his wife and unborn infant or giving up one of life's great pleasures.

One gentleman blurted out, "But that's her job—having babies is her job!"

Dr. Sadik countered: "No, that's not her job. Her job is to be alive, not to be dead from having your children."

Another officer argued, his voice rising: "I paid so much for my wife, and now you're saying I can't even have sexual relations with her?" This was a reference to the fact that in some remote frontier regions where there were few women, men must pay hefty dowries to the bride's parents in order to attract a mate.

To the husbands' great relief, Nafis explained that she was *not* saying that they couldn't have sex; she was merely saying that they couldn't get their wives pregnant. At this point she introduced the concept of the condom and demonstrated to the troops how to put one on by sliding the rubber over a pencil. In later sessions she realized that the pencil was perhaps not the best demonstration tool, and so she substituted her thumb.

By the end of the meeting she required the husbands to sign a contract with her, promising they would not get their wives pregnant. If they broke this agreement, she warned that she would take the woman and put her in the hospital for six months so she could be properly cared for until her delivery date. As she watched in amazement, all the army officers obediently signed the document. *After all, this doctor might be bossy, she might be brazen, she might even be crazy, but she has looked after the health of my family for several months now, even my daughter and mother and grandmother—and she needn't have. I can't afford to take a chance.*

One officer in Abbottabad broke his promise; when his wife announced she was having a baby, Nafis was furious, and he was enormously embarrassed. More urgent emotions were soon to follow. He was at wit's end when he discovered Nafis was good at her word. The pregnant patient was severely anemic, and Dr. Sadik realized that even though these women were the wives of officers and in a better economic position than the average villager, they were still undernourished. Local customs dictated that first the husband would eat, then any male children, then any female children, and whatever scraps were left over would be the dinner of the wife—certainly not suitable nourishment to sustain someone eating for two.

Nafis put the wife in the hospital so she would receive proper rest and nutrition, and her husband had to figure out who would care for the couple's four children. He was furious about the situation and yelled, "Oh, I'll go to the captain with this!"

"You do it—go to someone else, too—I don't care. It's my duty to make sure your wife stays alive."

Unfortunately the staff would only agree to keep the patient for a month before she was released. In the meantime she received blood transfusions and proper nourishment; in addition, by taking a break from the strain of caring for four young children, she was able to recoup her strength.

Azhar remembered much "sniggering and snickering" in the community about what his beloved was up to, because no one had ever interfered in the sex lives of the troops before. True to her nature, Nafis was too busy forging ahead to stop and worry about public opinion. During the course of her mission, she saw that some men couldn't care less about their spouse's health, while others were genuinely worried about their mate's welfare. The problem was, they couldn't afford to display this concern in front of their peers, because they didn't want to be labeled as weak. The men wanted to come across as warriors who feared nothing and treated their women anyway they chose. But Dr. Sadik had made good on her threat by sending the pregnant wife away from the home to be cared for at the hospital, and this action sent a message to the soldiers: comply or else . . .

It was during this era that the seeds took root in the young doctor's mind, seeds that would later grow into her work at the UN. Nafis had seen the effects of poverty and social strictures on women's reproductive health in the United States, but this was different. This was her own country, a world that was paradoxically familiar and yet foreign to her. She thought she was coming home to live in Pakistan, and yet she found herself working in remote mountain villages on the frontier, facing a mentality she didn't understand: here were intelligent men willing to sacrifice their wives' health to have a son. And even more alarming—it wasn't just the men. Many times it was the mother-in-law or even the woman's own family who just didn't care that much for her well-being; they were ready to let her die if it meant having a baby with a penis in the house. And saddest of all, the woman herself seemed resigned to this fate. With no education or income of her own, she had no more authority than the children she begat, and no control over her own destiny. If her loved ones expected her to reproduce every year like a broodmare, then she must obey. And if she died trying, well, there were plenty of relatives left to raise the children.

This was the system that had been in effect for most of history, but this system had not been part of Nafis's personal history. Having grown up in a family that celebrated her femininity, valued her wishes, gave her the same educational opportunities as her brothers, then encouraged her career and independence, she was discovering how different her reality was from that of most women in Pakistan.

In 1955 family planning was a new concept, and one of the world's first family planning clinics had just started up in Karachi. Still the vast majority of people had no access to information about how they could prevent pregnancy or the concept of spacing births to give the mother's body time to recuperate—or even that planning their families was an option for women versus the domain of almighty Allah or almighty Husband. When Nafis witnessed her first desperate patient dying as a result of a self-induced abortion—a woman who was married and already had several children—she realized that something must be done.

In 1957 Nafis returned to the site of her former job, the army hospital at Rawalpindi, for several reasons: the hospital was close to her home in Abbottabad, she knew all the staff, and she hoped to resume her bridge addiction while she convalesced. The purpose of her visit was to give birth to a second child. The delivery went smoothly, and she returned home with a baby girl, Ambereen. But this time Azhar's colleagues didn't even bother to call on the couple. "It was almost like they wanted to console him that he'd had another daughter."

Little did anyone realize that this was just the beginning. Nafis had followed the advice she gave her patients and spaced two years between pregnancies. However, as she continued her medical career, she would be raising five children.

Rubima Javed | Tetral, Pakistan

Zooming down the freeway from Islamabad, we pass beneath a sign on the overpass that reads: "Life is precious: do not risk it." I smile, noting this is an appropriate message for the morning, and I will think about that slogan many times in the hours and months to come.

I am with Pamela Sequeira, a native Pakistani who today works in UNFPA's country headquarters. Our driver, Monabar, has radioed in our whereabouts, destination, and estimated arrival time as we head 135 kilometers south, to the city of Chakwal, to see UN field operations, part of their program to improve maternal health in the district.

After visiting the overwhelmed maternity hospital at district headquarters, where they deliver about 150 babies per month, we drive through the hilly green countryside, sparsely dotted by dusty acacia trees; the Kalar Kahar mountains rise blue and hazy in the distance. Leaving the freeway, the UN SUV bounces along the cratered roads, passing numerous examples of "truck art," Pakistan's mobile gallery of buses, vans, and trucks that are trimmed with metal filigree and decorated with ornate paintings. They look like brightly colored tapestries combining paisleys and floral motifs—sometimes even incorporating landscapes and tigers.

When we reach the village of Tetral, Monabar slows to the pace of the rickshaw in front of us, which is carrying two women in burqas. Winding into the heart of this village of five thousand people, the driver squeezes the 4x4 down tiny alleyways formed by walls of tan sun-dried bricks. I hold my breath and thank the Lord I don't have his job.

We arrive at the home of one of the "lady health workers." The name is self-explanatory; these are women employed by the Pakistani Ministry of Health and trained by the UN to help their communities' medical needs in this remote region. The project strives to take reproductive care to the doorstep of clients, knowing that the vast majority have no means of reliable transportation. The team is working to reduce maternal mortality, and their success ratio is impressive: of 16,195 births in 2004, only 31 mothers died. This is a ratio of under 0.2 percent, better than the United States, with all its technological advances.

The lady health workers set up shop in their own homes, where those in need can visit, omitting the need (and expense) for a separate care facility. The workers identify two or three drivers in the community who have cars, and instruct the expectant mother's family to contact the driver when the patient goes into labor so that he (in this region few women drive) can take them to the hospital for delivery.

Today we are discussing the issue of family planning at the home of worker Asiya Rajput. She has placed a circle of chairs around her front room, a space with cement floors, a beamed wooden ceiling, and plaster walls covered by posters illuminating the female reproductive system. It is a darkened oasis from the bright sunlight. With traditional Pakistani hospitality, our hostess serves us all candies, cookies, fruit, and Coca-Cola.

Seated in the circle are about twenty women of all ages, and the atmosphere is brightened by the lively colors and sparkling whites of their fashions. They wear a humbler version of the same female uniform I've seen in Islamabad and Karachi: the *shalwar kameez*.

This garment consists of loose trousers covered by a long overblouse extending below the knees; it's modestly cut with a high neck and long sleeves. The shalwar kameez is usually covered by a voluminously draped scarf, a *hajib*, which hides the woman's glory—her hair—a treasure so valuable that only her husband may appreciate it. In comparison to Western women, precious little skin is visible: their hands, their feet peeking out of sandals, and their face, unless wearing a burqa. I am surprised to see that few women in Tetral have covered their faces, as many do in the city. None is wearing a hint of makeup. A few gentlemen from the health care agencies have accompanied me on my visit, and they are all wearing Western shirts and ties.

With Pamela translating I ask the women about their experiences with childbearing, and they shift uncomfortably in their chairs. I worry that I've gone too far, expecting them to open up and talk to this stranger about such a personal subject. Then I notice a few women glancing nervously at the men in the room. On impulse I ask the gentlemen to please leave us alone, and suddenly it's as if the room emits a collective sigh of relief. Immediately the women begin to chatter in Urdu and giggle. Ah ha. I have turned the key in the conversational lock, and we launch into a session of multilingual girl talk as if no continents or cultures have ever divided us.

I ask how many children the women have, and Rubima, a lady draped in a dark hajib says she has nine. When I ask if she would like to move outside so we can speak about her family life in private, she replies, "No, we are all women here."

With that she launches into her story, and I marvel at Rubima's presence. There is no self-consciousness, no hesitation at talking to this American journalist. On the contrary, she exudes great strength, and as she talks she looks me in the eye with an intense, confident manner, her large brown eyes fixing me with the keen, unblinking stare of a hawk. Rubima, a farmer, thinks she is thirty-two or thirty-three. I am shocked to hear her estimated age, as I would have placed her around fifty. She's at least six feet tall with broad shoulders, as big as a man—a fit, stout body useful for raising cabbages and kids. With faintly pock-marked skin the color of tanned leather, her features are also boldly masculine, offset by a gold stud adorning her nose. I notice the large hands of a worker resting on her lap, their orange fingers offering telltale signs of henna. But in contrast to her masculine appearance, this woman is dressed in the most feminine costume in the room—an embroidered pink-striped shalwar kameez.

Rubima tells me she married at approximately fourteen and was sixteen when she had her first baby. She worked all day in the field and then gave birth to her baby at home, the labor lasting only a half hour. An unskilled, untrained older woman delivered all her babies at home, until the last two, who were born in the community hospital. Rubima made this decision because she had begun to feel weak, a common symptom of anemia from having only a one-year gap between her last few pregnancies.

I ask Rubima about her family life. "My husband is a good man, he takes care of me and the kids, takes us to the doctor when we need it. Along with our children we run a farm growing carrots, cauliflower, cabbage, and okra. We raise livestock, cows and buffalo, and we own a horse that we use to take our vegetables to market."

I ask Rubima why she had nine children. "My husband was supportive of the idea of birth control," she says in her deep husky voice. "but I tried an IUD and it had lots of side effects like cramping and bleeding. Then my husband used condoms for a while, but we decided we wanted to have a boy." From this point on, Rubima tells a common story found in many parts of the world where boys are preferred: "We had five daughters first before we got a son. Then we wanted our son to have a brother and I became pregnant again, but this one was also a girl. Then the last two children were boys." After her ninth baby was born she made the decision to have her tubes tied.

All her kids are studying in school now, except for her two eldest daughters, ages seventeen and eighteen, who just finished high school; both of them are engaged to be married. Although they want to continue their studies, Rubima wants them to wed *now*. "It's according to Islam. Girls must marry before they're twenty," Rubima declares. Her daughters will start their families right away. By contrast, her eldest son is in tenth grade, studying electrical work; he plans to become an electrician.

"Would you have so many children if you had it to do over again?" I ask her.

"No, I would only have two or three. However, the best part about so many kids is that they are all around you. I prefer my daughters, because they do more work and they listen to their parents."

I ask Rubima for her advice to young women like her daughters who are just starting their married lives. "Take care of your husband, your parents, and your home," she replies with that same intense hawk-like stare, "and have two kids."

7 MOTHERS

Mothers and daughters possess a unique connection—perhaps because they understand their shared pain and joy, the knowledge that giving birth will produce both, and the poignant reality that they are forever intertwined: one creates the other. The mother becomes one through the birth of her child, and the child cannot exist without the mother. So it is with the existence of pain and joy; we cannot fully know one without the presence of the other, and therefore when it comes time for the daughter to become a mother, no one else can comprehend the profound mixture of emotions in store for her better than the woman who brought her into this world. This daisy chain of primal wisdom has passed down through the female lineage since time immemorial.

The lesson of pain and joy in childbirth had long ago cast its shadow across the Shoaib household. Nafis's *amma*, Iffat, had lost her own mother when she herself was born; in effect the infant's life cost her mother's life. When it came time for Iffat to have her first baby, she returned to her father-in-law Mohammed Abdulla's house, where she delivered Nafis. Then twenty-five years later, although they lived on two separate continents, the mother and daughter fell into the same pattern as their ancestors had for generations. And even though Nafis was a practicing obstetrician, she returned to her parents' home in Karachi when it came time to give birth to *her* daughter, so that Amma could look after her.

Nafis, an ob-gyn, had gotten pregnant on her honeymoon and was rather embarrassed about this fact. She was too shy to tell her parents for the first couple of months, and when they finally learned the news they were shocked she had kept the fact secret. At this point Iffat prepared to make the long journey from Washington DC to Karachi, where the Shoaibs still maintained the home they had established upon their arrival from Calcutta. Also coming along for assistance were Chicky and, for a shorter time period, Nafis's father. They would be bringing from the United States a steel trunk full of the baby's layette and dozens of diapers. As soon as the Shoaibs flew into Karachi, a very pregnant Nafis traveled alone, taking the day-and-a-half train ride to meet the family, as Azhar would have to stay at his army post.

Nafis delivered at Lady Dufferin, a women's obstetrical hospital and was attended by a female doctor. The birth itself was a normal one; however, the new mother's relationship with her first daughter would prove problematic from the moment the tiny human exited the womb. Auntie Chicky remembers that the baby "screamed her head off. I kept asking, 'Why is she screaming so much?'"

The other reaction to little Mehreen would also become commonplace: "She was a *very* lovely baby." So began the dichotomy, the wonder at her demanding nature and her beautiful countenance.

When Nafis brought the newborn to the Shoaibs' home in Karachi, friends and relatives queued up to pay the little princess a visit. Mehreen was the first grandchild, the first niece or nephew, and in this group of girl worshipers, she was a welcome addition. Unfortunately, the lovely baby spent most of her time crying, and the seasoned veterans from the child-rearing front clucked their tongues and advised the new mother: "Oh, she's going to have colic for three months!"

A concerned Nafis was thinking: "All night and all day with *this*?" The infant—whether she had colic or not—very quickly realized that crying produced lots of attention. "She liked to be picked up," her mother remembered.

Mehreen created quite a stir with those powerful lungs and looks. In Pakistan there was a preference for light skin, and the handsome Azhar's coloring was much fairer than Nafis's due to the fact that his mother hailed from Ireland, and on his father's side, the ancestors had originated in Turkey and Iran before migrating to Kashmir. Relatives rang up after the baby's birth, dying to know if the wee one had a pale complexion like her father. They couldn't figure out how to politely phrase this question to the dark-skinned mother, so they would simply ask, "What does the baby look like?" Catching their drift, Nafis perversely did not feel like satisfying their curiosity, so she would merely respond, "Oh, she looks just like me." And true enough, her features did.

After a month away from her husband and job in Rawalpindi, the new mother returned on the train from Karachi to present Azhar with his first child. When his kinfolks witnessed this adorable infant in the flesh, with pale skin, light hair, and blue eyes, they were dumbfounded. "But . . . she's so beautiful . . . so perfect. . . ." Everyone doted on the baby, and she—like most firstborns, and like her mother before her—enjoyed being the center of attention. However, Mehreen would not command the spotlight for long.

After Azhar's parents divorced, his father accepted a position in Iran as the Pakistani military attaché. There Asghar Sadik met Atiya Vijay, and after he returned to Pakistan and considered the situation, he married the young beauty, bringing her to live with him on a scenic horse farm in Probynabad. Asghar soon began a second family, with his new wife giving birth to two daughters: the elder, born in 1953, was Wafa. And in July 1957, Mr. Sadik became the proud father of another girl, Ghazala. She was four months younger than Azhar's new baby, Mehreen, which meant that he now had a sister and a daughter the same age.

Asghar and his wife were living in this remote region in Pakistan when Atiya developed an ear infection and sent for a local doctor. The physician administered a shot of penicillin, unaware of his patient's allergy; she immediately went into anaphylactic shock, and without access to the antidote, the doctor watched helplessly as she died. The young mother left behind a newborn and a chubby two-year-old toddler.

When the phone call announcing the tragedy came into the younger Sadiks' home, Azhar was out in the field on army maneuvers. Nafis, unable to reach him, made the decision to travel to the funeral and bring the three-month-old home with her to care for it. The neighbors marveled at this new arrival: "She's come back with a baby again! Every time she goes away, she brings back another one!"

Dr. Sadik still came home from work several times a day to nurse her infant daughter, but she now suddenly found herself with two babes-in-arms. After months of floor-walking Mehreen through the colic phase, she had a new charge, Ghazala, who was ill with a diarrhea infection and no doubt fretting for her mother, was not feeding properly. "I was petrified something was going to happen to this poor baby. I spent more hours with her, looking after her, than with my own child."

Following her own advice, Nafis waited until her daughter was two years old before she became pregnant again. As is usually the case, the birth of the second baby was a much less dramatic affair. For this delivery no one flew in from America. The expectant mother merely traveled from her home in Abbottabad to the location of her previous job at the army hospital in Rawalpindi, where she knew all the staff. She had arrived a few days prior to stay with a friend, a German doctor, who rushed Nafis to the delivery room as soon as her water broke. After a short, easy labor Ambereen was born on March 5, 1957, and a few days later Azhar drove to fetch mother and daughter and bring them home.

Within a few weeks of the baby's birth—since there was never to be a dull moment in the Sadik household—Azhar announced he had accepted an opportunity for further career training, a year-long army staff program in Kingston, in Ontario, Canada. The couple packed their bags to return to North America, this time with their two infants in tow. Azhar's half-sister, Ghazala, was now two years old, and she returned to live with her father. He at last felt capable of raising her, wishing to reunite the toddler with her older sister.

In order to relocate the remaining family, Nafis took a leave of absence from the hospital and got out the familiar packing crates to prepare for the move. Azhar went ahead, and in the meantime, Nafis traveled separately with the girls, flying into Washington DC to stay with her parents. The children's names were on their mother's passport, but as she entered immigration, the officer raised his eyebrows and informed her that she had a big problem. "Well, *you* have a visa, but your *children* don't."

"What do you mean, 'but my children don't?'"

"You've forgotten to stamp 'and two children,' so they can't enter the country."

"Okay, then in that case, I'm going in and you can keep the two children, because my parents are waiting for me."

"What! Lady, what do you mean? You can't just leave these two kids here! Okay, listen, here's what we can do. You can take them in with you, but you must get them a visa later . . . only don't do it here in Washington."

One of the primary attractions of a Canadian sojourn for Nafis had been the opportunity to spend more time with her mother and father, since the distinguished Mohammed Shoaib was still working at the World Bank in Washington. She was happy that the move would allow her parents an opportunity to spend time with their only grandchildren.

While they visited, Azhar scoured Kingston; it was a town of

35,000 people located northeast of Toronto on Lake Ontario. He was looking for a suitable rental property for his family, and when he found a furnished house, he sent for his wife and children; they arranged themselves comfortably in the passenger car of the Vermonter line, headed north on the long journey.

On a February night the train pulled into Kingston, and Nafis got her first glimpse of the place that would be home for the next year. But in reality she couldn't see Kingston—she couldn't even see the station—because the locomotive navigated through a tunnel between walls of snow piled on either side of the tracks. "I thought to myself, my God, where am I?" The train had to be delayed while she exited with two babies, and the porters piled their mountain of baggage on the frozen platform.

Nafis, arriving from the steamy subcontinent, had never lived in these arctic climes before. But planning ahead, the clotheshorse had had a coat with two linings tailored in Pakistan, a garment specially made for subzero temperatures. Unfortunately she realized too late that her wrap design was a fundamental error that permitted in the icy wind off the lake.

At the academy in Kingston, Azhar was studying his military staff college courses, which was an important step to getting ahead in the army. While he did this, his spouse settled into their new place, and as had become a recurring pattern for them, after a couple of months they moved to yet another home, and she settled in again. Mehreen was two and a half, and Ambereen nine months old. The lady of the house found herself without servants for the first time in her life, and so she plied her hand at caring for the children, cleaning, and learning how to cook.

Another new experience emerged during this era: for the first time ever she did not have an intellectual pursuit.

Azhar asked his wife, "Are you bored?"

"Yes. Very definitely."

At this point they began asking around for a housekeeper who could look after them and the children so Nafis could return to work. Azhar recalled, "People said, 'You must be mad. There's no such thing as this type of servant in Canada. You just hire a baby sitter.' Still, we looked through the papers and we advertised, but nothing happened." The circumstances were further complicated by the Sadiks' tight budget, what with Azhar attending school, and Nafis not yet earning a nickel.

Their fairy godmother arrived in the form of a Canadian widow named Rolene. As if she had been conjured precisely to answer their prayers, Rolene informed the couple that she could only accept a small salary; otherwise, if she earned too much money, she would not be eligible for her retirement pension.

As in any relationship, there was a brief adjustment period. Nafis remembered that the first time the new housekeeper bathed the girls she complained, "'I can't get all the dirt off their skin.' As I watched, she was trying to scrub them, and I said, 'Listen, that's the color of their complexion. I mean, don't take their skin off!'"

But Rolene proved to be worth her weight in gold. She learned to cook Pakistani food. She watched Nafis trying to press a sari and said: "I don't think you know how to iron. Why don't you let me do it?" She trained the children to go straight to sleep at night without the period of wailing that had previously ensued when they were put in the crib. And she quickly became so close to the babies that she asked if she could please take them home with her on the nanny's day off.

The couple had acquired a rattletrap jalopy for their temporary stay, and when it came time for the five-hundred-mile road trip to visit Nafis's parents in Washington, Rolene volunteered to take her new car. Then she told them to sleep while she drove all night to get to DC. Upon meeting the Shoaibs, she so loved Iffat that she wanted an opportunity to become one of their family. "Rolene was so sweet," Nafis remembered. "When we moved back to Pakistan, I remember her saying good-bye, weeping at the train station. We heard later she had died from cancer soon after we left . . . it was like she was just there for us."

On these Washington visits Nafis's family was thrilled to spend time with the first members of the next generation. Chicky recalled, "Mehreen was such an adorable little girl with this light hair, a lovely little thing. I remember picking her up and taking her to the Pakistani embassy to meet everyone there. And they were all loving her and playing with her. And Ambereen was a tiny baby, and big sister was lugging her around—they were so cute." Iffat was dying for Mehreen to come to Grandma, luring the child by offering her the world, but the toddler instead always clung tight to Mama.

After the Sadiks had found the perfect housekeeper, Nafis was free to look for work. She went to Kingston General Hospital, part of the local medical school, and the gentleman in charge asked, "How did you hear of Queen's University?"

"Oh, when I came here."

"Of course," he replied with withering sarcasm, "why should you hear about it? It's only been here a hundred years." After this surly interview, Dr. Sadik's hopes plummeted, and she didn't expect to land anything. As a result she was surprised when an offer came for a three-month position in obstetrics.

After Nafis finished this temporary assignment, the university offered her a research assistantship in physiology. The post wasn't in her field, and it required doing experiments on dogs, which she detested. Still, she was so eager "to do something" that she took it.

This new research appointment involved teaching, another adventure the doctor had never attempted before. At twenty-eight she looked like she was still in her teens. Having retained her shapely figure and sultry Eastern elegance—with the mixture of silken saris, diamonds, and Radha eyes—she was even more alluringly exotic here in the frozen North. "When I arrived to teach, the students thought I was one of them, and they were all wanting to date me. I said, 'Listen,

I'm your instructor. I'm going to mark you, so please be respectful.'
It took me a while to get them to calm down."

Rising above their professional demands, the Sadiks made the most
of their lives outside of work, creating a rich social life just as they always had throughout their marriage. Nafis got some Pakistani recipes
from her relatives, and she and Rolene experimented. They had dinner parties, inviting Azhar's classmates from the school. One was an
Indian man, Harish, who had been at the military academy at Dehra
Dun with Azhar and coincidentally wound up in Canada with him
as well. Harish's wife and children had remained at home in India,
so he was most grateful for a dinner invitation to experience the cuisine of the subcontinent. As a Hindu he was a vegetarian, and Nafis
would always thoughtfully point out when one of the dishes contained meat. Finally he complained to Azhar, "I don't know why
she tells me 'this or that has beef in it.' Why does she do that? If she
doesn't tell me, then I can eat everything." From then on, his hostess
thoughtfully remained silent.

Nafis and Azhar discovered the part of life in Canada that would
appeal to them the most: fishing. "In the summer this area is so beautiful that the people go crazy. They have a sunny day and everyone
is out." The Sadiks located a place where they could rent a boat, and
while the loyal Rolene cared for the babies, they would slip away
in the golden summer afternoons to glide across the water and toss
their lines in to catch mossy stones, old tires, and the occasional bass.

For the sake of her husband, Iffat had tried to make the best of living in Washington and mingling with his high-stakes political circle, even though it was not her nature. Meanwhile she missed the
closeness of their friends and relatives back home, and she longed
to return to Pakistan. As a result, when Mohammed was offered the
position of finance minister there, his wife was delighted. This appointment came at the perfect time, a lucky coincidence; they would

be moving back to Karachi in 1959 for Mohammed to join the cabinet of Ayub Khan, at the same time Nafis and Azhar were scheduled to return home from Canada.

But Iffat had developed high blood pressure, and according to Chicky she was quite careless about taking her medication. On one of the Sadiks' visits, Nafis realized her mother wasn't feeling well, and she advised Azhar to head back to Kingston without her. A few days later Iffat complained of a brutal headache that lasted the whole day. The doctor arrived, prescribed a sedative, and advised them to keep an eye on the patient; if she wasn't better by the next day, he would take her to the hospital.

However, she never saw the next day. That evening Iffat went into convulsions, and after racing to the emergency room in an ambulance, she died thirty minutes after arrival. She had suffered an aneurysm in her subarachnoid—a massive brain hemorrhage.

The mother of six was only forty-five years old, and her loved ones reeled from the trauma of losing her. Since Muslims do not believe in embalming, Islamic funerals are held within a day or two of the death; as a result the arrangements were made very quickly, which didn't allow time for relatives from overseas to attend. Azhar came down from Kingston, and Kemal came from Boston, where he was attending MIT, but the Shoaibs' eldest son, Iqbal, was living in Rangoon, where he worked for an oil company, and Hassan was still a student in London. They could not make it to Washington in time to see their mother buried.

Of all the family, the tragedy hit the youngest child, Tariq, the hardest. At ten years of age he had just lost his mom, making him the latest forlorn child for whom his big sister would become *amma*. As a girl, Nafis—being the authoritative eldest child, the one who looked after the younger siblings—had developed characteristics that she would brandish for life. And they would now serve her well. Unconsciously she stepped up to fill the void left by the sudden disappearance of the beloved Iffatara, becoming the matriarch of the clan. Now her brothers, sister—and even father—looked to this young woman as the female head of the household. She would later expand this maternal role into her professional life, but not in the warm nurturing way of her own mother. Rather, Nafis evolved an advocacy incorporating the protective maternal fury of a lioness, becoming the guardian of millions of harried mothers and helpless daughters alike.

Natasha Bankov | St. Petersburg, Russia

The female of the species instinctively protects its young and will risk its own life to do just that. I am reminded of this fact as I encounter a mother of two while cruising the St. Petersburg suburbs searching for prostitutes.

I am out in the field with the team from Humanitarian Action as they conduct their outreach mission to the region's sex workers, women who are predominantly heroin addicts. As we lurch along in a worn-out Winnebago, I look from the driver's seat—where Vitaliy steers in and out of traffic with a maniacal glee—to the back end of our conveyance, which sports a cooktop, cabinets, and a table with bench seats. There is no bed on board.

For two hours, the Winnebago inches along in rush-hour traffic heading from the city center to Leninsky Prospect. Translating for me tonight is Nikita Bulanin, a twenty-nine-year-old political science PhD. As he quizzes me on American politics, he scrutinizes me through his wire-rimmed spectacles. Nikita evidently has a mind capable of running on numerous tracks at once; he simultaneously translates the multiple conversations around us, runs his fingers through the long strands of his greasy sepia locks, chain smokes, and asks me to explain to him how a country like the United States

A pseudonym has been used to protect this woman's privacy.

could elect George W. Bush and Arnold Schwarzenegger into office. The van picks up speed along the busy four-lane street, which randomly becomes five lanes whenever another kamikaze Russian driver is seized by the urge to pass. One such maneuver forces Vitaliy to slam on his brakes, sending me, the staff, and boxes of condoms and syringes sailing across the camper. I feel inadequate to explain my country's electoral choices, so I'm grateful for the distraction.

Replete with big-box stores, car dealerships, and fast-food outlets (including a Pizza Hut, where we'll later break for dinner) the Leninsky Prospect region looks more like a soulless collection of L.A. strip malls than a historic European capital. Interspersed with decidedly non-Communist commerce are acres of drab Soviet-bloc apartment buildings, all mass-produced during the Khrushchev era to accommodate the 1950s population boom. The prostitutes street-walk along these bedroom community boulevards, working an area that contrasts radically with the graceful neoclassical architecture of the St. Petersburg city center.

They do not wait until it's dark to come out—for good reason. The sky remains light until midnight during the summer White Nights. The women know the route of the van, and those who need assistance wait for it. When Vitaliy pulls over at 8:45, we have our first client of the evening.

Natasha climbs up the stairs of the camper as if she's sleepwalking and glides into the booth across from me. With shoulder-length platinum hair parted by dark roots, and single-stroke penciled eyebrows, she's a sort of sad Jean Harlow parody. She's tall and skinny, dressed in a white eyelet blouse that hugs her frail body so tightly that I can see her oversized bra caving in. She wears platform heels and flashy jeans with silver studs—a sexy uniform that is pretty much de rigueur among young Russian women. But what sets Natasha apart from them is the tranced look of the heroin addict on her face. With pupils dilated to the size of dimes and brown eyes framed by stiff fake lashes, her fixed stare gives the appearance of a demented doll.

She tells Anna, the project coordinator, her name and age for the program's records. She reveals that she's twenty-eight, although with her rotten teeth and sunken cheeks, she looks much older. Natasha takes the plastic bag that the program distributes containing condoms, clean needles, tissues, and alcohol swabs. Although later most clients will enter feverishly, take the bag while muttering *sposiba*, Russian for "thank you," then depart quickly, this client stays to chat. With her eyes glazed and speech slurred, she launches into a story of how she began the life of a sex worker.

Natasha was married, staying at home to care for the couple's two young children, when her husband abandoned them. Finding herself with no means of support, she did the only thing she could think of to earn quick cash: she began working as a prostitute. "I started using heroin because I was so ashamed of being a whore." She had hoped the drug would blur the realities of her nightly grapplings with strange men, but recently she's decided to clean up in hopes of creating a better life for her children. She asks Anna for information on a detox clinic, and the coordinator obliges, also giving Natasha the address of a clinic where she can receive a free AIDS test.

Humanitarian Action's success has grown out of the trust clients place in the staff as a resource to which they can turn for nonjudgmental help. Besides their services to prostitutes, the NGO runs a similar outreach program for drug addicts and a tiny shelter in the city center providing food, beds, and counseling for St. Petersburg's estimated 25,000 street children. All these projects are conducted on a shoestring budget that provides the staff with even greater challenges than their work, although they receive some funding from UNFPA for training. Humanitarian Action sees its mission as that of a go-between, reaching out to the community's outcasts and connecting them with the governmental resources designed to assist them.

Alexander Tsekhanovich, the agency's general director, traces many of their client's problems to *perestroika*, the economic restructuring that took place during the transfer from a Communist system of all-inclusive social services to a modern era of capitalism. This new system saw diminished support for working-class families on many levels. During the ensuing globalization of the Russian economy, millions lost their jobs, resulting in depression, alcoholism, and drug addiction. Confused and angry by this new paradigm, parents were ill-equipped to raise their children after the abrupt disappearance of Communist support. Alexander sees how the positive options of a free economy have been accompanied by a dark side for many families—the ills of poverty and the resulting twin problems of addiction and prostitution.

As our next client comes aboard, the Winnebago's radio plays the old Del Shannon song "Runaway." It's an appropriate soundtrack for the evening's drama, as St. Petersburg and Moscow are full of poor young Russian women, runaways who left their villages in search of opportunity and then wound up on these urban streets as hookers. Anna says she has seen some of their clients show up at the van for the past five years. "They used to be quite beautiful and you could carry on a conversation with them, talk to them for hours. Now you can see the degradation. They're absent-minded and can only focus on getting drugs."

While the music floods the cramped space, a twenty-five-year-old woman who looks like a Russian Liv Tyler with ripe pink pouty lips enters. Upon closer inspection I realize those luscious mounds are pushed out to full flower by rather feral-looking buck teeth. Her pupils are dilated so large that her eyes appear like black marbles, and she stares at me with the wild desperate look of a hurt animal. Anna asks if she needs a referral to the free clinic to be checked for the AIDS virus. Liv responds there's no need. She already knows she's HIV positive. This is not really a surprise, considering Russia has the world's fastest growing HIV population.

As the night wears on, we stop for more clients. Lana, a

twenty-one-year-old blonde enters the Winnebago clearly about to come out of her skin for need of a fix. She stands hunched, hopping from one foot to another, sucking air through her teeth as her eyes dart around the camper. Lana reveals she has the jitters for more reasons than one: she bought seven hundred rubles worth of heroin from her dealer on credit, and if she doesn't have the money back to him today she's in big trouble. It's five minutes until midnight. She quickly takes her packet and exits the camper. But as we drive away we see the police stop and pull her into a squad car.

At 12:30 Vitaliy suddenly wheels the vehicle around, and we begin racing back to the city center. The staff explain we have less than an hour before the drawbridge rises over the Neva, the river that bisects St. Petersburg. Once the bridge opens to allow ships to sail in from port, the two halves of the metropolis are cut off from each other until morning—a convenient fact frequently used by philandering husbands as an excuse for not returning home. Passing a Russian Orthodox church, I notice its onion domes silhouetted against the periwinkle sky, still light after midnight. We speed home like Cinderella fleeing the ball, the vintage Winnebago our carriage, and with a bit of shame I thank God that I am able to flee, and not one of those women still standing on a corner of Leninsky Prospect.

8   FAMILY PLANNING

Always in motion, the Sadiks would soon be separated again. When Azhar completed his coursework at the academy in Kingston in 1958, he returned from Canada alone, reporting to his new post in military intelligence at army headquarters in Rawalpindi. Meanwhile Nafis stayed behind to help her father cope with her now motherless baby brother, Tariq. She also utilized her considerable packing skills, dismantling the Georgetown home to move the family back to Pakistan, where Mohammed Shoaib would become the new finance minister for President Ayub Khan. The young wife, now five years married, reached an agreement with her husband that when they returned to their homeland, they would once again live apart: Nafis would move into her father's place in Karachi, assuming the role of lady of the house, and Azhar would stay on the base in Pindi, commuting to visit his wife and little girls seven hundred miles away.

Once she had settled back into her parents' home, Nafis resumed her career as a civilian medical officer at the Naval Hospital, treating officers' wives in obstetrics and gynecology. During this era the clinician became increasingly frustrated at dealing with the same problems over and over again, exasperated at encountering illness and death fueled by ignorance, and a culture that reduced the feminine gender to chattel. Outside her elite group, the mothers she cared for held no more control over their own destiny than the children they bore. For the next four years she counseled each patient individually, repeating the same advice until the words echoed in her head like a prayer for the damned. Finally, fed up with her Sisyphean task, in 1963 she told her husband the unthinkable: she was going to retire from medicine and become a housewife.

Before she came to this decision, Dr. Sadik had worked in obstetrics, yet the cases that distressed her the most were from another ward. She had inherited a handful of patients with chronic TB, and Nafis was reminded of her trials with the army wives in Abbottabad and their struggle against anemia, as she fought a similar battle here in Karachi. "During a pregnancy the tuberculosis gets suppressed; however, immediately after the birth it becomes rampant. Really you should not be pregnant with this disease, but there again, I had great difficulty with the treatment because I couldn't just address the illness—I had to deal with the patients' whole social situation." In 1959 streptomycin had just come into vogue as the preferred remedy, "so at least we were no longer relying on fresh air and good living to cure the patients. We did have some drugs. But still they needed to be properly nourished, protected from infections, they couldn't be anemic, or pregnant—anything like that. Unfortunately, the women would often get well enough to leave the TB ward to go home; then they'd have a baby. At that point whatever treatment I'd given was undone. To help them, I got contraceptives from the hospital superintendent."

Nafis decided to repeat her method from the Abbottabad days, and she was lucky that even though family planning was still not routinely discussed in this era, the head of the Karachi hospital was much more open-minded than her previous boss. "He understood that it was absolutely essential for these women to avoid childbirth." When Nafis released a TB patient to go home, she gave her condoms and in return required the woman's husband to sign a contract agreeing he would use them. "And I'd take a lot of interest in these cases: 'When did you feed her? How much food did she eat?' You know, all these silly questions to make the point that her nutrition was more important than his. And I would say, "Who's looking after your children—is it your wife? Then she has to be well nourished.' I made all kinds of arguments with these husbands, short of saying, 'Your male attitude has to change'—you know, this macho attitude. He had to make a decision, a decision that his wife was as important as his children. I knew if *he* started to think his wife was important, everyone else would too."

As the good doctor carried on her valiant—and increasingly wearisome— effort to rescue the have-nots, her friends all advised that she should go into private practice, treating the city's haves. But Nafis was not interested in running a business or making money. She told them, "I can't be bothered with all that." Nevertheless, her chums all consulted her on their ills despite the location of her office.

After seven years away, Nafis, now thirty, had returned to the city of her youth and the full spectacle of Karachi society. The former ring-leader of the Pack of Roving Debutantes resumed a role verging on typecasting as she played hostess for her father—dining, dancing, singing, receiving heads of state. Like the rest of her coterie, Nafis outfitted herself for these society functions in silk saris and shalwar kameezes—conservatively dressed, yes, with long hemlines and high necklines, but she and the others did not cover their heads with any type of veil or scarf.

Along with the Debutantes, the Intellectual Society had grown up, married, and reproduced. One New Year's Eve Nafis organized a party for about sixty of her pals, taking over a nightclub in the Metropole Hotel. They danced and drank the night away—that is, all except for the hostess, who remained an infamous teetotaler. In spite of her extrovert status and her career as a devout partygoer, she had never even tasted alcohol. The thought of losing control was not only against her Muslim upbringing, it was also antithetical to her personality, one that embraced discipline, intellect, and accomplishment. She had no use for the numbing effects of spirits, and even though many in her social circle imbibed, including her brothers and husband (who was, after all, an army man), she never touched the stuff, even as an experimental youngster.

"In Pakistan, when I went to parties, I used to be quite interested in seeing how people's attitudes—their behavior—changed when they had drinks. Some became so wonderful, others became so awful. And you know, they used to think I drank. I don't know why. I guess many people used to think that because I'm always animated, that I'm having a drink. But they don't know that I also talk like that in the daytime."

In addition, there were periodic visits to the hundreds of relatives. On one of these calls Nafis paid a visit to Azhar's mother in Lahore, and when she arrived she found that Doreen was also entertaining a young lady named Salma, a dear old friend's daughter who had just returned from living abroad. "Oh, that's a very pretty girl," Nafis remarked in Urdu, thinking her comments would slip past the fair-skinned, green-eyed European.

"Why thank you," replied Salma. The beauty had come home from three years of graduate school in the United States, but she'd grown up in Lahore and spoke fluent Urdu. Nafis was a bit taken aback, but she did not let that derail her from an important family-planning mission of her own, part of her new role as matriarch: find a suitable wife for her brother. Hassan, or Sheikoo as the Shoaib clan called him, had finished university in London and was back living in Karachi. That day, though, he happened to be in the Punjab for business. And Auntie Doreen just happened to have a reputation as the matchmaker of Lahore.

Salma remembered: "After that day, Auntie Doreen asked me for tea, and I thought, why not? I often went to see her. So, I went to tea, and a young man was there, and we talked, and I didn't think anything of it. Then Auntie Doreen said, 'Why don't you drop Shei-koo at the airport, he's leaving for Karachi.'" Hassan was grateful for the lift, and he thought Salma was quite attractive; however, he didn't mention meeting up again.

The next coincidence occurred the very next time Hassan was in Lahore. He rang up Auntie Doreen, who said, "Oh, I'm so glad that you're here, because I want to go out tonight and have a good meal. Let's go to this nightclub over at the Sheraton Hotel." They arrived at the posh establishment—and lo and behold—who should be having a romantic dinner at a cozy table by the dance floor but Salma and a young gentleman.

Hassan admitted: "Of all things, Doreen got *chutzpah*, as they say, and she goes up to this table—and I'm kind of lagging sheepishly behind—and she says to them, 'May we join you?' And they were too embarrassed to say no. Even though they were obviously on a date, they said, 'Yes, yes, by all means!' and throughout the course of the meal Auntie Doreen kept this fellow, this Englishman called Adrian, entertained so Salma and I were able to chat. That night the two of us actually happened to hit it off very well, you know, and it was then that we made a connection. Afterward I made a point of visiting Lahore to call on her." What Hassan didn't know at the time was that Salma was engaged to this Englishman called Adrian, who worked for the British Foreign Service. He signed up for a posting in Vietnam when she broke things off to marry Hassan instead.

Besides matchmaking, Nafis discovered other myriad duties as matriarch. A year after her mother's death, in the fall of 1959, her father came to her and said, "I miss your mother so much that I want to get remarried." He was asking his daughter's permission.

She discussed the situation with her siblings and spoke on their behalf: "We all want you to be happy." With their blessing Mohammed married a woman with two children of her own, and they settled into his home.

At this juncture—instead of moving to Rawalpindi to join Azhar—Nafis and the girls moved into a place of their own in Karachi, and there was a reason for this. Her husband had never liked army life; he had always resented not being able to attend Cambridge with his friends, and the devoted family man was tired of uprooting his wife and children at the whims of his commanding officers. Now, at thirty-one, he chose to leave the service and join private industry, taking a management position with the Hashmi Can Company in Karachi.

The couple had Azhar's career change in mind when they chose to be separated and for Nafis to settle in Karachi and make it their permanent home. There was even more reason for this need to put down roots when in 1961 she gave birth to their third child, a son they named Omar.

What the Sadiks didn't know was that they would be expanding their numbers again very soon. In 1962 Azhar's father passed away, leaving his two little daughters with no parents. Ghazala was seven and Wafa was nine when they went to live with their half-brother and "Bhabhiji," the name they had always used for Nafis—bhabhi meaning "my brother's wife" and ji a term of respect.

"We had never even been to Karachi before," Wafa remembered, "and now my sister, Ghazala, and I were going to be moving there and be part of this big family, have two sisters and a brother. Somehow to me it was nice that I was going to have such a large family. I felt very secure."

Ambereen was five years old when her parents explained that their father's two young half-sisters were coming to Karachi to live with them. She remembered her and Mehreen's attitude: "We were thrilled. We knew the girls, so it wasn't like these strangers. They had come and spent summers, spent a fair amount of time, and when my parents told us they were going to come live with us permanently, I couldn't believe it. It was sort of like having a big sleepover—a slumber party forever."

Nafis determined that even though Ghazala and Mehreen were

only a few months apart in age, temperamentally the two oldest girls from each household had more in common and therefore they would room together. Perhaps this was the birth order issue again, because both Wafa, at nine, and Mehreen, at seven, were headstrong aggressive girls who liked to push the boundaries of authority. That left the congenitally shy Ghazala and her dolls to room with Ambereen, two years her junior. But years later Ambereen acknowledged that the two became, "very, very close. Till this day I'm closer to her than my own sister."

Nafis enrolled the orphaned girls in the Convent of Jesus and Mary school along with Mehreen. People in her set knew the circumstances of how she suddenly became a mother of five, but when she met outsiders and casually mentioned that her eldest daughter was born in 1953 and she and her husband had married in 1954—well, that statement certainly raised some conservative Pakistani eyebrows.

Now, with four daughters and a son in the household, Nafis set out to reenact her own childhood: in addition to enrolling the girls in Catholic school, she hired a Eurasian tutor (similar to the infamous Teacher) to help the children with their language skills. The clan's activities were also reminiscent of their mother's youth, which made sense because not much had changed within the strictly controlled cultural confines of Pakistan. There was still no television, few forms of popular entertainment, and, of course, in the early 1960s, no home computers.

Instead daily life revolved around the family, getting together with their aunts, uncles, and cousins several times a week. The children played games and went to Karachi's large urban parks every day. They participated in sports and went to polo matches, later mimicking these athletes at home by taking riding lessons with an instructor who brought the horses to their doorstep.

They wiled away the stifling afternoons lying about the darkened house reading books, and in the evening the whole neighborhood played hide-and-seek. On Sundays they went to the beach on the

Arabian Sea—a major exodus from the steamy city that involved families carting their children, friends, servants, and food out to their "hut"—a two- or three-bedroom house with a kitchen, wraparound porch, and showers, where they would spend the day, letting the children ride rented camels along the waterfront.

Another favorite pastime was visiting the Sind Club, an elite private establishment left over from Colonial England prior to Partition, when a sign hung out front saying, "Natives and Dogs Not Allowed." (The sign was removed the day after Jinnah became president.) The manicured grounds of the estate housed a Pakistani version of a British gentleman's club, and here, amidst the club's palm trees and bougainvilleas, the Sadik children swam in the pool and anxiously anticipated the monthly movies, which included screenings of Elvis Presley, currently the craze in Pakistan. Wafa caught the spirit, becoming one of the early Elvis impersonators; for the benefit of all comers she sang and danced like the King in their Karachi backyard.

Although the trappings of the Sadiks' lifestyle would suggest they were well-to-do, and certainly their social standing placed them in the Pakistani uppercrust, they were not in the same financial league as their peers. With no inherited ancestral wealth they lived on salaries, and Azhar's wages from the army had always been substantially lower than his colleagues in private industry—yet another reason for his decision to make the jump into the corporate world. Likewise, even though Nafis was a physician, her choice to be a civilian medical officer, albeit for the navy, put her at the bottom tier in earnings. The couple's solution: to pool their incomes and use their ingenuity to create a life as fulfilling, if less luxurious, than their friends maintained.

One of their financial priorities remained the youngsters' schooling. Like her father and grandfather before her, Nafis believed that education was the greatest gift she could bestow on her children, and so she and Azhar shelled out the high tuition for one of the best private schools in Karachi. As they found themselves raising a family of five on these same salaries, they had to cut corners. Nafis had remained close friends with Zeenat and Laila Haroon, her co-conspirators from the Pack of Roving Debutantes. These old chums remembered the year that Azhar's half-sisters came to live with the Sadiks, and a conversation as they all prepared for Eid-ul-Fitr at the close of Ramadan. "You know for Eid the children always wear new clothes, so we turned around to Nafis, and we asked, 'What are you making for the girls?' But she said, 'I find it very expensive on my salary. I cannot afford a new outfit for them this year.' And you know, what really hit us was her two daughters were not going to get new clothes either, because she couldn't afford new clothes for the other two girls as well. She considered them like her own daughters. Now, this was years ago when she was just on a small income, but this is the most remarkable thing: she was frank, she didn't even try to make an excuse like, 'I'm busy,' or something. She simply said 'I can't afford it.'"

In fact, the Haroon sisters' comment was echoed over and over by others who observed Nafis's determination not to favor her birth daughters over Azhar's sisters. As Wafa noted: "She was very careful with us, you know. To bring all five of us up, her way of doing things was that there shouldn't be any misunderstanding. She decided she was going to do things age-wise. That would suit everything. So, since I was the eldest, I was allowed to—for example, let's say if we wanted to put rollers in our hair—I don't know why, but I remember the roller incident—she would announce, 'Wafa is allowed to do that first because she is the eldest.' Then after a certain time, Mehreen would, then my sister, Ghazala, and so on. Since everything was done that way, we had no problems."

Prior to moving in with Nafis, Wafa had not had a real mother since her own died when the girl was two. Now she devoured this opportunity for maternal companionship, doting on Bhabhiji. "When she had to go out, I used to always ask her if I could choose the sari that she would wear, and pick out her bag and her jewelry, because it used to make me feel so good. And she loved it."

While Wafa played the role of Bhabhiji's dresser, as with most large families, the other four siblings struggled for their share of attention. But the matriarch made a special point of conversing with Ghazala to draw the child out of her timid cocoon, because the girl was frozen into silence when she had to speak to strangers. Like Nafis and Chicky, and Kemal and Hassan, these two sisters had assumed the roles of one extrovert and one introvert.

Nafis remembered how even the infant Omar got in on this competition to be noticed: "My son, growing up as a baby, was quite sickly for some reason and often got colds and diarrhea and always needed attention. He was the only one who eventually had to have his tonsils removed because he got repeated infections, and this in a time when tonsillectomies were not very common." Little Omar also developed bronchitis, jaundice, and, along with the rest of his siblings, chicken pox and malaria. "You know, it was like always one thing or the other was happening."

Life was chaotic on more than the home front. Maternity was a particularly difficult medical practice because patients delivered at all hours, and on top of it, the doctor's frustration with clinical work continued to mount. She complained that the whole business was so repetitious. "I was doing the same thing, saying the same thing to these poor women—and to their husbands—over and over again. And yes, it made a difference, but just one patient at a time."

However, the ob-gyn's contributions did not go unnoticed. Her patients sometimes penned heartfelt letters of appreciation, like the husband who communicated his gratitude after Dr. Sadik had nursed his wife through a complicated Cesarean section and long recovery: "Thank you from the bottom of my heart," he wrote, "and my wife's bottom, too."

In spite of these fan letters, Nafis was heading toward a breaking point without yet knowing which way to go. And as frequently happens at a point of crisis before a transition, she started looking everywhere for more factors to corroborate her decision to escape. In 1963 Dr. Sadik—who had fought with her relatives for the chance to become a physician, piled on the extra science courses throughout high school, slaved through five years of medical school, an internship, residency, and then practiced her trade in the United States, Canada, and Pakistan—resigned from the Naval Hospital.

After several years of treating military men's wives, she just knew she had had enough. "I told my husband, 'I'm going to quit working. Everyone else is relaxing, enjoying life—none of my friends work— why should I?'"

Fortunately Azhar was earning more money now in his marketing position so his wife's salary wasn't essential. Still, he knew her temperament. "Well, I'm not saying don't quit work—if that's what you want to do—but why don't you just take a couple of months holiday to start, and see how you like it?"

On the morning of her first free day, starring in her new role as lady of the manor, Nafis rose and stationed herself at command headquarters in the parlor. "I didn't know what everyone did at home, because I didn't do anything at home. My maid servant and my cook and my cleaner were all waiting for me to leave. But I'm hanging around the house asking, 'Have you done this? Have you done that?'"

"Of course, we do it every day."

After shaping up the staff, Nafis went to coffee parties. She met friends for lunch. She played bridge. And she "got so bored with it; I decided that this was really too much." Azhar had known his wife better than she knew herself, and she quickly determined that there had to be more to life than these relentless pleasures of the leisure class.

The same energy and drive that had propelled Nafis to become a doctor to begin with wasn't about to let this woman give it all up at age thirty-four. After two months of retirement, she began staging her comeback. It was then that she discovered the Planning Commission of Pakistan was seeking a new administrator for its health section. At this point the various threads of her life's work began to be woven together, producing a tapestry with an image she could recognize. From sitting on her father's knee she understood about policymakers and how they operated. Now here was an opportunity to continue what she had accomplished in medicine, except on a grander scale, because the public health approach would allow her to make more of an impact than dealing with individual patients one by one.

The physician also approached USAID, the United States Agency for International Development. The U.S. government created this organization to administer economic assistance, and in 1963 the organization considered sixteen-year-old Pakistan one of its pet projects, investing in development on multiple fronts. As a result USAID provided Nafis a scholarship to fund her study at Johns Hopkins University School of Public Health. She would be returning to Baltimore, where her medical career had begun over a decade ago.

With the Johns Hopkins scholarship in hand, she applied to the Planning Commission. She knew that she would be up against a sea of qualified candidates—and she could presume she would be the only female amongst them. With a little over a week to prepare for her interview, she set out to craft a grand plan for improving the nation's well-being. At this time few countries actually had a public health program, an organ that did planning on a national scale, so there was not much literature available. Nafis reasoned that she had an extensive knowledge of maternal and child health, which accounted for the majority of the population. She knew the other major concern was malaria, and here is where she put in the late hours, researching how to get basic services to the rural populations to prevent the disease.

The doctor arrived for her myriad interviews and exams and not surprisingly discovered that she would be questioned by a panel of all men. Although in her mid-thirties, she was still young for a position with so much responsibility; in addition, she looked even younger than her age. But she knew she was well prepared, and as she spoke, even more ideas came to her about the job and how she was going to tackle it. "I was actually interested in interventions that would affect more people rather than individual curative services. So I said that though my background is clinical, what we have to do is invest our money where we can do the most good with it. And that means getting to people in the rural areas, and 65 percent of these people are women and children. Then, I discussed programs that concerned everyone, like malaria, which affects the productivity of the whole population."

The fact that Nafis had already worked in the United States and would be returning for the certificate from Johns Hopkins School of Public Health impressed the commission. Nafis also outlined her community service with the maternity patients in Baltimore—her eye-opening visits to the ghetto mothers' homes—and her work treating and counseling the families in Abbottabad. She pointed out that she had acquired her education not merely through university credentials but through practical experience as well.

In an era when there were few professional women of any kind in Pakistan, Dr. Nafis Sadik became the new deputy chief of health for the Planning Commission. And after working there only a couple of months, she moved from Karachi to Baltimore to attend Johns Hopkins for six months.

Here it must be noted that it was quite unusual for a woman to achieve this kind of professional success during this era, and her husband's willingness to support it was rarer still. Even though the Sadiks had servants to tend to the everyday tasks, Azhar would be responsible for running the household of five young children, ranging in age from ten-year-old Wafa to two-year-old Omar. In addition, this couple seemed to never take the path of least resistance. They rotated around Pakistan and hopscotched back and forth across continents, packing and unpacking—usually with a newborn baby in one of the crates—if that's what it took to move forward in their work. Forty years later Omar would say that what set his mother apart from anyone else he knew was her phenomenal energy.

When his mother arrived in Baltimore in 1963, she discovered a much different city than the one she had left behind in 1954. And this surprise at the unexpected was mutual, because evidently the dean of Johns Hopkins School of Public Health had anticipated a much different person that the svelte creature who strode onto campus in her silk saris and diamonds. "Who are you?" he wanted to know.

"I'm Nafis Sadik."

"Are you sure?"

"I should be, shouldn't I? I mean I know who I am."

Because she was an officer of the Pakistani Planning Commission, the dean had expected a much older woman; now in a panic, he tried to convince his charge to live in the nurse's quarters for her own safety. The city center had crumbled into a burned-out slum with a high crime rate, and the university's strict instructions were the most frightening part of all: "When you come out of the building, do not turn left, only turn right. Do not talk to anyone. Do not walk after dark."

There were other surprises. Nafis marveled that the maternity ward of nearby City Hospital, where she had brought scores of babies into the world, had closed as a result of changes in the post-1950s baby boom birthrate and the region's economic decay.

Nafis thoroughly enjoyed her courses, studying health economics and planning, where she learned techniques for prioritizing preventative health versus curative measures. One contact at Hopkins would prove to be a major influence on the rest of her career: Eileen Toyber, a famous demographer. Nafis would later fashion this instructor's lessons into policy for millions in the area of population growth. Toyber discussed ideas that were new at the time: the concept that governments must plan for future numbers of citizens, and that the fewer citizens you had, the better life you could provide for them. As the population increased, funding had to increase proportionally to provide the same level of services. Otherwise quality of life would begin to deteriorate for the masses.

An invigorated Planning Commission deputy arrived back in Karachi full of theories, ideas, and plans. On the trip home Nafis decided that she needed to obtain all Pakistan's data on various programs, such as maternal and child mortality and morbidity, to begin putting her newly acquired planning knowledge to work. "Then I discovered that there was no data!" She was shocked to learn her country's leaders were making policy choices that affected the entire population with no real basis for their decisions. "I realized the process was completely uneven. If someone asks for more money and somehow makes a good case, then they get it, and if they don't make a good case, then they don't get it."

"Next I went to WHO, the World Health Organization, thinking surely they must have the data I need. But they said, 'Well, we want to get it, but we don't have it yet.' I said, 'But you must have some idea. Otherwise, how do you provide assistance to Pakistan? How do you decide priorities? How do you decide how much money should be allocated to a health center, or a rural area, unless you know how many people come and what kinds of illnesses they have?'

"WHO said, 'Well, we talk to the minister of health, and then we just sit down and decide.' I mean, I was quite disappointed. I realized this lack of information was really bad, and that this was one of the things we must include in our plan, how to get data so we could measure progress. They told me, 'You're thinking like in a Western country, but we don't have all those statistics. The politicians decide where the funding goes.'"

Here Nafis had encountered it again: the notion that people in positions of power should make decisions that influence the lives of millions, but with no systematic basis for those judgments or any way to measure their success.

Caught in the bureaucratic snafu of needing to formulate a plan of action before she had all the data, she did her best to estimate the public's needs by extrapolating the figures she could obtain, such as the overall birth and death rates in Pakistan. Nafis knew the approach was flawed at best, with no regional or local information, but she deduced that the current allocation for the nation's public health programs was merely one-quarter of the need. "I was quite distraught, and I wrote to the chief economist and said, 'Our proposal starts with the statement that the objective of the National Investment Plan is 'to raise the quality of life for the people.' Therefore you must increase the funding for our health programs because at this rate you're not going to improve the quality of life for anyone. On the contrary, they are going to be ill a lot more or die, because there's no money invested in health. In fact, if you see projections of the population, you will see that in order to maintain the same standard of living, we will have to invest much more, and to improve even slightly, we'll have to invest more still."

Professor Toyber had taught her student well. Nafis may have been the only woman heading a division of the Planning Commission, but her concerns were not ignored. Economists from Harvard University aided the commission with their strategy, and it no doubt helped that Nafis spoke their language. Not only had she memorized these points on planning from her courses at Johns Hopkins, but the fact that her father was a world-renowned economist and Pakistan's finance minister couldn't have hurt either.

Her level-headed assessment of the country's needs earned her respect from a host of colleagues, including Joint Chief Economist Mahbub ul Haq, who would later go on to become a leading global development economist and minister of finance for Pakistan. In the evenings she further enhanced her status by playing bridge with her counterparts from the office; one of them—impressed by her skill—called her "one of the best bridge players I've ever encountered." This seemingly innocent pastime allowed her to bond with these men socially while proving herself a coolly calculating intellect capable of beating them at their own game.

Nafis Sadik has stated on numerous occasions that she had never encountered professional discrimination in Pakistan, a country some would regard as a bastion of male domination. In fact, she says she never in her life felt discriminated against for her gender until she arrived at the United Nations. Her brother Kemal explains this paradox by noting that there was no need for discrimination in their homeland, because women in Pakistan did not pose a threat. "The people that threaten you are the ones you want to sort out; Pakistanis are terribly nice to the menials, or the people that are the peons and drivers, more so than they are to their colleagues."

A different theory was posited by one of Nafis's friends, Shahida Azfar: "In our part of the world women get a lot of their credibility by who they are related to—husbands, brothers, etc."

In contrast to Nafis's personal treatment, the doctor recalled meetings where the Planning Commission discussed education for Pakistan's women. The thinking ranged from their deep-seated fear that "girls will become uncontrollable" if educated, to a hand-waving dismissal: "It's not our highest priority."

"But you know to me it was a priority," she concluded. "I wasn't that assertive and aggressive about those things at that time," she admits, "but I used to believe that you have to be educated. Because, otherwise, you can't read anything. You can't understand anything. You can't read labels. You won't even know how to take medicines. However, the thinking at that time was that you just raise the economy and everything else would become okay."

Nafis would wait and fight this education battle another day. In the meantime, she went to see the secretary of health, a man twice her age, to tell him what needed to be done on the funding issue.

She became a hero in the provinces, the outlying regions of Pakistan, which were thrilled that she had maneuvered more money for their health programs.

Ironically the current administration of President Ayub Khan, which had come to power in a military coup, created a more progressive and democratic era in the Muslim nation's politics than previous administrations. This was an era of greater opportunity for women in Pakistan, as the new political leader passed a number of laws restricting polygamy and increasing women's rights—alongside reforms that would soon create hostility between him and religious leaders.

At a time when family planning was a foreign notion to most of the world, the Planning Commission received the green light to launch one of the first such programs in history, and Nafis's background in reproductive health made her a natural leader in this agenda. In order to assess the population's position on this new service, she began to tour the country, venturing into every outpost, including East Pakistan (modern-day Bangladesh). This rough travel into remote regions involved navigating through some of the planet's tallest mountain ranges, requiring a stamina that was not for a frail damsel.

In keeping with her own guiding philosophy, that people's needs must inform policy decisions, Nafis set out to gather knowledge. She was no stranger to the challenges ahead of her, having encountered the mentality of the frontier in her Abbottabad days, and so she prepared her strategy. She might have been a scientist, but the deputy was first and foremost a woman, and she would begin with her wardrobe.

"I did not wear a sari. I wore a shalwar kameez and a scarf that covered my head. So I dressed more in line with what the locals wore. Because if you want to speak to someone on the village council, the local political leaders, they are mostly men, and they are generally very uncomfortable talking to women or they don't talk to women, period. So you know, to make them comfortable, first you tell them you're a physician, and what you're doing and why. And then they'll usually nod, because you are willing to look after their family. You are really looking to find out what they think are their needs. For me at the Planning Commission, I sought to find out what people actually thought about health, what they thought they needed, and what they wanted." Her strategy of respectful inquiry worked.

Old friends who have observed Nafis in her myriad roles—from bridge player to mother to diplomat—note that one of the most fascinating facets of her personality is that she never changes her persona. Her wardrobe, maybe, but not her personality. As an acquaintance from this era, Akhtar Isphahani, remarked, "Nafis stays Nafis—she doesn't become Dr. Nafis Sadik because she is in a meeting. It is only the subject matter that changes. She doesn't change. A lot of women, to get a job done, we might go out and try to flatter the male ego. She never does that."

As Nafis helped create the new family planning program, her wisdom in health and finance proved invaluable, since this new government operation would require both. She had already ascertained the connection between well-being and capital. The fledgling agency followed the old socialist model of multiyear planning, formulating strategies for the next five to twenty years. Nafis, working side by side with hardcore economists, set targets in each sector within a broader context. However, by being in an arena where multiple goals were discussed in relation to their ability to affect one another, she understood the interconnectedness of development: to uplift the people's standard of living, the populace must progress simultaneously on all fronts. And as Nafis learned, once you understand these interlinkages, you can persuade governments to accept them.

As she prepared the next five-year plan for the health sector, she inadvertently created her own future job by including a strategy to provide women with access to birth control. In 1965 Nafis went to work for Pakistan's newly created Family Planning Program. Because she had already worked so much on its conception by gathering information and writing the report, the government asked Nafis to join the agency, and she became its first director of planning and training.

President Khan's administration was receptive to the concept of planning the nation's population, realizing that, as projected by demographers such as Eileen Toyber, if Pakistan's numbers continued to multiply at current rates, the nation's economy would have to accelerate at exponential proportions in order to keep up. But the idea of a government involved with private citizens' procreation was met with resistance. First, it was seen as anti-Islamic, and an organization of religious teachers called the Mullah Group opposed it. And there were many more obstacles for the nascent program yet to come.

Nafis remembered some of the lessons from these days of pioneering: "When the family planning programs were first introduced in Pakistan in the 1960s, they were directed to women. But what we didn't realize is that men actually controlled a lot of the decisions. And many men, because they didn't know enough, felt ignorant. So the reaction to their own ignorance was to forbid the wife to use birth control. And it was only much later that we started to realize that you have to involve men as well.

"At the time we thought, 'It's women's health that's affected, so they must have control. How dare anyone else decide!' But in time we realized if you want to achieve your objectives, you must also involve men, not ignore them. Because sometimes ignoring them had the opposite effect.

"In Pakistan, in one of the clinics, a man brought in his wife who was using an IUD, an intrauterine device. And he said, 'She's had it inserted without my permission.' The doctor said, 'You know, the law is that she can have it. It's her decision.' The wife said, 'No, no, I want it removed,' because she was scared of the husband. So anyway it was removed. And then he said, 'Now reinsert it, because now I give my permission.'"

As time went by, their family planning team's approach matured.

"We learned to listen to the women and ask them what they wanted. Women generally wanted some method of birth control which they would not have to bother with, not have to use continually. At this time the IUD was one of the main features of our program, but we started to note that many women didn't like the IUD because it produced bleeding. And then they said they didn't have enough follow-up help.

"When I used to come back from many of these research trips, I would write these reports and say that we have to improve our follow-up care, otherwise the program was just going to disintegrate. Because there was a lot of gossip then about the IUD, as these rumors spread by word of mouth people started to distrust it. But the director general didn't want any bad things to be said about our program, and he warned me, 'Oh, my God, you can't do that. You can't write that in your report.' I said, 'Well, that's what I found, and this is my report. If you want to change it, then you change it.' So he doctored the report. But of course I used to go around publicly telling people about what I'd found.

"Then gradually we started to introduce oral contraceptives, which had less side effects, although at that time they possessed a very high dosage of estrogen. Also, it meant taking pills every day, so some of the women didn't like that. And some of the women used to take home condoms for their husbands. Many never came to get anything for themselves. Some of the wives used to manage to persuade their husbands to use condoms, and of course our program's male worker used to go from house to house and sometimes try to persuade individual men as well.

"There was also a sterilization option as part of our service program. In the beginning, many men came for vasectomies, but always after having numerous children, not after, you know, just a few children. Then many of them wanted their wives to be sterilized, not themselves. Interestingly enough, lots of women didn't want their husbands sterilized, either, preferring to have the procedures themselves, because they said, 'Oh, my husband is the breadwinner. If something happens to him, that will be bad.' So they had this mindset, that the men were more important to the family than they were. The women thought if something happened to themselves, it didn't matter."

Nafis and Azhar decided to build a home in the Defense Housing Society, a posh suburb of Karachi. Ambereen remembered how exciting the process was, working with the architects as they drew up the plans, visiting the site each day, and visualizing where everything would be as the foundations were being laid. Of course, it was tempting fate for the nomadic Sadik clan to put down such deep roots, as they would have been better served by dwelling in a gypsy caravan.

When their new showplace was complete, the family did settle in—albeit not for long. Built on a hillside, the home was a split-level design, and because of the slope of land, it felt as if the visitor entered on the second floor. In traditional Muslim fashion—where the facade of a home's exterior should be modest so as not to appear flashy, the architect created a lush central courtyard with a fountain and positioned the layout of the rooms around it's perimeter. At the same time the living room, dining room, and four bedrooms also faced the huge yard; a big veranda wrapped around the upper level, with a staircase leading to the garden below. Landscaping rolled down the hillside of the 1,500-square-yard lawn, providing an Edenic setting where the Sadiks frequently entertained.

But while the parents were away earning the money to pay for their fabulous property, the children took advantage of this opportunity. The girls would steal the Volkswagen Beetle, "mother's sort of scooching-around car," and cruise the neighborhood. They would all pile in, along with the perennial houseguests—in one case the son and daughter of one of Nafis's friends, children who lived with the Sadiks for a year and a half while their parents were posted in Indonesia.

During one such excursion the wide-eyed explorers were sputtering around the block in first gear, since Wafa, the driver, didn't know how to shift, when they passed their mother, who was hurrying home with tickets to take her little angels to the movie theater. Imagine her surprise when she passed her own car jerking down the street.

Ambereen remembered how she lined all of them up and gave them a thorough tongue-lashing, with her topmost concern being the potential bodily danger to the houseguests: "What would I tell their parents? My children have just killed your children?"

More than the Volkswagen was out of control. The older girls had hit puberty, and their hormones guided them to an overweening interest in members of the opposite sex, resulting in behavior that was considered scandalous in conservative Karachi. Wafa began inviting a young man named Nadoo into the bedroom she shared with Mehreen, thinking the house was so huge that they were sufficiently insulated against their parents, especially when their mother and father left them in the servants' care.

One night the young lothario was visiting until 10:00, lounging around, when Mehreen left the room to fetch a glass of water. Wafa dutifully locked the door, and when a knock came she opened it, only to find Azhar standing there staring in disbelief at the boy sprawled across her bed. The only good news was that Nadoo was fully clothed, an asset, as he tore past the startled father and streaked down the hall.

"Catch him!" Azhar screamed to the servants as he raced after the intruder. In the confusion Amosh, the Sadiks' driver, believed his master had surprised a thief, and Nadoo broke into the type of sprint that only a testosterone-infused teenage boy on the brink of death can muster, outrunning the whole household.

Unfortunately for Nadoo, his cousin was married to Nafis's brother Kemal, so there was no real escape; the whole tribe became judge and jury, conspiring on the disciplinary process. In the end Wafa and Mehreen were grounded, and they spent the entire time bickering about whose fault it was that they had gotten caught.

Her bad behavior aside, Wafa greatly admired her adopted mother. "I was really fascinated by Bhabhiji, and I used to just sit there watching her. The driver would pick me up first from school, then pick her up from work to go home for lunch. She had this small, little office, and her table was piled high with papers. And there was a line of men with files in their hands who used to be waiting to see her, a line that went all the way from her desk to the doorway, then out of the doorway down the hall. They were waiting for her to sign those papers, and the work had to be done before she could leave. So I used to sit there in a chair, watching her. And she went through the files quickly, signing them, and I used to say, oh my God, so much work!"

Many years later, as an adult and mother herself, Wafa reflected back on the fate of the two orphans when their father died: "I was scared before the decision was made that we were going to move in with Bhabhiji and my brother—scared because I didn't know what was going to happen to us." There was talk of separating the sisters because various relatives felt they could only take one child, but not two, and the youngsters could have wound up in any number of less than ideal situations. "But Bhabhiji spoke up and insisted that we should both be with them.

"She, herself, was very young at that time. It didn't register on me then, but now when I think about it, I wonder if I was in her place, would I do it? To suddenly have five children to look after, with two brand new? At that time, as kids, we took things for granted, of course, because we were so young. But now when I look back and I think about it, I wonder if I would take that on. Because it's not just feeding two children. There is so much more that comes with it, the education, the growing up. She's seen us through all that—everything—until I got married in New York."

As many a vulnerable waif before Wafa has learned, and as Nafis knew, the right guardian could change a child's life forever, especially a little girl's.

Vianca Ivonne Huerta Garcia | Mexico City, Mexico

She corrects me when I ask about the man who raped her. "*Men.*" At first I believe we are having a communication breakdown between her Spanish and my English, but as she continues I realize I have understood her perfectly. "I was raped by three men," Vianca says matter-of-factly. "My step-father, my uncle, and my grandfather." For years she lived in a situation of sexual abuse that began when she was five years old, and her alcoholic stepfather started molesting her while her mother was at work. "He drank a lot and took a lot of different drugs," she explains almost apologetically. When she tried to report what had happened, "Mama didn't believe me—she said I was crazy." It didn't help matters that the other relatives in question are the mother's younger brother and father, the latter a man who instead of being his descendant's protector was more of a predator than the girl's stepfather. The grandfather also had sex with Vianca's twin sister.

Today both teenagers live at Ayuda y Solidaridad con Los Niños, a center for street children located in Mexico City. Instead of returning after school to their own home and parents, they pass through the blue steel gates and graffiti-covered walls of the shelter, located in Vallejo, a rough area of this enormous city of nine million people. I note with bitter irony that the twenty-five girls who reside at this institution are sealed inside a fortress for the their own protection; they live like prisoners behind bars, while the men who have molested them run free.

At fifteen, Vianca's looks belie the tragedy of her childhood: smooth skin with plump rosy cheeks, animated dark eyes, small white teeth, shiny black hair pulled back into a ponytail. She wears a mismatched outfit of Teva sandals and socks, the gray trousers of a track suit, and a lavender top covered by enormous flowers. Underneath her blouse is the apparent contradiction of budding breasts on a tiny maiden barely four feet tall. As I interview her I see the phenomenon of other girls' heads popping up at the darkened windows, and as they watch us talk, their hands reach up to cover their mouths to stifle the giggles.

These refugees from the Mexico City slums hail from a variety of heartbreaking circumstances: parents dead, parents in prison, parents disappeared, or parents so addled by drugs and drink that their daughters would be better off if they disappeared. Many of the children have lived on the streets for years before they make their way to Ayuda y Solidaridad; some have experimented with drugs, and all have seen more before elementary school than most individuals will witness in a lifetime.

Vianca wound up here after her stepfather, in one particularly brutal binge, raped the thirteen-year-old for seven days in a row. She ran away to a neighbor's house, and then the neighbor took the girl to stay with her best friend. Vianca's mother arrived and tried to convince her daughter to come home, but the stepfather was still there in the household, just as he had always been. Soon *he* began to show up at the home where the girl was staying, trying to coerce her to come back. That was when her foster parent, realizing the danger, took Vianca to a government-run agency, and they placed the child at Ayuda y Solidaridad. During this whole ordeal, she was agonizing over the fact that she had left her sister behind, and when the director of Ayuda y Solidaridad informed Vianca one day that her twin was coming to live with her, the girl's white teeth flashed into a Cheshire cat grin.

The shelter is an independent nongovernmental organization affiliated with UNFPA. Though they receive no funding from the Catholic Church, the nuns visit to provide religious instruction, and the residents attend mass on Sunday. The program strives for two main objectives: (1) socialize the young women, taking into account what they've been through, and (2) help them become independent and function in society. The counselors agree that their biggest challenge is to make it clear to their charges that they can't change their families and they can't change the past. "They must accept their situation, which can be difficult. Sometimes a lot of aggression comes out, and because they've had such a difficult past, it's tough to think they can have a better future."

Vianca says she loves living at the shelter, especially now that her sister has joined her, and she vows that she loves the director, Mariamar Estrada, "because she always calls me 'princess.'" The teenager likes to work in the library and help out in the kitchen, where she assists with making *sincronizadas*, a dish with layers of tortillas, beans, ham, and cheese.

Vianca has embraced this place as home and no longer talks to her family. The last time she called her mom was two years ago, to wish her a happy Mother's Day, and the woman asked, "Why are you calling me?" The mother has told her daughters they are welcome to come back anytime, but she still lives with the stepfather who raped Vianca and does not believe her daughter's stories of abuse. At least the uncle who tormented the girl is no longer a threat. He's serving a term in prison for killing a man.

When I ask about school, Vianca admits that she's not so great at math, but declares Spanish as her favorite subject, and with a pencil gripped in her pudgy fingers (which are tipped by glittery nail polish), she begins to draw a gigantic bumble bee to show me her other passion: art. She raves about a third obsession—Harry Potter—and I can see how the magical powers of these fictional children, youngsters who can conjure the ability to escape from harm's way, would appeal to Vianca's imagination.

Her career goals are a bit vague, but she's narrowed them down to becoming a singer (because she loves rock in Español) or a veterinarian, and in a moment of déjà vu, I am reminded of the extreme career options of another fervent go-getter—the young Nafis Sadik.

When I ask the diminutive adolescent if she would like for me to use a pseudonym when I tell her story, her confident comportment, direct gaze, and authoritative manner further remind me of a young Nafis, and I have an eerie glimpse of what the diplomat must have been like at this molten age before she hardened into obsidian. Vianca nods at my notebook and says, "Oh no, you use my real name. I want *everyone* to know who I am."

9 THE UN

The ever-bold Nafis's name became internationally known as she charged forward with her work at the Pakistani Family Planning Commission. Her aggressive management style incorporated the spirit of community building, a technique that would become a trademark throughout the doctor's long tenure working for women's rights. To this end she decided to host a global symposium to enable the sharing of information on methods to control fertility. She called the event "Beyond Family Planning," a title that foreshadowed a showdown she would face in Cairo twenty-five years later: the battle over who has the right to control a woman's uterus—the woman herself or the government that wants to impose its demographic goals?

In 1969 Nafis organized a conference in Dhaka, the capital of East Pakistan, and almost immediately ran into massive security issues, another situation she would face in Cairo. By comparison, however, her Dhaka organizational challenges were a joke . . . literally. Someone had advised that her opening speech should start off with a joke, but the mistress of ceremonies was so nervous that she couldn't remember the punch line. At the point where the audience was supposed to burst into gales of laughter, she was greeted by raw silence instead.

Considering all the possible pitfalls she had to negotiate to put the event together—this being the first major one of her career—a flat one-liner was the least of her worries. She had asked USAID for guidance on the creation of such an undertaking, and they had sent out a seasoned veteran who advised how to organize a conference of this magnitude, one attended by VIPs from all over the globe. Nafis soon realized that the informational panels were just one facet of the experience; she had to consider protocol, booking flight and hotel arrangements, receiving 250 guests, meals, entertainment—oh, and the safety of some of the world's most important leaders.

She chose Dhaka for the conference's location because the city was so densely populated that it served as a living testament to the necessity for population control. (This theory was confirmed two years later after the region was renamed Bangladesh, and the media focused a horrified gaze on the nation's plight of overcrowding, squalor, and starvation.) Nafis reasoned that if the vehicle of a visiting dignitary even paused at a stoplight, the VIP would be swarmed by hundreds of beggars, and this experience alone would do more to demonstrate the dangers of letting your population outpace an economy than any speech from a podium.

Her government's Ministry of Foreign Affairs was stunned when they learned that Nafis had invited all these individuals to Pakistan without informing their office—but typical of her style, she had decided what she wanted to do was the right thing to do and then didn't wait around for permission. The problem with this approach was that East Pakistan was currently the scene of much political upheaval, with the citizenry rioting as they demonstrated against President Ayub Khan, demanding their independence. This chaos and the ensuing curfew were well publicized on the nightly news in the United States, and participants who had confirmed began to back out. Nafis assured them all that she had everything under control and to come ahead.

"I then went to East Pakistan's governor and told him I needed some passes for the conference guests so that they could avoid the curfew.

"'Okay,' he said, 'how many?' I said, 'Around 250.'

"He said, 'What! You're not allowed to organize meetings of more than five people!' It took some negotiating, but I finally got him to agree to give me enough passes for two busloads so that I could pick up the guests arriving at the airport. Then I had to put everyone in the Intercontinental Hotel, and agree not to let them out into the city. I spoke to the hotel's management and said for goodness sake, be sure you have enough food, because these people will be eating breakfast, lunch and dinner here for four days." Talk about a captive audience!

"Next, I knew I needed to arrange some sort of entertainment. The Intercontinental brought in some violinists—they also had to stay on the premises and couldn't go out. But mainly what the conference is remembered for is that we had to amuse ourselves every evening, and so many hidden talents were discovered. Someone played the piano, a few sang, others danced."

Naturally this was an area where Nafis, our Leo in the limelight, had some expertise, and she felt right at home leading the charge. The whole stay produced a wacky camaraderie, and at the end one speaker came to the podium with a redux of Jonathan Swift's satire *A Modest Proposal*. His name was Phil Hauser, a professor at the University of Chicago and pioneer in the fields of demography and urban studies. His work argued that if international economic growth did not happen proportionally to population growth, then that disparity would lead to poverty, political instability, and war. But on the podium that day his speech offered an alternative—that the best demographic strategy beyond family planning was cannibalism. "On one hand you increase the food supply, and on the other hand you decrease the population." The audience howled at the spoof, but being sequestered on the premises under martial law must have cast a shadow over their mirth—not to mention that in a couple of days their departure busses would be wading through the hungry throng again.

Other men in the audience that day listened keenly to the speeches, and they would later prove to be important partners for Nafis's future goals. U.S. general William Draper, who had become very interested in population issues, had brought along an entourage of American politicos and wealthy businessmen from Xerox and IBM—individuals who would later become donors for the cause. Dr. Sadik had organized the conference as a medium of information exchange, but in the end it also served as an opportunity to showcase her own talents and thus proved to be a pivotal point in her career, although these developments would take years to materialize.

Of course, in Dhaka in 1969 she did not know what the future had in store. But typical of Nafis, she didn't wait around to find out. Instead—aggressive as ever—she solicited funds for her fledging family planning agency, understanding that without capital, they could have a game plan of pure genius but be incapable of buying a single condom.

Sweden had already sponsored some programs in Pakistan, and so Nafis decided to approach USAID and the Canadian government, asking if they would be interested in supporting her mission. Both governments expressed their theoretical approval, but declined, stating, "at this moment, family planning doesn't fit with our priorities or policies." This was a sign of the times, and the fact that the notion of reproductive rights was still regarded with queasy dissent, an issue too sensitive to be endorsed by most religious and political bodies. However, the private individuals interested in Nafis's agenda were not so hesitant.

In a city very different from Dhaka, along the broad shady lanes of Colonial Williamsburg, lay the red brick buildings where the founders of American democracy orated ideas that would launch a revolution. Nearly two hundred years later another group of innovative thinkers convened there to discuss a different type of revolution. Among them sat John D. Rockefeller, who in 1952 financed an organization called the Population Council; the assembled agreed on the need for solid science to guide in addressing population questions. According to Rockefeller, the reason to care about population was "to improve the quality of people's lives, to help make it possible for individuals everywhere to develop their full potential."

When Rockefeller later visited Nafis in Pakistan after the Dhaka conference, she received him at the airport in the middle of the night. The millionaire had expressly requested a single room with a bath, but when she escorted him to his hotel, he discovered that he was booked into a luxury suite. The philanthropist became quite upset and declared: "I do not want to waste my money on this room."

Nafis explained that he would not be charged the extra cost. "I don't want the Pakistani government wasting their money on this room either!" The man whose name was synonymous with wealth impressed his host by his sensibility; she saw that he would prefer monastic quarters in order to use his fortune where it would do the most good.

After the Dhaka conference, other developing nations considered Pakistan's family planning program a role model and Nafis a leading authority in the field. She traveled to other newborn family planning programs as an adviser, visiting Indonesia, Egypt, and Tunisia. Partnerships evolved between the governments and NGOs. These outfits, such as Planned Parenthood, were in many nations responsible for dispensation of all birth control (even when they were quietly funded by the government), a situation that neatly side-stepped the regimes' involvement in the moral equation and the need to answer the question: Who controls a woman's uterus—the woman herself, the government, or God?

These questions jumped to the forefront back home in Pakistan as Islamic leaders began to object to the notion that the government should have any say over how many children a couple produced. In 1971, when Ayub Khan was driven from office and replaced by

Zulfikar Ali Bhutto (father of Benazir Bhutto), a more conservative era ensued. One of the leader's first steps with the very visible family planning program was to make it fade into the background; he began by renaming it "Family Welfare," which had the ring of a bureaucracy involved in everything except sex.

In this same year Nafis positioned herself in the hot seat at the head of the family planning table, when she took over as director general running the program. By this point political support from the president and other government agencies had evaporated. Pakistani radio and television stations refused to publicize any of her initiatives, lest there be a backlash against them.

The fundamentalists began to make headway with reversing progressive political gains, especially for women's rights, turning the country away from its Western-leaning British past to align it with a more extreme interpretation of Islam. One of these was Bhutto's overnight declaration that instead of observing Sunday as the Sabbath as the West did, Friday, the Muslim holy day, would now be observed as such, and Sunday would become a regular work day. Nafis and her progressive friends noted the changes with a type of vigilant dread, watching closely as the country their parents had created with such enthusiasm began to lose its identity as a modern secular nation inhabited by Muslims to become a conglomeration of Muslim sects.

The upper classes began to evacuate the country, relocating to London or New York or Zurich or Dubai, not wanting to raise their children in an environment that was steadily moving toward an Islamic theocracy. As Zeenat Haroon reflected, the situation "made all of us very fearsome, because we found that it is not going to be what it was when we started out. Children are not going to enjoy the same liberties and modernity." Soon the Haroon sisters left, the Shoaib brothers left, and Nafis and Azhar began to consider their own options as they watched their government, the one that had been birthed with such fanfare and hope, turn inward, closing itself off from the international community. The cream of Karachi society became afraid to question the motives of the Bhutto regime. They stopped assuming that religion was a personal choice, rather than a state mandate.

Clearly the problems came about from conflicting ideas concerning what Pakistan was destined to be at its inception; the fundamentalists looked at the country as their haven, their chance to break free from the slights of the British who had oppressed them, their chance to break free from colonists who had regarded Muslims as second-class humans. The trouble was that most of these fundamentalists tended to place women in this same slot, as second-class humans.

Naturally Nafis wasn't accepting this attitude.

In 1967 George Herbert Walker Bush was the U.S. ambassador to the UN when the organization first broached the topic of creating an agency to "assist developing countries, at their request, in dealing with their population problems in the forms and means best suited to the individual countries' needs." Until this time the topic of family planning was so controversial that the United Nations couldn't even agree to *discuss* it. However, there were some fearless individuals involved in the story, among them Ambassador Bush. In spite of the pro-life policies he would later endorse as president, his position supporting access to family planning was not actually that surprising. Rather, it was more of a family legacy, considering his father, Senator Prescott Bush, had been one of the founders of Planned Parenthood. In this era population control was a Republican agenda, with one reason being that the exponential rise in the number of babies born in developing nations was seen as a security threat to the United States. What happened when two billion starving people, seeking a solution to their survival, started eyeing the agricultural surpluses of history's wealthiest nation?

Bush worked in conjunction with a small group of activists such as General William Draper, who persuaded UN Secretary-General

U-Thant to create a trust fund. This endowment opened under the guidance of the UN Development Program, with the mission to create censuses, statistical systems, population policy, and—for a few countries—family planning. With this directive, the United Nations Fund for Population Activities was born. The United States donated 50 percent of the capital, matching contributions from Sweden and India. Located on Lexington Avenue and 45th in Manhattan, in 1969 UNFPA opened for business.

Six professionals were hired to staff the brand-new agency. Each representative was assigned to cover a different region of the world, a chore they orchestrated from a couple of offices tucked in back by the kitchen, and to say these six staffers had their work cut out for them was an understatement. Only a fraction of countries even had family planning programs in 1969. The few that were interested, like Kenya and Egypt, didn't have the internal infrastructure to implement any initiatives. Most other African nations had laws banning contraception. The USSR and the Arab States wanted to *increase* their populations. Because of the historical position of the Catholic Church, the Latin American countries were against "family planning," and in parts of Asia diplomats literally couldn't even say those words without being deported. And yet, UNFPA's initial surveys had shown overwhelmingly that a large percentage of women and couples wanted to limit the size of their families but had no means to make that happen. So, the missionaries commenced their mission.

These pioneering UN optimists strolled into a minefield of international controversy, as could have been expected from any topic that involved sex, power, money, and religion. As Nafis noted in a speech thirty years later: "There were people who thought that there could be no development without solving what they called 'the population problem,' and that family planning was the solution. There were people who thought that 'the population problem' was a diversion from the real problem of under-development, and that family planning had no part to play. Some people thought it was a plot against the poor.

"People who talked about 'population control' didn't seem to realize that they were dictating to women how they should manage their lives. On the other hand, many men who opposed family planning have actually told me that it would make women promiscuous. They seemed to think that the risk of getting pregnant was the only thing that kept women faithful to their husbands. Neither side seemed to have much respect for women.

"In 1970 there seemed to be no common ground between population and development. But no one reckoned with Rafael Salas. Mr. Salas was a very farsighted man. He understood that demography was important for development. But he also understood that behind the demographic figures were real figures—individual women and men, making their own decisions. He had a very clear idea that women should and would play an equal part in development."

Rafael Salas, from the Philippines, headed the tiny staff. Back home he had been a deputy to President Ferdinand Marcos, the chief of his cabinet, and had run Marcos's first presidential campaign. Later he had run his nation's rice sufficiency program and then represented Asia at the first human rights conference in Tehran in 1968. He had a reputation for being scrupulously above board, and in 1969 he left the creeping corruption of Marcos's regime to head the United Nations Fund for Population Activities—perhaps an odd job for a Catholic.

After the Dhaka conference in 1969, Nafis, the woman of science, decided she wanted an independent, outside review of the progress of Pakistan's Family Planning Program, an objective appraisal of the agency under her aegis. She turned to a colleague at the Population Council, Bill Draper, for advice. He in turn referred her to the United Nations and suggested she ask them to evaluate.

The UN agreed to the task and sent a team to review Pakistan's program. What ensued, though, was far from the helpful guidance Nafis had sought. When their report had not landed on her desk after six months, she began writing New York repeatedly, inquiring on the progress. The response was that "it was being edited," but as time dragged on the situation at home in Pakistan turned grim. Gossip fermented that the review *had* arrived, but its results were so damning that Nafis had suppressed them.

No one could have guessed the absurd truth behind the delay: that although the review team visiting Pakistan had approved of the nation's program, the World Health Organization overruled its own representatives' positive verdict. In fact, WHO had a policy against family planning in general and did not include it in their global health agenda. While the interagency debate raged on, the UN was not willing to finalize and release the requested information. Finally after nine months—the same gestation period as a baby—the report was delivered and held high praise for Pakistan's family planning program along with some suggestions for improvement. But by this point Nafis, thoroughly disgusted with the whole experience, wished she'd never heard of the United Nations.

Nafis Sadik's first encounter with the United Nations Fund for Population Activities occurred when the agency asked if they could visit to observe Pakistan's family planning methods in depth and discuss the country's needs. Nafis, feeling proud of her agency's accomplishments, was pleased and told them to come ahead; she set about to make all the arrangements for her esteemed colleagues. After spending thirty days working with the UNFPA representatives, she asked, "Well, how much assistance do you think you can provide us?"

"Oh, at the moment we don't have any money, but when we do . . ."

"You wasted a month of our time for *you* to learn, rather than to assist *us*? This is not how I expect the UN to operate. You are supposed to be working for *our* benefit, not for *your* learning experience!"

Their experts returned to Pakistan in 1970 to offer assistance. Since the core staff of UNFPA was a skeleton crew, their experts were borrowed from other UN agencies: the main headquarters of the UN; United Nations Educational, Scientific and Cultural Organization (UNESCO); the World Health Organization; the International Labor

Organization; and the Food and Agriculture Organization, among others. Some of the agencies not only refused to communicate with one another, they flagrantly vied for dominance. Nafis began "going quite crazy" dealing with the cast of characters . . . not to mention egos.

Luckily some experts were just that. "Very sensible and knowledgeable advisers who also had worked in developing countries, and sometimes knew more about Pakistan than we did, because they had read up a lot, they had traveled, and they were interested. But there were also some really irritating individuals, and it seemed the less they knew, the more arrogant they were."

She was referring to one health guru in particular who informed Dr. Sadik: "Now, we must organize caucuses for the midwives in these villages—they must come into headquarters periodically." Nafis, whose medical practice had begun fifteen years prior, chugging up dirt track mountain roads in a Jeep to visit her ob-gyn patients, explained the situation: that in these remote regions midwifery was a handed-down career, with the knowledge passed on from mother to daughter, and in many cases the women were not literate. "Have you ever visited these midwives? Have you ever even *talked* to them?" she inquired, knowing the answer—that this consultant had never been outside Karachi. "You're going to have meetings and conferences with them? They won't even understand what you're talking about—the first thing."

"But that's how we operate."

"Well, maybe *you* operate like that, but they're all uneducated. And *you* have access, communications. You just go and live with them, before you come and tell us how to bring women from all these different villages to a caucus."

The setting of Bellagio offers colorful contrasts; here the blue backdrop of the Alps frames red terra cotta rooftops, and the glassy water of Lake Como reflect the ochre sunbaked estates surrounding its rim. At this luxurious Italian resort the Ford Foundation organized a conference in 1971 on population and invited Nafis to attend. This upset her boss, the health secretary, who complained that the invitation should have gone to him. He understood that the heads of all the UN agencies would be present and so would many donors, like Robert McNamara, the president of the World Bank. What the secretary was just beginning to grasp, however, was that Nafis was already playing on a field he had not even glimpsed, meeting VIPs and making an international reputation for herself.

She did attend the conference at Bellagio and met McNamara there. Her father had left Pakistan in 1966, returning to Washington DC and the World Bank as vice president. When McNamara came home he told Mohammed Shoaib, "I met a very, very bright Pakistani woman at the meeting, and I believe I'm going to hire her for the bank."

"Well, think about it," Mohammed responded, "because it might have been my daughter," which would have disqualified her from employment at the same agency. Sure enough, it was Nafis.

In Bellagio she also met Rafael Salas. He, too, wanted to hire Dr. Sadik as a technical adviser, and he wooed her to come to New York to work for the two-year-old UN agency. She couldn't resist the opportunity to tell him of her impression of his organization based on previous encounters. "Well, then we need someone with your kind of experience to come and help us," he concluded suavely. Who could resist this invitation? Nafis agreed that if she came to the United States she would visit him to discuss possibilities.

As fate would have it, that same year the University of North Carolina invited her to help them develop their population and environmental policy program. After spending a month in Chapel Hill, she headed north to Manhattan to talk to Salas. "Oh, I'm very keen that you must join. Look around, and you'll see that you can do a lot more from here," he told her. A smooth operator, he knew to play the card that would win Nafis's interest, the dictum that she could affect change on a global scale. Being a seasoned diplomat, he instinctively played his trump, appealing to her ego and, although he didn't know it, her lifelong mission "to change the world." He then urged her to speak to UN personnel about salary.

Reluctant to abandon Pakistan, Nafis first discussed Salas's offer with her father, who advised her to at least talk to the UN to see what they could offer her. And so she did. Mr. Fin, the personnel representative, made the forty-two-year-old doctor an offer to come aboard as a technical adviser at the rank of P4. In her discussions at the agency she had already ascertained that all her male colleagues were P5s. When she pointed out this disparity and asked why she, too, wasn't being offered the higher rank, the gentleman responded sarcastically: "Oh, well, what do you expect? To become the head of the agency?"

"I'm not sure, but what's wrong with that? What is it to you what I want to become?"

Little did he know. And so it was here, for the first time in her professional history, Nafis encountered gender discrimination, extended by the organization built on the concept of promoting global justice for all.

"I'm not going to come," she told Salas in a huff. "It's just a matter of principal." And with that she returned to Pakistan. However, he kept pressing the hire, so for the next nine months Nafis haggled over her rank and salary as she negotiated with UN personnel. She stubbornly demanded the same compensation as her male colleagues before she would agree to take the job. During this time, personnel countered by suggesting that at forty-two she was too young for such an exorbitant salary, and even asked, "What's wrong, doesn't your husband work?"

Yes, he did work, and that was one of the problems. A point of serious contention arose around this fact, as Azhar's job was located in Karachi. She had followed him from post to post, packing up the well-worn crates and hauling along the kids. Now with Nafis's job offer, the couple had to make a difficult decision; not only whether or not to move to the States, but which opportunity would best benefit their children, their income, their personal futures, and their marriage.

One of the biggest concerns revolved around Azhar's job prospects: would he be able to find a job of equal wealth and prestige in New York? He currently worked as sales manager for Caltex, a firm created by a joint venture between Standard Oil of California and Texaco. Even though the company had a limited number of top management positions in New York headquarters, their charter stated they could not operate in the United States, and so that meant the forty-five-year-old middle manager would not be able to transfer.

Azhar was faced with one of the biggest quandaries of his life; like his earlier career impasse, where instead of studying at Cambridge he had headed off to the military academy in Dehra Dun—a situation brought about because his father had run short of cash—his family life had now pushed him into the position of another sacrifice. And at his age, he felt sure the move to the States, where he had no professional connections, would permanently dwarf his potential. As he made inquiries, his fears on his ability to land a new job were confirmed.

There were other factors to consider: in Pakistan the political climate continued to worsen, and yet the majority of their extended family were there. He also knew the easy life of domestic help and a luxurious home would be a mere fantasy if they moved to New York City. The children would be uprooted; then again, in the United States the options available to them would be significantly greater. They could attend American universities for a fraction of the cost they'd pay as international students, and afterward avail themselves of the lucrative American job market—the very thing that was now beyond the reach of their father.

If Nafis took the UN job, for the first time in their fifteen-year marriage she would be the primary breadwinner—an unusual position for an Asian man. Azhar's choice was further compounded because the work his wife would be doing would be important; he had not forgotten his days as a cadet on patrol back during Partition, the vulnerability of the women, their naked bodies lying in the village streets of the Punjab. He understood that in order for Nafis to make a major contribution to history, he would have to make a tremendous personal sacrifice.

Finally he and his spouse compromised on a trial separation; she would move to the States alone and make sure she liked it there and that she liked the job. After all, her opinion of UNFPA had not been the best so far. Azhar would hold down the fort at home in Karachi and keep working for Caltex. After six months they would reassess.

The stalemate over Nafis accepting the UN job carried on for several months, until finally the organization agreed to hire her at the same rank as the men. In October 1971 she made the decision to take all five children and move to New York.

The next challenge was to inform the children. When their mother flew into Karachi after she had finalized her appointment in New York City, the whole family came to pick her up at the airport. "We're moving to America!" she said.

The girls began wailing, but Omar, delighted, said, "Why are they crying? It sounds like fun!"

His sisters had their own idea of fun, and as their departure time drew near and they adapted to the notion of moving, they grew excited about the journey because they would be touring Europe en route to the States. For years, their mother had brought home Western artifacts from her travels, Beatles' albums and *Vogue* magazines, so they had definite visions of what was in store for them in Swinging London and on the continent. But the media images did not quite match up to reality—as travelers the world over have discovered— and as young Ambereen would soon learn.

"When we got to London, we actually knew people there. Tariq, my mother's younger brother, was much closer to our age—he was only twenty-three—and he had gotten tickets for *Hair*, which was the first play I'd ever seen. I was trying very hard to be sophisticated because I was fourteen, but I'd never seen anyone naked before, let alone in public, and here the performers came out into the aisles nude. Swinging Sixties was one thing, but in *Hair* it was another reality!

"My uncle took us out to a discotheque after that. Someone came up and asked me to dance, and I said, 'no thank you.' Uncle Tariq said, 'How embarrassing.' And I said, 'I don't know who he is, how could I dance with him?'

'Oh, God, you're so conventional!'

'But I haven't been introduced—how can I possibly dance with this stranger?' We'd really been quite sheltered.

"London proved to be a lot of fun, but really dirty, gray, and yucky. However, I'd expected that everyone would look like they had just walked out of *Vogue*, and that was a huge disappointment to me. HUGE! Because nobody looked like *Vogue*. I was hard pressed to find one person who looked like they were into high fashion."

Nafis left Azhar alone in the grand Karachi home, set in its lavish Garden of Eden, while she headed off in search of the Big Apple. With this latest move, the Sadik clan had truly transformed into nomads, now wandering in several different locations all at once: Azhar was back in Pakistan, Wafa and Ghazala had stopped off for a visit to their deceased mother's relatives in Iran before coming on to the States, and Nafis stayed with some friends in Queens, while she packed her other young vagabonds off on the interstate bus for points south.

In the way of foreigners—strangers in a strange land—the family did not think it odd that the children should arrive at the Greyhound bus depot in Washington DC, only to be greeted by their grandfather's chauffeur, who held up a placard simply saying "Sadik." Their fellow Greyhound passengers eyed the Pakistani youngsters curiously—the stunning sixteen-year-old Mehreen, her fourteen-year-old sister, Ambereen, and their ten-year-old baby brother, Omar—as they shuffled through the station after their driver.

Meanwhile, Nafis was charged with feathering her brood's nest in New York City. One of her colleagues at UNFPA, Halvor Gille, was planning to go to Geneva for a month and had generously offered the use of his Westchester home until the Sadiks could get settled, handing Nafis the keys and a neighbor's phone number, "just in case."

She had declined his offer to move in, saying she preferred to find something in the city. Nafis completed all this very quickly, renting a nice house for an amazingly cheap rent; it had the added benefit of being close by her friends' home in Queens, where she was staying temporarily. Then she picked out some used furniture—beds, dressers, a sofa, dining table and chairs. She proceeded to equip the house down to the lamps and linens, and just that morning she'd put the finishing touch on the arrangements by calling the Marsh & McLennan firm to arrange for renter's insurance.

On this chilly October evening the vagabonds had returned triumphantly from their journey to DC—along with a servant, Shamshuddin, the same chauffeur who had taught their mother how to maneuver the car through the early morning traffic back in Calcutta thirty years ago. Mohammed Shoaib had sent the elderly driver along to help his daughter. Nafis picked them all up in a taxi to deliver her family to their new home in America, proud that she'd been able to pull everything together in just a couple of days.

As they drove through Queens, the kids—hyperalert to everything in this unfamiliar place—commented on the proliferation of fire engines in New York City. They noticed that the closer they got to their rented house in the Jamaica Estates neighborhood, the wail of sirens was becoming deafening.

As the taxi inched across the borough, through the streets clogged by fire trucks, they could now smell the smoke. "Oh, wouldn't that be funny if it were our house on fire!" yelled Omar.

When the taxi driver reached the address he'd been given, everyone exited the cab. At 6:00 on an autumn night, they watched the flames leaping against the darkened sky, a view that was rhythmically strobed by flashing red lights, as the immigrants stared at their new home in America burning to the ground.

Nafis paid the driver and told him to leave their bags on the curb while she spoke to the firemen. The kids slumped down next to their luggage, and Ambereen remembered preparing to cry until she saw how calmly her mother was handling everything; the girl decided then it must not be that big of a deal after all. Instead, she waited, watching the fire, while Nafis went in search of a phone to make some calls.

"Lillian Miller, this is Nafis Sadik. I talked to you this morning about my house, insuring the contents and all that."

"Yes, darling, it's done. It's done, dear. We do things on the telephone!"

"Good. I just wanted to confirm that my insurance is valid, because my house is on fire."

"The house burned? What? What? Oh my god."

Next Nafis rang up Halvor Gille's neighbor (who also worked for the UN), and while apologizing for the late notice, she explained that they would be arriving at Gille's home later that evening. Her next call was to order another taxi. She went back and collected her menagerie, and with the house still burning, they abandoned Queens and set out for parts unknown in Westchester County.

Next they stopped for their first experience with New York City cuisine: McDonald's. Upon arrival, the driver—taking pity on the forlorn family—charged them a fraction of the real cost of their thirty-mile cab ride when he dropped them off at the formerly sight-unseen house in Tarrytown, just before 10:00 p.m.

Sara, the woman next door, came over immediately to welcome them, bringing along some milk, cereal, and bread so the new arrivals could have breakfast in the morning. She showed them around the lovely vintage home and gave them the keys to Halvor Gille's Volvo station wagon so they could get around.

In the morning Nafis got the children up and enrolled them in school as if nothing had happened, then went to her office. This episode immediately earned their new employee a place in UN lore and a reputation as truly intrepid. Less than twenty-four hours after becoming homeless, she had a new house in Westchester, her kids were in class, and she was working at her desk in Manhattan. "I can't believe you wouldn't be in a state of shock!" said one of her coworkers.

"Who is meant to be in a state of shock? The house is burned, that's true, but there's not much I can do about it," she replied sensibly.

The insurance adjuster stopped by Nafis's office, and she told him her claim was fourteen hundred dollars total. Now *he* was in a state of shock. "Are you sure? That's all?" She explained she didn't have any receipts because she'd bought all the furniture secondhand, but the linens were new.

The adjustor wrote her a check on the spot, and as he pushed it across the desk he commented wryly, "You should have asked for a lot more."

The culture shock that had begun as the Sadik children toured Europe only intensified once they arrived in New York. After the siblings had sat on the curb and watched their house burn down, they started school in suburban Tarrytown the very next day. Nafis drove them to campus that morning, but after that they rode the school bus along with their neighbors.

The other students were fascinated by this exotic tribe who had suddenly invaded their quiet community. "They'd never even seen a person from France before," Ambereen remembered, "let alone Pakistan. They were crowding around us, in every class and at lunch." The teachers took advantage of the situation and, "made us go off to classes and lecture on our country. We used to feel really foolish because we didn't think we were equipped to talk about anything."

To the amusement of their classmates, the siblings, trained in convent schools, leapt to their feet whenever the teacher asked them a question, a habit that seemed to take an eternity to break. However, their convent education did come in handy. One student remarked: "God, you people must be really smart in Pakistan. You know, you've only been here in New York for a couple of weeks, and look how good your English is!"

Their mother, in an attempt to provide some stability, called a real estate agent and asked if there might be another house available in the area, because her colleague, Halvor Gille, would be coming home in less than a month. Happily for the homeless family, why yes, there was a place close by for rent.

And this is how the Sadiks came to move into an ancient brick house that was the first mansion built in Sleepy Hollow, a historic locale on the Hudson River just north of Tarrytown. Their new home seemed constructed straight out of the children's imagination, with chandeliers in the living room, a grand ballroom, enough bedrooms for the whole clan, a sprawling lawn sloping down to the river—even secret passageways that had been part of the Underground Railroad. Nafis bought more used furniture, and again the household was up and running. The only problem was that she had never had to manage financially on her salary alone, and she wasn't quite sure how they were going to get by.

Enter Wafa to the rescue. She and Ghazala had arrived from Iran, and the eldest child set about putting things to rights. She was ready and willing for the challenge of running the show . . . if not, as it turned out, altogether able—because at eighteen, the teenager had never cooked in her life, having grown up surrounded by servants like the rest of the bunch.

The scenario was ripe for a family comedy. Exit servants. Shamshuddin, the chauffeur, had returned to his master in DC, leaving them to fend for themselves. The mother and supporting cast of five continued to perform on location—with all the panache of aliens having landed on an unchartered planet.

Nafis said, "I remember the first time we went out, I drove the car to the grocery store. We didn't know where anything was or what was for what. We were asking the clerks, 'What should we buy to clean the bathroom?' They were looking at a grown woman who didn't how to buy cleaning products." She didn't mention she also didn't know *how* to clean the bathroom.

In this rare void of authority, Wafa emerged as the domestic dominatrix, and her dominion began in the kitchen. She discovered Shake and Bake and put it to good use, serving the same dinner to each lucky recipient every night: one chicken drumstick dipped in the dusty coating, a boiled potato, and a handful of green peas.

Finally after a few weeks of this, Bhabhiji gently suggested that she thought they could afford to branch out a little on the food and have more than one piece of chicken per night. But Wafa disagreed: "One is enough. Nobody needs to eat so much . . . everyone is okay."

However, the crew was on the verge of mutiny. "Why did you bring us here! We thought we were coming to this developed country, and here we are slaves. And we're starving to death! We have to slog—raking leaves, making beds." Daily the litany of woes continued. Before they had left home the youngsters had known that they would not have servants in the New World, but they had never considered what that actually meant. No longer could they drop their clothes on the floor and find them neatly washed and ironed, waiting in the closet.

But the best surprise was yet to come. In December the snow started to fall on Tarrytown. The neighbor children outfitted the Sadik clan with hand-me-down ice skates and whizzed them around the frozen lake. However, Nafis wasn't having nearly as much fun; she had to commute into the city each day, taking the train into Manhattan. This also meant that she had to drive from the house to the train station and back. "When I came home one night the car was buried under snow, and I didn't know what to do. So I'm cleaning it with my hands, and people were quite solicitous, they were telling me, 'In your car, you must keep an ice scraper to clean off the windshield,' showing me these plastic things, which of course I didn't even know existed. They mentioned using salt, but I still didn't know what we were supposed to do with it."

Once Nafis made it into the office, she had a whole new set of challenges in store for her. The usual conflicts existed between the various departments within any organization: the financial side of operations threw a wet blanket over the political agenda of individuals in management—not to mention the interagency fighting that had driven Nafis mad in her previous dealings with the United Nations. And all these groups clashed with the technical side of UNFPA's mission: to supply women with the tools to control their own fertility.

These struggles produced enough friction, but on top of it Nafis found herself to be the only woman at senior-level UN meetings. Of course, being a distinct gender minority was nothing new for the doctor. She had howled as the lone she-wolf for twenty-five years, negotiating medical school, hospital hierarchy on two continents, the Pakistani armed forces, the bureaucracy of the Planning Commission and later the Family Planning Program, while appeasing two different presidential administrations. The work itself might have been difficult, but she had never felt disrespected for being a woman. Until now.

"Salas wanted me to be chief of projects at the time. I would be quite differential and respectful of someone else's expertise, but people have to do the job they were assigned to do, and if that means instructing someone—then so be it. I paid no attention to the gossip about me, and later on Salas was quite hilarious because he recounted all the things that were supposedly said or done to me, which I didn't know about because I was oblivious. I have this mind-set of disregarding things that are not helpful to me, or over which I have no control. I just pretend they're not there."

She couldn't deny the fact, however, that she was being ignored in top UN staff meetings. "I would propose an idea, and everybody would look at me like a secretary had spoken—like 'Why is she talking? She's not supposed to.' And then the meeting would continue until one of the men would repeat my suggestion, and they would all exclaim, 'Oh, what a wonderful idea!' I knew it sounded childish, but I would speak up. 'I said that ten minutes ago, and you didn't pay any attention.' I started to see why Western women were so aggressive, because you really have to push yourself to be heard." The doctor developed other survival methods.

"I never let anyone dictate to me. If I was supposed to do something, I wouldn't be intimidated by anybody, regardless of who they were. So that came as quite a surprise to people, because they used to think, 'Oh, she looks so decorative, so well dressed.'"

She tried to formulate a theory to explain this intellectual discrimination. At first she thought perhaps it was because she was outside of medicine now, but then she had not encountered this attitude in Pakistan in the planning agencies that had employed her. There, if she had a point, everyone was eager to listen, even her male colleagues who were much older, or living in the remote provinces. And if she needed their advice, everyone was happy to help. "They didn't treat me in a paternalistic manner."

Nafis considered perhaps her current coworkers—who hailed from all over the world—were uncomfortable with Eastern women. But in the end she concluded that it was women, period, that unsettled them. In 1971 governments tended to nominate men for these posts, so there were no females put forth into the UN system from her colleagues' own nations either. There were very few women professionals in the UN setting, and none of them were supervisors. "I realized I had to be much more aggressive and assertive to be heard. Other people with whom I've discussed this don't disbelieve that I felt undervalued at the UN. But what they find difficult to accept is that I didn't have the same problem in Pakistan. Well, I say, that's my personal experience."

The good news was that in her own tiny enclave of UNFPA, they knew of Dr. Sadik's know-how, and her coworkers valued her opinions. Because of the nature of their agency's work, her femininity was considered a plus, and Salas went out of his way to encourage her contributions. In an unexpected way, he would make it possible for her to become the head of the organization and get the last laugh on her detractors.

Salas had hired his female doctor for a variety of reasons: First, for the very gender that caused her trouble in the staff meetings. Second, because, like him, she came from a developing country and could understand the limitations facing implementation of their agenda. Third, she had the rare professional qualifications of having run a family planning program in the early days of this virgin discipline. Fourth, she combined these traits with her technical training in obstetrics. And fifth, she knew all the donors willing to bankroll family planning programs.

However much respect he had for his acolyte, Salas politically could not make her second in command at UNFPA because of her youth and inexperience within the organization. And although Nafis may have thought she was "quite differential and respectful" of her colleagues' expertise, that was not a view wholeheartedly shared by those colleagues. Alex Marshall, a speechwriter who joined the fund in 1973, remembered: "She was the number three spot. The number two was a cipher. I mean, a nice guy, but you know he was just there to fill a spot for political reasons. But she was the power. In fact, she used to treat this deputy something terrible—awful—very, very rude. She just didn't have any time for people who weren't significant, and the fact that he was technically above her in the pecking order didn't help either."

In the halls of the United Nations, Nafis presented a walking contradiction. The field of diplomacy requires the unique combination of brains and charm; Nafis definitely had it, but it was on her terms that she chose to parcel out the latter. In one day she could laugh with an associate until her mascara ran, treat another unfortunate soul with contempt, and then be downright coquettish with a third.

By the time she was in her forties, she was still by all accounts a very attractive woman. Like many at the UN, she continued the tradition of her native dress and would swoosh into the Manhattan boardroom for a meeting with the male minds, meticulously groomed, wearing designer sunglasses, high heels, and saris. The trouble began when she removed the glasses and the Radha eyes took the measure of her counterparts; if she found them lacking, the eyes did not offer the mediocre object of their scrutiny the luxury of self-deception. Rather, an icy gaze broadcast her estimation as clearly as the scoreboard at Madison Square Garden.

Her looks also created other dynamics in this time when few women were in the professional arena. Many men felt challenged to make a pass at her, and even though Azhar was fourteen thousand miles away, she did not acquiesce. A congressman asked if she wanted to spend the night with him, and without even batting one of the Radha eyes, she replied, "No thank you. I wouldn't dream of it."

The diplomat learned tools to handle such overtures. "I never got angry at those things; I just treated them as really stupid behavior. And I think men can't stand to be considered foolish. When they would tell me that, 'Oh, you are so beautiful, you're so blah, blah, blah,' the next time I saw them I would say, 'You're so handsome, and look at your clothes, your tie. It would make a lovely sari!' One man told me, 'You shouldn't congratulate men on their clothes.' And I said, 'Oh, and why not? You praise my clothes, so why can't I do the same to you?'"

More than one observer has noted that Nafis is an intriguing combination of male and female attributes. Some credited her confidence and intellect to the daughter's imitation of her idolized father. Her old friend from Karachi, Zeenat Haroon, commented, "She hasn't got this gossipy bit about her, or a mean nature. She's more like a man who is well placed—successful and not having to worry about how he got there. She hasn't stepped on anybody's toes getting where she did."

Back in Tarrytown the Sadik children were rapidly developing their own personalities in response to their new environment. All her life Ambereen had chafed at her lack of autonomy, because everywhere the youngsters went they were accompanied by a relative, a servant, a driver. When she heard about the French Metro, she had fantasized about moving to Paris so she could be independent, riding the subway alone. But in Karachi, the only place the siblings had been permitted to go solo was the Sind Club, where everyone knew their parents. Now in Tarrytown, for the first time the teenagers were anonymous.

Intuitively they understood that this new life was different. "We realized this was much more of a serious world. In Pakistan you felt like nothing bad was going to happen to you. There we always felt we would never go to jail, somebody would get us out—that we were quite safe doing anything. I don't think we would ever consider zipping out in Mummy's car in New York. We were smart enough to realize that there could be serious consequences here."

Their transformation followed the universal story of immigrants. In the children's rush to blend into the community, they lost the connecting thread to many of their family's traditions; they spoke English, and their understanding of Urdu faded. The mother may have worn saris, but her daughters wore jeans. In keeping with her upbringing, Nafis acquired two servants: a cook and a driver. But preferring their independence, the teenagers rode public transit into the city—unchaperoned.

They were thrilled to see all the first-run movies the week they came out, rather than waiting years for them as they had in Pakistan. The kids attended rock concerts and saw bands they had only read about, like the Grateful Dead and the Rolling Stones. Ambereen felt guilty about it years later. "My poor mother worked quite hard because she used to have to drive us in, hang out somewhere while the concert was on, and be there to drive us back again. To be honest, I don't think the children appreciated how tedious it must have been for her to do this."

She and Ghazala tried dating as they got older, but in retrospect these attempts must have been quite confusing for the American male. "We went out with boys in a sense, but only if we were serious, which is how it is in our culture. I'm sure we used to scare the life out of these guys. We'd go to dances with them, and we'd say, 'Sorry, can't be kissing you unless I'm planning to marry you.' I'm sure they thought we were very funny, because in some ways we were so Westernized, and in other ways our attitudes probably came out of left field." Meanwhile for Wafa and Mehreen migration to the New World was marred by missing beaus they'd left behind, as it had been for Nafis and Chicky a generation before them.

At first Nafis mitigated her homesickness by driving to Washington each weekend to see her father. Over the course of the next two years Azhar came to visit a few times, along with a steady parade of relatives. They returned to Karachi and complained to Chicky that her sister must not be paid very well, because she didn't even serve lunch at the house. They weren't capable of seeing over the fence of the cultural divide, that unlike their daily routine in Pakistan, in America there was normally no one at home in the daytime to eat lunch.

Ermelinda da Silva Ximenes | Tibar, East Timor

On a July evening Ofelia was awakened by a strange man knocking at her door. She threw on some clothes, grabbed her bag, pulled on her white helmet, and then hopped on a motorbike to shoot off into the night. She was headed to his house, although the stranger did not go with her. The woman wound up the treacherous hairpin turns of Fahi-Ten Mountain, avoiding the hazards she knew were waiting for her in the dark: the free-roaming goats, dogs, and cattle, and of course the other drivers who would hurdle around a blind curve dead in the center of the narrow thoroughfare. On top of this Mother Nature had voided the plan to introduce civilization here in the wilderness, creating an obstacle course by washing boulders and uprooted trees down the slope. The resulting condition of the roadway proved to be more rutted earthen track than smooth concrete, and in spots the surface suddenly dropped several feet in jagged tiers; in other places the pavement had washed away altogether, leaving potholes several yards wide, yawning like jaws as they waited silently to swallow the unsuspecting rider. And the rainy season had not yet begun.

As I retrace Ofelia's route in daytime, in an off-road vehicle, I cannot imagine navigating this course in the black of night. On a dirt bike. My driver Carlos sits stoically behind aviator sunglasses as he steers along the edge of a cliff. The valley lies hundreds of feet below, the view slightly hazy as the fresh morning air suspends dust particles from the arid hillside, and the scent of dried grass and minty eucalyptus rushes in the open window. We round the bend and come upon what I initially take to be a pond covering the road, reflecting blue sky. Carlos cuts the wheels sharply, and as we careen around the edge, to my horror I realize that it's not water we're avoiding; rather, the cliff has eroded, and I am staring through a gaping hole larger than our truck into the void. He has just saved us from dropping through nature's manhole to free-fall through the heavens and flatten one of the unsuspecting thatched huts dotting the basin below.

It's not an unusual occurrence for Ofelia to have men awaken her in the middle of the night. She's a midwife in this remote district in East Timor, the world's newest nation, and she delivers twenty to thirty babies a month. Everyone in the district knows where she lives, and so when this gentleman's wife went into labor he rushed straight to the midwife's home to summon her. The dutiful husband had waited hours for a bus to pass by the winding, isolated route down Fahi-Ten Mountain, and there is no phone service in this region, where even the health professionals communicate by shortwave radio. When he finally reached Ofelia she dressed quickly and leapt aboard her Honda Supra X Astrea, a bike built for rough terrain, and headed up the treacherous road in the dark to deliver Ermelinda da Silva's baby. Unfortunately, she did not succeed.

Ofelia Soares Madeira is part of a program called Midwives on Motorbikes, an operation begun by UNFPA in 2003, where the maternity professionals of Timor use motorcycles to traverse the mountain passes of this country bordering Indonesia. The agency ordered sixty-five cycles from Honda, and the manufacturer threw in another fifteen for free. Local health care workers also ride the dirt bikes to reach their remote clientele for other services, particularly to deliver immunizations.

After sixteen years on the job Ofelia has lost track of the number of babies she's delivered, and in addition she now coordinates the entire midwife program. Her professional training was thorough—attending nursing school for three years followed by a year of midwifery courses. Her husband taught her how to ride the Honda and sometimes accompanies her on missions. She thinks the motorbikes are a great asset to health care workers' ability to reach patients, but she laments the poor communication options in the district. If she runs into problems with a delivery, she must ride back to the clinic to radio for an ambulance, wasting valuable time that has cost lives.

Today I am traveling to visit the home of the man who summoned the midwife in the middle of the night. As we climb, I take in the breathtaking tropical scenery of mountain vistas, the leafy green of banana and coconut trees, the brilliant magenta bougainvillea, the delicate feathery limbs of acacia trees sheltering the coffee plantations, the gatherings of thatched huts built of bamboo and palm fronds, the baby goats and full grown cows meandering aimlessly, the vans barreling around blind curves as Catholic schoolchildren amble across this same road in their spotless white shirts and dark trousers, heading to morning mass.

On this sunny September morning we find the new mother, Ermelinda, sitting on a bench outside her hut, a one-room box built of twigs topped by a corrugated tin roof. She is a petite woman, with mahogany-colored skin and large eyes luminous with worry; her ebony hair sweeps back from her face into a bun. She is dressed in a simple black cotton skirt and blouse with tailored lines and fitted, puffed sleeves, an outfit that looks oddly formal for life in the wilderness. Ermelinda holds two-month old Maia, whose face is contorted beneath a shock of wild hair. The infant howls until her mother removes one breast to nurse, and it's clear this newest member of the family has a healthy appetite.

As mother and child stare transfixed into one another's eyes, they form the hub for the melee of life swirling around them: the newborn's six siblings—some teenagers dressed in T-shirts and base-ball caps, some naked toddlers wearing nothing but dust. Other vil-lagers in this outcropping called Aldeia, a name that means "small community," come out to meet the visitors. A neighbor walks up balancing a plastic jug of water on her head, while roosters crow, baby chicks peep and peck around our feet, goats endlessly search for something to eat, and puppies look for playmates. A gray mon-key studies us solemnly with his tail curved around his feet, and the morning calls of songbirds float down from the palms.

I am accompanied by Cecilia da Silva from UNFPA and the mid-wife, who tells me the story of what happened on the night Maia was born. While Ermelinda's husband made his way into the village, his wife lay at home alone in labor. Before Ofelia arrived the mother had pushed her tiny daughter out on her own, but she was fright-ened because even though at thirty-two she had already given birth to eight babies, only six had survived. Of additional concern was the fact that on this night the mother's placenta had not come out, a situation that could cause hemorrhaging because the uterus won't contract, and she could bleed to death.

When Ofelia arrived at the hut on that dark night, she set to work cutting the umbilical cord, then massaging the top of Ermelinda's uterus while pulling steadily on the cord to deliver the placenta. This procedure allowed the patient's womb to begin contracting, thus returning to its normal size—a necessary step that ceases the flow of blood.

With her patient stabilized, the midwife packed up her equip-ment and boarded her Honda Supra X for home. Now the sun was rising, casting a golden light over the coffee plantations as she rode slowly back down the mountain, dodging the obstacle course. Ofelia yawned, hoping she could get some sleep before another baby decided to enter this world.

Nafis giving an interview in 1981.

(*top*) Nafis, as assistant executive director for UNFPA, being interviewed for the television program *World Chronicle* in 1981. Interviewing her, counterclockwise, are Brian Saxton, BBC News; Ewa Boniecka, *Perspective Magazine* (Poland); Iftikhar Ali, AP of Pakistan; Kathleen Teltsch, *New York Times*.

(*bottom*) Rafael Salas and Nafis at a population and development conference in Tokyo, 1978.

(*top*) UNFPA meets with officials from the People's Republic of China
to discuss their population policy. (*First row from left*) Tian Jin, Li Xiu,
Nafis, Chen Mu Hua, Rafael Salas, Deng Xiao Ping, Nessim Shallon, Shi Lin, S. L.
Tan, Chen Xing Nong, (*second row*) Shu Sheng, Luo Zhen Tao,
Siri Melchior-Tellier, E. Kerner, Ye Yuan Ge, Wand De Lun, (*third row*) Chen
Jian Ping, Yao Wen Lung, Xu Shu Yun, Zhang Ying Fang, Ho Yi Quin, Zhu Wen.

(*bottom*) Nafis leading a conga line in Colombo, Sri Lanka;
behind her is Paul Micou, director of UNFPA's Asia Division.

Nafis at ICPD in Mexico City in 1984.

10 THE DIRECTOR

As the gestation of her career advanced, Dr. Sadik was required to birth more than babies. She had arrived at UNFPA in October 1971, and in 1972 Executive Director Rafael Salas sent his new technical adviser to Yugoslavia with the dictum to raise capital. He was eager for Eastern Europe to support his fledgling fund and sent an ob-gyn to deliver contributions.

This mission came shortly after Nafis's very first assignment: to prompt the creation of more methods of birth control—the project she worked on in the daytime between leaving the five kids at home while she took the train into snowy Manhattan and returning home to eat her Shake and Bake drumstick and frozen peas. Luckily she was well fed, because Nafis would need her strength. Salas had determined the need to stimulate advances in contraception after witnessing a disturbing trend: "The private sector at that time was moving out of investment in research and development, so Salas suggested I organize a meeting by inviting some of the people I knew, like the Population Council and the donors."

Dr. Sadik set to work and discussed strategy with her colleagues at the UN. At the time UNFPA, the tiny start-up agency, was under the umbrella of the UN Development Program (UNDP), a much larger branch assigned the staggering task of eliminating world poverty. But it seemed everywhere the doctor turned within the gigantic bureaucracy, instead of finding assistance to help resuscitate research on birth control, she met with skepticism about this project—even from her friends there. They commented that this was not an appropriate undertaking for UNFPA, which was merely a funding agency designed to dispense financial assistance to developing countries. "They felt we shouldn't get involved in 'substantive matters.'" She informed everyone: "Salas has given me this assignment, and I'm going to do this regardless of whether you help me or not. Just because I don't know the UN people very well doesn't mean I don't know lots of other people in the field."

And with that, Nafis fired off personal letters under her own signature, writing to the men she knew, such as General Draper and the other top brass at the Population Council, the folks at the Rockefeller and Ford Foundations, major donors like USAID, and the heads of major pharmaceutical companies—all of whom she had dealt with in Pakistan—and consequently all of whom attended her meeting in New York City.

Reporter Kathleen Teltsch covered the event for the *New York Times* in a story headlined "Family Planners of 23 Nations Voice Optimism at UN Parley." "Salas wanted to know how I got this interview and I said, 'I didn't. She just came to me, and I invited her to join the conference.'" He had been trying since UNFPA's inception to get some coverage from the *Times* and was particularly impressed by this breakthrough. Nobody deduced the real reason for the press coverage: in the early 1970s era of women's liberation, having this female in such a visible position of power was noteworthy. Not coincidentally, rather than discussing the fine art of contraception, about 50 percent of the copy was devoted to Nafis: "a slim sari-clad woman with a cloud of dark wavy hair, she volunteers that her own children, aged 17, 15 and 11, were 'well planned,' and adds, 'I say with certainty that regardless of country or culture, no woman in the world wants a baby every year.'"

Fresh on the heels of this victory, Salas sent Nafis to garner a contribution from the Yugoslav government. When she arrived at the airport in Belgrade, nobody was there to greet the diplomat—her first clue to what lay in store for her on the rest of the trip. Luckily as she wandered through the airport, she ran into an old friend, Iqbal Akhund, the Pakistani ambassador to Yugoslavia. Akhund asked Nafis where she was staying, and when the bleary traveler—fresh off an international flight—told him, he replied, "Well, that's not a very nice hotel. You better just come stay with me and my wife."

The next morning the ambassador supplied Dr. Sadik with a car and driver, and she arrived at the UN Development offices fresh and ready for business. Clad in her signature sari, she swooshed into the room and asked to speak with the representative in charge of Yugoslavia's mission. The secretary left to speak to his supervisor, then returned. "The representative wants to know what level you are?"

"I'm a P-5, but what has that got to do with seeing me?"

"Well, in that case, I suggest you see his deputy."

"Tell him if he doesn't want to see me, I don't have to see him."

The UNDP minion carried this message to the inner sanctum, and when he returned, he asked: "Well, what is it exactly that you want done?"

"I want an appointment with Yugoslavia's minister of finance, minister of foreign affairs, and minister of health." The secretary, obviously stunned, rushed back to tell his boss, who was finally prompted to leave his desk and talk to this upstart in the lobby himself.

"It's not your level to meet with these ministers," he told Nafis emphatically.

"I don't know what the level has to be, but I need to see them to get a contribution for UNFPA."

"Very well. Because this type of proposal must come from my level, I will write them a letter and request an appointment for you."

"But I don't have time to wait for a reply. I want to have an answer for Salas when I return home. I need to talk to the decision makers directly this week."

"You can't do that, it's impossible."

"*You* can't do that, but *I* will." And with that she turned on her high heel and strode out to her waiting limo.

She rang up a friend of hers, Vida Tomsic, a Yugoslavian parliamentarian and official at the country's Planned Parenthood operation. The two women had worked together before at several conferences, and Nafis explained that she had been sent to Belgrade to land a financial commitment of support from the government. Tomsic immediately agreed with Nafis's strategy for success, that she must speak with the minister of finance, but warned it would be difficult to get an appointment at such short notice. However, Tomsic, through considerable wrangling, was able to arrange the meetings between all three ministers and UNFPA's newest employee; the diplomats agreed that in exchange for their donation, Dr. Sadik would set up a small family planning program in Kosovo, which at that time was part of Yugoslavia.

When Nafis returned to New York, and the UNDP honcho learned that she had met with three cabinet ministers, he wrote headquarters complaining that this insurgent had violated protocol. Salas, on the other hand, was pleasantly surprised that she had managed to accomplish her mission. When he asked her how she did it, Nafis—with characteristic humility—replied: "You know, Mr. Salas, I just decided that since you had asked me to do it, and you were very keen on it, that I was going to do it. I mean, I used unorthodox sources to get it done, it's true, but that's how life is."

Her new boss told the rest of the staff: "Nafis is a jewel." However, his jewel had learned a valuable lesson about writing ahead to schedule appointments.

Dr. Sadik was the first physician to be hired by the United Nations Fund for Population Activities. Salas knew they needed her expertise, but she did not fit seamlessly into the mix. For one reason, Nafis was not exactly the girl one sent into the fray to maintain the status quo, and for many of her colleagues—men secure in their positions of expertise and power, yet engaged in jobs that by definition were designed to affect world change—their sympathies were conflicted.

On top of this lay the problem of an organization, the UN headquarters, overseeing twenty-nine other organizations, all of which dealt in negotiations with parties that were radically different, from the enormous atheistic Soviet Union to the tiny Catholic-controlled Vatican.

The United Nations had grown out of the trauma of World War II and the desire to settle future conflicts without the carnage modern-day combat had produced. Fifty nations met in San Francisco in 1945 to sign its charter, providing a vehicle for peacekeeping. The myriad challenges the UN would take on in the coming decades would multiply exponentially, a system that seemed more and more vital as member states acknowledged the interdependence of their actions and the delicate balancing act required between national autonomy and international cooperation.

To synchronize all its global initiatives, a resolution was passed in 1946 to create a governing council of all UN agencies; it was originally called the Administrative Committee for Coordination, a name later changed to the Chief Executives Board. While the name changed, the council's task remained the same: to oversee the activity of all its branches, ranging from the fledgling UNFPA to the powerful World Bank.

Thirty years after the creation of the UN, the focus in the postwar era was not exclusively how to keep people from being blown up, but—growing out of the 1950s baby boom—included how the population itself was exploding. Even the violent language of the time frightened leaders, particularly Paul Ehrlich's call to action, *The Population Bomb*.

In one scene Ehrlich describes his first trip to Delhi, an account that might have come straight from the journal of one of the visiting dignitaries to Nafis's first conference in Dhaka:

My wife and daughter and I were returning to our hotel in an ancient taxi. The seats were hopping with fleas. The only functional gear was third. As we crawled through the city, we entered a crowded slum area. The temperature was well over 100, and the air was a haze of dust and smoke. The streets seemed alive with people. People eating, arguing, and screaming. People thrusting their hands through the taxi window, begging. People defecating and urinating. People clinging to buses. People herding animals. People, people, people, people. As we moved slowly through the mob, hand horn squawking, the dust, noise, heat, and cooking fires gave the scene a hellish aspect. Would we ever get to our hotel? All three of us were, frankly, frightened.

Ehrlich, a professor of biology at Stanford University, dropped his missive on the American public in 1968, and the fallout from it drifted across the continent's cultural landscape. After he excoriated U.S. politicians for their lack of action, he then called for the planet's developed nations to work with the UN to create a plan that would "involve simultaneous population control [and] agricultural development"; thus UNFPA began operations in 1969.

At that time Ehrlich estimated unless drastic changes were made to the birthrate, the earth's population would double in thirty-seven years. Along with Ehrlich, demographers, such as Nafis's professor Eileen Toyber from Johns Hopkins University, had also mathematically extrapolated the current growth rate to predict a cataclysmic "population explosion," and it was hard to argue with the coolly calculated data.

During the early 1970s the term "population control" was prevalent, and the philosophy, both in governments and aid organizations, was that the need to control population grew out of the need to promote development—hence the reason UNFPA was initially positioned under the aegis of the UN Development Program, the group knighted as the crusaders to eliminate poverty. Governments saw the quality of life for their citizenry sliding backward, indirectly proportional to the birthrate. The same spending that would provide a home, health care, and education for one family, when spread thin enough to cover a hundred, was not even enough to keep them from starving. In many quarters the vision for economic prosperity took on a singular focus: women simply had to stop having so many babies. But the vastly male power structure did not take into account one small factor: how many babies did the women—the people most involved in this decision—*want* to have?

Catholic countries, including several European nations and most of Latin America, were fundamentally opposed to contraception. Many African rulers saw the notion of population control as a plot by the North to reduce their numbers; they felt their continent was so big, with such a wealth of minerals, that they needed a large labor force to develop their resources. And then there was the inherent macho notion that the bigger you were, the more important you were, a subconscious drive amongst the powerful that extended beyond muscle, to mass.

All of these ideas were not only in conflict with each other, but with all the survey results UNFPA did, which showed that most women—some secretly—wished to drastically reduce the number of babies they were bound to birth and feed. Dr. Sadik came to the UN as someone who had taken part in hundreds of face-to-face conversations with such women, and as she traveled, she realized nothing had changed since her days back in Abbottabad: "In the 1970s I went to India and Africa and so on, and they were still asking the same questions there in the rural areas: 'Can you please give us something that we can just take—like a simple injection that prevents pregnancy? Then when we want to be pregnant it can be reversed? Something we can hide from our husbands?'"

From husbands to heads of state, everyone wanted a say over who controlled these women's wombs, while they themselves carried the baby, gave birth, were charged with its sole survival if the husband disappeared, and their government shrugged its shoulders and looked the other way. And sometimes the mothers didn't have to worry about what happened after childbirth, because many died in the process. For example, in Africa one in twelve women would not survive her delivery. Dr. Sadik determined that the final say over bringing a child into this world *must* belong to the person whose life was on the line.

UNFPA originally thought the only thing stopping women from using contraceptives was being able to obtain them. After all, the mere physical challenge of reaching their clients seemed almost insurmountable: how to extend services into mountains and valleys and jungles and deserts and farms and ancient villages where people still lived like they had for thousands of years, transporting their goods to market on the backs of camels and donkeys? The agency set out on their daunting challenge, but after about a decade they saw that their results had plateaued; only around 15-20 percent of the population used contraceptives. Their research showed that beyond the cultural, legal, and religious barriers, they must overcome this problem of distribution and access.

In response they broadened their web of outreach to include women's groups and environmental NGOs. Then they expanded their network to labor unions, which already offered social services; UNFPA persuaded them to offer health care in addition. The fund began working with the military—an approach that Dr. Sadik already understood well—reasoning that the armed forces had established capable hospitals in many countries, and UNFPA should take advantage of these facilities. They trained existing health care workers on how to dispense oral contraceptives. Next they advanced to "social sector marketing," promoting birth control options such as condoms—which required no follow-up care—with the same distribution network already in place to supply soap and tea, using private companies to expand family planning options into rural communities everywhere. In this vein, they also took advantage of agricultural colleges and extension workers, because they offered the largest number of people working in the countryside. "We used all of these channels for education and information and advocacy," Nafis recalled.

Many developing countries utilize health care workers, practitioners who work in clinics or visit patients at home but whose skill level is beneath that of a registered nurse. UNFPA discovered that these workers were not being taught family planning methods as part of their training. The agency worked on reversing this practice at its root. "We spent quite a lot of effort to incorporate family planning education into the curriculum of the medical establishment."

More good came out of the doctor's journey to Yugoslavia than delivering a contribution for UNFPA. Nafis's promise to start a mission in Kosovo provided women there with availability to birth control, as previously the Eastern Bloc nations had used only abortion for family planning—a policy that was quite contradictory, because simultaneously the USSR promoted motherhood by awarding medals to women who gave birth to a prodigious number of children. Abortion at this time was mainly performed under anesthesia, so some females had undergone eight, ten, sometimes fifteen operations in a lifetime. Contrary to popular belief, most terminations take place amongst married women who simply don't want to have another child, a decision that imposes much emotional anguish on the parents, suffering that could easily be prevented by having access to contraceptives.

In 1973—the same year that the Supreme Court ruled abortion was legal in the United States—the Helms Amendment passed the country's Congress, stating, "No foreign assistance funds may be used to pay for the performance of abortion as a method of family planning or to motivate or coerce any person to practice abortions." In theory this new law supported UNFPA's position; instead, it would later cause much bad blood between the agency and one of its leading allies.

Azhar and Nafis now had a bi-continental marriage. Since she had left for the Big Apple, he had remained in the grand house in Pakistan, working at Caltex. Even though he lived alone as a bachelor, he kept all the servants. "I didn't cut a single one." That's because he needed them to look after him. "For instance, I couldn't even boil water. I wouldn't have known where to start, how to put the kettle on."

At the same time Azhar carried on in Karachi, his wife bought a home in Tarrytown. The old estate the family had rented in Sleepy Hollow sold to developers, and Nafis's real estate agent conveniently advised his client, "You know, in America everyone *buys* their house."

"But I haven't got any money."

"How much money can you get?"

"I don't know . . . maybe three or four thousand dollars."

Then on Fremont Road, the agent found a cute house built in the 1950s, with an L-shaped living area, a large family room, a dining room, kitchen, a master suite, two smaller bedrooms, and a basement. The cellar wasn't finished, but Nafis figured they could redo it as a place for the servants. And it was located on a lovely pond where the children could go ice skating. The only problem was that the deal required a down payment of ten thousand dollars. At this juncture Nafis reminded her agent: "But I don't have ten thousand dollars."

This enterprising gentleman had a solution, though. "Tell you what, you put down whatever you want. I'll give you the rest of the loan for the down payment, as a second mortgage." Nafis bought the house, and now she needed a new car for her commute, so she bought that, too. She was quickly becoming acculturated to life in the States and to the American way of borrowing.

The Sadik clan settled into their new home, in a secure neighborhood where no one locked their doors. And they set about creating their social whirl there immediately, in true Pakistani fashion, hosting a New Year's Eve celebration with a hundred guests stomping and dancing. "I think the whole neighborhood must have wondered who these people were," Nafis remembered.

Life for the mother and her brood settled into a routine. She commuted into the city each workday by train, frequently arriving home at midnight after attending a diplomatic function. The older children graduated from high school, and the younger ones took the bus to campus. Some weekends Nafis drove the family down to DC to visit her father, and on other weekends she would take a couple of the kids into Manhattan for the theater. The siblings had to take turns, as she couldn't afford to bring them all at once. And the fatherless family would entertain a good deal, inviting neighbors and UN compatriots out to Westchester to their suburban home.

Reminiscent of the time of their courtship, in 1974 Nafis and Azhar had now been separated for over two years. Yes, they visited, they talked on the phone, they caught up on family, children, and the happenings of their day-to-day lives. But the pair maintained two separate households on opposite sides of the planet. As time dragged on and they debated about what to do, a few things became clear: First, Nafis was committed to her work at the UN. Second, because of company rules at Caltex, Azhar could not transfer to New York permanently, and—as he had feared—after two years of trying he was not able to find a suitable U.S. position. And third, Azhar was very unhappy with the status quo. He kept remembering a conversation he'd had on one of his visits to the family. "We went to a barbecue in Westchester where I met a Swedish woman, and I said to her, 'Do you plan to stay on here in the States, or will you be going back to Sweden? A natural question to ask, I thought. She said 'For the present moment I'm here because it's my turn.' I said, 'What do you mean 'it's your turn?' She said, 'My husband and I take turns. One looks after the children and one does a job. I've got this job opportunity here in the States so I'm taking my turn." Now, after two decades of marriage—twenty years of Nafis packing the crates and following him around the globe from post to post—Azhar considered that perhaps it should be his wife's turn.

In the end the future of the children determined the choice. The parents felt that they could afford to send their son and four daughters to excellent colleges if they lived in the United States, and like her father before her, Nafis believed the greatest gift she could offer her progeny was education. The Sadiks feared that paying the tuition for five international students—especially by converting rupees into dollars—would be a financial disaster. After Azhar's disappointment when it was his time to head off to university, he doubtless didn't want to sit down and have a similar conversation with his own offspring, explaining that the money had run out . . . and so had their options. Thus like many an immigrant family before them, the couple decided to take a gamble, to set sail from the known commodity of their homeland in order to provide their children with a better way of life.

In 1974 Azhar finally finagled a one-year contract with Caltex, which would have him working in the General Motors Building on Fifth Avenue, not far from Nafis's office at the UN. He arrived in New York, and only then did he inform the clan that he'd sold their home in Karachi . . . along with all the possessions they'd left behind. Nafis's enthusiasm about being reunited with her husband was somewhat mitigated by this news, because they had discussed keeping the home and returning to Pakistan someday, possibly in their retirement, to rejoin their families. However, the man of the house felt their place was too large and would therefore require considerable upkeep to maintain. "Besides if we are going to move to the States, we don't need a house in Karachi."

After his arrival, Azhar joined the routine in Tarrytown, which meant he soon shared Nafis's disdain for commuting. They realized their recreational lives also centered around the city, as they found themselves hopping on the train nearly seven days a week to attend cultural and sporting events. Additionally Nafis had concerns about Omar's education. "My daughters used to tell me, 'Your son it growing up to be illiterate. He's learning nothing in this country.' I said, 'But he's getting stars on his homework.' They said, 'Well, he may be getting all the honors and the stars, but he doesn't know anything.'

And I started to get quite worried, because I looked at one of his assignments, and there were so many spelling mistakes. I went to see his teacher, and she said, 'But this is social studies.' I said, 'Yeah, but I mean, look at all the spelling mistakes, and they're not even circled or marked.' She said, 'That's done in English class, not in social studies.' I said, 'School is school regardless of which class.' Anyway, I got a little bit worried then when the girls kept saying Omar's going to be illiterate. Finally, in '75 we decided that we would move into the city, and I would put him in the UN school."

Azhar set to work researching Manhattan real estate, and the man who hailed from the Punjab was astonished by what he found in the epicenter of the great superpower. For its filth and crime, New York City had become the butt of jokes on national TV, and the mayor announced the municipality was teetering on the verge of bankruptcy. Even long-time urbanites were fleeing for the suburbs, and as a result housing prices had plummeted. Nafis, eager to utilize her lessons from purchasing the Tarrytown property, wanted to buy a place in Manhattan during this down market, but Azhar was much more cautious and decided they should rent. Landlords were begging for tenants, and in the end they chose an apartment in a high-rise in Midtown, with four bedrooms and four baths, conveniently located between their offices.

In the coming years UNFPA became increasingly more established, and clearer in its mission, which coincided with growing international concern about the ticking "population bomb." Governments valued the neutral position of the UN and turned to them, as did many of the NGOs, for technical expertise and guidance on how to implement family planning initiatives tailor-made for their citizenry. By the end of 1974 UNFPA had expanded to eighty-nine staff members in headquarters and twenty field coordinators. Salas had been busy fundraising, aided in this effort by General William Draper, who had devised a matching grant formula with the U.S. government. Their success had netted fifty million dollars in voluntary contributions, and this money had to cover the cost of the 1,200 projects UNFPA had taken on in ninety-two countries. Yet the requests the agency received for help still far exceeded its capabilities.

In 1974 the UN helped communist Cuba—which already had a good maternal health service—reduce their dependence on abortion by introducing family planning services and making contraception available. The government embraced this plan, to the extent it even created facilities to manufacture birth control pills and IUDs. Officials in Catholic Chile, where the government had banned abortion *and* contraception, had done their own study. The results shocked them: 90 percent of the obstetrics wards were occupied by women who were recovering from the effects of unsafe illegal abortions, and these patients were using over half the hospitals' blood supply. Like Cuba, the Chilean officials asked UNFPA to help them implement family planning and introduce contraception. In many Latin American countries the laws didn't ban birth control; it was merely government policy due to coercion from the Catholic Church.

Other political events were woven into the changing landscape of the 1970s. Many African nations had become independent from their colonizers in the 1950s and 1960s. When the nationals took control of their own affairs, they realized that they had no idea how many people actually lived in their country, which made it impossible to do any kind of accurate economic projections. In the 1970s UNFPA helped leaders from twenty-two countries organize their first census, a critical tool so they could accurately measure their rate of population growth with a second census in the 1980s. Before this, most of these nations had only a vague idea of the total number of citizens. The second census proved what a fallacy these estimates were, when officials realized their actual growth rate.

Demographers created a formula to estimate how long it would take for a nation's population to double: dividing the number 70 by the percentage of growth. For example, if the growth rate was 1 percent, the population would double in 70 years. However, after the census most African nations realized they had a 3 percent growth rate—which sounded like an infinitesimal increase until they realized that meant the population would double in 23 years. In 1968 the Population Reference Bureau had already calculated the doubling rate for some other populations: Turkey, 24 years; Indonesia, 31 years; Philippines, 20 years; Brazil, 22 years; Costa Rica, 20 years; and El Salvador, a mere 19 years—a scale so accelerated that it would not allow their leaders time to put a development strategy in place and reap its reward before they were forced to provide for twice as many citizens.

UNFPA outlined a plan of action to offset this terrifying eventuality. Their family planning recommendations suggested several immediate steps: spacing children would limit the number of births and improve the mother's health. They also encouraged parliamentarians to outlaw child marriage; raising the marriageable age of girls would reduce the number of years they would be reproducing. Again, this step would decrease problems such as maternal mortality and obstetric fistula, plus have the added benefit of allowing girls more control over their own lives. Nafis had learned early on when dealing with heads of state that it was much easier to appeal to their desire for a brighter economic future than their shame over human rights' abuses.

Dr. Sadik pushed the philosophy that "population policy" was not just passing out condoms. UNFPA's main strength grew from their belief that while population policy was a government responsibility, all countries must have family planning as part of health care. Furthermore, responsible policy must address education and environmental reform to ensure a financially stable society. The English-speaking African nations changed their policies rapidly to embrace these ideas, but the francophone countries were bound by the Napoleonic Code, which mentioned that contraceptives were illegal. This took more time to change, but many of their rulers put programs into practice, *then* changed the laws later.

The debate over these controversial issues pointed to a need for a broader dialogue, so Nafis again plied her trade at community building with the first World Population Conference in 1974, held in Romania, which at this time was part of the Soviet Bloc. The primary conflict that raged on the floor of the forum was the question: Who has the right to decide on pregnancy—the couple or the individual? As Nafis remembered thirty years later: "from the beginning, UNFPA sought the role of honest broker. We responded to countries' own priorities, and we developed programs based on *their* needs. On that basis we tried to assist the search for consensus, for the middle ground, at the international level. Given the sharp differences of ideology, it was surprising that a consensus emerged. But it did: after much discussion and dissension, the World Population Conference in 1974 adopted the World Population Plan of Action, and UNFPA used that document as a basis for our programming."

By signing the World Population Plan of Action, 137 countries agreed that, "the family, as the basic unit of society, should be protected by appropriate legislation and policy. All couples and individuals have the right to decide freely and responsibly the number and spacing of their children and to have the information, education and means to do so." It further asserted that women had the "right to equality in all aspects of social, economic, cultural and political life."

It's interesting to look back from the perspective of history and note that at the conference, countries like China and Algeria were adamantly opposed to family planning as a way of promoting health or reducing fertility. And others, like Mexico and Chile, had introduced programs in their own countries and so supported the concept.

In one of the preparatory meetings leading up to the conference, Nafis gave a formal presentation to the U.S. State Department. One gentleman in the audience stood up and said, "Dr. Sadik, you sound like you are anti-men."

She beamed her most charming smile and replied: "I hope I don't give you that impression. As a matter of fact, I love men, but I love men who behave themselves and who know how to respect gender equality. But you know, there are too many men with bull syndrome who simply want a lot of children. If we are talking about this syndrome, then we ought to put these men in the pasture like we do with bulls, with eight strands of barbed wire around them. We'll keep them there for only when they're needed."

Nafis's progress drew notice within the other UN agencies, and Bradford Morse, an administrator with UNDP, sent for her. When she sat down in his office, he offered her a position as their representative to the Philippines. "When I declined, he was stunned. He said, 'But everyone wants to join UNDP from all the other organizations.'

"I said, 'No, I never want to do a job that I don't know much about, or which I'm not sure that I can bring any personal sense of commitment to. I'm very happy with the job I'm doing—I have an important position, I'm the chief of programs. I don't worry about whether I'll go up in the agency or not.'

"So many people in the UNDP tried to persuade me: You'll become the number three, the number two. I said, 'Really, it's not that I'm not ambitious, but 'What will I become?' isn't what I think about every day of my life. What I think about is, 'What change can I make?' You might think I'm being sanctimonious, but I feel very strongly. I'll never, ever, in my life, do a job in which I go somewhere and find that all the people below me know more than I, and here I am trying to direct them."

By 1980 the family planning train had picked up speed, and things were changing at an accelerated rate; along the way, UNFPA had doubled its resources to $112 million in contributions. Even in countries such as Brazil, where the UN representatives had been forbidden to utter the words "family planning," the government climbed on board.

It should be noted here that the different reasons governments gave for adopting family planning were deeply divergent. Some governments could accept the idea of saving women's lives, but were philosophically opposed to the idea that these same women be allowed to eat birth control pills like candy and lead lives of reckless sexual abandon. Other leaders didn't care about women's promiscuity *or* their health; they just wanted fewer mouths to feed. Ironically, the process was the same. The difference was in how the regime packaged their game plan for public play.

And Nafis was earning her stripes as a diplomat and rhetorician, making unorthodox decisions to get things done at a variety of levels. While the UN Development Program offices in Brazil refused to work with nongovernmental organizations, she talked with various NGOs and found that particularly women's groups were quite receptive to what she had to offer. During this era she learned the same lesson over and over: "You had to do a lot of education and advocacy, even with your own colleagues, before hoping to persuade others." It was at this point that UNFPA spread its wings, leaving the oversight of UNDP, to become a full-fledged and autonomous member of the UN body, answering directly to the secretary-general and the executive board. And the importance of their work was becoming increasingly clear.

As the census data began to emerge in Africa, attitudes shifted dramatically. "I remember visiting the president of Cameroon, and the thing that struck him was how his minister of health and his minister of education wanted more money just to keep the services at the same level with no improvement. And he was not interested in maintaining the current level of services, because it was so low. Their access to health care in Cameroon was only like 3 percent, and enrollment in schools was very low. It started to strike the president that these census numbers were really much more devastating than he had ever imagined. He wanted to improve their situation, so the country had to have a program that dealt with all these needs at the same time."

Like Cameroon, the attitudes of other governments changed toward population numbers, and they began introducing family planning as an element in their development strategy. At one time these African nations had been high-yielding agricultural producers and exporters, but they saw the demand of populations catching up and surpassing the food supply. And to make matters worse, the growth of residents and their settlements took away from the land that had been used for cultivation. When the Brandt Commission Report, a study on international development issues chaired by West German chancellor (and Nobel Peace Prize winner) Willy Brandt, released its findings in 1980, the authors cited rapid population growth as one of the strongest factors shaping the future of human society and, along with excessive consumption, as a prime source of alarming ongoing ecological changes.

With these developing nations' desire for progress came more obstacles to overcome, as Dr. Sadik pointed out. "The program was all right for those to whom birth control was available; it was okay for those women who could actually use it. But the methods were not necessarily the most suitable for all women. In particular in Africa, you often heard the statement, 'our men will not use condoms.' So men could not be expected to have any responsibility to plan their families. The responsibility and the onus fell solely on women. The effort became how to get women more self-reliant, more able to make decisions. We introduced programs like economic activities for women along with health education and family planning, because then they'd be a little more economically independent, which would give them some autonomy." Nafis realized that a woman with money in her purse had more freedom to control her own destiny, and thus she lobbied governments to provide their female populations with business opportunities.

"Our executive board was not happy. They thought we were off our mandate. And I kept trying to explain to them: the idea is not just to provide contraceptives, but to enable people to actually use them. And to use them, especially if the programs were directed towards women only, the women had to make decisions for themselves. You can see how our policy evolved over a whole period of time."

The expression "bleeding-heart liberal" usually refers to a person's political persuasion, but in some cases it can be an eerily apt metaphor, particularly when the heart in question belongs to someone engaged in heartbreaking business: daily immersion in the most sordid side of humanity. These activists are not able to merely change the station when the photo of the emaciated child comes on screen; rather, they're forced to let the image burn into their retinas while they focus on the reality of the ruined lives of the starving, the sick, the abused, the maimed, the raped, the enslaved. Until one day, the bleeding-heart liberal's heart explodes.

By 1982 Dr. Sadik had hit her stride, and she was the chief of the UNFPA programs division, overseeing all agency projects worldwide. She was traveling the globe, spending more time on airplanes and in meetings than she spent at home in her Manhattan apartment. The diplomat was in demand everywhere as the concepts she'd been promoting her entire career finally caught fire, and governments requested her expertise as a pioneer in family planning and public health.

On top of this, for many years Nafis had had another man in her life besides Azhar. In fact, Salas and Sadik formed quite the team. He had the charm and diplomatic know-how to woo heads of state, and saw his role as primarily that of an executive and fund-raiser for UNFPA. He had hired Nafis to provide the technical expertise he lacked: her knowledge of medicine, family planning programs, and women's issues. He also appreciated the fact that, like himself, she came from a developing country and had worked in the field for years, an asset that provided the benefit of hands-on experience rather than merely textbook theories. By 1983 the twosome were seeing their twelve-year union pay off handsomely in measurable results.

While no romantic involvement existed between the colleagues, they were in many ways kindred spirits. Salas appreciated Nafis's ambition and can-do approach; he never criticized her for getting above herself. On the contrary, he enabled her to push for change, both in the administration of world governments and within the UN's own labyrinthine system. He even taught Nafis to fill her champagne flute with ginger ale when they were toasting at diplomatic functions, so she could blend in. Her supervisor was grooming the doctor to take over his position, but once again things did not turn out the way he'd planned.

Nafis and Werner Fornos from the Population Institute had driven all night from New York to Washington DC to do a lecture at American University. Fornos had planned the event, but what he had not planned on was getting lost. The pair finally found their way, and Nafis, as usual, was lugging a huge stack of papers for her talk. As they hiked up a hill in the cool morning air, Nafis began to have trouble breathing.

However, like most doctors, her own health was not a priority, and she ignored the symptoms. But to be fair, she had every reason to believe she was well enough. Nafis had signed up for swimming classes at the YMCA, feeling that at fifty-three it was time to finally conquer her childhood fear of the water. Before diving into the pool, she'd had a check-up, including a cardiogram, and had received a clean bill of health. But then as she struggled to stay afloat, her swim instructor kept asking, "Are you okay?" She just assumed she'd lapsed into bad shape from years of desk duty and needed more exercise.

After the meeting in Washington with Werner Fornos, she ran into another colleague, Dr. Isadore Rosenfeld, with whom she had interned back at Baltimore's City Hospital. She casually mentioned the incident, and Rosenfeld looked at her solemnly. "It's not like I'm looking for patients, but you're a friend of mine, and you really should come in and have a checkup."

An angiogram showed Nafis's main artery was 70 percent blocked. Her response? To sneak out of town for a conference in Saudi Arabia without informing her cardiologist. When Rosenfeld found out, he tracked her down and called her hotel in Saudi Arabia. "What on earth are you doing there? Do you want to get me in trouble? Come back immediately!"

His chastened patient returned to Manhattan, and the two doctors conferred on the best course of action for Nafis's condition. Rosenfeld sent her angiogram to Emory University Hospital in Atlanta and shopped around for alternatives to open-heart surgery; but in the end it was the only course of action if Nafis didn't want to live like an invalid at fifty-three.

On March 9, 1983, she went under the knife; the bypass operation went smoothly, a routine procedure performed daily at New York Presbyterian Hospital. But the moment Nafis came out from under the anesthesia is where the normality ended. She had scheduled her hairdresser to come to the hospital to shampoo and style her postoperative hair. Then the patient slipped into a handsome caftan and greeted her numerous visitors in style. She remembered that "They were quite shocked. 'How is it that you look so well?' I said, 'Why should I look awful in the hospital?' You know, for me how I appear is also how I feel."

Her family, friends, and colleagues took over the whole waiting room, bringing a festive feel to a place normally so sterile and rife with grief. Nafis had instructed her guests, "Don't bring me flowers, I want some food, because the food in here is awful." They did as told, and a nonstop smorgasbord emerged with the arrival of cheese balls, spaghetti, lasagna, and an array of desserts to satisfy her sweet tooth.

After a week she went home to her Upper Eastside apartment and began one of the more original physical therapy programs on record. Ambereen, now twenty-six, was getting married, and mother and daughter combined cardiovascular exercise with trousseau shopping. "My doctor said I was supposed to walk a mile everyday as part of my recovery, so I had measured the distance to the department stores. It was five blocks to Bloomingdale's; five blocks to Bonwit Teller, seven blocks to Bergdorf's; and ten blocks to Saks."

Giving new meaning to the expression "retail therapy," her method worked. Six weeks after her bypass surgery Dr. Sadik flew to London for yet another conference, and for the next four years she would circle the globe countless times, flying hundreds of thousands of miles, spreading the gospel according to Nafis. "Before the operation, everyone kept saying, you'll be incorrigible, you'll have even more energy. When you were supposedly half dead, nobody could keep up with you." She would soon need that renowned energy, and then some.

As she remembered in a speech years later, "By the second World Population Conference at Mexico City in 1984, the controversy about family planning seemed to be over. This was the result of ten years' practical experience with maternal and child health programming, which in most cases included family planning.

"Much of this activity was funded by international donors: one of Mr. Salas's great achievements was to make funding for population programs acceptable to both donors and recipients. His watchwords for UNFPA were neutrality, flexibility and responsiveness, and on that basis he increased UNFPA's programming budget ten-fold in its first ten years. By 1984, over 140 developing countries had requested our help.

"The Mexico City recommendations filled a gap in the World Population Plan of Action by referring to the role and status of women. I recall that these recommendations were not in the original draft: they were inserted at the last minute by a group of concerned women delegates, in a sort of guerrilla action while delegation leaders were busy elsewhere. But they reflected the growing acceptance that women and their reproductive choices would be critical to development. At about that time, we started using the umbrella term 'reproductive health,' to include family planning, safe motherhood and treatment and prevention of sexually transmitted infections. It also covered gender-based violence, the focus of action for the growing number of women's groups."

However, this speeding train of progress was about to slam into the White House. Ronald Reagan, re-elected as president in 1984, sent a conservative delegation to the Mexico City conference headed by James Buckley. They objected to any language relating to abortion and instituted the infamous "Mexico City Gag Rule," meaning that any aid organization that received funding from the U.S. government could not mention abortion as an option to any clients. Already the Helms Amendment forbade any U.S. funds from being used to cover the cost of terminations, but now it was as if the procedure did not exist, meaning that a teenage girl who had been impregnated by her father could not be advised by her health care practitioner that she could terminate the pregnancy. In effect, the term "abortion" had been wiped clean from the slate of human history.

Buckley supplied the rationale for the envoy's decision: "This reflects a sharpening of focus to make U.S. foreign assistance programs more responsive to true needs and more reflective of fundamental values." And in sharp contrast to most other 146 member states in attendance, "The main argument of the Reagan administration was that population growth and economic development are not related."

In the end Reagan reversed the twenty-year history of U.S. support for family planning and pulled the plug on all aid to the UN Population Fund. The stunning irony was that Reagan punished the very organization that had worked tirelessly to *prevent the need for abortions*. The UNFPA Crusaders watched as—with the stroke of a pen—25 percent of their operating budget disappeared, and with it their ability to continue the mission they had begun. International Planned Parenthood Federation also watched their U.S. financial assistance disappear overnight.

The continued great irony was that Reagan's second in command, Vice President George H. Bush, had been an integral part of UNFPA's creation, and now, to win support of the conservatives, he had abandoned this earlier position in anticipation of his own forthcoming presidential run. Nafis met with him on several occasions, but he was unwilling to change the position of the United States and renew the agency's funding.

Rafael Salas, by all accounts, had been the perfect choice to head UNFPA. He was Asian, Catholic, and hailed from a developing country, the Philippines, where he had run the presidential campaign of Ferdinand Marcos, and he later became a cabinet minister.

Salas had also been a presidential contender himself, and he had let it be known that he intended to return home shortly to fulfill this dream. At UNFPA he'd been considered by all as a charismatic leader, a thoughtful supervisor, and despite his association with Marcos, his UN colleagues felt assured he held none of the negative attributes of corruption associated with his former boss and the shoe-mongering Imelda. He even originated model procedures to monitor the agency's expenditures and programs. "Salas was a very straight arrow."

The United Nations mandate forbade officials from accepting gifts, as it was believed this might sway their judgment. The only reward they were permitted was the awarding of honorary doctorates. And it became a source of great amusement around the office that Salas had set out on a quest to garner as many of these honorariums as he could fit on his résumé. And he'd logged twenty-six so far.

Through the vast Palladian windows of Ceremonial Hall at Sofia University, the afternoon sunlight streams in, reflecting off the domed white ceiling. A long parade of professors files down the aisle in their flowing robes, a holdover from medieval times; the garments' colors, hoods, chevrons, and ornamentation provide a complex map of each faculty member's own academic history. Their heads are covered with black velvet tams—a sign that they have already earned their own doctorate the hard way. On the podium sits a pleased Rafael Salas, ready to accept yet another honorary degree. His devoted technical adviser sits in the audience, listening as the orchestra's cello and bass sections, low and hushed, begin a primal, unaccompanied rumble. The violins come in later with the countermelody, and bit by bit the rest of the orchestra joins in—winds, horns, timpani, until all voices are present, a veritable wall of sound that exalts the spirit and thunders through the hall. Seated next to Nafis is the French director of the population division who, recognizing Beethoven's Symphony No. 9, turns to her and announces with satisfaction, "This is the Ninth."

Startled, she corrects him. "Oh no, this is the twenty-seventh."

This misunderstanding became a joke oft-repeated, told when the Crusaders returned stateside after a mission, and took a moment to gossip around the water cooler, next to the kitchen offices that served as headquarters.

Because the team frequently traveled together, they learned much about each other that they might not have noticed in a static work environment. Like the fact that their leader, the recipient of degree number twenty-seven, read a book a day when he was traveling. Salas was a philosopher and thinker who wrote his own books on overpopulation, and even in an environment full of brilliant minds, his stood out. As his UN colleague Alex Marshall observed, "I've come across people who came out of his office visibly shaken. 'What a great man,' they'd say."

As Nafis remembered in a tribute to her boss years later, "He made it his business to visit the head of state of every country in the United Nations. His great strength was that he had no ideology, nothing to sell. He didn't join either side in the 'population versus development' debate—or rather, he ignored the controversy altogether. Instead, he would ask governments what they wanted from UNFPA. This was quite a novel approach on the part of an aid agency—in fact I sometimes think it still is—and it was highly successful."

"He was, and was seen by others, as very smart," agreed Stirling Scruggs, the senior resource development officer for UNFPA, and one of the few Americans employed by the fund. Among his other sobriquets Salas had earned the title of "Mr. Population," and he had adopted a punishing work schedule. In February of 1987, Scruggs took a trip with his supervisor to Manila, where Rafael Salas was known to his old pals simply as "Paeng." "His Manila schedule had been daunting. He had several meetings with officials of the new Aquino government by day and with many of his friends by night. They all carried the same message: 'It is time to come home, Paeng. Your country needs you.'"

On this journey, Salas confided to Scruggs that he was planning to accept this invitation. At the age of fifty-nine he determined it was time to leave UNFPA and return home to seek political office, perhaps to head the cabinet of Corazon Aquino. "I asked him who he would like to succeed him if he returned to the Philippines. He said, 'Of course, Nafis. She deserves it and she's very good. It could be no one else, and Stirling, you and the others are going to have to see to it that she replaces me.'" The UNFPA team had visited members of Congress several times to solicit support for their agenda, but now they had new problems to worry about besides the Gag Rule and the disappearance of their budget. The U.S. position had changed again, with additional contingencies that had to be met before the president would consider restoring their funding. This time Ronald Reagan wanted UNFPA to pull out of China, abandon its mission there, which Dr. Sadik refused to do.

Now, on the heels of their Manila trip, Salas and Scruggs took another junket in an attempt to restore the $46 million in funding they'd lost. "On Monday, March 2, we visited with Representatives Peter Kostmeyer and John Porter and Senator Daniel Inouye. We were scheduled the next day to meet with Representative Jim Moody, Senator Alan Simpson, and the Chinese ambassador."

At the Capitol, Salas had run into a compatriot from his home town and had happily agreed to have supper with him that night. However, after the long day, as he and Scruggs took the elevator up to their separate rooms, Rafael announced he was exhausted; he canceled those dinner plans and ordered room service instead.

"We arranged to have breakfast the next morning at 8:00 a.m. in the hotel restaurant with Werner Fornos, president of the Population

Institute. I joined Werner at about 7:45 for coffee and to await Mr. Salas. When he didn't arrive by 8:10 I called his room, because he was always punctual. But there was no answer. Then I went out the front door of the hotel to look up and down the street as he frequently took early morning walks. By 8:20 I was worried and asked the hotel manager for a key to Salas's room. The manager sent the house detective along with me to open the door.

"I found Paeng's body on the far side of his bed, with a book lying on the floor next to him. His bed was still made and pillows were propped up against the headboard, as one would do if they had been lying there reading. He was wearing an undershirt, his suit pants and socks.

"I remember rushing over to him, kneeling beside him, and saying, 'Please wake up.' The house detective said, 'He's dead, sir.' I knew it was true, but for a moment I refused to believe it. I had tears in my eyes as I knelt there beside him and thought of his wife, Menchu, his sons, Ernesto and Raffy. And I remember thinking that his country had lost a national treasure at a critical time in its history." They would all learn later that Salas had suffered a massive heart attack, fallen off his bed onto the carpet of the Capital Holiday Inn, where he'd died alone that night.

His deputy, Heino Wittrin, who had been the number two man at UNFPA, was now in charge of the organization. He was out on a mission and so was Nafis, and they had to fly back home upon the news. Wittrin announced that he was the only one who would be flying back to the Philippines for his boss's funeral because the expense of several international plane tickets would look bad to the auditors. But the number three person in the pecking order responded, "Rubbish. I'm going and so is Stirling and the senior Filipinos. He's the only executive director we've ever had, and now he's gone."

Already Sadik and Wittrin were vying to replace their boss as they both set off on the plane for Asia. When they arrived, Nafis went to the UN offices, closed the door, and, using an old manual typewriter, plunked out her eulogy for the funeral. On another flight Rafael Salas's widow and sons accompanied his body back home. When their plane landed in Manila, waiting on the tarmac stood President Aquino, her entire cabinet, and a one-hundred-person honor guard.

The services were held in an open-air chapel where hundreds of mourners' sobs dissolved into a steam bath of smoldering humidity. The ironically named Cardinal Sin officiated while three women sat together to comfort each other: the widow and Corazon Aquino, who both held Nafis's hands until she walked up to the podium, where through a river of tears, she delivered her tribute to the man she noted had made great contributions to humanity. He had also wooed her to join this mission, then mentored her throughout the journey for sixteen years.

The politicking to line up the new head of UNFPA had begun even before they left Manila. Scruggs, who had worked in the Philippines for many years, asked some of Aquino's cabinet members to put in a word for Nafis. He knew that not only would she be competing against Heino Wittrin, but other doctors, diplomats, and politicos from around the world who would see this job as a plum assignment. And Dr. Sadik herself was quietly campaigning, not leaving anything to chance.

In 1987 Javier Pérez de Cuéllar was the UN secretary-general; the choice of whom to name as the next executive director for UNFPA would be solely his decision. The "SG" as the secretary-general is known in UN parlance, had been a member of the Peruvian delegation to the General Assembly at its inaugural session back in 1946. An attorney and career diplomat, he was no stranger to controversy, having served on the UN Security Council and as a special envoy to negotiations during the wars in Cyprus and Afghanistan.

Two weeks after Rafael Salas died de Cuéllar appointed Nafis Sadik as the first woman to head a UN agency—a bold move on his part. As one observer noted, "It was, I think, a wonderful announcement to the world when the UN was willing to appoint a Pakistani woman to be the head of a major UN agency, replacing a man. That was important to the movement on women's issues and women's health."

However, Jurgen Sackowski, one of her colleagues, felt that her gender didn't play an important role. "The essential characteristics of Nafis, which made her good for UNFPA, are not those that you normally say are the typical characteristics of a woman. She was actually a good man, if you want to call her that."

Politically it was a given that the person—male or female—appointed to run the agency needed to be from a developing country, especially considering the current heads of UNDP and UNICEF hailed from developed nations. The approval of the major donors was also a critical factor, considering UNFPA was voluntarily funded. If, say, Japan, as the top donor, had strongly objected to Nafis, her chances of promotion would have been slim. Or as Sackowski opined, "Powerful supporters are not needed. It's rather more important not to have powerful enemies."

At the same time, she had been highly visible in her tenure at the agency. Another UN diplomat, and fellow Pakistani, Shaukat Fareed, observed his friend Nafis for thirty years at the organization. He noted that Rafael Salas would always bring his technical adviser to conferences and meetings with heads of state because "it was Nafis Sadik who worked the delegations, and convinced them about the programs. She was very, very good. She had the capacity, the capability, the guts, the fire in the belly. You have to have the fire in the belly, and she had the fire."

Alex Marshall remembered her promotion. "She was gratified, I think, by the appointment, not necessarily overwhelmed by it. She pretty much thought it was her right. And she took to it like a duck to water. She was a bit nervous going in. I remember I wrote the first speech she ever gave as executive director to the governing council, what's now our executive board. She was nervous as a kitten. And she made a tremendously good impression, simply because people could see she was a little vulnerable, you know. After that she picked up and went for it . . . that was in the spring, and by the summer, she was full steam ahead."

Shaukat Fareed, who was the deputy representative at the Pakistan Mission to the United Nations, had trained as an economist. He outlined theories on development, theories that his colleague Nafis shared and that she would now—with her new authority—put into practice: "It's said that economists invent a theory after seeing life experience. They know this has happened, then they go back and develop a theory to explain *why* this happened, and that becomes an economic theory. So, the human factor that affects development is immeasurable, very difficult. But bottom line is that development also has a security dimension: without rule of law, without human rights, you can't have development. So, now the new concepts are that everything is so closely interlinked that you can't make progress in one area without also demanding progress simultaneously on one hundred other fronts. You can't have education by itself. It doesn't mean anything. What do you do with these people when they are educated? And you can't have child survival if you can't give them education when they grow up, and you can't have education if you can't find them employment. It just goes on and on and on, and there is no end to it. So I think people don't appreciate this point very well. They think UNFPA is an organization which is just limiting the growth of population through abortion or contraceptives— that sort of thing. But the fundamental aim is to make sure that the population is healthy. Because what good is a mother when she dies in childbirth after giving birth to six kids? I mean, that dimension of the work of UNFPA is somehow lost on people. It's an integral part of the developmental process."

With these concepts in mind, Nafis began to steer the rudder of her organization into choppy waters, sailing out into the high seas of social change, where she would not only provide condoms to couples in need but also demand "progress simultaneously on one hundred other fronts." Needless to say, this exponentially increased the workload and challenges her organization faced, but she saw it as the only viable way to accomplish their mission.

Dr. Sadik took to her new position "like a duck to water" for several reasons. As Fareed pointed out, "Nafis understood these interlinkages, and when you understand them, then you can persuade governments to accept them. Governments get sidetracked by their own internal political constraints. For instance, in Islamic countries, a lot of their resistance is spread by ignorance. In America, at the so-called abortion clinics, people have been throwing fireballs, they've killed doctors. This is ignorance that people believe in. Nafis was successful because I think she promoted her agenda with passion, but without sentimentality."

In addition the new executive director had a personal commitment to the issues, or as Fareed described it, "the fire in the belly." She also inspired her staff to be dedicated to *her*. They would do things for her that were above and beyond the call of duty, and even senior executives at the other UN sister agencies began to comment to her, "Oh, your UNFPA staff seems to be so committed."

Nafis responded: "They just do it because they want to get their mission accomplished. And they do it because they believe what they're engaged in is something that will make a difference."

UNFPA's new leader continued with the vision established by her predecessor, including a documentary in production by Turner Broadcasting System, *Day of Five Billion: A Day to Celebrate, A Day to Contemplate.* The film chronicled the birth that put the world population over the five billion mark and featured an interview with Nafis, along with contributions from such heads of state as Rajiv Gandhi, Kenneth David Kaundra, and Oscar Arias. Many artists weighed in on camera also, such as authors Arthur C. Clarke, Isaac Asimov, and Kurt Vonnegut; joining them were musicians Stevie Wonder, José Feliciano, and the aptly named Crowded House, who sang, "Now we're five billion strong, I can hear them calling." The credits offered a memento mori: "Dedicated to the memory of Rafael Salas."

While their fallen Crusader was missed by his colleagues, it was quickly apparent that the agency's new leader would not be a Salas duplicate. As was her lifelong pattern, Nafis went about her business in a way that was uniquely Nafis. Her former chief of staff for fifteen years, Mari Simonen, noted: "What was very special about Dr. Sadik was that she knew every person at UNFPA personally—and we're talking seven hundred employees. She knew all the people working in the field worldwide by name. One thing absolutely phenomenal about her is her memory."

The boss used her phenomenal brain to propel UNFPA forward, and Shaukat Fareed watched Nafis rise in the overall profile of the UN as well. She was invited to sit on numerous committees and more importantly the UN Executive Board, the global governing council that oversaw all twenty-nine United Nations organizations. "She is able to get to the issue straight away, no nonsense, and she knows what's she's talking about. Most people, men or women, don't know what they're talking about, and so they talk in circles and circles and circles. But one of the things you cannot ignore, is the fact that she's a woman. She has a personality, she dresses very well. She speaks very well. So you know that she's a woman, you can see her, but the way she deals . . . she knows what she's talking about and she has an argument that is very persuasive. You cannot deny her." Gone were the days when she sat at the conference table surrounded by men who regarded her merely as a decorative secretary who should keep her mouth shut and fetch the coffee.

Mari Simonen remembered accompanying Dr. Sadik to meetings with heads of state. "She didn't miss an opportunity to put forward points of view that aren't necessarily theirs, or raise issues that are difficult. I mean she's a very, very savvy diplomat in the best sense of the word, a negotiator and creator of change. Depending on the situation, she would use different tactics, including, obviously, her charm, her considerable charisma." By comparison, others who have observed Nafis in action have agreed she's charismatic, charming—even coquettish—but they have also characterized her as rude and downright abrasive.

Simonen argues, "I think she's just a really complex person who has lots of qualities, different qualities, and they are all very strong, very eccentric, and because she is extremely intelligent, she's using all of them. Sometimes the abrasiveness probably was accentuated if she was under considerable stress, which comes with these jobs. You travel constantly, you are totally jetlagged all the time. You are constantly bombarded with information. You have to make quick decisions, you know everybody comes to you for something. Every person who comes to you usually has an ulterior motive, so there is the presentation they come with, plus something else, which is not being presented. These are very stressful jobs, and I assume that if the so-called abrasive side was too strong, or maybe used in some place where it wasn't needed, the reason is also a bit cultural, based on where she grew up and how women in her class and in her milieu acted if they were to succeed professionally. They were expected to be relatively authoritarian."

Or as one colleague put it: "People used to say she ran UNFPA like a Pakistani estate."

So not everyone was genuflecting to the new chief. Mari Simonen noted one source of agitation amongst the tribe. "Dr. Sadik would really know what was going on. She would know what the people's motivations were, what their personalities were, what their strengths and weaknesses were. She was a decisive leader, and she didn't have much patience for letting people go on with things where she had already seen long before what the conclusion should have been. So often times, she was criticized for being extremely direct and very fast in her decision making and sometimes abrupt."

Jurgen Sackowski put it more bluntly: "Some people called

her—jokingly—a cowboy. Why? Because she shot from the hip. And frequently she got the target."

"If I give her grades, I give her an A+ in industriousness. I have never had, among all my supervisors, someone as hardworking as she. After a trip, she was at her desk, and she went through her mail, and you got a decision, right or wrong, but she had done her homework. Superb, no question about it. But given that she knows everything, and she does, she gets a B- in listening. Why waste time to hear the rubbish of A, B, or C, if she knows it's not the case? And then half the time, she interrupts. She can be rather rude and that has consequences. People are not comfortable to be interrupted, especially by the boss."

And he had other issues with her imperious style. "Notably, that she scared people, which is really risky. Once I told her, 'Nafis, do you know what your real problem is? People don't tell you what they really think. That, as a senior official, you can't afford. And why don't they tell you? They are scared of you!' Do you know what her reply was? 'They should be, I'm the executive director.' Now that, with all due respect, is not what they teach in Human Relations 101. You don't have to go to grad school, that you could probably learn in junior college."

Stirling Scruggs added, "Nafis can be very gracious. If somebody has something wrong in their family or something wrong medically, she is absolutely your best friend in the world, but she can cut you off, or treat you like a slave sometimes, too. I don't think she even comprehends it. And she's got a mercurial kind of temper when something goes wrong—she'll just fillet someone."

Alex Marshall had his own take on the situation. "To be in that top position, you have to be a chess player, you're always thinking three or four moves ahead. Those who are still a little bit slow have some problems catching up . . . then they do something wrong. She just couldn't—absolutely couldn't—believe that you'd done that without doing it deliberately, and if you did it deliberately, then you were attacking her, and that was, you know, disloyalty. Any form of opposition at the organization, or to the organization's mission, and that was an anathema to her. So once or twice she got it into her head that I was trying to do her in because of my stupidity. Who me?" Life was tough for these mere mortals struggling to play in the same league with Nafis.

"The problem was, in many ways, she was cleverer than she gave herself credit for. She was actually further ahead of the game than she knew. So, Nafis would sort of assume that you knew stuff, and you couldn't possibly. I was always amazed by her encyclopedic knowledge."

Besides his other duties, Alex Marshall worked as Nafis's speechwriter, and the two developed a symbiotic partnership, with him expressing her unique perspective. Sometimes he'd work late into the night and drop her speeches off with her doorman on his way home, and many times he accompanied her on a mission.

Once they journeyed together to Rio de Janeiro for an important conference. Marshall decided to give the director of UNFPA communications the slip so he and a cohort could venture into the Amazon rainforest. The director, Hiro Ando, kept trying to call to check on the status of Nafis's speech, but Alex solved this problem by answering his mobile phone, and while crumpling paper into the receiver, mumbling that the call was breaking up.

Later, as the executive director was seated on stage fuming, while she prepared to ad lib her talk, she saw a hand shoot out from the potted palms and lay some papers down next to her. She picked up her speech, walked to the podium and began to deliver her address to the packed house.

This was a rare occurrence, however, and for the most part the two worked smoothly as a team all over the globe. "I've seen Nafis bouncing off the plane after a fourteen-hour flight, then walk straight into a meeting, and start talking to people as if she'd known them all her life. And she knew stuff about their country, and their program, and the details of their business. She would just sort of turn herself on. You could see her changing practically from one moment to the next. Coming from the airport, she'd be sitting in the car with her head slung. As the car slowed, she would go like this, head up, door would open and she was *on*. Bang! Extraordinary."

Even her detractors had to marvel at her legendary energy, especially for a fifty-eight-year-old woman who had survived open-heart surgery. Werner Fornos recalled how they had traveled together to Bulgaria for a European conference. "When everybody else was weary and tired she went up to the top floor of the hotel and played the slot machines late into the night."

The staff soon learned her ways, particularly that she was a notorious night owl who would stay up until dawn hashing out an agreement, but don't expect to see her at breakfast. Or as Salas—ever the quick study—had realized years before: "Never wake Nafis up in the morning—she's useless."

With this in mind her assistants scheduled everything as late in the day as possible, avoiding at all costs the dreaded early morning flights. Nafis developed her travel methods for coping with the UN schedule after logging hundreds of thousands of miles on airliners. As soon as she boarded a flight she set her watch to her destination's time zone, and refused to think about what the hour was back in New York. She never ate the food placed on her tray table, but rather utilized one of her greatest natural abilities.

"Many colleagues used to travel with me and think oh, they'll have my ear, because they'll be sitting next to me. But I used to say, please don't disturb me, I'm off to sleep. I just have this habit of being able to sleep whenever I want. So even when I travel, let's say I'm tired in the daytime, then I say, I'll have a quick nap, and I just go lie down for fifteen minutes and go to sleep. I get up and I feel fine. I can do that many times a day if I need to.

"Often when I'm taking a journey from A to B, it's like an hour drive, so I'll talk to my hosts for half an hour, then say, 'Do you mind if I just close my eyes and go to sleep?' This also I learned from Salas.

He said, 'You should just say, can I take a nap? Don't stand on formality, that you have to sit there and stay awake, because, you are the one who will be running around.'"

Having skipped the in-flight gruel, Dr. Sadik was now free to indulge at the state dinners, where even her dining habits became exercises in diplomacy. "Sometimes you get so overfed at these affairs. At one point I announced I had diabetes. I didn't have it, I just used to say to people, 'You know, my blood sugar is a bit high, so I can't eat all these sweets.' Otherwise the hosts are offended if you won't try something. You're so well fed at all these luncheons and dinners, it's impossible to maintain your weight." She also used to pick up a lot of colds from the germs circulating through the plane like biological warfare; but that ceased once she discovered flu shots.

With all the hours spent on the road and the demands of her position, it could be assumed that she had precious little time left for her home life. Mari Simonen watched this dynamic at close range and found the opposite to be true. "Talk about work-life balance—Dr. Sadik was a pioneer. She worked very hard, but she left the office—not too late—around 6:00, 6:30, but never later than 7:00 each day. And that was it. Unless, you count the fact that she attended some kind of official function almost every night. But when she went home, that was it, and she almost never took papers with her. She didn't spend time on the weekends and evenings working. She was very clear about that. She had a life, she had a family, a big family, lots of children and grandchildren, and other relatives who were very important to her. So, she wasn't alone. She wasn't going home to an empty house like many career women these days. First of all, they don't have a family, and then it becomes self-defeating. When you're alone, you have more time to work, to fill up the void—the space or loneliness. You continue to work at home and everywhere else. So, obviously, she never had that situation, and I think it was very important for her not to.

"In addition she had all these other interests: sports, bridge, shopping, the theater—all kinds of things. So she was absolutely incredible in terms of being able to maintain all these different lives very intensely. Yeah, that was quite impressive to me, to see that. And this is a lesson I think for all women, or anybody else who wants to have a life that's successful both personally and professionally. Obviously, she had help at home, but not like excessive amounts of help. And she had five children!"

What was Nafis's secret? "You know, I work hard when I'm in the office; I don't do other things. I just work, all the time that I'm there. I want to clear my desk and inbox before I leave every day. I read very fast, and I write a lot of notes on the side and I expect someone to decipher them. I have a way of reading so that I don't go from the first line to the last line. I read the summary and then I look at some items which stick out, which I think might be important."

Down through the years Simonen watched her mentor close at hand in order to make Dr. Sadik's traits her own. "She's just phenomenal in terms of being able to process things, but not dwell on them. I think that's very important. She took on a lot of information, and processed it, and then made a decision. And she always said that it was okay to make a mistake, but not to repeat it many times. But it was better to make a mistake than not make anything. We needed to move on. There were many people here who would procrastinate—any bureaucracy has those—but she couldn't stand it."

Dr. Sadik chastised her male subordinates for working all hours in the office. "I mean, I'm sure once in a while they have to do something, but not every day! I think some men preferred to be out of the house, than to be in the house. I told their wives, 'It's not me who is telling him to stay at work, so you better find out what he's doing.' Because they were going in every Saturday. What are they doing on Saturday?"

Her mentors may have been male, particularly her father and Rafael Salas, but most of Nafis's management methods were uniquely female—like the habits she learned growing up in a traditional Pakistani family, that of paying homage to a massive number of relatives on a routine basis. Except Nafis adapted that technique to her work environment and managed to keep track of not only family but also friends and colleagues who lived all over the world, and this in an era before the Internet. Whenever she would fly out for a mission, she would take along her address book for that city, and upon arrival she called up everyone she knew who lived in that town to say hello.

This type of social skill allowed her to maintain a friendship with Zeenat Haroon for sixty years, decades after they moved to separate continents. "You know, I have a flat in London and she stays with me whenever she comes. Without fail, she has this list of about ten people she knows, and the first thing she will do, she will call them. And, she will say, 'I am in town, I don't think I will be able to see you, but I just wanted to be in touch. How is your daughter, or how is your grandmother, or how is your . . .' But you know the minute she hears that somebody has died, then she'll make a point of going to condole. He may have died about six months before, but she turns up."

This tactic would pay off with dividends over the years, as Nafis spun an enormous global web of support, a network that would aid her in myriad ways besides connecting with friends: to understand the diverse cultures that made up her clientele. "I always want to be invited to someone's home to see how people actually live. You can't always get that done. And even when you do, I know that you'll be going to visit families who are better off economically, but still you can get some idea of the culture and what people actually think, and all that. Just meeting government is not seeing the real society, the real people."

Nafis Sadik continued to be a walking contradiction. As she had her entire life, the UN diplomat merged the most extremely masculine and feminine attributes in such a way that she jarred the ability of her observers to place her in a tidy cultural cubbyhole. While much of her management style may have been uniquely female, and she was known for being a gracious hostess when she entertained at home, she quickly adopted a policy of not serving tea or coffee to visitors in her office. Back in Pakistan it had been the custom for a "peon" to run for refreshments, and people ate and drank all day long. However, in Manhattan there was a noticeable absence of peons on the staff, and Nafis quickly realized that she would spend her entire day entertaining those who dropped by wanting to ingratiate themselves. Not wanting to encourage this behavior, she maintained a dry office geared more for efficiency than hospitality. In addition she frequently ate at her desk while she worked, only going out for official business luncheons.

And she had a way of dealing with high-ranking executives that was boldly male. As one of her subordinates, Stafford Mousky, observed, "Sadik has a quality of getting along with senior males in different organizations who treat her as an equal, and the fact that she's female doesn't enter into the equation almost at all. Her behavior has a long history; it was already evident in the early '70s when she joined UNFPA—she had a take charge, no-nonsense side to her, and would argue with almost anybody about anything. And often—more often than not—carry the day because she had more determination, more facts, was willing to push for her views, willing to put more chips in the center of the table, than most bureaucrats.

"And men in power respected her for that. Many may have understood [reproductive health] was a sensitive area, one in which they didn't know a lot, and they were willing to listen to what she had to say."

Then again, Nafis could come across as more macho than a testosterone-crazed warlord, especially when dressing down a subordinate who had given a lackluster presentation. Mari Simonen recalled, "If she didn't agree with something, or she found somebody to not really contribute in the proper way, she didn't hesitate to say it in front of everybody."

But Simonen understood how her boss had developed this

aggressive stance at the outset of her UN career: "In those early days, Dr. Sadik was the only woman, and a woman from an Asian country, from a southern country—and remember, she was relatively young compared to her colleagues. So basically she quickly realized that unless she stood up and made a point in a much stronger and confrontational way than the men, nobody would ever listen to her. And it served quite well the causes that we stood for, because unless you really speak out in that kind of very passionate way—not aggressive—but really direct way, and with the kind of eloquence that she was able to put forward with intelligence—it's very easy for naysayers to dismiss these issues."

And yet her loyal assistant, Mari Simonen, would have to slip the boss notes when they met with foreign dignitaries, telling Nafis to shut up and let them speak. "There were so many times when she met with people and she had so much to say—she could have gone on forever—but the people, the audience, were absolutely stunned by the amount of information which was coming from her; she has this phenomenal capacity to deliver. It's just amazing. And, in fact, could be too much for some people to absorb. I would pass her notes. 'Let the others ask questions.'"

The comment that the executive director ran UNFPA "like a Pakistani estate" had other dimensions to it. As Dr. Sadik began to stamp the agency with her own imprimatur, she inculcated it with her personal management philosophy, and one of these practices—namely that of hiring several Pakistanis for senior positions, earned UNFPA the nickname "The Pakistani Fund."

Women were the other linchpin of her hiring preference, as Nafis felt that an agency created to help them should be representative of their gender. By the time she left office she had seen to it that females held 60 percent of UNFPA's top administration jobs in New York headquarters and 40 percent at the country level. In order to achieve this goal she made other unpopular decisions, like replacing Stafford Mousky with a woman.

Mousky had been chief of the office of the executive director under Salas. He had a background in history and political science, had served as a naval officer and then as a high-ranking official for USAID in Washington and Peru. "When Sadik took over in 1987, she called me to the office and said, 'I want you to move, taking half of your responsibilities with you. I'm going to put a woman in your spot because I'm going to be placing more women in various high-ranking positions around UNFPA.' So, I then moved to what is now IERD [Information and External Relations Division], taking a bunch of my functions with me, including being Nafis's sherpa."

While Dr. Sadik may have solved the problem of gender inequality by hiring lots of women into management positions, she couldn't change the eternal dynamic that happens when powerful men interact with women. "Men think if they are powerful, women are attracted, because women let it be known that they are attracted. So I think it's not just male behavior, it's also a response to what a woman wants them to do sometimes. It's like encouraging them. In my case, I don't think I was encouraging, but then I thought to myself, you know I have this way of talking which is quite familiar. Sometimes, I'm very playful, I may pass frivolous remarks—flirtatious, not in the sense of having an affair—but you know to be friendly. So that can be taken as I'm interested. Then you just have to learn to deal with the consequences." She learned to accept compliments graciously, but not dinner invitations to dine solo with gentlemen.

Her staff recalled incidents of traveling on the road with her and counseling their contemporaries not to waste their time making passes at Nafis. Alex Marshall observed one statesman at a dinner in Asia who had not heeded this advice. "She was a very attractive woman, actually, and because she had this sort of force, she was very attractive to a certain sort of man. So, this guy thought he was in like Flynn, and she just . . . whoosh! Like napalm, like a flamethrower. She didn't say or do anything particularly rude or nasty, she just showed the guy he couldn't get away with this, which was quite funny."

With the territory of her new position came the unpleasant responsibility of adjudicating over sexual harassment claims amongst her own UNFPA employees. A few of her new hires protested bitterly about overtures made by their male colleagues. "Some women complain about this. I said, 'Well, you'll always have passes made at you. You'll just have to learn to handle it. The men can only try. They can't make you have sex unless somebody's violent.'"

Dr. Sadik's opinion was that female employees would sometimes use sexual harassment claims as a political tool. "We've had cases that went through all levels of investigation and were found to be totally frivolous. And sometimes men are harassed by women supervisors as well, and men don't object as much because they're too embarrassed, though you hear more of it now. Unfortunately I think the ones who are really harassed don't come forward to complain as much as the ones who maybe are manipulating the system, which is tragic because I think a lot of this goes on. I have no doubt that it goes on. It's a subject that has bothered me a lot, how to protect everybody on the staff and how to get those who are really being harassed to come out. So it's a subject that we don't have the answer to."

The dialogue of male/female dynamics extended beyond sexual harassment. "Of course, some feminists project this image of hating men, which is, I think, quite ridiculous. Why would you hate men? I mean, what you're asking for is equality and equal opportunities. And that's not against men; it's *for* women, but should not be seen as *against*. I have difficulty with some women's attitude. When I would say 'We must also talk to male leaders,' and they would reply, 'Why are you bringing men into this?' like they're our enemies. And I think that's the most ridiculous thing, because if you're fighting for equality then everyone has to be equal. I mean men also have *their* rights."

Just when everyone had decided that Nafis was really one of the boys, she would sneak out of an important summit meeting to go shopping. She became notorious amongst the staff for her shopping mania, and they were even instructed to book time in her foreign travels for this pastime. Imelda Henken (who took over as chief of staff when Mousky was reassigned) told of traveling to Viet Nam with her supervisor. When they landed in Hanoi, the driver picked them up at the airport, took them straightaway to a shop to buy fabric, then to a tailor. When Nafis and Imelda arrived for a state dinner with government officials that evening, they were wearing their new *ao dai*, long form-fitting silk tunics over pants.

Nafis Sadik's fashion-plate persona became the source of endless jokes. "In the office, they make fun of me. 'Well, of course you can't go to the village unless you have on your diamond earrings, can you? or your gold Rolex watch?' I said, well, it's not like I bought them with someone else's money. I bought them with my own money, so I can do whatever I like with my earnings." She had fulfilled the prophecy she'd made to her mother forty years earlier, that she would buy her own clothes and jewelry.

Whether self-serving or not, Nafis believed that her shopping obsession provided a useful purpose beyond boosting the GNP of a developing nation. "I feel that unless you go to the shops, even if you don't buy anything, you don't get an idea of the country. When you go, you learn what people do, what kinds of things they like. You can see it firsthand.

"When I go to India the media often ask me about my shopping. I made the mistake of once telling them at some press conference, I said, I love coming to India because I can find my clothes here. 'So how many saris have you bought?' they asked. I said, 'Oh, one suitcase full, at least.' I mean, I said that just to be flip. After that, every time I go to India, they ask me about my shopping, as if that's what I came for. Now the Indian government always reserves some time in my schedule so I can tour around." The UN's first female head— with no self-consciousness whatsoever—admits to having thousands of saris.

These garments have served more than a sartorial purpose,

however, because over the years Nafis learned that her gender could be transformed from a detriment to an advantage. As Mari Simonen observed, "She dressed in her traditional saris—not only that, but in these absolutely gorgeous saris. She had this incredible collection, and every day she'd come out in another more beautiful silk one, and beautiful jewelry, so obviously, while she may have done that for her own pleasure, I think it was also a strategy. It was a big part of her personality, a good way to add to her charisma, *and you would remember her*. She would be stunning, coming into a room, first of all because everybody else is probably a man in a dark suit, and she would be in these bright colors with gold jewelry, and then she would be remembered. 'Oh, that must be Nafis Sadik.'"

Who would think a sari could have political power? Stirling Scruggs witnessed this phenomenon. "Once when I'd been meeting with the staff director of the appropriations committee for foreign operations in the Senate, Nafis and I went to see the chairman. We thought we were going to discuss various things with Senator Inouye from Hawaii. But he was more concerned than anything else about how a sari worked. And so Nafis was showing him and unhooked part and showed him this and that, and he kept asking questions, and then he asked questions about Pakistan—why did women start wearing saris?—all kinds of things. This went on for forty-five minutes. We had gone beyond our appointment time, and then the senator looked over at us and just nodded, as if to say, 'Don't worry, everything's going to be all right.'"

Like all great showmen in her beloved theater, Nafis, our Leo in the limelight, had learned to use all the tools at her disposal—wardrobe, mannerisms, speech, and her forceful stage presence—to transmit the kilowatts of maximum star power. When Mari Simonen arrived at UNFPA in 1980, her boss had already been there for nine years, mastering the art of navigating the minefield of male egos. "By then, she had already clearly developed this way of operating when she entered the room. You would know that she was in command, basically. When men would disagree with her ideas, would try to argue against her, or dismiss her or whatever, they were very quickly diminished in their attempt. She really didn't give them a chance, because she knew so much."

This forcefulness served her well, as another colleague noted. "She can meet the secretary-general, she can meet a head of state, she can meet the pope—anybody—and hold her own."

Juliana Di Tullio | Buenos Aires, Argentina

After wading through the layers of security in the lobby of La Can-cillería, I am waiting in the reception area to interview Foreign Re-lations Ambassador Juliana Di Tullio, a diplomat who, among other tasks, has the challenging assignment of making sure that Argentina complies with the Beijing Agreement on women's rights. In a few minutes some bombshell comes out and kisses me on one cheek—the Argentine greeting—and I think, *oh no, this can't be her.* The woman before me looks more like a soap opera star than a politica—tan and lean with long honey-brown hair, wearing a fitted pantsuit and skin-tight blouse sporting more cleavage than Pamela Lee Anderson. But something about her suffer-no-fools expression tells me that this is *la embajadora,* and I follow meekly as she sashays in backless stiletto san-dals to a corner suite. Watching the authoritative manner in which this woman plops down and tosses one arm over the back of a sofa seals any further debate about whether this is an intern or a cabinet member.

Her enormous office is filled with contemporary black leather fur-niture and provides a view out over the electric purple jacaranda trees of Plaza San Martin. I notice several portraits of Eva Peron displayed, along with a homespun cloth wall hanging of a woman with enor-mous hands; this last artifact seems out of character with everything else in the surprisingly masculine room.

When Juliana tells me her career history, the dichotomy makes sense: she was appointed to her political post as ambassador by President Néstor Kirchner; at thirty-five she is the youngest ambassador in the world. Then at his urging, she mounted a congressional campaign, and last month she was elected to the Argentine legislature.

While leading "an intense family life" with her husband of fourteen years and two adolescent children, performing her duties as ambassador, and running her congressional campaign, Juliana is busy completing a degree in clinical psychology. I assure her that a working knowledge of deviant behavior could only aid her political career.

Like other women I've interviewed here in Buenos Aires, she combines her political activism with her social conscience, her *feminismo*. "You can't separate the two," she emphasizes, and as the ambassador talks she waves her hands with characteristic Latin passion, puncturing the air with her index finger to make a point, then throwing both clenched fists back to her chest to show how issues affect her. When I ask why Argentina has such a strong movement of women in politics, she throws both hands up in the air and shouts: "It's Evita!"

Juliana is a Peronist; the figure of Eva Peron has been very important for her as it has for the whole women's movement. Because of Evita, Argentina passed female suffrage laws in 1947, allowing women the right to vote. "Her work in the nation had a focus on rights—not just for women, but social rights, rights for workers, with a focus on dignity. And this was fifty years ago!" In this struggle Eva Peron organized females in the public sphere, and this women's movement has remained her legacy to Argentina.

One example is the Madres de Plaza de Mayo, a group of mothers who circled the Plaza de Mayo each week in protest of the military dictatorship that ruled the nation from 1976 to 1983. With white scarves on their heads, they carried photographs of their husbands and children, loved ones who had been "disappeared" in the conflict. But the ambassador says these heroines paid the ultimate price for their activism. "Many were kidnapped, disappeared, and killed while the whole society looked the other way. But they persevered, and managed to help the dictatorship fall." During this period even much of the armed resistance to the junta was carried out by women, so much so that the dictatorship had special techniques of torture targeted just for them, like raping them in large groups and taking away their children. However, to this day the Madres continue to circle the plaza every Thursday, carrying their photographs as a reminder of Argentina's tragic past.

The legacy of Evita's activism can also be seen today in the Piqueteros movement that began in the 1990s, representing people who had been excluded from the labor market. About 70 percent of this group of roughly one million Argentines are women; through their picketing, their occupation of abandoned factories, and their battles with police during these struggles, they have forced attention to the plight of unemployed workers in Argentina. In 2001 when the economy crashed, women blocked the roads with their tractors to stop the agents of the banks from coming to take their property. After this physical offensive the women managed to change the law so that they had juridical protection from the creditors' appropriation of their homes. They take their *feminismo* seriously here in Argentina. I notice that like the contradiction of the word *feminismo* itself— the word for feminism is a masculine noun in Spanish—these activists manage to be intensely feminine physically, while their actions would be considered aggressively masculine.

And this is where Ambassador Di Tullio comes in. Ten years ago she worked with the National Women's Council during preparations for the Beijing Agreement, and today part of her official duties include making sure that Argentina is in compliance with its commitments made at the Beijing and Cairo Conferences. This latter agreement is a point of particular embarrassment for Argentine feminists, because in direct conflict with their wishes, Carlos Menem, who was president of Argentina in 1994, sent a conservative anti-reproductive rights delegation to Cairo, making this nation one of the few who refused to sign the program of action without reservations.

Today Juliana has seen that those reservations have been removed at subsequent follow-up meetings and that Argentina complies. This role would be a test of anyone's diplomatic skills, requiring her to negotiate with groups as diverse as the radical Piqueteros, the Madres de Plaza de Mayo, the Catholic Church, the labor unions, the political parties, President Kirchner, and the UN. And for the first time, at the 2005 Summit of the Americas, where leaders from the governments of North and South America met, gender was an issue on the agenda. And it was put there by Argentina.

Ambassador Di Tullio came from an activist family, which explains her success at such a young age. A few years after the fall of the dictatorship her mother founded Creative Hands, an NGO operating in the workers' neighborhoods on the outskirts of Buenos Aires where many residents—especially union laborers—disappeared. Her mom was a teacher, and she began by helping the mothers at the school who had lost their children or husbands. They wanted to create individual and collective histories of their neighborhoods; they used fabric as their medium, fashioning wall hangings from recycled cloth—making their art from stuff people had thrown away. Hence the humble reminder, the homespun creation hanging on the ambassador's wall today.

Juliana herself became an activist at twelve during the time of Argentina's military dictatorship. She remembers going out with her parents to hand out pamphlets, and now she's doing the same thing with her own children.

She confirms that she was raised and educated as a Catholic, and I ask how she squares her faith with her feminist viewpoint. "I grew up Catholic, but over the years I have become a rational person, and I don't agree today with much of what the Catholic Church says." She feels that throughout her personal and political history the church hierarchy has not played the role it should have. In fact, the total opposite. "For example, during the dictatorship they were not with the good guys." Her experience was different in that she was educated by liberal French nuns from the Sacred Heart order, a branch of the church that was very politically active in the 1970s. Unfortunately these activists disappeared during the dictatorship, but their remains have recently been discovered, solving the mystery. According to forensic experts, their captors tortured them, tied rocks to the nuns' bodies, and then shoved them out of an airplane into the Atlantic Ocean.

And yet, the ambassador's advice to women who are considering going into political life is: "First of all, to do it. Don't say no. But political life is very hard for women in general, especially to have your family accompany you in that life. However, women have a way in general of decentralizing themselves. They think about more than themselves—they also think about the collective project. The democratic life in Argentina is getting better and will continue to get better for women with more of us in politics."

I ask Juliana what made her decide to run for congress, as she so clearly enjoys her current position. "It was not a personal decision. President Kirchner asked me to run for office and that's a great recognition; it's like stepping up in the hierarchy. It's not easy for me to leave this office because it's in the executive power. This is the place where the more concrete things are done and you can see faster results. But if you're part of a collective project, you can't say no if the president asks you to run."

While pondering her political future, Juliana shared a phrase from Evita: "I will come back and I will be millions." That explains the whole strength of the women's movement. Evita came back in millions of women organized and fighting here in Argentina.

11   THE VATICAN

Hailing from 179 governments, thousands of women organized and prepared to fight as they shipped off to Cairo in 1994. In countries around the planet they had held strategy meetings, talked on the phone, met for lunch, and hosted fund-raisers. Then they simultaneously packed their suitcases with policy notes, tape recorders, business cards, and high heels. They were headed to join Nafis at her penultimate community-building experience, the biggest gathering of its kind ever held. It would be a watershed moment where they would have an opportunity to hold a dialogue with world powers, build a global consensus, and forge a historic pact: this is what women want, and they were asking their leaders to sign on the dotted line as a promise to deliver it. Some of the women attending the conference *were* those leaders, among them Prime Minister Benazir Bhutto from Pakistan and Prime Minister Gro Harlem Brundtland from Norway.

Nations from Argentina to Zimbabwe sent delegations, and during the first week of September, the twenty thousand attendees arrived at Cairo International Airport aboard a squadron of planes. UNFPA's executive director had even found funding to fly in her poorer sisters from Lithuania, Latvia, and Estonia—along with representatives from the other nations newly independent from the Soviet Union—so that their long-silent voices could be heard. In preparation for the conference Nafis herself visited one country that would be sending no women: Vatican City.

This Muslim had been granted the wish of millions of devout Catholics, a private audience with the pope. As Nafis packed her bags, she reviewed the memo she'd been given by his staff. They advised that in order to meet with His Holiness, she should cover her head, wear a garment with long sleeves, and the color should be black. She would have to abandon the power of the sari for this occasion, because it would show her bare arms. No problem. By this point Dr. Sadik was sixty-four years old, and after decades of meeting with heads of state, little rattled her. Besides, she'd learned to dress for the occasion at the start of her career when she would drive a Jeep into the mountains in Pakistan and talk to the tribal chiefs about their women. She carefully folded the long-sleeved tunic and pants of a shalwar kameez and placed them in her suitcase along with a scarf. However, crammed into the overfilled closets of her Manhattan apartment were no solid black garments, so the pope would have to cope with a print fabric. This, she felt, was not asking too much. After all, she hadn't made any special requests for what *he* should wear to their meeting.

As one always eager to maximize her efforts, Dr. Sadik flew into Rome, where she had scheduled additional appointments. She also met with one of her contacts from the Holy See, who advised the diplomat on what to expect in her conversation with the pope. He asked if UNFPA would be issuing a press release after the meeting, and when he confirmed that the Vatican did not plan to issue one, Nafis said, "In that case neither will we."

On the day of her audience she donned the shalwar kameez, placed a filmy scarf over her dark hair, and instructed the driver to deliver her to the Vatican. He took her as far as the car could go, to the gate of St. Peter's Square, the perfectly elliptical plaza outside the basilica, ringed by 140 statues of martyrs and saints. Here is where thousands of pilgrims gather to shout *Il Papa! Il Papa!* hoping their leader will make an appearance at the window of his study and wave down to them. In 1978 here in the *piazza* is where they had waited patiently for days, watching for a sign. And finally on October 16 it arrived—white smoke wafting toward heaven, announcing that Karol Wojtyla, the archbishop from Krakow, had been chosen as their new pontiff, and from this moment on he would be known as Pope John Paul II.

The 1,400-room compound of the Vatican Palaces would become his new home. And today, when Nafis arrived, she walked to the right of the ellipse, under the colonnades designed by Bernini, to another of the artist's creations, the Bronze Door. Stationed at the entrance were the Swiss Guards, a regiment assigned to protect the pontiff back in 1506. Today the Swiss Guards still wear their traditional uniform: gold-and-blue-striped pantaloons, a ruffled collar, and a silver helmet topped by red ostrich feathers. Nafis approached the sentinel who stood at attention with his white-gloved hand holding a halberd.

She was escorted on the long walk to the private papal chambers, her footsteps echoing on the marble floor. She found herself wanting to stop constantly to admire the antiques and priceless masterpieces lining the walls—the statues, frescoes, tapestries, and paintings—because she knew she'd never have the chance to see these objects again. When they arrived at the door to the pope's study, a photographer approached Nafis and said that at the end of their session, he would be called in to take her picture with His Holiness. The diplomat spent the next fifteen minutes waiting in the shadowy light of the wide corridor, rehearsing the plea she would make to one of the most influential mortals in this world—a man one billion Catholics consider a small step below God, their connection to the next world.

The stakes were unusually high for today's meeting, as Nafis knew the outcome of this conversation could affect the lives of all Catholics, both the ones living today and those not yet born. Even though Dr. Sadik negotiated with the powerful on a daily basis, today's meeting was different. The young Nafis had been educated in convent schools, and she steeled her nerves, fearful that the awe of being in the Holy Father's presence might unsettle the diplomat to the point where she'd botch her mission. What she couldn't have predicted was an even greater danger: meeting with the pope would ultimately lead to threats against her life.

The last international population summit had been held in Mexico City ten years ago. As Alex Marshall noted: "Just thinking back, things change so slowly over the years, and then you suddenly wake up and say—God!—it really is different, you know. These ten-year milestones really show how things have changed. If you look at the '74 Population Conference, which mentions women, sort of, but mostly it's mothers and fertility. And around paragraph 99 they say, it's a jolly good thing for women to be equal. Then I remember what happened in '84: a group of women waited until the men were busy electing conference presidents and vice presidents on the second day of the meeting, and then they slipped in several paragraphs on women, virtually while no one was looking."

However, it was also at this meeting that the feminists felt they lost a lot of the gains they'd made in the previous decade. They had watched Ronald Reagan's delegation enforce the Global Gag Rule that forbade them from mentioning abortion. Then they subsequently watched UNFPA and Planned Parenthood lose their U.S. funding. And this dichotomy illustrates the point made by many critics of the UN system: they spend their efforts talking and very little real change occurs. But perhaps because the change happens at such a glacial pace, it requires the long-range perspective of history to examine how the agency has affected the day-to-day lives of individuals, how their options differ from what they were fifty years ago.

One example of this evolution is the paragraph Alex Marshall referenced, and as a speechwriter, his realization of how words can ultimately shape lives. Up until this point most of the language in government policy documents had referred to women simply as "mothers." In this regard the Crusaders harken back to the same time-worn view of females that had so disgusted Nafis at the start of her career forty years ago: the notion that a woman's only real human value was that of a breeder designated to propagate the species. Leaders might feign interest in a woman's welfare insomuch as it affected her ability to give birth to a healthy baby, but once that factor was removed from the equation, very little concern was paid to their female constituents for their own sake—as individuals worthy of human rights equal to any male's. And some feminists felt demographers were primarily interested in probing into the wombs of females for statistical value, logging births like counting parts coming off an assembly line.

All the players had learned from past experience and had adapted their game plan accordingly before they came together in Cairo for the next round, where thousands of men would join their female colleagues to discuss the global agenda on population and development. As Alex Marshall remembered, the UNFPA team went in armed with a new strategy, one that would shift away from the paradigm of past diplomatic talks where "it was never women as women. They were always mothers, or wives, or units of production, or something like that . . . economic actors. Even when they talked about migrants, women were ignored. They were assumed to be traveling with men, and they weren't and they still don't. About half of women migrants travel alone. But a woman was never referred to just as a woman with feelings and desires and ambitions of her own—you know, separate from her family, separate from her father, her husband, or her kids."

In 1992 the Egyptian Boutros Boutros-Ghali became secretary-general of the United Nations, and it was due in part to his influence that the International Conference on Population and Development came to be located in his homeland. With fourteen million inhabitants, Cairo had always been considered as too great a security risk for such a sensitive venture that would bring many of the most important leaders in the world together in one spot, a situation that would provide a dream opportunity for terrorists to make their mark. However, with the same logic Nafis had used when she brought decision makers to Dhaka, Boutros-Ghali felt that navigating this crowded capital would bring home the notion of what the whole planet would look like if the current birthrate continued. And, of course, Nafis Sadik, a Muslim woman, would be the natural person to appoint as secretary-general of the conference to be held in a devoutly Islamic nation.

She had already begun her preparations for the population and development summit four years prior in 1990 by organizing a series of roundtable meetings on topics that she knew would be difficult, such as reproductive health, adolescent health, migration, and women's rights. The executive director brought in experts to tell her what they knew about these issues, and what the current evaluations and programs were. Then she conducted regional meetings around the globe with governments to garner their recommendations on the Program of Action.

At the time George Herbert Bush was president. "I met with Bush a couple of times, and I asked him to restore UNFPA's funding. He said, 'Oh you have to ask the USAID administrator. He's in charge of those policies.' Mr. Bush is very charming and all that, but it was disappointing that he was not willing to do anything on this, especially since I had met him a long time ago, I think in 1967 when I was visiting the States and looking at some population centers. Because in Pakistan we were going to set up a center, and the USAID people took me on a round of visits with some senators, and there was Bush and Ralph Yarborough and Hubert Humphrey. I was quite impressed with them. They were all supporters, because at that time, Pakistan was a favorite country of the U.S.'s and they were interested in our plans. So Bush's change was a real disappointment for all of us who had known him earlier. Mexico City was under Reagan. In fact, that era was the first change in the American policy toward UNFPA. So I believe Bush watched what the president did and saw that he was successful; as his vice president he was preparing to run then, and the conservative groups obviously were going to support him only if he stuck to the Reagan policies." What later added even more controversy to this topic was the public announcement by President Bush's wife, Barbara, that *she* supported a woman's right to choose abortion.

In spite of a lack of U.S. support, positive changes had occurred in family planning since the 1984 World Population Conference. Alfonso Lopez Juarez, former deputy of Mexfam, Mexico's pioneering family planning agency established in 1965, discussed one of Dr. Sadik's legacies to the field: "Her scheme offered a new approach, not to stay in the big clinics, but to go to the community and establish small medical *consultorios*. These centers aimed at her philosophy, that clinics should not only provide family planning, they should provide all services which are demanded by the community." They felt that if mothers brought in a sick child, and the clinic treated that child, the mother would grow to trust the staff and be more inclined to return for family planning. As a result Mexico opened over six thousand *consultorios* offering health care for men, women, and children, a product of a successful triumvirate, with Mexfam providing services, UNFPA offering technical support, and Japan donating funding—a truly international effort.

Another Mexfam program called Gente Joven joined this community-based innovation, a plan that offered services to the youth, because up until that point all UNFPA's efforts had been geared toward adults. In fact, Gente Joven would prove to be a controversial departure because it acknowledged that, with or without their parents' consent, many young people were sexually active, and in most regions offering them advice and services was illegal—seen as condoning their sexual activity. But in 1981, like something from a sinister melodrama, AIDS marched onto the global stage. Now Dr. Sadik realized that UNFPA's role had to expand; they could not just advise governments on how to steer teenagers away from pregnancy or venereal disease. Another priority shot to the top of their agenda: keeping these children alive. As a response to the crisis, UNFPA partnered with the Japanese Organization for International Cooperation in Family Planning to produce what many believe are the best series of sex education films ever made, an informational series geared to youth.

Nafis Sadik may have been executive director of the United Nations Population Fund, but she was now moving headlong into a polarized position against someone much more powerful than she: Pope John Paul II. In truth, the two leaders had much in common: they had both considered a career on the stage in their youth, and while they'd chosen other paths, these theatrical skills would serve them well. While John Paul's path might have been religion, he was a renowned diplomat, and both he and Nafis would extend their hand to the battered populace left when the Soviet Union crumbled beneath its own weight. They were both notorious for their athletic ability, their indefatigable energy, their nonstop global travels. Behind their backs colleagues complained about their dictatorial management styles and their penchant for surrounding themselves with their countrymen in the workplace.

However, the major irresolvable difference lay in the fact that the pontiff had made his bans against contraceptives and abortion one of the cornerstones of his papacy, and his conservative positions were well documented, all the way back to 1966, when he helped dissuade Pope Paul VI from lifting the papal ban on birth control. Of course, as a man who had devoted his life to religion, he surely felt that his missives were transmitting the will of God. On the other hand, even though his adversary was a woman of science, Dr. Sadik also felt like her position involved divine guidance. "As I was telling the Catholic Church in one of my discussions with the representatives of the Holy See in Manhattan—I know it may have sounded a bit pompous—but I think God has put me in this position to make sure that even girls without a good father like I had are still able to thrive, to achieve the things that I have. This is their *right*, and we should enable them to exercise this right. God has given me this responsibility, I believe."

These two world figures squared off in a replay of the omnipotence paradox: what happens when the immovable object meets the unstoppable force? In this case that force would definitely be Nafis, who sought to move the position of the papacy—a position that had not budged in two thousand years.

Everyone got into the debate, and it wasn't just the pope and the U.S. Republican Party that wanted to derail the family planning train. Even some women's groups criticized Dr. Sadik, saying that her emphasis on these issues felt coercive. Anti-women. She responded heatedly, "This was not true. We suggested to those groups that *they* should go and survey women to find out what they actually want, as we had done." The scientist still practiced what she preached, and collected data from a variety of sources: government agencies, NGOs, and other aid organizations such as USAID. UNFPA financed not only many services but also the analyses of these services.

"In the late 1980s when Daniel Ortega was still president of Nicaragua, and his brother, Humberto Ortega, was a cabinet minister, UNFPA went to visit. We were trying to have a national seminar on population policies, and in the morning we had a big meeting of national health officials. This minister gave me a long speech about how in his country women wanted to have more children, and they wanted to increase the population of Nicaragua, and blah, blah, blah.

"We knew there were a lot of younger teenage mothers in Nicaragua, and I quoted him the percentage. Most of them had become pregnant in spite of themselves. They really didn't want a baby at this point in their lives. The country's incidence of illegal abortion was growing, and we had collected some figures on the increasing number of girls that were resorting to abortion. We also had figures of maternal mortality, which were quite high, and infant mortality was high amongst young girls delivering. I said, 'You know there was a survey on attitudes of women and girls, and they said they didn't want to have the number of children they had, and that they didn't want to have pregnancies at this early age, but that they didn't receive the information they needed to prevent this situation. So the data we have seems to be somewhat different than yours.

"Our UNFPA Nicaragua representative was kicking me under the table, meaning I shouldn't be saying all this. But I went on. I just looked down and I thought, *now this minister is going to tell me to leave the country or something*. But at the end of my statement, all the women in the room started to clap. They were so happy. Then the minister said, 'But Dr. Sadik, you never let me finish my statement. It's because we know that women want these changes,' and here he turned around to look at the other women in the room, 'that we need your help!' It was the most hilarious encounter."

Dr. Sadik had tried to schedule an appointment with the Nicaraguan president but was told that he couldn't meet with the UNFPA team; however, his vice president would see them. "We went to visit the vice president in the afternoon, and all the while he was talking to me, he was looking at the door every two minutes. And I thought, such a rude man, he wants someone to come in and tell him that he's got a telephone call or something. Suddenly President Daniel Ortega bursts into the room wearing his fatigues. Our earlier conversation must have been reported to him by his brother. So Ortega decided he must meet me. He is quite interesting—very charismatic. I went through the same discussion with him, but he didn't make the mistake of saying that Nicaragua's women wanted more children."

In 1987 Nafis also went on a mission to El Salvador to meet with President José Napoleon Duarte. She had a half hour on his calendar, but he wound up taking her home for lunch, then canceling all his other appointments to spend the whole day with her, discussing ways that UNFPA could help him create a national population policy. He later attended Dr. Sadik's press conference and announced that his cabinet planned to approve her program for El Salvador, even though she felt certain the cabinet had made no such decision yet. "This shows that what the head of state wants can be done. But if he or she does not want it, then nothing moves. They are not totally democratic, some of these countries, even though they have an election process and all that. Rather the decision making is very much in the hands of the one individual at the top, and that is why we often work with heads of state. In fact, Salas used to organize meetings with the leaders' spouses, saying, 'She is the last person that talks to him every night, so if you can influence her to put a word into the husband's ear, maybe policies will change.'"

Unfortunately no spouses were available to help the Crusaders with their biggest challenge, because these gentlemen were not married. This situation was especially problematic in Latin America where the politicos kowtowed to the Catholic bishops because their endorsements held huge sway.

At the same time, the pope forbade the leftist members of the clergy from preaching liberation theology—sermons supportive of the socialist regimes in Latin America, like Ortega's, which tended to be more liberal and coincidentally more supportive of women's issues than the dictatorships they replaced were. His Holiness considered the positions of these priests as a challenge to Vatican control and said, "When they begin to use political means, they cease to be theologians." Of course, he did not follow his own advice as he conspired with President Ronald Reagan and the CIA to bring about the downfall of Communist control of Poland, his homeland.

Unbeknownst to the Latinos, the pope had entered into a secret deal with Reagan, who would apply military pressure against leftist regimes, secretly funneling arms to the Contras. The last thing the Great Communicator wanted was to see Marxist governments establish a toehold in his hemisphere.

And here is where Reagan sold his soul to the pontiff. In exchange for John Paul's influence in Latin America, to encourage Catholics to support the conservative dictatorships, the president agreed to promote the pope's agenda by choking off the funding to family planning and created the notorious Mexico City Gag Rule that forbade the utterance of the word "abortion." At the same time the Catholic conservatives were threatening the faithful from Mexico to Argentina with hellfire and damnation if they popped a birth control pill or filed for divorce.

Dr. Sadik logged hundreds of thousands of miles over the course of the four years she planned the International Conference on Population and Development, coordinating with religious leaders and governments around the world as she prepared for their confluence in Cairo. She gained a reputation for being willing to say anything—voicing the notions that needed to be said, but everyone else was afraid to utter. According to Stirling Scruggs, she told Yasser Arafat "that he had to do a lot better job of taking care of women's health and making sure they had safe deliveries. Some of his ministers met with us afterward and said, 'None of us would have ever talked to him the way Dr. Sadik talked to him.'" She discussed her agenda with China's President Jiang Zemin, President Yoweri Museveni from Uganda, President Hosni Mubarak from Egypt, and President Fidel Ramos from the Philippines, among others.

Jurgen Sackowski talked about the tricky business of going into negotiations at this level and observed his fearless leader in action when he accompanied her on many such missions. "The real question is not, do you get 8 percent approval or 12 percent. In both cases, you are lost. The real question is, do you get 48 percent or 52 percent. It just sort of flips to the other side. This is tricky in the UN. You try to avoid getting a negative decision, because if something is decided, it's cast in stone. If you feel you're not going to get your decision, then you try to avoid a vote and bring up the matter again in a better climate, rather than having it discussed and voted down in full. But the overall question is always, will you make it or not?

"The decisions that we get are normally from legislative bodies, so if it was discussed and the argumentation wasn't found strong enough—meaning there was hesitation to approve—that leaves a door open of coming back. Which you can do when dealing with group decisions. If you are dealing with an individual, eventually either you get it or you don't, making it a bigger risk if you are turned down. But mostly when I went with Nafis, it was actually to group decisions, where you can sense the tone of a negative situation and maneuver so that it doesn't close a door for good.

"Nafis was a master at this; she would argue her case and she would never say something totally unbelievable. In other words, there would always be a good rationale for us, and then eventually, she would say, 'Well, this is the way we see it, and we think this should be done. If I couldn't convince you, give me some time to rethink it and to be a little bit more nuanced the next time we meet.' Oh, no, she was good. No question about it."

At the heart of the dictum banning Catholics from using artificial contraception is a singularly miraculous and unique concept: the infallibility of the pope. In other words, the wisdom of a cleric with no wife or children—indeed, a man who by the vows he's taken promises to engage in no sexual activity of any kind—dominates the sex lives of a billion Catholics and controls any limit on the number of babies they will bring into this world, the number they will be honor-bound to feed, clothe, house, and educate.

After the invention of the Pill in 1960, Pope John XXXIII asked a commission of six nontheologians to study the questions of birth control and population. When John XXXIII died, the new pontiff, Pope Paul VI, enlarged the commission to seventy-two members including sixteen theologians, with an executive committee of sixteen bishops.

In spite of the large number of clergy present, the Birth Control Commission voted overwhelmingly in 1968 to allow Catholics to decide for themselves about the use of artificial contraception. All members of the commission, except four theologians, agreed with the report, and this includes the bishops present.

Pope Paul decided to ignore the vote and in direct contradiction wrote *Humanae Vitae* (*On Human Life*), banning artificial contraception and maintaining the status quo. Supporting him in this endeavor was his acolyte, the archbishop from Krakow, Karol Wojtyla, whose research and philosophical writing morphed into the majority of the text that would galvanize the church's position on contraceptives, issuing a mandate to be followed around the globe. The encyclical decreed that the devout follower should roll back the clock two thousand years and use the same birth control methods that had been available to the first Catholics in 30 AD.

What's mysterious is that Italy, the nation that surrounds the Vatican, has the planet's lowest birthrate, 1.2 children per mother, a fact that seems very hard to imagine using the only church-sanctioned birth control methods of rhythm and abstinence. In addition, in a country that is 90 percent Catholic, the Italians voted to legalize abortion.

The inescapable conclusion is that Catholics living within earshot of masses ringing forth from St. Peter's Square use a variety of contraceptives in quiet defiance of the papal ban. As do millions of other Catholics the world over. In fact, priests and nuns at a community level, those on the ground who see the daily suffering of their parishioners at close range, encourage couples to do just that. This fact was witnessed by Stirling Scruggs, who began his family planning career as a young man in the Peace Corps and remembered what happened when he arrived with his wife in the Philippines. "These people surrounded us on our first day in this village and asked, 'How can we stop having babies?' The women said, 'How can we have contact with our husbands and not get pregnant?' So we prepared ourselves, got some information and materials, and gave a few seminars in the barrio. There were a couple of Catholic missionaries around the province, and they would come to the barrios and hold services on a rotational basis. A Catholic priest heard about us—this couple going around in a Jeep to talk about contraceptives—and he got to know about our work. Eventually a couple of priests came to see my wife and me and said, would you help us tell other people about family planning—babies and mothers are dying. They have so many children, and there's so much malnutrition.

"Next, this priest started setting up these meetings for us all over the place, and we'd take off—he had me going out all over the place. And then the schools found out, and it went on and on. I became a missionary of sorts for them. But that story is not unique. It happens all over. In UNFPA we worked with the Catholic Church in many countries, but very quietly. Some church leaders—who could cause a lot of problems if they wanted to—just look the other way. Of course, other church leaders do cause a lot of problems."

But Dr. Sadik wanted this conflict to end, and she dreamed of the day when no Catholics would fear losing their mortal souls by secretly using birth control. Her desire was to unite the power of the United Nations and the Vatican, to combine the technical expertise of her organization with the unlimited persuasive powers of John Paul II in an unprecedented opportunity to change history. When this enormously popular pope had visited Mexico, he had drawn record crowds, estimated at five million people, so Nafis understood the sway he held with Catholics, particularly in Latin America. With his blessing, UNFPA could provide these women with access to contraceptives and aid them in determining the size of their families, choosing to have only the babies they wanted and could afford to feed. In a generation, she calculated that this diplomatic and religious union could redraw the global landscape, reduce the population, decrease malnutrition, disease, and poverty, and increase the empowerment of women.

To this end she and her staff had tried for several years to maintain a congenial relationship with the well-manned and powerful delegation of the Holy See in New York City. Even though they were philosophically on different sides of the fence, they'd laugh and drink coffee together—diplomatic foes, yet friends. That was until the preparatory committees began meeting as part of the buildup to the International Conference on Population and Development.

Like most massive organizations, the UN functions on a proprietary language of argot and acronyms, jargon inscrutable to the casual observer. To this end the International Conference on Population and Development became ICPD for short. The United Nations Fund for Population Activities was shortened to the United Nations Population Fund, and yet they mysteriously decided to keep the old acronym. And in the same vein, the preparatory committees, formal détentes that met to iron out differences amongst warring factions before a major summit meeting, became known as "PrepComs."

In the lead-up to the ICPD finale in Cairo, three official PrepComs were held at the UN in Manhattan. Unfortunately, during these preparatory meetings it quickly became clear that the coffee-drinking camaraderie between UNFPA and the Holy See had evaporated like steam from a cup. As Stirling Scruggs remembered, "The Holy See had people who would come to these negotiating sessions along with several priests. These were trained professionals from the outside, who were either hired or were volunteers. I worked with them, very smart people, who would influence governments, trying to do what they call 'put in brackets' words like 'reproductive health' or 'adolescent services' or 'condoms for HIV/AIDS.'"

Putting phrases in brackets meant that these passages were areas for future debate, that the Vatican was not willing to endorse phrases committing to the use of "condoms for HIV/AIDS." Nafis took on the church relentlessly, arguing that the UN's agenda should not be a religious one, that international agreements were universal, apolitical, and nonsectarian.

She and the UNFPA crew were not the only ones trying to persuade the Vatican to reconsider their position on artificial contraception and women's issues. Within the Catholic Church, the Jesuit order held a more liberal position, as did many of the bishops in Germany, the Netherlands, and the United States; one from the Congo, Ernest Kombo, even challenged the pope in person, expressing "horror at the discrimination and marginalization to which women are subjected in the church and society." In addition, UNESCO executive director Federico Mayor, a Spaniard and devout Catholic, met with John Paul himself. Mayor expressed his view that the decision to use birth control methods was not a matter for the Catholic Church to decide—rather, it should be the personal prerogative of the individual. He recounted the pontiff's reaction: "The pope was really concerned and interested, and I found more comprehension of the problem from him than from his entourage. I thought there was hope for a change, of a dialogue, because the pope had made very courageous decisions in the past.

"For example, I remember when UNESCO celebrated the centenary of Albert Einstein, and the pope joined in. I think that was a positive gesture on his part, because Einstein was a very big scientist, but also was a person that was not precisely in the Catholic Church. We were having a wonderful ceremony, and then suddenly, John Paul said, 'I beg your pardon for what the church did with Galileo Galilei. We were wrong. Our field involves the spiritual and your work is the scientific. And they are different—you are dealing with things that you can demonstrate and we are dealing with things that we cannot demonstrate.' I was sitting to his side and he told me, 'Finally it's not important for the church and for the Christian belief if the earth is round or not and if it's moving around the sun or not.'"

This analogy to the church's earlier insistence that the earth was the center of the universe would resurface again in the PrepCom debates. Never one to shy away from controversy, Jane Fonda spoke to a packed house at the UN, attacking the Vatican directly. As reported by the press, she commented on the Catholic Church's reluctance to face reality, comparing their denial of the need for contraceptives to their earlier denial that the Earth orbits the sun. "It was only last year that they officially admitted Galileo was right!"

Predictably, the Holy See had a fit over this cheeky sarcasm appearing in print and complained to Sadik and Boutros-Ghali directly. Nafis replied sweetly, "Well, there's not much you can do about the press now, is there?" The Vatican complained further that Nafis shouldn't be seen as supporting this type of coverage, and finally that UNFPA's name had appeared first. "Perhaps," Nafis reasoned, "that's because this is a population conference?"

The abortion dispute raged on from the private papal chambers to the U.S. Supreme Court's chambers, where the justices attempted to examine the ethics of abortion by answering the utmost question: When does life begin?

After the court ruled on *Roe v. Wade*, making abortion legal in the United States, the Religious Right was galvanized into action. In the States they began to acquire television and radio stations, a strategic move that built their base of power exponentially. Subsequently they became more successful electorally, with the result that in 1980, six pro-choice Democratic senators and seven congressmen were defeated.

Next came the terrorist tactics of the movement, as Operation Rescue engaged in dozens of illegal acts such as violent blockades, assaults on abortion center staff, trespassing and destruction of property, injecting noxious acid into buildings, and planting bombs to blow up facilities. Clinic workers were also harassed at home and on the phone. One caller phoned the mother of a doctor in the middle of the night and told her, falsely, that her son was dead. This was nothing compared to the murder of physicians who performed abortions. During the investigation of Operation Rescue activist Rachelle Shannon, who shot a doctor in Wichita, Kansas, "an anonymously written 113-page booklet called the 'Manual of the Army of God' . . . was found buried in Ms. Shannon's backyard—with instructions on how to make C-4 plastic explosives, homemade ammonium nitrate bombs like the one used in Oklahoma City, and the suggestion that doctors providing abortions should have their hands cut off."

In addition, the anti-abortion movement fought a secretive misinformation campaign against UNFPA on a global scale, and the elusive nature of this movement made it nearly impossible to fight. To these groups Nafis Sadik became "the archenemy."

Dr. Sadik recalled one of their strategies when she gave speeches: "They would try to pack the room. In one conference, I remember the room was packed with reporters who were not reporters, these anti-abortion enthusiasts who had gotten themselves accredited as press people, but were really all from right-to-life organizations. They started asking all sorts of provocative questions—I mean a lot of the time was spent on these questions—until the real reporters got wise to it and they said, 'Sorry, we want to ask Dr. Sadik questions,' and then they started to assert themselves."

Jill Sheffield, president and CEO of Family Care International, recalled seeing Nafis in action in one such situation. "We had been working in the area of maternal mortality reduction, because it's a terrible thing, every minute one woman dies during pregnancy, childbirth, or immediately after. And most of it's preventable. We had started the Safe Motherhood Interagency Group, and when that effort was ten years old, we had a big do at the World Bank in Washington. We asked each of the heads of agencies to come and speak, and to help us move forward in the world's agenda—women and their reproductive health, particularly motherhood. So, there we were in the World Bank with all these important guests—I mean there were several hundred people stuffed into this meeting room. And someone asked a provocative question of Nafis, about abortion. And I guess the situation then was pretty much as it is now, it's not a favorite topic. It's not even an issue that some people want you to work on, even to save women's lives. So, Nafis drew herself up to her entire height, and she was in this spectacular sari, and she said, 'You know, I don't think I've met anyone who on any given day would say, "Let's have sex, so that maybe I'll get pregnant, and then I can have an abortion." Do you know anybody who would say that? Now, what are you talking about?' And then she got right down to it and said, 'Let's just stop this.' In the World Bank. I thought my socks were going to drop."

When Nafis first joined UNFPA in 1971 UNICEF, the United Nations Children's Fund, existed as an organization geared to the betterment of children; they were joined in this noble effort by many Catholic charities. The agency promoted infant and child health, along with maternal health, and as such UNICEF saw providing birth control to women as part of their mission. Thus the procurement and distribution of contraceptives initially happened through this much larger and well-established agency, and they coordinated their efforts with their baby sister organization, UNFPA. A couple of years later UNICEF's secretariat announced they would no longer be involved with contraception, but didn't really give a reason. Nafis and company shrugged their collective shoulders and took steps to take on sole responsibility for distributing contraceptives to their global clientele. Only much later did Nafis discover the reason UNICEF had walked away from the birth control business: pressure from their Catholic partners—donors who controlled the purse strings for a sizeable number of the agency's operations.

The Catholic Church played a particularly strong role in the determination of political policies in Latin America. Politics are one thing, but when we are talking about laws that control a woman's right to contraception, a woman's right to abortion—even in cases where she has been raped, even in cases where the rapist is her father, even when she may die if she carries her father's baby to term—now the political has become the personal.

One such uncompromising ideology emanated from Carlos Menem, the president of Argentina, who presented one of the more polemic viewpoints amongst the disparate creeds influencing ICPD. Interestingly Menem had previously been a Muslim but had converted to Catholicism before he ran for president. In return for the support of the church, he promised to ban abortion. The delegates he sent to negotiate with UNFPA were conservative, to say the least. Nafis recounted a conversation with one of the president's men, an Argentine diplomat: "I said, 'In Argentina, their policies allow abortion for the life and health of the mother and in cases of rape.' And this man, in a meeting, said, 'Well, in my country, abortion is against the law, you know.' I said, 'No, that's not exactly true, because we have the study on abortion policy, and there are only a very few countries which don't allow abortion for any reason whatsoever. And there in Argentina, abortion is allowed for certain extreme reasons. He said, 'Oh, who made those laws?' I said, 'I don't know. Perhaps it was your parliament.' He said, 'Well, I don't care what our parliament says. I get my instructions from a higher being.'"

In spite of these disagreements, even before ICPD the UNFPA Crusaders were able to reach a consensus with all 179 governments on 90 percent of the document that would provide guidelines for the world's population and development. Dr. Nicolaas Biegman, who at the time was the Dutch ambassador to the UN, chaired the PrepCom meetings. He admitted that his interest in this job grew out of his fears of global overpopulation, rather than women's rights, but still he was impressed by the results of the negotiations. "I've never seen an organization that did so well as UNFPA did during the run up to Cairo, and Cairo itself."

He described the PrepCom process in effect: delegations made speeches presenting their views on the Program of Action, an accord by nations joining the UN consensus at the Cairo conference. Members' signatures denoted agreement to abide by a twenty-year plan for handling population, health, education, and development challenges. UNFPA's job was to support the proceedings with facts, noting participants' positions and objections. At the end of each day's session, the secretariat drafted a new document incorporating the revisions, and the next day the assembled would continue to move through the objections, working toward consensus. The infamous passages in brackets—the controversial portions that were the root of heated disagreements between the various factions—remained as items to be ironed out later.

Nafis, throughout her career, had developed numerous uniquely feminine traits in her management style: her community-building mania, her peculiar insistence that in each town she visited she look up old friends and colleagues, and yes, going shopping to get in touch with the local culture. Another goal during her travels was to be invited into someone's home and to meet with the local women's groups, which she felt had a different perspective on the issues than government, because the official legislative bodies were most likely male dominated and operating at a level so far removed from the daily life of most of the populace that they were incapable of connecting to the needs of ordinary people.

In this vein Nafis made a radical decision to include the NGOs in the negotiations at Cairo and invited them to join the PrepComs. This was not a unanimously popular decision; in fact, it was seen by some as tantamount to permitting the moneychangers into the temple. But Nafis was guided by her long-held philosophy that the reality of life on the ground should inform policy; she had seen the dangers of simply accepting a verdict that wafted down from the ruling body on high. Just as many Catholic priests and nuns at the community level held a much different perspective on the needs of their parishioners than their superiors in the Vatican possessed, so too did the workers dealing daily with teenage mothers have a different view of the issues affecting the girls' lives than did the nation's cabinet ministers, as in the Nicaragua example.

Nafis realized she had an opportunity *and* a challenge when the Soviet Union dissolved in 1991. She wanted these fledgling nations represented at Cairo because their women's reproductive health needs differed from much of the rest of the developing world. In comparison, these were poor regions with poor health care; and yet in contrast to their sisters in Latin America, they had a declining birthrate and relied solely on abortion for family planning. However, the perennially understaffed UNFPA didn't have the man- or womanpower to organize these groups, so Nafis turned to her old friend Werner Fornos and asked him to take on the project. Fornos recruited government and nongovernmental representation from all the former Eastern Bloc nations and wound up leading a 128-person delegation to Cairo, consisting of many freshly minted NGOs, most of which had never attended an international conference before.

In 1993 the U.S. participation in the global population debate took a radical tack with the swearing in of Bill Clinton. During the first week of his administration Nafis recollected that she was in a meeting with some donors when her secretary, Sheila Murdock, came into the room and whispered, "'The president is calling.' And I said to her, 'Which president is calling?' So Sheila, who's American, said, '*The* President. Of the United States.' I said 'President what?' I still didn't understand. I thought, what is she talking about? She said, 'The President of the U.S. Bill Clinton's office is calling, so can you take the call?' I told my guests, 'Oh, Mr. Clinton is calling me.' Of course he wasn't, it was his office calling, so they said, 'Oh, please take the call.'

"He invited me to the White House because Clinton was going to sign a bill lifting this Gag Rule. Could I come down tomorrow to witness the signing ceremony? I said yes, I would go there—it was quite exciting—and there was the signature ceremony, and he announced that he was going to re-fund UNFPA's programs. Then Gore came into the room and kissed me on both cheeks. I said, 'Oh hello, hello. I'm not sure what I'm supposed to call you now.' He said 'You can call me Al.' So I said 'No, I think I'll just say Mr. Vice President.'"

Nafis had met Mr. Vice President for the first time when he was Senator Gore. At that time he was already quite concerned about the environment; never one to miss an opportunity to promote her agenda, Nafis said, "Well, if you are interested in the environment, you have to know something about population and how the numbers affect the environment, especially in the world's poorer countries."

"Actually I am very interested. I don't know enough about it so I'm willing to be educated. But at this moment I have five minutes. What can you tell me in five minutes?"

"I speak very fast, so I can tell you a little bit. However, I don't think you can retain it, so we need to get some more time." Nafis gave him her five-minute spiel and then promised to send him more information. Senator Gore promised to study the issue on his own as well, and by the time they met again at a conference for parliamentarians in Moscow, he delivered a dramatic speech on the effects of population on the environment. He stacked chairs on the stage to demonstrate the historical perspective of population growth, with the chairs representing the earth's number of human beings. The display showed how many years it took for the total to reach one billion and demonstrated how that number was doubling at an alarming pace. It was clear to Nafis that he had done his homework.

As the Cairo conference drew near, the preparations heated up, and so did the tension. Consequently so did the press coverage. At an ecumenical meeting of different Christian denominations in Germany, Nafis was approached by *Die Zeit*, a newspaper published by former chancellor Helmut Schmidt. Accompanying her was Stirling Scruggs, then UNFPA's director of communication. "The reporter was asking Nafis all these questions, and really focused on the Vatican and on the church. The German bishops had come out and said that they supported many forms of family planning, including contraceptives and condoms. There had been a big brouhaha in the paper about that. And there were a lot of conflicts between the church and the Catholic bishops from Belgium and Germany. But the Germans were the most outspoken. And at one point this reporter said, 'Dr. Sadik, would you like to see the next pope be a German pope?' I said, 'Wait. You can't ask her those kinds of questions.' And I said to Nafis, 'You can't answer that.'

"They talked about something else for a couple of seconds and then she suddenly turned around and said, 'Yes.' I said, 'Nafis, come on.' And so, afterwards, I took this reporter out, I don't know how many beers I bought him, but I said, 'Come on, we don't need that. We don't need to take on the Vatican. It's hard enough working with these Latin American countries and some of the others, as it is.' So, a couple of days later, I see *Die Zeit*.

"Across the whole top page of the paper was a headline which basically said 'Sadik calls for German Pope,' and here is Nafis's picture, and here is the pope's picture. I told this reporter later, 'You owe me a lot of beer.'" Needless to say, this media drama would add fuel to the controversy with the Vatican in the coming months.

Nafis held ulterior motives for encouraging the NGOs to join the conference process. She knew that their position tended to be more radical, for several reasons: they were on the ground, dealing with women's problems on a one-to-one basis and had a clearer perspective of the challenges. They also were not elected officials and did not have to placate voters. This freed them from kowtowing to the Catholic Church in conservative countries such as in Latin America, where the church tended to be all-powerful. This also meant that on average, these groups, most of them devoted to women's issues and women's health, tended to be further left of center, closer on the political spectrum to Germany, the Netherlands, the Scandinavian countries, and Nafis herself.

One of the concepts being debated was the idea of "reproductive health" versus "family planning," terms that the casual observer might regard interchangeably, but at this policymaking level, they definitely were not interchangeable. The commitment to provide "family planning" meant basically that couples would have access to information and contraceptives, whereas "reproductive health" ensconced a much broader range of services—family planning, yes, but in addition, maternal care, preventative care such as pap smears and mammograms, and treatment for sexually transmitted diseases and HIV. In other words, "reproductive health" involved any issue connected to the female reproductive system.

Dr. Sadik held conferences with the Holy See in New York for over a year. "I wanted to accommodate their view and yet not exclude all the other points of view. In the Program of Action for Cairo, in the fertility and family planning section, we had wording which said that all safe and effective methods should be known about, and the choice should be left to the individual. This, I thought, would be acceptable to the Vatican, but of course, they have their point of view, which is no methods should be available to anyone, only abstinence or 'natural methods,' as they call them. I said, well, that could not be, because the whole world is not Catholic, and we have to base our recommendations on scientific fact, not on ideology or religion."

To further exacerbate their disagreement with UNFPA, the Vatican's representatives argued that condoms did not protect anyone from AIDS. Only abstinence did that. And another of their main objections to the Program of Action was that it proposed offering birth control services to married and unmarried women alike. Several heated exchanges took place during the debates. After Monsignor Diarmuid Martin said the UN's plan had no ethical or moral basis whatsoever, Chairman Fred Sai shot back, "You want people to believe that there is one set of ethics for the whole world! The people who are assembled here have their own ethical principles, and secondly this secretariat organized a group workshop on ethics and cultural issues just a few weeks before we met. That report is in the back of the room, for those who care to look at it."

After these meetings ended in gridlock, Nafis Sadik decided she would orchestrate a bold move: she would appeal to Pope John Paul II himself, who had been following events at the PrepComs closely. The meeting of these two leaders was chronicled by Carl Bernstein (who broke the Watergate story for the *Washington Post*) and Marco

Politi (who covered the papacy for twenty years for *La Repubblica* and *Il Messaggero*) in *His Holiness*, a biography of John Paul II. What Dr. Sadik didn't realize, they reported, was that from the get-go she held little chance of negotiating with the pontiff, who considered her "an angel of death."

And now here in the Vatican Palace, as she waited in the hallway to be admitted into the pope's private chambers, the diplomat reviewed her strategy. As any astute student of rhetoric would advise, she reasoned she'd begin her conversation with all the points that the UN and the Catholic Church share in common.

When Nafis entered the impressive *appartamento nobile*, full of Renaissance frescoes by Raphael, objets d'art, and oriental rugs, she found the Holy Father sitting alone behind a polished mahogany desk in the center of the room. He stood as she approached, and she noted his pale face, snowy hair, his white cassock and gold pectoral cross gleaming on his chest. The woman facing him wore a flowered shalwar kameez, a pink scarf framing her brown skin, with a glimpse of pavé diamond earrings peeking out.

The seventy-three-year-old cleric indicated that his guest should sit in the chair to the side of his desk, and this is when the doctor noted his trembling hand, that to steady it he had to grasp the furniture. She later commented to her Vatican contacts that their leader had Parkinson's Disease, an assertion that was vigorously denied.

Nafis recounted the conversation from her audience, noting that her carefully considered strategy was immediately derailed. Without preamble the pontiff began by saying, "This is the Year of the Family," a comment referencing the UN General Assembly's designation of 1994 as the International Year of the Family. He spoke to her in English, one of his eight languages. The diplomat thought he might be confused about who she was or why she'd come, although before she could respond, he continued, "but it seems to me the Year of the Disintegration of the Family."

"Yes, this is the Year of the Family, but I am the Secretary-General of the International Conference on Population and Development," she said, feeling uneasy about this antagonistic opening volley.

"Oh yes, I know that." He went on to express his concerns about the current discussions within the UN, that many governments felt that the whole idea of family had changed, and he advised they should remember that families—which consist of a father, mother, and children—are the basic unit of society.

Nafis responded, "As far as we are concerned, we are not dealing with that as an issue. We're just addressing population in relation to fertility, and fertility is defined very clearly. In any case, in our parts of the world, the family as a single unit doesn't really exist. We have very extended families, which creates a concept of the family being a support structure that looks after its members—those that are better off look after the other members of society." She still didn't think that there was any connection between the concept of population and his definition of the family, but obviously in his mind there was.

The pope was quite strong in his disapproval of the Program of Action, and he asked, "Why has UNFPA taken this approach, this individual rights approach?"

"What other approach can there be? Human rights are individual rights."

"Oh no, they should not be individual rights, they have to be couples' rights."

"Well, couples' rights can exist only if both members of the couple have an equal say in the decision making and especially in an area where the effect is basically on women. In many parts of the world, certainly women don't have equal rights in decision making. In fact, in many places they don't have the right to make choices for themselves at all. Decisions are made for them, and it's expected they will acquiesce to the wishes of their husband or family. So often their health and their life suffer."

But Karol Wojtyla was adamant. "No, it should be couples' rights and the couple should follow the natural, spiritual, and moral law."

"Well, whose moral and ethical laws should they be?"

"Oh, there is only one set of laws, and they should be followed by the UN."

"I don't think that can be, because in any case, how many Catholics do you think there are in the world?"

"As many Muslims as there are," he shot back.

"No, the purpose of my question was *not* how many Muslims or Catholics, but rather to say that most of the people in the world are not Roman Catholics. I mean there are 5.8 billion people, and one billion may be Catholic, but the rest are other religions. And all other religions are not opposed to family planning. How many Catholics do you think are following the teaching of the church on family planning?"

"They all do, except the materialistic societies of Europe and North America," he replied with obvious irritation.

"Also, I don't think that is correct. In my view, Latin America has the highest incidence of abortion and therefore, they are not following the teachings. They are resorting to abortions, so they are not using family planning, but they are doing something much worse for their health. Women resort to abortion because they don't want that pregnancy, and they are unable to protect themselves, not necessarily by using contraceptives, but also by denying men the right to have relations with them. Because they are not in control. Many times, men are drunk, or men are violent—there is a lot of sexual violence even in a woman's own home."

"Don't you think," the pontiff interjected, "that the irresponsible behavior of men is caused by women?" Nafis's jaw dropped in disbelief and she struggled to contain her anger. John Paul saw the look of shock on the diplomat's face and tried to change the subject, but she was not willing to let this comment go.

"Excuse me, I must respond to your statement about the behavior of men. In most of the developing countries men look on marital relations as their right and the women have to comply. Men come home drunk, have sexual relations with their wives, and the wives get pregnant. Or they get HIV without having any control over their partner's behavior and their own situation.

"Violence within the family, rape, in fact, is very common in our society. The most upsetting thing about all this is that only women suffer the consequences. Many women, you know, wind up abandoned. Latin America is full of abandoned families, full of women who are left as the heads of households, with children to look after, while the men go off and start another family somewhere else."

None of this changed John Paul's demeanor; instead, his pale blue eyes continued to stare at her coldly while he jumped to yet another topic. "Adolescents," he said, "they must only abstain. This education and services for adolescents is out of the question."

"Again, the objective of that section in the Program of Action is to promote the health of adolescents by choosing abstinence, but it doesn't say *only* abstinence, because many young people are sexually active. And as far as we're concerned, as development workers, we must protect the health of young people, regardless of what we think is moral or not moral, sanctioned by religion or not sanctioned. They have to be advised on how to protect their health. And it's like your own children, you might want them to behave a certain way and have a certain value system, but on the other hand if they do something, you try to help them. You can't condemn them. It's not for us to just sit in condemnation; we are trying our best to educate and help."

The pope also returned to Nafis's comment on her mission as a development worker, and challenged, "Who does more development work than the Catholic Church?"

"The Catholic Church does a lot. They have education and health. I, myself, went to a Catholic school. But in the area of family planning, the church doesn't do anything, and this is an area where women and infants and children suffer a lot because of the consequences of lack of information and services."

"That is not true. That is God's will." He suggested that if everyone followed the natural laws properly, then everything would be okay.

"We are certainly not promoting the disintegration of the family," Nafis responded, "because we want the family to be happy and healthy, and we want the parents to have the number of babies that they can actually look after, support, and feed, and not have children that they just use as labor, who are not educated, children who are abandoned or run away and wind up on the street. There's the problem of trafficking in children which grows out of poverty. So all these things come from the fact that parents have more offspring than they are able to look after. The church can do a great service if they promote responsible parenting."

"That's what we promote, responsible parenthood, which means natural methods of family planning. Because it is irresponsible to use scientific methods."

"Responsible means having the children you can afford, and that is what we are helping countries to do, to provide information and services so parents can have that number of children."

After forty-five minutes of this, Nafis realized that there was no way they were going to be in agreement on anything. About this time she learned her audience with John Paul had come to an end when he suddenly pressed a silver medallion into her palm and said, "God bless you and the people of Pakistan, and may God show you the right way."

"May God bless you, too, Your Holiness, and show you the right way, too." As the diplomat exited the pope's chambers, he did not summon the photographer to document their meeting.

During the PrepComs in Manhattan the first and second documents contained a small percentage of "bracketed" text, areas of the draft that were still under debate by member states. Primarily these sections contained language about educating adolescents, or the terms "reproductive health," which drew fire from conservative quarters, and "unsafe abortion," which the Vatican demanded be struck from the document.

The activity that followed this friction offers an example of how the inclusion of the NGOs changed the debate. A group from the International Women's Health Coalition, including its vice president, Adrienne Germain, decided to insert themselves into the drafting process in an attempt to influence the third and final version of the Program of Action that would go to ICPD. These activists lobbied heavily to join their government officials as part of their national delegations. As the negotiations were coming down to the wire before the September deadline for ICPD, according to Germain, "The governments were still very far from agreement. By that time I was on the U.S. Delegation for Cairo, and the International Women's Health Coalition was also at the same time helping our friends from other countries, mainly Asia, Africa, Latin America, get on their country delegations, so we had—at least in that third prep—about six to ten NGOs from countries of the south represented on their delegations. And in addition, the coalition was also helping to mobilize NGOs to come to New York as an NGO lobby. On top of the official delegations, these women's groups would be present in the balcony when the governments were negotiating the final document." Here she is referring to the process that allowed observers in the gallery to monitor the debate but be unable to participate in the proceedings on the floor, much like observing congressional proceedings on Capitol Hill. However, the NGO's presence would act as a powerful force, not only as fans cheering on their team—but they would be able to pass notes to the official delegations during the proceedings, lobby them outside the hall, and serve as witnesses to the views these emissaries attributed to their nation.

Adrienne Germain remembered the final meeting as they created the document that the secretariat would take to Cairo as the foundation for the Program of Action. "I think it was about eleven o'clock at night, but it could have even been later, because it was certainly dark outside, there was no doubt about that. The NGOs sit up in the balcony above the plenary floor, and there were not that many people left by this time, because it takes a lot of stamina to get through these meetings, and we used to try to rotate. Just two of us remained from the U.S. delegation.

"There came a moment when obviously most governments in the room were basically ready to sign off on a set of paragraphs—the chapter having to do with family planning, what is now Chapter 7. And the Vatican just was not willing to back off of its very narrow perspective about family planning. They had been obstreperous all the way along. Very, very difficult.

"In the context, you have to remember, Cairo was a conference about population and development. So their opening salvo always was, No. 1, that we should be talking about poverty reduction and alleviation, that is the development side—not population. No. 2, if we have to talk about population, the most we should talk about is natural family planning, but not contraception, and then just the way the Bush administration would later see abortion around every corner, the Vatican saw abortion in every word, somehow. You couldn't talk about anything to do with sex, or young people, or women's health without them seeing abortion hidden in it. They were driving us all crazy because this was a consensus process, and if any delegation didn't want to join the consensus, then they could hold up the whole process because generally in the UN they don't want to go for a vote on this kind of document. They want to have a consensus. And the Vatican is a single-minded, single-purpose member of the UN. They are hugely skilled at what they do; however, even they were getting desperate by this time, because we'd managed to get virtually all governments in the room to join the consensus, including the Islamic states—which the Holy See always wanted on their side. But the Islamic groups weren't joining them.

"We were discussing condoms at the time, as I recall, and suddenly we heard Renato Martino, an archbishop heading the Holy See's delegation, say if the African governments did not reconsider their position on this paragraph, and join their concern about condom usage, that the Vatican would have to reconsider their provision of health services in Sub-Saharan African countries. And then they reminded those countries that the church provides substantial health care in Sub-Saharan Africa—which is true—all their missionary health services, and so on.

"You know, literally, there was a gasp in the room. It was such a horrible thing for them to say. Now, years later, it might not sound so shocking, because the Vatican has been against condom use even in the context of HIV, but at the time, we were stunned. Imagine. Threatening the African countries to withdraw all basic health services just because the Vatican doesn't want the word 'condoms' in a paragraph about family planning."

Dr. Sadik was at the podium, and she leaned over to the chair and told him to take a five-minute break. As soon as she did this, pandemonium broke out on the plenary floor—and in the balcony, where the NGOs were already rising out of their seats to head down and join the fray. Martino, the Vatican delegate who had threatened to pull the church's African funding, "was a very short man, a very tiny person. Joan Dunlop, who was the president of the International Women's Health Coalition at that time, is a very tall, very present British woman. She's actually taller than most people in any situation, but the visual in this room of Joan towering over this tiny person from the Vatican, and then being joined and surrounded virtually entirely by women . . . and there's Nafis up at the podium . . . .the other government delegations were sort of making their way across the floor toward the Vatican, but then they realized they didn't have to go there because the NGOs sort of had it under control, and it was just . . . it was a wonderful moment."

That five-minute break wound up lasting about an hour and a half. "It wasn't Nafis's role to come down to the plenary floor, but she demonstrated her political sense that night to take a break. She knew Joan very well and knew if she gave her the opportunity, the NGOs would be on the case immediately. And what happened after that night . . . that was a real turning point before Cairo. From the next day forward, Nafis's message—not simply to the governments—but basically to the sort of standard friends of UNFPA in the NGO world, was to say, 'Look, the women have the moral high ground here. They are the ones who can confront the Vatican the best. It is their bodies and their lives that are at stake. So, we need to moderate what we're doing here, and the women need to take the lead. It was really a major moment."

When the meeting resumed, the Africans refused to ban condom use, and the Vatican had to back off. "The chair can give a delegation an option in a case like this, and say, 'Following consultations, would the delegation of the Holy See be willing to allow consensus to go forward and take an explanation of position?' It is some formality like that, and that's basically what happened, so we moved on."

But let none assume that this minor defeat represented the Vatican's skill level as debaters. Germain continued, "During the Prep-Com, they would prey on people's feelings, talking about 'killing babies' and how the church is 'saving people's lives,'—as though we weren't. In addition to that, when you negotiate, what you have to know, is that it's so intense, which is why when it goes on for so many hours, it's so terribly exhausting. And you must be extremely skilled. It's not just that you have to know your current document; you have to know all the precedents that came before. You get to a point where you just want to strangle people."

When Dr. Sadik strode out of the pontiff's chambers, she was in a fury. She flew back to New York and held an executive debriefing at the UN to apprise them of the situation. Years later she reflected on her shock at meeting the Holy Father. "I was disappointed, because while I know that the Vatican has very strong views on contraception, I expected more concern for the situation of women—especially poor women—around the world. And one of the things I was saying to John Paul was that the church can do a lot by condemning violence and recognizing that violence does take place, and to promote natural methods of birth control requires the cooperation of both members of the couple.

"I thought for a pope who has traveled around the world, he should be more in touch with the situation, because he's really visited all these countries. So, either, you know, he is totally disconnected from the real people, or the real people are not allowed to speak up."

After their meeting it was clear that the diplomat and the pope shared a mutual contempt for one another, and the battle lines were drawn. In spite of the Holy See's earlier statement that they would not issue a press release following Nafis's visit, His Holiness penned a six-page letter directed to the doctor herself and released it to the media immediately. Among his ten points, he opines that "every woman is equal in dignity to man." Later he goes on to add, "In the family which a woman establishes with her husband she enjoys the unique role and privilege of motherhood," and writes that "support should be given to programs which aim at decreasing maternal mortality, providing prenatal and perinatal care, meeting the nutritional needs of pregnant women and nursing mothers, and helping mothers themselves to provide health care for their infants." A doctrine that might as well have come out of the UNFPA play book, but John Paul had chosen not to play on the same team.

Many believe Pope John Paul's views on the role of women was firmly etched in his childhood, starting when he lost his own mother at eight, a woman whom he adored. As a boy growing up in an impoverished home, he had two options to a better life: the priesthood or the military. His father had chosen the latter, and fulfilling the dream of his mother, her youngest son chose the Catholic Church. But his vow of celibacy helped to typecast Eve's gender in Wojtyla's passion play, confining them to eternally act the part of

Mother, a part he extolled as "their mission to bring new life to the world." Or as one scholar noted, this was a man who had "consciously chosen to devote his life as a teenager and afterwards to the cult of the Virgin Mary."

The same compassion he devoted to the sick, dying, and downtrodden did not extend to any female who wanted to deviate outside of her role to propagate the species, or to any modern male who balked at supporting a brood that numbered in the double digits. This position on family planning, while personal to John Paul, mirrored the long-standing views of the Vatican, as expressed by Paul VI, who advised in a speech at the UN: "You must strive to multiply bread so that it suffices for the tables of mankind, and not, rather, favor an artificial control of birth, which would be irrational, in order to diminish the number of guests at the banquet of life."

In reality, outside the Vatican Palaces the banquet of life becomes less celebratory with an unchecked guest list. Dr. Sumner M. Kalian, a professor of pharmacology, summarized the inevitable outcome of unlimited births in devoutly Catholic Columbia: "Each child adds to the impossible financial burden of the family and to the despair of the mother. . . . The average mother goes through a progression of attempts to limit the size of her family. She starts with ineffective native forms of contraception and moves on to quack abortion, infanticide, frigidity, and all too often to suicide."

According to Carl Bernstein and Marco Politi, the pontiff's biographers, His Holiness took unprecedented action after meeting Nafis Sadik. He called for a gathering of the Vatican's 140 nuncios, his papal ambassadors from around the globe. "John Paul II had decided to declare his own state of war against the United Nations."

These nuncios did the bidding of their superior, a man who many forget is not only the religious leader of a billion Catholics, but who also serves as a head of state for the Vatican, a position that gives him a seat at the diplomatic bargaining table.

John Paul intended to disrupt the progress of Nafis's agenda in Cairo, her mission to provide women with access to birth control. "How can one fail to be disturbed by the fact that certain agencies are prepared to spend huge sums of money in order to spread ethically inadmissible means of contraception, while refusing to develop the great potential of natural family planning?" The "natural family planning" methods to which John Paul refers are, of course, the Vatican's cherished tactics that offer the faithful the same discipline the priesthood has embraced: abstinence. This includes the rhythm method, which is simply another form of abstinence practiced during the woman's fertility cycle—in other words, an opportunity to suppress sexual urges. Paul Ehrlich discusses the rhythm method in the *Population Bomb*: "Unfortunately, people who practice this method of contraception are commonly called 'parents.'"

According to the *New York Times*, Wojtyla's nuncios voted to oppose "a pervasive feminist influence at a forthcoming United Nations population conference, saying measures on abortion and women's rights sponsored by the United States reflected 'cultural imperialism.'" The cardinals "warned that the measures would legitimize 'abortion on demand, sexual promiscuity and distorted notions of the family.'" And this is the message they carried as they fanned out around the globe from Libya to Bolivia to sow dissent, bonding with unlikely allies like Islamic extremists to enlist them in the holy war they planned to wage at ICPD in Egypt. The *Times* noted that the Vatican felt "the future of humanity" was at stake. Thus they orchestrated a pincer movement marked by "the most vehement and concerted diplomatic campaign the Vatican has waged in recent years to influence international policy." And all this from a pope who had said of his Latin American clergy: "When they begin to use political means, they cease to be theologians."

While John Paul's actions might not be ones most would attribute to a theologian, this gauntlet thrown down against UNFPA represented a side to the pope not visible to the public. Dr. Anna-Teresa

Tymieniecka, his collaborator on volumes of philosophy, described the Karol Wojtyla she knew before he became pontiff: "People around him see the sweetest, (most modest) person. They never see this iron will behind it. . . . The work going on in his mind . . . His usual attitude is suavity. His iron will is exercised with suavity and enormous discretion."

His iron will included his dismissal of a report issued in June 1994 by the Vatican's own papal advisory body, the Pontifical Academy of Sciences, warning that refusal to deal with the issue of population growth could create "insoluble problems" for future generations. Ironically, as ICPD approached, a newspaper cartoon lampooned the situation, showing the pope speaking from his study to the masses in St. Peter's Square. The throng replied: "We know how to multiply, but where can we go forth to?"

That summer John Paul II even took on President Bill Clinton for his aggressive support of abortion rights and of UNFPA's Program of Action. When the two met on June 2, 1994, Clinton came away admitting that the two leaders had "genuine disagreements" that could not be bridged—the same conclusion Nafis had come to after her conversation with the pontiff. The U.S. envoy to the Vatican said, "the Pope has never expressed more anger about a position and an issue than he has on this UN document." John Paul's spokesman, Joaquin Navarro-Valls, next issued personal attacks in the press against Vice President Al Gore, accusing him of misrepresenting ICPD's intention on abortion. The Vatican representative claimed that the Cairo Conference threatened to become "a session called to sanction a current life style in minority circles of certain opulent societies." As the *New York Times* reported, "By attacking Vice President Gore and seeking to highlight inconsistencies in the American position, Mr. Navarro-Valls also seemed to be reaching to a wider audience in the Islamic world and the third world, seeking to win allies for the Vatican's cause by damaging the United States' credibility among those long used to questioning American intentions."

Surely, however, His Holiness could not have anticipated the reaction to his edict to stir up dissent against UNFPA as they all marched to Cairo, or that this edict would place Dr. Sadik's life in danger. Richard Snyder remembered attending a meeting at headquarters in Manhattan, shortly before ICPD. Senior UNFPA staff sat around the table listening to Mike McCann, head of UN security, somberly address Nafis: "He said, 'You know, we are very concerned for your safety. We have received all kinds of death threats against you. For the next several weeks your office and your whole operation are going to be inconvenienced because any piece of mail addressed to UNFPA is going to be checked by us. We are concerned about letter bombs. We are going to be screening virtually all your communications, and you're going to have to bear with us—we hope nothing happens, but we really do have concerns for your life.' When he finished, Dr. Sadik sat there and just laughed. She said, 'Well, you know, if they kill me, then I'll be a martyr for the cause, and it would undo everything that they want. Either way, I don't think I can lose this one!'"

Richard Snyder is not easily impressed, yet he was stunned by her reaction. "She's got guts. Oh yeah. I mean she's got *real* guts."

Even Nafis's sister, Chicky, was worried. "Before Cairo, Nafis said, 'People actually telephone me and say, don't take part in this Cairo Conference, because religious elements here are threatening you.' Of course the family didn't waste their breath trying to persuade her to stay home."

To further intensify the situation, it wasn't just Nafis Sadik who was being threatened. As Abubakar Dungus, another UNFPA colleague, remembered, "Just before the Cairo Conference, a lot of militant groups let it be known that they might kill some of the delegates coming to the conference—could be UN staff, NGOs, delegations, anybody could get it. They warned they'll kill people—of course, hoping to get publicity for their causes through the crime."

Now the Egyptian government grew progressively more concerned, as they were charged with hosting the conference and keeping the expected twenty thousand conference participants alive. This agitation by the Vatican turned up the heat on an increasingly tense political situation, as Mubarek, already a hunted man in his own country, saw Muslim fundamentalist groups respond to the assertions about ICPD—a diplomatic event that was clearly sanctioned by him. John Paul even went so far as to inform heads of state around the world, including Bill Clinton and Boutros Boutros-Ghali, that the UN's Program of Action might bring on "the moral decline of humanity." No small feat for an eight-day conference!

Next the U.S. government joined the fray, warning the Vatican to call off its disinformation campaign. The level of terrorist threats compelled U.S. security forces to operate on red alert, sending advance teams to plan escape routes out of the conference hall in case of a security emergency. The Clinton administration would be sending Vice President Al Gore to Cairo, along with other high-ranking officials, and they did not care to have them murdered or kidnapped.

Teresa Lanza | La Paz, Bolivia

Considering she's four foot nine, a mother of two, an attorney, and an activist, Teresa seems an unlikely person to conspire to stage a kidnapping. However, it was her role as an advocate for Católicas por el Derecho a Decidir (Catholics for the Right to Decide) that led her down this twisted path.

As Teresa Lanza sits against the picture windows of my hotel room, behind I see her red brick homes rise up the hills of La Paz to the blue November sky. As she recounts her story, I can tell she's a seasoned public speaker, poised and calm, no doubt a reflection of her legal career. Her Indian heritage is apparent in a slightly hooked nose, but her skin is light and unlined, belying her forty-eight years and the harrowing battles she has waged in Bolivian politics. Her sharp brown eyes scan my face intensely as we talk, looking for information, and occasionally her chubby childlike hand tucks a stray strand of straight auburn hair behind her ear.

"I wasn't a feminist my whole life," she admits. But today she puts her legal skills to work for an organization whose bedrock philosophy is a belief in the Catholic religion, yet the group firmly rejects the Vatican's mandate against contraception and abortion. She also admits that she's been called a traitor to her faith. "They say if you don't agree with the Catholic teachings why don't you just leave your church? And I say, no I don't want to leave my church. I am a Catholic; I was baptized in the church; I got married in the church; I was confirmed in the church; I live as a Catholic, and I am a good Catholic. I merely want some changes inside of my church. The hierarchy has to hear what Catholic women really think about their teachings. We are silently not adhering to their teachings, yet we feel we are not sinners. We feel that these issues have to change because they are killing women and they are destroying their health and their lives. So I am not going to leave my church. I am going to be Catholic until the day I die."

Teresa was raised in a liberal Catholic family but was educated in a Jewish school. "My parents were very Catholic, but they were always pro-choice, because they saw how abortion was constantly present in our lives in our own family. Maybe it shouldn't be, but it was.

"My parents were very young when they started their family—my mom was still in high school. I saw some photos of them when they got married, and my parents are small like me; in this picture my father and mother were sitting down and their legs didn't even touch the ground.

"They had three kids by the time they started college, six children total. My father was raised in a good middle-class family, and he worked so hard to support us. My mother has nine brothers and sisters, and she had to take care of her younger siblings and her own kids at the same time, while she studied and worked. They grew up in La Paz and lived here all their lives. I am very Bolivian," she proclaims proudly.

"I always say the number two is very important in my life. I was married twice, and from my first marriage I had two kids; my second husband had two kids, and I raised all four of them. My husband is a journalist, the vice director of *El Diario*, and he's studying law. I have two dogs. And last week I was elected the co-coordinator of the Latin American office of Catholics for the Right to Decide, a task I'll share with my colleague, who's a psychologist."

Her family thinks her work is important, and Teresa's husband supports her; when she travels he looks after the house, shops for groceries, and takes care of the whole family life. "He is my feminist husband."

Monica was an eleven-year-old who already had enough strikes against her. She was a slight, skinny child with learning disabilities. Then when her father raped her, the unthinkable happened: she learned that she was pregnant with his child. This nightmare gets worse, because in conservative Bolivia, where Catholicism is the official religion and the government pays the salaries of the priests and bishops, abortion is, of course, illegal. In desperation, Monica's mother turned to a local feminist NGO in her home city of Cochabamba, which in turn contacted Catholics for the Right to Decide, looking for help.

Enter the tiny warrior, Teresa Lanza—perhaps not much larger than the child she would help rescue—but a formidable opponent nonetheless. She went to the magistrate and presented the child's case to receive authorization for an abortion, which qualified on three counts: the pregnancy was a result of rape, of incest, and due to Monica's small size, her life could be at risk during delivery. Teresa cited the penal code, Article 266 allowing for abortion under extenuating circumstances, but the judge didn't know what Article 266 was, so the attorney had to educate him on its contents. Once she had finished presenting the case to the magistrate, he did write a court order requiring the public hospital in Cochabamba to perform an abortion.

During the proceedings, however, the press had gotten wind of the case and started to publicize it. Soon a firestorm of protest against the abortion ensued, and picketers surrounded the child's home, the NGO's offices, and the law offices of Monica's attorneys. "The right wing of the church and other evangelical pro-lifers started making a war against us and the mother of the girl, saying that Monica had to

A pseudonym has been used to protect "Monica's" privacy.

have the baby because God says so. So the doctors in Cochabamba said, 'No, we are not going to do the abortion. We don't care if the judge sent us a judicial order, because we are very moral and very Christian and very Catholic, and we are not going to kill a human being. Our ethics won't allow us to do this.'"

With the clock ticking, and Monica growing bigger every day, Teresa and the legal team returned to court to obtain an order to permit them to get an abortion anywhere. They found a physician in La Paz who agreed to perform the procedure, saying, "I'm a doctor and my first priority is the life of the girl. I don't care if they excommunicate me."

Teresa and her colleagues at Catholics for the Right to Decide found themselves working around the clock. They spoke with the media, the judges, the doctors, the nurses, and they raised money for the operation.

And then the moment came when they had to spirit Monica out of her home in Cochabamba and get her to the hospital, without the picketing circus of evangelicals catching on and disrupting the process—or worse still—following them in hot pursuit to the hospital in La Paz. The rescuers donned costumes to protect their identity and also disguised Monica and her mother; then they left the house undetected and delivered their eleven-year-old charge to the doctor for her abortion.

By now she was seventeen weeks pregnant, and the procedure had become a much greater risk for everyone involved. As the girl went into the operating room, Teresa, the devout Catholic, was praying to the Virgin Mary to help Monica survive the operation: "You are the only one who can save her now."

Today, after counseling, Monica is doing fine. Her parents divorced, and her father is serving a prison sentence.

Teresa recounted how at conferences she'd had many moments of illumination, namely realizing what Pope John Paul II was willing to do to prevail with his agenda. Her conclusion was, "I believe the UN should not allow the Holy See to participate as a government, because they don't have many elements required to be a country. But they are sitting in the UN as observers and are constantly telling the governments what to say, how to vote.

"Bolivia is a very poor country, we have very few policies that protect the poor, and our government agrees with the Vatican's teachings. They repeat like parrots what they hear from the church. I was in the Vatican—it's a palace! You can't write laws from a palace, from a wonderful place where there are no children suffering, where there are no women dying because of botched abortions, where there are no men starving because they don't have food to eat."

In 1994 Catholics for the Right to Decide planned to travel from Bolivia for ICPD, but the Holy See even approached the Egyptian government and asked them not to provide visas for the group. When I ask Teresa why the Vatican was so aggressively opposed to the NGO's work at these conferences, she says: "They were afraid, because Catholics for the Right to Decide were prepared to let the world know that Catholic women have the right to decide reproduction issues and sexual reproductive rights. They were afraid that the world would find out that Catholic women use contraception, that Catholic women get abortions, that Catholic men use condoms—even though they are still good Catholics, and not sinners, not immoral people."

But the women from Catholics for the Right to Decide persevered. They did obtain their visas from the Egyptian government, they organized their agenda, they raised the funds for their trip, they boarded the plane for Cairo, where they gave their presentation on Religious and Ethical Perspectives on Sexuality. At the conference itself, during the roll call for private caucuses, certain names were not recognized. The Catholics for the Right to Decide discovered that spies, members of a Catholic "right-to-life" group, had infiltrated their sessions. And the drama was just beginning.

(*top*) UN Secretary-General Boutros Boutros-Ghali standing next to Nafis in front of the Cairo International Conference Center during ICPD.

(*bottom*) The dais at ICPD; (*from left*) Joseph Chamie, Nafis, Boutros Boutros-Ghali, Hosni Mubarak.

(*top*) Nafis and Benazir Bhutto.

(*bottom*) Nafis with Al Gore in 1993.

ro, Egypt

(*top*) Nafis with NARAL president Nancy Keenan, Al Gore, and Bill Clinton in 1993.

(*bottom*) The dais at ICPD. (*From left*) Nafis, Al Gore,
Gro Harlem Brundtland, and Sonny Ramphal.

12   CAIRO

Over the course of the coming week, dignitaries from around the globe will be arriving for the International Conference on Population and Development, their limos gliding down a grand circular drive lined by palm trees and a colorful cornucopia of national flags. They will stop at the VIP entrance to the conference center, a sleek white circular building featuring arched windows—a design reminiscent of a space-aged Roman Coliseum. When the passengers exit their cars, they'll look out upon a wide expanse of green lawn and manicured trees. Peeking up above those treetops, they'll be able to see the point of a contemporary pyramid marking Anwar Sadat's grave—a poignant reminder of the risks those dignitaries will face when they enter this facility.

Egyptian president Sadat may have won the Nobel Peace Prize for his diplomatic efforts, but that didn't save him from dying in a pool of his own blood when terrorists machine-gunned him as he sat a short distance from this conference center, watching a military parade. In the reviewing stand alongside Sadat that day were the future secretary-general of the UN, Boutros Boutros-Ghali, and the man who would become the new president of Egypt before that day was done: Hosni Mubarak. Thirteen years later, as this Arab nation's head of state, he would be responsible for protecting twenty thousand dignitaries from violence by the same type of fundamentalists who had murdered Anwar Sadat.

So for Mubarak—who had served as a military man for three decades, who had been seated just to the right of Sadat and watched him die, who had himself escaped multiple assassination attempts in his lucky thirteen years as president—the importance of security during ICPD was a very real concern, not just another perfunctory item on his administrative checklist. With four thousand journalists in town and the eyes of the international community focused on Cairo, he did not want any deaths—least of all his.

Part of the president's strategy to prevent this was to station ten thousand armed troops around the city—circling the conference center, along the streets, at the airports—and to position soldiers and metal detectors at every hotel. A member of the U.S. delegation said the omnipresent security could border on the comical at times: "Our entire delegation and other invited guests spent one night on the Nile for dinner, a sort of relaxed evening. And ringing us on the river were police boats. They were just cruising around us, good and slow, making sure that nobody else came close." In the meantime the leader of the U.S. team, Tim Wirth, wore a bullet-proof vest under his suit jacket.

Stirling Scruggs, as one of the UNFPA spokespersons handling the conference, remembered being coached on what to do in case someone was killed or taken hostage. "The White House Advance Team and the Secret Service from the U.S. government came in and laid out this map to show me where the U.S. was involved and where the vice president's escape routes would be if there was an attack, or anything like that. There were fundamentalist threats against the U.S.—some of the dignitaries and Al Gore—but there were also threats concerning the issues." Gore, hobbling around on crutches after surgery to repair his Achilles tendon, had better hope he didn't' have to beat a hasty retreat on foot.

Interestingly, many members of the UNFPA team did not know

about these warnings, and years later Boutros-Ghali also declared that Nafis Sadik had never mentioned to him that she was a marked woman. But the tensions began to grow just before the conference opened when Muslim militants in the south completed the forth deadly attack in a week, killing two policemen. This news accompanied demonstrations in places like Manila, where Cardinal Jaime Sin and President Corazon Aquino burned drafts of the Program of Action in Rizal Park to protest the document's contents.

At ICPD Scruggs had the unenviable job of heading UNFPA public affairs. Before the meeting even began, he was called to give a press conference and showed up to find roughly 150 journalists waiting, most of them Arabs. "For the first question, a reporter held up a local conservative newspaper featuring a photo of two men in drag, one wearing a brunette wig, the other a blond wig, and it said something about 'Delegates arriving for the Cairo Conference.' Then they asked me, 'Since President Clinton was unable to create an all-homosexual military in the United States, it looks like the U.S. is trying to force that behavior on the world through its social policies.' And he asked for my comment.

"I said this conference hasn't anything to do with gay rights. I wanted to say, 'Although I wish it did,' but I didn't. And, then I got some other remarks like, 'There's a death threat for all gays coming to Cairo, and there's going to be people at the airport to turn them back.'"

In other countries fundamentalist groups were also busy, and various media outlets conveyed their disapproval of the Program of Action by encouraging their government officials to boycott the summit meeting. Much to Nafis's dismay, these scare tactics made an impact. UNFPA's Richard Snyder had the job of reading all the daily news releases at this time, and he remembered the coverage on one particularly famous speaker: "When Benazir Bhutto came to Cairo, all the traditional press in Pakistan was saying that she can go to Cairo, but she can never come back home again. There was a double entendre—they did mean it both ways. It was very clear that they meant that once an Islamic leader, especially a female Islamic leader, is tainted with the kinds of stuff going on in Cairo, you can never come back and lose that taint. It's kind of like being scarred for life, but it also had this innuendo in there that her life was in danger. It was very clear—and I know I wasn't reading into this—that a similar idea would apply to Dr. Sadik."

Bhutto had intended to back out at one point—no doubt capitulating to this pressure—but Nafis called and persuaded her to attend. She was not so successful with the prime ministers of Bangladesh and Turkey, both of whom were Muslim women, and although they did not admit it, the UNFPA leader felt that they had canceled at the last minute out of fear.

Dr. Sadik flew in three weeks prior to the conference opening, and as soon as she hit the tarmac, she was under the watchful eye of Mubarak. As she traveled throughout the capital, UN bodyguards sat in the car with her. Two others, holding automatic weapons, hung out the windows of her limo on either side; this dynamic was repeated by the Egyptian security in the lead car in the motorcade and the car to the rear. As she walked around the conference center she became a very popular woman indeed, followed by four men: one in the front, one on either side, and one to the rear. They searched the ladies' bathroom before they permitted her to enter; they accompanied her at lunch and sat at another table, with some staring at her throughout her meal while others scanned the perimeter; they monitored her conference command headquarters, which became a real nuisance as she was running this enormous event. "My office had two doors, one to enter and one to exit, and once I went out of the entrance door to look for some staff members. My security opened the door for something and when they found out that I wasn't there, they went crazy and shut everything down. They said, 'You can't do that, you have to leave from this door and we have to see that you're leaving.' I said, 'Well, obviously, you should have had somebody guarding the other door!'"

Under all the pressure, her speechwriter, Alex Marshall, recalled that his boss was acting edgy from the get-go. "She had a big assist at ICPD from Al Gore and others, from many, many people, but she was the person on the front line. I remember going into Cairo, she was sweating bullets because she was afraid she'd gone too far, you know. She thought the draft that was being presented to the conference was too extreme, pushing too much one way. And it wasn't really until the second or third day of the proceedings that she got her nerve back. She was very, very, very nervous in the early days of that conference—just tense, you know. With Nafis, though, she'd always have her game face on, and that is the face she wears most of the time you're with her."

One situation Nafis found particularly annoying was an announcement by the security team that forbade her from visiting the NGO Forum, the gathering of thousands of activists housed in a separate building. The security staff reasoned that with 4,200 attendees present at the forum alone, and no control over the clearances for those nongovernmental operatives, it would be too easy for one of these groups to be infiltrated by terrorists intent on wreaking havoc. Many of the participants had just assumed that they would have easy access to the main conference halls where the government officials would be debating issues. However, it was determined that only NGO members with special credentials could enter, and that number was roughly one in ten.

While Nafis may have been inconvenienced by her four body guards, Mubarak frequently traveled with ten times that number. So you can imagine the security melee on the opening day of ICPD, when on the stage simultaneously were the Egyptian president, the U.S. vice president, the secretary-general of the UN, the prince of Swaziland, the prime minister of Pakistan, the prime minister of Norway, and the ringmistress of the event herself, Nafis Sadik.

The ceremony was held in Cheops Auditorium, an impressive space holding 2,500 people. Behind the stage a cerulean blue backdrop featured an image of a pyramid, and inside it was a globe, interestingly a design quite similar to the back of the U.S. dollar bill. "The International Conference on Population and Development" was written in English above and Arabic below this image. The cabinetry of the speakers' area, painted a pale yellow, permitted the guests to face the audience while discreetly hiding their legs. The podium, decorated by the UN logo of a blue earth with a laurel wreath, had five microphones attached, so no one would miss a word.

The audience reinforced the notion that this was truly an international gathering, as in UN tradition the delegates assembled in native dress. The majority of them were male, donning the usual Western business suits; they were joined by many female colleagues who mimicked this tailored approach. But also present were Arabs, who floated through the corridors in flowing white *thawbs*, with their heads draped in the red-checked *ghutra* popular with Saudis; African women in wild print dresses with matching headgear; African men in *galabya* and skull caps; bearded muftis in dark robes and turbans; and clerics in black suits with white tabbed collars, stiffly starched.

UN Secretary-General Boutros Boutros-Ghali opened the gathering with his signature smooth-as-silk diplomatic flair, but he felt compelled to nod to the controversy that had cartwheeled through the press in the preceding months and consequently landed on his desk: "Clearly, these are extremely delicate questions, for, let us be quite frank about it, even behind the most technical problems we shall be called upon to discuss, choices by society can implicitly be discerned. And consequently, the fears, hesitations, and criticisms that have surrounded the preparations for this conference are understandable." He then suggested his "principles of conduct" for the proceedings: rigor, tolerance, and conscience.

Next up, President Mubarak, as the local host, welcomed the delegates and then talked of his own struggles with the dilemma they had all gathered to solve: "Egypt's population doubled in a quarter of a century. This problem has been exhausting development revenues and threatening standards of living, necessitating more services with limited resources. We could neither meet the growing aspirations of the people for a better life nor cope with a demographic growth rate that was the highest worldwide."

Nafis Sadik now stepped into the spotlight wearing a sky-blue sari color-coordinated to the setting; her dark hair was styled into a smooth chin-length pageboy. When she took the microphone, she began by recognizing the contributions of her staff. At this juncture, the voice of the woman with a reputation for being a hard-nosed authoritarian broke as she struggled to keep her emotions under control. But she continued in a positive and congratulatory tone, thanking the assembled for their preliminary efforts leading up to ICPD: "The result of all your work is a draft Program of Action that you will discuss and finalize in the days ahead. You have already agreed on nine-tenths of it." This wise diplomatic tactic gave the delegates pride in their accomplishment and a sense of ownership over the end result of the historic summit—motivations they would need in the long hours of gridlock that lie ahead.

Then Dr. Sadik directed her comments pointedly to the Pakistani prime minister seated to her left on the dais: "About Mrs. Bhutto, what can I say? You will be recognized by the world community for your courage and conviction. This is what leadership is all about." Chilling words to note, as in years to come Bhutto's courage and conviction would lead to her assassination.

From the moment the bell rang to start the conference the politicos came out swinging. Prime Minister Gro Brundtland from Norway, dressed in a hot pink suit and gold choker, talked about the need to decriminalize abortion because women should not be made to suffer for pregnancy, especially since they frequently got pregnant against their wishes. Years later, she recalled the reaction she received: "Maybe the speech that made the most headlines during the Cairo Conference was my speech. That was because I spoke out directly about the churches and the religions that placed themselves against the basic needs of women and their future. So, it became a big furor."

Al Gore, tan, fit, and—in spite of limping on crutches—looking every bit the "stud muffin" handle he had earned while campaigning, came appropriately dressed in an Uncle Sam ensemble of navy blue suit, red tie, and white shirt. He launched into a speech that would address the recent personal attacks made against him by the Vatican. "The United States Constitution guarantees every woman within our borders a right to choose an abortion, subject to limited and specific exceptions. We are committed to that principle. But let us take a false issue off the table: the United States does not seek to establish a new international right to abortion, and we do not believe that abortion should be encouraged as a method of family planning." The A-word had been mentioned exactly one time in the past population conference in 1984 . . . to eliminate it as an option for family planning. But it was already clear from the opening ceremony that the Mexico City Gag Rule had been feverishly rejected here in Cairo, and the talk of the town for the next eight days would be abortion, abortion, abortion.

Next up, ignoring her critics, Benazir Bhutto presented "a brilliant speech" that would be quoted in newspapers around the globe. She stood in front of the gathering looking more like an exotic intellectual queen than a politician, a classic beauty with enormous dark eyes hidden behind huge horn-rimmed spectacles, her upswept black hair draped in the white scarf she wore in deference to her traditional heritage. "I come before you as a woman, as a mother, and as a wife. I come before you as the democratically elected prime minister of a great Muslim nation—the Islamic Republic of Pakistan. I come before you as the leader of the ninth largest population on Earth." Seeming to address her fundamentalist detractors directly, she continued: "This conference must not be viewed by the teeming masses of the world as a universal social charter seeking to impose adultery, abortion, sex education and other such matters on individuals, societies and religions which have their own social ethos. . . . Leaders are elected to lead nations. Leaders are not elected to let a vocal narrow-minded minority dictate an agenda of backwardness." She went on, however, to make her reservations clear, a reflection of her divided loyalty between her progressive, feminist goals and the demands of her conservative constituency: "Regrettably, the Conference's document contains serious flaws in striking at the heart of a great many cultural values, in the North and in the South, in the mosque and in the church. In Pakistan, our response will doubtless be shaped by our belief in the eternal teachings of Islam," which as she added, "rejects abortion as a method of population planning."

Most sobering of all, though, Bhutto—like Mubarak—chose to discuss her own nation's challenges: "In Pakistan, in a period of 30 years—from 1951 to 1981—our population rose by 50 million. At present it is 126 million. By the year 2020, our population may be 243 million."

Mubarak's presence on the stage signaled his support of ICPD and what it stood for, once again pitting him against the Islamic radicals who had literally been gunning for him since the day they shot Sadat, and his vice president took office. Mubarak had always been a supporter of family planning, a smart fiscal move in a desert country that imports 66 percent of its food supply. The first lady, Suzanne Mubarak, also played a key role, as she had made issues of women's health a cornerstone of her agenda since her husband had become president. But the couple's position was in contrast to some of their other countrymen, such as the Islamic fundamentalist groups that had originally been opposed to ICPD and all it stood for—or what they thought it stood for.

After hearing the papal nuncios rail against the UN's proposed Program of Action, which the Catholic Church claimed "authorized abortion, homosexual relations, and free love," even Egypt's grand sheik of Al-Azhar University, Gad el-Haq Gad el-Haq, got into the act. He took the UN to task for promoting an agenda that was offensive to Islam—a statement that Nafis, the devout Muslim, had difficulty swallowing. And it was particularly annoying considering UNFPA had gone to the trouble of funding a major research study at Al-Azhar, which was published under the title *Family Planning in the Legacy of Islam*. The author gathered the views of leading Muslim theologians and jurists and came to the conclusion that "Islam has been endorsing contraception for fourteen hundred years."

One of Dr. Sadik's tasks when she flew in before the conference began was to try and resolve this conflict. "During '94, the Catholic Church convened some meetings of Islamic religious leaders at the Vatican. And they said, oh, they always had these meetings, but in fact, this was to try to get the muftis to be opposed to the Program of Action at Cairo. And they got some conservative groups to agree. Interestingly, none of them had read the Program of Action. They just went by what was told to them by the Catholic Church. Based on this information, many of them said attending the conference would be going against their religion, and so they condemned it. As a result we had to work very hard with all the Muslim countries to make sure that they attended." As if things weren't difficult enough, top Islamic scholars in Saudi Arabia concluded that policies proposed by the Program of Action would transform Islamic society into "one of disease-ridden sex perverts without morals" and called on all Muslims to boycott the conference.

"When I went to Cairo, there were headlines, newspapers in Arabic condemning the conference. So, I kept asking what were these newspapers saying, and they wouldn't tell me. I said, 'I have to know.' This was like ten days—or maybe two weeks—before the conference, and then they told me the strange headlines, that this was a conference that promoted sexual promiscuity, and free love, and blah, blah, blah. I don't even know where they got all those things from. So, I went to see the sheik of Al-Azhar, which is the leading Islamic university, because he was quoted in the press as having condemned the conference. So, I said, 'Why are you doing that? Have you read the Program of Action?' And he said no. So, I said, 'Then in that case how can you condemn it?' He said, 'Oh, well, the Vatican told us that this is what is in it, and we believe them because they were there in New York at the PrepComs.' So, I said, 'Yes, they were there . . . but, maybe you misunderstood them.' You know, I didn't want to say, well, maybe they were misrepresenting us. I said, 'Why don't you read the Program of Action yourself? Please, I'll send you a copy, there is one in Arabic.' Anyway, they did read it and then they said they didn't care for some of the terms being used, because in Arabic apparently they did not have the right meaning. But they realized that there was really nothing majorly objectionable in this document." Arab translators from Egypt and the UN resolved the issue, changing problematic language, and one more obstacle to consensus was out of the way.

After all the mudslinging in the press and the PrepComs, by the time the warring conservative and liberal factions arrived in Cairo, there was much bad blood between them. The Holy See delegation arrived en masse, with a highly experienced team of negotiators having memorized past international agreements, chapter and verse, and carrying the standard of Pope John Paul's ban on contraception, condoms, and abortion. But during the days ahead, it became clear that there was more at stake than family planning methods. As Nils Daulaire, a member of the U.S. delegation commented: "I think that this conference, as it evolved, became much more of a threat to the Vatican's view of the world and of women."

In Cairo an American named John Klink served as the Holy See's strategist. His credentials included representing the Catholic Church's interests on UNICEF's executive board. When describing this gentleman, Steven Sinding, who at the time headed the Population Sciences program at the Rockefeller Foundation, didn't mince words: "He is just a nasty piece of work." But he had to give credit where it was due. "Klink was very effective; in fact the whole Vatican delegation was very effective in working with other nations to create havoc. I mean Cairo succeeded despite enormous efforts on the part of the Vatican to create trouble in the UN system, which only takes one delegation to raise objections, to put brackets, as they call it, around language. You know once the language is bracketed, you can debate it endlessly, and it means that you have to sort of work for compromises. And so the Vatican made us spend untold hours in every PrepCom and at Cairo debating the language."

In the United Nations, Vatican City maintains permanent observer status, a designation that does not allow them to vote; and the governing body of the Holy See holds sovereignty over the state of Vatican City, with the pontiff maintaining the ultimate authority of a monarch. When Pope Paul VI went to the UN in 1965 to request permission to join, he drew "attention to the Vatican state as a protected zone or a space of freedom that permitted the church to preserve neutrality towards and distance from political events while devoting itself to its own tasks." However, at conferences like ICPD, the Vatican is granted equal voice—and vote—with all other nations, which means that while this sovereign state of a thousand residents may be tucked neatly within the city limits of Rome, and although it's one-eighth the size of Central Park in Manhattan, it wields an equal vote to the entire United States.

While many may have disagreed with the Holy See's positions, at the same time, their foes still commented with respect on their opponents' power; after all, the papacy antedates every political institution in the world. In fact, other than the UN, no other organization possessed tentacles that reached into every country. This access allowed the Vatican to call heads of state while the conference was in progress to complain about the positions their national delegations presented on the floor.

The old axiom about politics making strange bedfellows was never truer than it was in Cairo that September. "The Holy See had officers running around talking to various Latin countries. You could see it all happening in the conference room." And while they might be celibate, the clergy did attract some interesting partners to share

their political bed at the conference: Malta, Cote d'Ivoire, Honduras, Argentina, and the anti-abortion American NGOs. Some of the
Islamic nations chose to join the church's protest by shunning the
conference outright: Sudan, Lebanon, and Saudi Arabia.

While a legitimate case could be made for the alliance between
Catholic and Muslim conservatives, since Islam and the Roman
Catholic Church both oppose abortion for the most part, the Holy
See's mission to woo Islamic factions caused concern. The *Houston
Chronicle* reported, "The diplomatic campaign has begun to draw
criticism in some quarters, mainly Western governments fearing
that the Vatican is allying itself with radical Islamic forces backing
the overthrow of governments in the Islamic world." The Holy See
admitted that its envoys had held talks with officials in Iran and
Libya. But what really raised eyebrows was the announcement by
the Libyan news agency, JANA, that "Vatican diplomats were supporting Libya in efforts to resolve differences with Western governments over the bombing of the Pan Am jetliner over Lockerbie, Scot-
land in 1988." The pope even announced a "visit to war-torn Sarajevo
September 8 in a gesture of solidarity with the Muslim populations
there." The timing of John Paul's goodwill mission to Muslims did
not escape political analysts, who noted that it happened to land in
the middle of ICPD.

In Cairo, on the other side of the conflict, an equally strange mix
of bedfellows gathered in the liberal boudoir: the Scandinavians,
the Germans, the Dutch, and organizations like Population Connection, the Rotary Club, the Sierra Club (which maintained that
overpopulation was the number one danger to the environment),
and the Union of Concerned Scientists (a multinational organization containing 104 Nobel laureates). All were joined by Catholics
for a Free Choice, whose members Rome considered traitors to their
faith. In addition, most of the other 1,500 NGOs present joined this
rollicking party, where you could also find the literal bedfellows of
CNN mogul Ted Turner and his wife, movie star Jane Fonda. And

last but not least, enter the Americans—who had flip-flopped from being on the Vatican's team in the last go-round in Mexico City. The U.S. delegation contained such high-ranking politicos as Vice President Gore, Representative Patricia Schroeder, and former U.S. senator Tim Wirth. As the Catholic Church continued to rail against the U.S. delegation's support of legal abortion, one bishop called for "American Catholics to walk away from the Democratic Party."

Tim Wirth had served in the U.S. Senate before becoming undersecretary of global affairs for the Clinton administration and heading to Cairo, where he would put all his political acumen to the test. He remembered dealing with the ICPD crises daily: "We began for the first time to see the organized right wing from the United States. I'd never run into these organized right-to-life groups before, who were trying to disrupt these meetings. We had a big NGO meeting every day and then had a big press conference every day, and I had various members of the delegation handling these. Nobody had ever done that before. And you know there is a vulnerability that comes with that, because the right-to-life groups would come and pick out a few words they objected to, and attack you. They got pretty shrill—pretty shrill stuff came out. I hadn't seen them before, these groups, behaving in such an aggressive political way."

Unlike Wirth, Nafis was an old hand at dealing with the religious extremists and had developed techniques to handle her detractors. "I always treat everybody's question as the most serious question—and they really don't know how to react then, because they want me to be angry and respond. I pretend that when they talk about natural methods—and they say those birth control methods are the best, claiming that we were advocating all these unnatural things—I'd say, 'Well, that's part of life. When you get ill, you take unnatural things to heal you, but you do it for the greater good. So, I suppose, in that sense, yes, probably, abstinence is the most natural. But contraceptives are for the greater good to prevent someone who's anemic, or cannot afford to have another child for whatever reason, from getting pregnant—rather than be forced to do something after she's pregnant.' At this point they usually get very upset, and then they start on ethics, on values. Then my response is, 'Ethics and values are everybody's personal business. So if your value says you should not use contraceptives, well, then that's what you should do. But I think some values can't be imposed on other people and certainly not in the UN. So long as it's within the internationally accepted principles, we will support it, and we support programs that are based on evidence and science.' Then they argue, 'But science has often been wrong,' to which I respond, 'Until it's proven wrong, you have to believe that science.' I think the more questions they ask and you just reply to them rationally, they get really frustrated, because they want to show you in a bad light. So it's important not to give in to your temper."

Meanwhile Dr. Sadik sat at the podium each day as secretary-general of the conference, shaping the debate between the eleven thousand delegates. She was joined in the hard work of running the conference by Dr. Fred Sai, a Ghanaian gynecologist who had served as president of International Planned Parenthood and as population consultant to the World Bank; he had also previously chaired the PrepComs in New York, so he was well versed in all the issues. The Dutch ambassador to the UN, Nicolaas Biegman, ventured to Cairo as well, in a reprise of his PrepCom role, as did UNFPA staffer Jyoti Singh, as the executive coordinator of ICPD. As the days wore on, they listened to 249 speeches on the plenary floor, from all manner of participants seeking to shift the debate in their favor.

Steven Sinding, on the U.S. delegation noted: "On June 29, 1994, Tim Wirth arranged a really remarkable event in Washington in the run-up to Cairo. It was the meeting of the U.S. delegation with a huge cross-section of different groups and individuals from American society: academics, journalists, business people, labor leaders, political figures from across the spectrum. It was a symposium held at the National Academy of Sciences, and it was really an opportunity for the U.S. delegation to present its ideas about the position it would take at Cairo and to get the responses and reactions from this broad cross-section. It was Tim Wirth using his political instincts to reach out and to make people feel part of the process."

All of this "civil society" participation was new, something that had not been done with UN conferences in the past, including the enormous participation of the NGOs in the drafting process. Prior to Cairo this approach had been seen as too messy, less preferable to the status quo of having meetings with government officials behind closed doors.

Steven Sinding and all the American liberals felt enormous relief at being able to head to Cairo sans the cloak of shame they had worn to previous conferences. "From 1984 to 1992 we have the Global Gag Rule in effect, so I would go to the general national meeting from Mexico City onward, representing the U.S. government, and feeling really despondent—as a population person and as a reproductive health professional, ashamed of my government's position. But the first thing Clinton did when he took office was to throw out that Mexico City Gag Rule and refund UNFPA and IPPF [International Planned Parenthood Federation]. At the third PrepCom, the last one before Cairo, Tim Wirth gave a speech on behalf of the U.S. delegation. It was a memorable, inspiring speech, and I was sitting behind Tim as he was delivering it, and tears came to my eyes . . . I mean I was suddenly proud again to be an American in this field, and I can't describe to you the pride I felt in our government . . . at the words Tim was uttering."

The whole forty-five-member U.S. delegation made a serious impact on the outcome of ICPD, a fact made possible for the first time in years because all the stars were in alignment for the liberals, meaning the executive branch and both houses of Congress were in favor of the UN's goals. Dr. Fred Sai, who chaired the Main Committee in charge of drafting the program, commented on this. "Tim and the Americans played the kind of role that you would like to see a powerful nation play, that is to underplay power and use persuasion instead."

But more importantly the Americans worked as a unit to support

UNFPA. Wirth noted, "Our job was to try to help to knock down all the barriers that existed politically regarding a consensus, and so I met with Nafis every day to discuss all the problems that existed that we could have an impact on. Also Nafis and I worked very closely with the host country, with Egypt and Maher Mahran, the doctor who was in charge of the family welfare program there. But Mrs. Mubarak really called a lot of the shots."

Probably one of the most important things that only the super-power nation could do was a little financial arm-twisting. Before the conference even began, Wirth enlisted all the donor countries and insisted that they show a real commitment by agreeing to what amount of resources they'd provide. During Cairo he met with the Germans to encourage them to contribute more funding, and he elicited monetary commitments from Japan, the Netherlands, Great Britain, and the United States itself.

Arguably the most flamboyant member of the U.S. delegation arrived in the personage of Bella Abzug, who at this time ran WEDO, the Women's Environment and Development Organization. One of her staff members recalled flying into Egypt for ICPD with Ms. Abzug: "At the time of the Cairo Conference I traveled with Bella on the plane and I carried her hat box. A colleague of mine said that from Bella's perspective there were two kinds of people in the world—people from whom she wanted something, or people who were her assistants. And no matter where you might be in the world, if you were moving with her, you were in the assistant category."

Heading into Cairo, her hat boxes stowed in the overhead bin, Abzug was seventy-four years old. As Nafis had developed the power of the sari, Bella had adopted the power of the hat, which brought her attention, respect, and recognition. Where Nafis had overcome heart disease, Bella had survived breast cancer. A former civil rights attorney, she had also served in the U.S. Congress, run an unsuccessful New York City mayoral campaign, and had settled into her latest political incarnation when she cofounded WEDO.

Back in the United States, Nafis had set out to woo Bella into becoming a collaborator, because initially WEDO was not going to support UNFPA's agenda. As Alex Marshall remembered: "At some point in the run-up to ICPD, the feminists seemed to be on a collision course with the process leading to Cairo. Some of the feminists thought that what was going on was a male-driven, population-control campaign, a means of controlling women's fertility and controlling their bodies, and therefore it was a demographic thing, it had nothing to do with women's well-being, a line you would hear often in the '70s, and to some extent in the '80s.

"Bella and her delegation came to see Nafis, and they came in armed for battle. But they came out like lambs. She convinced them that she herself had been fighting this lone battle against the population establishment to steer family planning away from a paradigm where women were merely pawns in a numbers game. She pretty much won them over, but more than that, it was a personal thing between the two women. Nafis and Bella Abzug had a very strange and beautiful relationship."

Abzug became a formidable ally because she was a strong voice amongst the coalition of women's organizations, and they were influential in Washington. It had been a crafty maneuver on Nafis's part to co-opt this seasoned politico into her conspiracy because, as one colleague put it, "Bella remembered the power of caucusing in Congress, and so she brought that experience and that power from there to the global community looking at women's issues." Abzug organized an NGO meeting every day and invited government delegations to speak to them, an equal forum for everyone to express views. The Women's Caucus also invited Vatican representatives to attend and answer questions.

Nafis's commitment to having the NGOs at Cairo is well documented, along with the fact that she went to great lengths to find the funding for organizations that wanted to attend. However, Steve Sinding tells the story of how UNFPA's executive director decided to include these groups: "Nafis didn't want the NGOs playing a major role at the conference, certainly not a decisive role. She recognized there was going to be a need to have some kind of an NGO event, but she wanted it to be very low-key, far away from the conference, and preferably at a different time. And she was very much under the influence of her staff in that opinion. At the same time, the women's health movement was gaining momentum and was absolutely determined to have an impact on that conference. And some of the leaders of that movement knew that I was very close to Nafis at the time because I was at the Rockefeller Foundation in New York. So these NGO leaders—Joan Dunlop and Adrienne Germain from the International Women's Health Coalition and Carmen Barosso from the MacArthur Foundation, among them—came to me and said, 'Do you think that you could get Nafis to agree to meet with us so that we could talk about these issues?' So I called her and I said the feminists really want to talk to you about the role of the NGOs in the process. And Carmen hosted the meeting in Chicago. Nafis agreed to go.

"So that meeting occurred, and it changed Nafis's mind. I mean she completely did a 180-degree turnaround and decided then and there that she needed to open Cairo up. I think what persuaded her was the realization that if she didn't, she stood to lose a great deal more than she would gain, because she would lose the support of all of those groups, and they were powerful enough to make real trouble. And she didn't want that. So from that moment on, it became inevitable that the NGOs would have a real impact on Cairo."

One of the ways they made an impact was lobbying delegates on the floor, as Jill Sheffield, an NGO representative, noted about her organization. "We had a lot of contacts because of this group of 117 countries that we'd mobilized, and a lot of them, in fact, were government people. And they were from every region—countries in Africa, Asia, Latin America, and the Caribbean. We had lists of names—government officials, women, men, Europeans, it didn't matter. And unfortunately for them, we knew where they were all staying," she laughs.

Once Nafis was on board with the NGO plan, she found money from government donors and foundations to help fund their travel expenses so they could attend. She also told them that they should attend the PrepComs "because just coming to the conference and having a meeting of their own is not contributing." She explained, "You really have to come to participate. And they said to me, how are you going to enable us to participate? So, I just decided as the secretary-general of the conference that I would invite them to come and sit in the gallery, which had never been done before. Then during the PrepComs, whenever they agreed with something, they would clap, and when some government said something they disliked, they would hiss. And the Vatican came to complain to me that this is not right, we are speaking as a state. And I said, 'I am not controlling them. I wish I had that kind of controlling power—I could have done so much more with that power.'"

Occasionally Dr. Sadik made an intervention on an issue to which she was really committed. In one such instance, discussing the fact that about two hundred thousand women die each year from the complications of illegal abortion, she said: "If you want to reduce maternal mortality, you have to address unsafe abortion. And while I'm not saying how or what you should do, you can't pretend that it doesn't exist, and sweep it out of the Program of Action—or else you have to change the objective to say that you don't really care about the health of women. You don't really care whether maternal mortality is reduced. You really just want to make sure that women do what they're told to do. Or you think that women who do not agree with your values should be condemned." At this point the NGOs seated in the gallery burst into applause.

Cairo's sobriquet as Umm al-Dunya, "mother of the world," marked the capital as a fitting place for a conference on women's reproductive rights. In fact, before Cairo was a Muslim city, it was a Christian city, and for over two thousand years before that, since the time of Ancient Egypt, this region fell under the sway of the goddess Isis, the divine ruler of motherhood and fertility. Many scholars even believe that worship of the Virgin Mary was the early Catholics' attempt to court followers of Isis.

Today, on the west side of Cairo bordering the desert, still lie the pyramids built during the time when the goddess's cult thrived. As one travels east through the city and crosses the Nile—the physical giver of all life in Egypt—one will witness yards of black fabric flowing gracefully as women in *hajib* cross the streets clogged by donkey carts and cars. The nimble pedestrians weave through the morass of traffic, past ancient monuments and skyscrapers; some of them will head to Al-Azhar University, Islam's oldest and most prestigious center of learning, which today allows females to attend classes, albeit in a separate facility from their male counterparts. Further east toward the airport on the outskirts of the metropolis are the domes and minarets of the university's modern campus. And across Nasser Road from the madrasa is the Cairo International Conference Center.

Inside this compound thousands of females have gathered to voice their opinion on the issues of population and development, a gathering unparalleled for its sheer size, scope, and diversity. They will witness something happen here during these hot September days, a sort of germination of the seeds that have been sown over the past couple of decades, seeds that were painfully slow to unfurl and blossom to full flower.

Whereas in 1971 Nafis was once the lone she-wolf at the UN, more and more females have entered the diplomatic corps, parliament, and even taken the top spot as presidents and prime ministers. But the arrival of the NGOs in Cairo in 1994, bringing 4,200 activists, the vast majority of them women, tipped the balance of power. In fact, never before had so many women participated in policymaking. These groups had formed a sisterhood as they caravanned around the globe to summit meetings, until the Women's Caucus grew into a force, a governing force that knew no boundaries nor national ties. Their tie was gender, and they were not fighting over land, money, or oil. Rather, the women were fighting simply for the power to control their own destiny, and with that mantra in mind, they functioned together like a well-greased machine. The assembled contributed their individual areas of expertise and helped to draft language into the Program of Action by presenting their ideas to government delegations for presentation on the floor.

Jill Sheffield, who represented Family Care International at the conference, remembered: "There was a big gulf between the gallery and the floor. But the fact was that if you had friends on the floor, you could get notes to them. You could capture them at coffee and water breaks and all sorts of things. So that was easy to do. It was frankly wonderful, because we had the luxury of going between the government negotiations and the NGO Forum, which was really interesting and lively. It was just a hot walk between the two buildings."

The veteran activists who attended tutored the virgins, as some of the groups had entered the international field for the first time. Indeed, a number of participants had never left their home country before boarding the plane to Cairo.

Dr. Sadik had always been a firm believer in the power of community to solve problems. But two female researchers have discovered that when a woman is under stress—unlike the usual male response of fight or flight—a woman's body releases the hormone oxytocin, which encourages her to tend children or gather with other women. This tending and befriending behavior in turn releases more oxytocin, which has a calming effect. Apparently females have an evolutionary response to crisis that compels them to bond together.

From its conception, Nafis knew that she wanted her ultimate community-building experience, the third World Population Conference, to be vastly different from its predecessors, to encompass all that she had learned in her forty years in the field. Since she took over as executive director of UNFPA in 1987, after Bucharest and Mexico City, this would be the first opportunity for the doctor to make her mark.

Yet it would take years for her vision of this conference to emerge from its primal ooze, and Steve Sinding takes part of the credit for influencing her ideas on the philosophy behind ICPD. "A year before the PrepComs started, International Planned Parenthood Federation was celebrating its fortieth anniversary. This period, 1991–92, was one of intense conflict between the feminists and the traditionalists, among whom I was certainly one, as was Nafis. We were basically committed to existing population policies and family planning programs that believed that demographic targets were the right way to go. There was really a very, very intensive struggle going on. I was unsympathetic with the feminists' view because I thought that there was a real danger of throwing the baby out with the bath water if they were so determined to get rid of population policies—since they believed those led to coercive programs. I was afraid they would demolish what was a very effective movement, and I didn't want that to happen." Sinding was not alone in his concerns, as the defenders of traditional family planning pointed out that their methods were a known commodity, having already reduced the world's population by four hundred million.

"So I was really struggling intellectually with what might be done to build a bridge or define common ground between the two positions. And I finally came up with something, an idea that's often called 'the unmet need for contraception.' This is a measure we have from the demographic and health surveys in several countries, answering how many women wish to limit their fertility, either to terminate childbearing or to space the next birth. In other words, who would use contraception if it were available to them, but they were not using it? I looked at the level of unmet need and asked if we could satisfy all the need that was there, what level of contraceptive use would you have compared with the targets that the countries had set for their demographic goals? We have that information for seventeen countries, big ones—Nigeria, China, Indonesia, India—countries that had demographic goals. And we did the analysis and discovered that in all but one, satisfying unmet need would produce a higher level of contraceptive use than the targets the governments had set.

"At IPPF's Fortieth Anniversary Conference in New Delhi in 1992, I presented that paper with a conclusion and recommendation at the end: that we do away with demographic targets. We don't need them. Satisfying the needs of individuals, in the aggregate, would produce more favorable outcomes than pursuing the targets, and the field worker quotas, and all of that. And I remember I gave that paper, and Nafis sat there and she thought about it. She looked over at me and said, 'Very good paper, Steve, but I don't know about this business of dropping targets.' I never forgot that because of course two years later at Cairo, that's exactly what we did, and she was in the forefront.

Ever the woman of science, Nafis would reevaluate her approach based on research. By the time Bella Abzug arrived in her office, Nafis had adopted a new position that was far beyond what the feminists sought: that of demanding a ground-breaking upgrade in the status of the world's females, a push that would become the vehicle to population control.

As the PrepCom phase progressed—even after conducting five regional conferences, even after years of meetings with heads of state, medical advisers, and population industry experts, even after hosting roundtables on the issues and analyzing mountains of data—Dr. Sadik still felt like the Program of Action they were drafting was lacking in this revolutionary shift she had envisioned. The UNFPA chief wanted something new and dynamic, and she knew that what she had wasn't there yet.

A little known fact is that between the second and third PrepComs she and Steve Sinding agreed to call a brainstorming session to see if they could come up with a fresh approach. Sinding remembered,

"Nafis said she wanted to keep this session off the record because it would be outside the UN process, and if people became aware that we were doing this, they would feel as if we were bypassing the prescribed approach, and the delegations would not be happy.

"We brought together at the Rockefeller Foundation a very distinguished cross-section of leaders, mostly from developing countries, but the head of the Population Council was there, the head of IPPF was there, prominent women's leaders from around the world were there, senior people from the World Health Organization, people from the women's movement, and so on. And we met for two days, two long days of discussion. Then we hired a woman named Sharon Camp, who had been a leading lobbyist for population funding in Washington, and asked her to take the input from these various constituencies and produce a new draft for the third PrepCom to consider. And, in very large part, that draft that Sharon prepared later became the Program of Action."

The result of these years of analysis meant that heading into Cairo, Nafis presented a fundamentally different paradigm from the one that had been considered at past population conferences, which had not, by the way, included the word "development" in their moniker. This tectonic shift in theory came from the concept that both agendas referenced in the name International Conference on Population and Development would be conveniently solved by the same action: the empowerment of women. Hence the strategy to solve the world's population problem would spring from perhaps an unexpected source—that of girls' schooling, a natural conclusion for the doctor whose father and grandfather had both viewed education as the single most important gift parents could bestow upon their children. Education was the fundamental building block to allow women the freedom to control their own destiny—which would lead to having fewer babies, which would in turn lead to less strain on a nation's economy. And women's increased productivity as skilled workers would boost a nation's development. In the end the strategy she would put forth at ICPD refined all the complex conundrums under her aegis at UNFPA down to a single issue: rights.

"In my opinion, the basic problem of women as far as their role and status is concerned, arises from the fact that they have no control over their fertility and that is used to keep them out of everything else. For example, in our countries, girls are not educated—the excuse being that the girl will get her economic security from marriage, from her husband. Parents say, 'If we have enough money, we must educate the boy.' But not the girl. So no matter how brilliant the girl might be, she's not given a chance. And from that so many things happen to her: she is not educated, she is not able to be independent, she does not know her own rights, she doesn't know much about her own health, and all that. She is married off at a young age, and then no matter how mistreated she might be by her husband and her husband's family, she can't really get out because she doesn't know what to do with herself. She can't go out and earn a living because she is not prepared, she hasn't been equipped to do that. Her parents are usually too poor to take her back, and most of them don't want to anyway.

"She is in bondage then, so she puts up with violence and all sorts of things. Many women lose their lives, and so many things happen to them because of the basic fact that their status is decided for them at the time they are born, almost literally."

Another major evolution in the decade between conferences came with the transformation of the focus on "family planning" to the more encompassing "reproductive health," an expansion that included everything from information on contraceptives and spacing pregnancies, to pre- and postnatal care, deliveries, pap smears, and treatment for sexually transmitted diseases. In other words, ministering to the woman's entire reproductive life, and not just the prevention of pregnancy.

The UNFPA team had an ace up its sleeve guaranteed to get the attention of everyone in the population field, even the most heartless bureaucrat: the numbers game. The UN demographers' research showed the earth's population in 1950 was 2.5 billion; in 1994 it was estimated at 5.8 billion. If nations implemented a rigorous approach to reduce current trends, they could hope to see the population stabilize in 2050 at 7.8 billion. However, if their recommendations were ignored, they warned that by 2050 the world would likely be inhabited by 12.5 billion people, raising the specter of mass poverty and starvation. And yet at the same time so much was at stake, a UN study showed that 120 million couples would limit their family size if they had access to contraceptives. These statistics prompted J. Joseph Speidel, president of Population Action International to proclaim of ICPD: "This is not just another meeting. The long-term fate of this planet is in the balance." Or as one agricultural scientist from India put it, "If our population policy goes wrong, nothing else will have a chance to go right."

Other parts of the new paradigm came from the expressed concerns of the developing world. They felt that they were always looked down upon as the problem children at the UN, because 98 percent of population growth took place within their borders. But they pinpointed another major concern for the global environment, namely the issue of consumption. For example, the United States, while possessing 5 percent of the world's population, used 25 percent of the world's resources. This was also sometimes referred to as a North-South conflict, with most of the world's industrialized nations in the Northern Hemisphere and the developing countries in the South. The numbers put this little debate into perspective: "each American, on average, causes some 70 times as much environmental damage as a Ugandan or Laotian, 20 times that of an Indian, 10 times that of a Chinese, and roughly twice that of citizens of Japan."

One of these problems to be solved at ICPD would have taxed the wisdom of Solomon, and Dr. Sadik's diplomatic skills were being put to the test as she sought to guide the proceedings in finding solutions. In order to do this, she knew she must deal with the conflict while trying to maintain a positive demeanor that all is well. Her chief-of-staff, Mari Simonen, watched her boss close at hand. She observed that one of Nafis's management methods was to maintain her distance, allowing the negotiators to take charge, and to intervene only when there was a critical problem and she needed to push it forward. "Overall, that whole conference was extremely tense, very, very stressful, mainly because we didn't know until the end how it would come out. Throughout, you could really see Dr. Sadik's incredible stamina and capacity to convey to the outside her total belief that in the end it would be resolved. So she was able to provide the kind of leadership that a real leader conveys, although inside, she must have known that we really didn't know. We didn't know which way it would turn out, and there were lots of potential problems."

Simonen remembered that Nafis had her own way of handling the stress. "During all this tension, almost every day when she didn't have an official luncheon, she and I alone would go to a nearby hotel and have lunch together . . . and it was as if the world didn't exist. We would talk about everything else but the conference for an hour, hour and a half, and have a very leisurely meal. And next door, two tables away were the security people, shadowing us. That was her way to deal with all this incredible tension, the stress level of work. She would turn it off, like you turn off the light."

At one point toward the end of their journey, the two even got a little shopping in, making their way toward a jewelry store. Of course, they were accompanied by the requisite UN security professional, who mentioned en route that he was getting engaged. He was delighted when the ladies helped him choose a ring for his fiancée. At Khan el-Khalili bazaar, all the shopkeepers recognized Nafis from her daily appearances on TV, and within minutes she was laden with gifts.

As the eight days of Cairo played on, Nafis realized that the vast majority of those present—thousands of them, in fact—were in agreement with her vision of how the world should be treating its women. As Shaukat Fareed, one of her UN colleagues, commented: "She led that conference intellectually, every bit of it. She had all the strings in her hand, but she delegated to all her chiefs, giving us our duties and assignments. Every evening she orchestrated a roll call, asking what had happened, what we should be doing. Nafis knew exactly what the outcome should be at ICPD and worked towards it."

The conflict over certain issues had begun at the PrepComs, but now the friction grew hotter than the Cairo midday sun. Thousands of media, though not permitted inside the negotiations, interviewed delegates outside the private chambers and broadcast the coverage worldwide. As could have been expected, the word burning everyone's tongue was "abortion."

On this subject two major points had already been agreed upon in drafting the Program of Action before the document left New York: "First, that abortion is not to be treated as a method of family planning, and second, that abortion should be treated as a major health issue." The only issue left open was how to deal with unsafe abortion.

In spite of this major consensus, for the next five days wrangling over the subject proceeded well into the dark of night, with the parsing of terms filling up the majority of the discussion. The hullabaloo centered around the Program of Action's Paragraph 8.25, until by the end of the conference "8.25" had become a synonym for controversy. At one point Egypt's minister of family welfare, Dr. Maher Mahran, asked in frustration, "Does the Vatican rule the world? We respect the Vatican. We respect the Pope. But if they are not going to negotiate, why did they come?"

In general, the process involved in these negotiations vacillates between soul-deadening boredom, angry tirades, and tearful pleas. On camera Archbishop Renato Martino gave an impassioned speech condemning abortion and contraception. A middle-aged man wearing glasses and the simple black suit and clerical collar of the priesthood, his voice broke with emotion as he read from his notes:

"Countries are urged in similar texts to provide in the coming years services of pregnancy termination for persons of all ages."

In some cases—certainly when ironing out issues surrounding the A-word—the roller coaster ride progressed into the wee hours of the morning. The system worked thus: all governments had a seat at the plenary, the primary floor of debate for delegates, over which Nafis presided as secretary-general and Fred Sai served as chair. It was the job of this body to reach a consensus. The chair broke the negotiation of the document down into pieces, and in smaller rooms these portions were debated by countries with the most divergent views until they came to an agreement. The participants would do line-by-line edits on the text, working through any areas in brackets.

U.S. delegate Adrienne Germain described her experience: "So what is it like in the small rooms? First of all it is very, very intense. It requires enormous concentration—not just on the sentence you're negotiating—but all the sentences that came before and all the sentences that come after." One particular session at ICPD sounds very similar to serving on a jury: "In Cairo, my focus—because it took the entire conference to do it—was on Chapters 7 and 8. Chapter 8 is on reproductive health, and 7 is on fertility regulation, and there is one session that I remember the best in these small rooms. Hernando Clavijo, a delegate from Colombia, was leading the negotiations, and he was a very good chair, very helpful. But we were there day after day till 2:00 or 3:00 in the morning, because when you're sent to the small room by the plenary chair, you don't come back until you have a solution.

"They were carving out the precise definitions of reproductive and sexual health, and another paragraph on rights. And we had in this room Iran, Pakistan, and the Vatican. Two or three Europeans—the Scandinavians, the Dutch, maybe the British, Canada, the U.S., and I think we had Brazil and India. The opening paragraph was supposed to define 'reproductive health.' We like-minded wanted—without naming abortion—we thought we could use 'fertility regulation,' because it's a scientific term, it has a meaning."

The delegate was referencing the World Health Organization's definition of "fertility regulation" as including "family planning, delayed child bearing, the use of contraception, the treatment of infertility, the interruption of unwanted pregnancies and breast feeding." But some countries objected to this interpretation, saying it implied an acceptance of abortion.

Germain continued: "We thought using 'fertility regulation' was a way to get reference to abortion without naming abortion in the definition of reproductive health, and maybe that would be a way out from the Vatican and Iran—who by then was an ally of the Vatican—even though abortion is basically not an issue for them. So, we thought we were making good progress toward using the term 'fertility regulation,' but the Vatican wanted to put in 'methods of fertility regulation that are not against the law.' And we were just dead set against that. But Iran and Pakistan chose to side with the Vatican, and we were getting nowhere.

"We kept trying all kinds of things, and it just was not working at all. By 2:00 in the morning, the space was filling up with empty coffee cups, candy wrappers, papers and stuff. This room had a couple of little windows very high up near the ceiling, with an air-conditioning unit that sort of jutted out from the wall. It was higher than chair level, and the Vatican every day chose to sit on top of that air conditioning unit—even though there were more than enough chairs to go around. So, there they were, looking down on us all . . . and I want to tell you, being claustrophobic in that room until 2:00 a.m., night after night . . . it really got to you after a while."

The Catholic Church had insisted that several terms implied support for abortion, a fact that had driven their opponents mad before the conference had even begun. Gro Brundtland had already addressed this business in her opening day speech in Cairo: "In a forward-looking Program of Action, it therefore seems sensible to combine health concerns that deal with human sexuality under the heading 'reproductive health care.' I have tried, in vain, to understand how that term can possibly be read as promoting abortion or quali-fying abortion as a means of family planning. Rarely, if ever, have so many misrepresentations been used to imply meaning that was never there in the first place."

And yet Monsignor Peter Elliot, representing the Holy See, told the press: "The people who drafted the first text, they did that—they're to blame. They caused all this, we didn't. When the firemen come to put out the fire, do you blame them for the house being burned down? No way."

Nafis insisted that her opponents were missing the point: never did the Program of Action suggest the legalization of abortion; it was up to nations to decide their own abortion policy. Rather, the conference must address the proliferation of "unsafe abortion" and protect women from its consequences and complications. Countries must examine why such a prevalence of this problem existed within their borders. The Vatican did not want to accept that family plan-ning offered the best alternative to unsafe abortion and its attendant health risks.

While the wording of the conference agreement may have evolved, the insurmountable obstacle in the debate never changed, because, of course, there can be no compromise with abortion. You either accept it morally, or you don't. Almost every country in the world allows for the termination of pregnancy in certain extreme cases, such as to save the life of the mother. However, impassioned pleas were presented by the Vatican against this practice because, as they pointed out, abor-tion always results in death for the fetus—a fact that is hard to dis-pute. However, the Holy See's intransigence eventually caused them to be abandoned by the Islamic countries, who felt that the life of a grown woman held more value than that of an embryo.

Other issues that put the Vatican at odds with the majority posi-tion, including the use of condoms to prevent the transmission of HIV, had been dealt with already in New York. But other controver-sies remained, particularly the idea of supplying information and services to youth. Dr. Sadik had already had the confrontation with John Paul II on this topic during their meeting in Rome. And it remained a painful thorn in the crown of the Holy See, perhaps second only to abortion. Nafis remembered their fears: "It was like girls would be sexually active if they had these rights. I said, 'They're sexually active whether they have the rights or not. So, what we need to do is deal with the reality of issues that are, that exist today.

"Along with the Vatican, many of the Muslim countries were very opposed to education, especially for girls—feeling that if you give them information, they will become sexually active, and if you have services, then they will of course be promiscuous because they can control their fertility. So what you are saying is that girls should be punished for being sexually active by becoming pregnant, because then that is a deterrent, and that is quite wrong."

Cultures throughout history have taken a variety of measures to control girls' sexual activity, whether voluntary or at the hands of predators, including the practices of sequestering the females at home, hiding them under burqas, locking them in chastity belts, cutting off their clitorises, sewing their genitals shut, even threatening to stone them to death for relations with a man—all actions intended to make sure the girls retain their virtue. The ban on contraceptives and abortion sends the same message: your only choice to avoid announcing to the world your sexual activity is to remain chaste; for breaking these strictures pregnancy is your punishment.

Nafis recalled the words of one Spanish delegate attempting to breech the divide as he spoke to the congregation: "I am a Catholic, and I believe in Catholic teaching, but I have a different set of values from my children. However, I do recognize that my children shouldn't have to suffer and pay with their lives, because of my value system."

Nafis had support from other fronts. "And even several Catholic countries like Mexico were very strong on adolescent education and services. They kept on saying, 'We have to talk about the realities of our situation, and in our countries we have to provide services. It is not enough to just give information or education."

The Holy See was adamant that adolescents could not seek reproductive counseling without their parents' permission. Alfonso Lopez Juarez, deputy of Mexfam, Mexico's family planning agency, spoke out on the issue. "Very few people were talking on the floor, but Mexico was not aligned with any other groups, so we could talk as much as we wished, and that was good for me. Most of the Europeans didn't want to counterattack the Vatican because they are very respectful, but they were passing me cards with their comments as I spoke. I remember that one gentlemen wrote, 'Please ask the priests, when adolescents go to confession, do they have to go with their parents?' There was a big laughter over that one."

Dr. Sadik insisted on adding other controversial topics to the platform for international debate, issues that no one had ever dared to discuss in polite society, much less at a conference, such as rape, incest, and female genital mutilation. Stirling Scruggs recalled the reaction: "Nafis brought FGM to the forefront, and she brought it in a vigorous way. A lot of people said, 'That's cultural, it's none of your business.' And she said, 'Women being harmed is our business.'"

The Crusaders had anticipated a fight on their hands regarding this issue, especially in Egypt where 99 percent of females are circumcised. However, this is not the way the drama played out. Just as the conservative press had condemned the conference before it opened, creating difficulties for UNFPA, the media was also capable of turning the tide in a way that created smooth sailing for them on FGM. CNN International aired a documentary on female genital mutilation the night before this issue was scheduled for debate. The film showed pubescent girls being led to a goatskin in the bush where they would lie down and, without anesthesia, have their clitorises cut off. They were forbidden to cry out as they were cut, because that would bring dishonor to their families. Afterward the camera zoomed in on the faces of the victims as they sat huddled together in shock, showing their expressions as they tried to cope—the haunting, unforgettable looks of anguish, bewilderment, and pain that flitted across those dark young faces as they tried to process this eagerly awaited "gift of womanhood."

Nafis remembered the response to the documentary at ICPD. "This film was shown the night before, and the next day this recommendation [to eliminate FGM] went through immediately. Nobody said a word, nobody objected. So, I was telling CNN that they should do more things like this. They wouldn't believe that it had such an effect."

In the final version of the Program of Action's Paragraph 7.40, the world agreed that "Governments and communities should urgently take steps to stop the practice of female genital mutilation and protect women and girls from all such similar unnecessary and dangerous practices."

It was not a coincidence that a film showing a female circumcision ritual played in the middle of ICPD. CNN founder, Ted Turner, had come to the UN through his work as an environmentalist; he had collaborated with Rafael Salas on a series of documentaries on population issues, sending a journalist named Barbara Pile out on assignment to India, China, and other locales. Around 1992 Nafis went to visit the media mogul, to tell him about the work she was doing with ICPD, but by that point he was already Nafis's fan.

Turner, who would later establish the UN Foundation by donating an extraordinary $1 billion, invited Nafis to address his global conference of reporters. When she arrived, they asked what they could do to contribute to the population debate. She suggested they do a series of documentaries around the issues that would be covered by the conference, discuss some of UNFPA's success stories, and provide extensive live coverage while the summit was in progress by interviewing delegations. All of which they did.

At the same time, Nafis was busy answering questions from journalists who asked how she squared her strident feminism with her

Muslim faith. "I said, just tell me what things in Islam can I not reconcile with? 'Oh, well the situation of women,' they said. So, I replied, 'Well I'm a woman, I'm a Muslim, and my situation is quite good. Then they said, 'But the fact that many women in your countries have a low position, or low status, they're not well educated.' I said, you cannot relate that to religion, because our religion says that every girl and every boy must be educated. It says that very clearly. The Koran has a whole chapter on the rights of women, which didn't exist in any religion at that time."

With four thousand journalists on location, no other UN conference had received the type of media attention that resulted from ICPD. The headlines had gone on for months, plastered across papers around the globe. Stirling Scruggs said, "On the second day of the conference alone, we were told there were sixty-five pages of print coverage by the media in Europe." As the summit got underway, the print media was joined by live coverage on broadcast news. Meanwhile publications from *Scientific American* to *People* magazine ran profiles of Nafis, and an *L.A. Times* interview quoted her views on the abortion conflict: "The subject of control is what concerns religious leaders. Throughout history, anthropological, cultural, social and religious norms have supported fertility control. That has been used to subjugate women."

In the United States the *New Yorker's* cover of the week showed an overpopulated Manhattan with businessmen walking on stilts through the skyscrapers. Inside, an editorial titled "A Manageable Crowd" declared that ICPD "marks a transformation of genuine historical importance—and one that has gone mostly unnoticed in the United States and Europe. For decades, the 'population explosion' ranked with the Bomb as a terrifying and seemingly permanent feature of modern history. But, just as the Cold War radically diminished the threat of global nuclear war, so the astonishing success of the family-planning movement has defused the exponential increases in global population." The author continues to ask readers to guess what proportion of couples in the developing world use contraceptives: "the figure is fifty-five per cent—much closer to the seventy-five-per-cent contraceptive prevalence in the industrialized world than to the under-nine-per-cent prevalence that existed in the developing world when the international family-planning movement got under way, in the mid-sixties. At that time, women in the developing world averaged 6.1 children apiece; by 1990 they were averaging 3.8, and the total fertility rate is continuing to fall. This dramatic decline results largely from the voluntary use of public and private family-planning services, not from coercive measures, and it has required very low investments."

So as any politician could tell you, the media giveth, and the media taketh away. Enter a press consultant who learned this lesson well in Cairo: Joaquín Navarro-Valls. By all accounts this Spaniard is an impressive gentleman: a handsome, worldly, educated, articulate polyglot. A physician by training. An author of several books. A foreign correspondent. And as a devout Catholic on assignment in Rome, he accepted the calling to become the director of the Holy See's press office. In his dapper tailored suits, the spokesman conducted his press conferences with great professional skill, and it was a measure of John Paul's commitment to the outcome of ICPD that he sent Navarro-Valls personally to represent the views of the Holy See. As the conference opened, his editorial in the *Wall Street Journal* defended the Holy Father's position, noting that, "something more is going on here than a mere exercise of political will. Civilization is at stake."

Navarro-Valls, the voice of the Vatican, is also a member of Opus Dei, a conservative Catholic organization with strong ties to John Paul II. Twenty percent of Opus Dei's members are "numeraries," devout lay people who, though not part of the clergy, reside in group homes segregated by sex and pledge a lifetime vow of celibacy. They also perform "self-mortification," the practice of wearing a spiked chain around their thigh for two hours daily and flogging themselves with a whip weekly. Interestingly, only the female assistant numeraries are assigned to do the domestic chores of cleaning, laundry, and meals in the women's *and* men's facilities.

It's easy to see how the ideological struggle between this type of conservative Catholicism and Nafis's brand of feminism came to be such a bloody battle. However, as she reports, "The Vatican was very upset during that whole conference, because I think they felt that they were taking a beating." Indeed, Navarro-Valls's confrontation with Al Gore was seen by many as a serious miscalculation, one that reflected poorly on the Holy See and its delegation. William Safire called the incident "an unprecedented papal meddling in U.S. politics" by the pope's "arrogant spokesman." But nowhere was the friction greater than his rivalry with Nafis.

At one point CNN coverage showed the two opponents side-by-side on the screen discussing the conference, with Sadik looking light-hearted and laughing, and Navarro-Valls looking dark and disturbed. In reflecting on his entire Vatican career in an interview years later, he commented: "The toughest days were during the United Nations Conference on Population and Development in Cairo in 1994. It was not easy to assert an interpretation of the human being in the face of opposition from too many pressure groups that appeared to think only in quantitative terms and disregard the person's essential needs."

One day toward the end of the conference Nafis gave her bodyguards the slip, jumped into a car, and instructed the driver to take her to the stadium on the other side of the football field. He looked at her in shock, as did a security guard who happened to be sitting in the passenger seat; he was quick to put an end to this plan. "No, no, no, no! You cannot go to the NGO Forum; we've told you that it's just not safe, especially after that business yesterday." An incident had occurred where a right-to-life activist had smacked the microphone away from a speaker for one of the women's groups. The culprit had been ejected from the conference, but the security risk was palpable in a stadium with thousands of people packed into bleacher seats reaching up to the rafters.

Britain's minister for overseas development, Lady Lynda Chalker, had witnessed the zeal of these groups and their hatred of Nafis.

> Now, I'm very anti-abortion personally . . . but Nafis was abominably abused by some of the so-called right-to-life campaigning groups at Cairo, abused verbally—what was said and written about her. I mean slander and libel. No, no bounds with some of these groups! She got angry, of course, but she withstood it, with good humor much of the time. And I think that's one of the things I admired so much about her, her ability to really rise above this vindictive, and very often erroneous information directed toward her and the people around her.

Alex Marshall also understood why the security advisers were concerned. "The opposition had been so strident. Abortion was, and is, a very emotional issue for people who oppose it, or certain groups of conservatives who are using abortion as a peg to hang other things on. But for some women, and actually more for some men, I think Nafis has become the symbol of everything they hate. They don't like her frankness; they don't like the fact that she's winning. That's what they really find objectionable. They feel on the defensive, and she's leading the attack."

But the object of their anger was fed up. "When I got up that morning, I said, you know, why am I buying into all this pressure to stay away from the NGO Forum? That's exactly what those who are opposed want, and so I'll go. But, I didn't tell the security my plans—I didn't tell anyone—because I knew if I told them, then they would definitely say no. But when I got into the car, I saw the security man was sitting there. 'I'm going to the NGO conference,' I told him. 'Now they don't know I'm coming, so there are no bombs obviously, nobody's organized, so I'm going, and I'm going whether you take me or not.'"

Unannounced, Nafis entered the stadium, and in her sea-green sari she strode up to the front of the room and took the microphone. People recognized her and began to cheer, thousands of women and men who knew they wouldn't have been here in Cairo without her. She spoke loudly to be heard over the din: "I believe the momentum is now in favor of accepting all of the recommendations for the Program of Action. Today they will be discussing Chapter 7, the other contentious chapter. But I keep my fingers crossed that by the end of today, we will have completed the work on the Program of Action—thanks really, and I mean this very, very sincerely—to the work of all of you." The tough cookie's voice broke with emotion, as it had on the first day when she thanked her staff. Nafis then acknowledged the NGOs' help in using their expertise to draft language and their skills to make sure the edits landed in the hands of delegates. She discussed the shift that had been wrought as a result of these few days gathered together in Egypt. "There's a subtle change in the atmosphere, a change in the relationships, and I believe that governments are going to look to you a great deal more to reflect the grassroots voices. They'll ask you to be very much a partner with them in the implementation of the movement and the monitoring of the program."

She finished by saying, "I wanted to show you my sincere appreciation and my deep, deep gratitude for all that you have done." By now, everyone in the room was on their feet, cheering, whistling, clapping. Word got around that she had arrived, and more NGO delegates flooded into the room as she spoke. As the thunderous applause continued, she turned her head away from the mike at one point and mumbled, "Oh my god, I'm so embarrassed."

"No, don't be," said a woman at the speakers' table, "because you're the one taking the risks."

Later Nafis recalled, "People there wanted to touch my hand, and I felt like I was a goddess arriving at the forum. They knew I had been told not to come, so I think they appreciated it even more."

The inclusion of the NGOs in the negotiation process had been just one of the many watershed accomplishments at Cairo. Another first was the hard currency initiative that put the *D* for "development" in the ICPD: real budgets to pay for the agreed-upon services and the resulting financial promises from donors to fulfill this need. They committed to increase funding from the current level of $5 billion to $17 billion by the year 2000.

It was this exact same generous allocation of funding that created such animosity on the part of the Holy See, according to Frances Kissling, president of Catholics for a Free Choice. Kissling, quoted in the *Washington Post*, felt that the Vatican's vociferous protests at ICPD hid another agenda—one much more prosaic than their esteemed moral or religious concerns. "The way church officials see it, the greater the percentage of foreign aid budgets that is allocated to family planning, the less money there will be for education, health care and disaster relief." And as reporter Hobart Rowen went on to explain in the article:

> It's not generally known, but Catholic Relief Services (CRS) in 1992 received 77 percent of its $290 million budget directly from U.S. government agencies, including the U.S. Agency for International Development (USAID). CRS, the overseas aid program sponsored by American Catholic bishops, provides a legal and valued humanitarian service. Other nations also use private Catholic agencies as a delivery vehicle for relief purposes. [Catholic Relief Services] is one of the largest nongovernmental agencies distributing food and grants provided by USAID and is especially active in Africa. But because of budgetary stringency, the total aid pie is not going to increase any time soon. Therefore, if the Cairo conference spurs greater U.S. expenditures for condoms, legal abortions, and other population-limiting programs, the money is going to come directly out of the wonderful tap the Catholic Church has on AID money, reducing its overall influence in less developed countries.

Frances Kissling summed it up rather more succinctly: "They need the money." The French expression *cherchez la femme* instructs detectives seeking an explanation for strange behavior amongst men to "look for the woman." In a less romantically inclined universe, however, this sentiment should be revised to *cherchez l'argent*, or "look for the money."

Whatever the root of the Holy See's objections to the Program of Action, be it divine guidance or the quest for filthy lucre, for the first time in history they signed the consensus, albeit with reservations. In these recorded reservations they were mainly joined by a handful of supporters from Latin America who maintained that life began at conception: El Salvador, Honduras, Nicaragua, Paraguay, Ecuador, Guatemala, and Peru. Dr. Sadik noted: "I think in the end the Vatican felt very isolated, because they really lost there. In the beginning, they were allies with some of the Muslim countries when they hadn't really read the document. But Egypt, Pakistan, and Iran played a very important role in getting all the Muslim countries together to say that we support family planning, and we support abortion, as most of them do for the life and health of the mother. They felt these were issues they could not afford to give away to any other religion. 'We support life, and it is the mother who's alive.' So, with that, the whole group of Muslim countries, several that had been undecided, separated themselves on these issues, on abortion and all that. And then the Vatican opposition just dwindled down, with only these few countries supporting them in the end. So they felt that they had really lost face. Then for the first time the Vatican joined the consensus, as it's called. They agreed to let the Program of Action go through, while they registered their objections to certain sections, as governments are allowed to do.

"In the end, the African nations were very irritated with the Vatican, because out of the eight days of the Cairo Conference, five days were spent on one paragraph, 8.25, which dealt with abortion. The Africans said they wanted to look at poverty and relationships with population and the access to services, and you know all these big issues that we didn't get a chance to get into. The agenda just had to be hurried to get it finished."

During negotiations many problems were resolved by the inclusion of a paragraph reading: "The implementation of the recommendations contained in the Programme of Action is the sovereign right of each country, consistent with national laws and development priorities, with full respect for the various religious and ethical values and cultural backgrounds of its people, and in conformity with universally recognized international human rights."

The conventional wisdom is that a woman forgets the pain of childbirth immediately upon the joy of holding her new baby in her arms. While the twenty thousand assembled in Cairo might not forget the pain of birthing this agreement immediately, they were happy to be part of a significant event: the signatures by all 179 governments present on a plan of action to deal with population and development for the next twenty years. That these disparate factions, which started out so far apart on September 5, had come together in agreement by September 13 was a stunning victory; the *Washington Post* called the consensus "a resolve to make a lasting difference that is rare for any international parley." It was this very feeling of resolve that brought about a congratulatory mood that swept through the conference hall, hard-won relief and triumph at being part of history. In her closing speech, Dr. Sadik once again drew the participants in to share the glory:

> You should not be modest about your achievements. Compared with any earlier document on population and development, this Programme of Action is detailed in its analysis; specific in its objectives; precise in its recommendations and transparent in its methodology. In our field, it represents a quantum leap to a higher state of energy. Thanks to the media, it has already drawn the interest of people

worldwide; I hope that this process will continue so that everyone can contribute to its objectives.

Speaking on behalf of the United Nations system as a whole and for the United Nations Population Fund in particular, I can assure you that we stand ready to provide all the advice and assistance we can, whenever and however you ask for it. I give you my personal pledge that I will spare no effort in the coming years to ensure that the agreements you have made here become a reality. I remain committed to building the future by building the power to choose.

As Dr. Sadik finished her speech, the assembly packed into Cheops Auditorium burst into applause. It was unheard of in the UN for delegations to give a standing ovation to a secretariat staff member, but here they were—the whole hall on its feet—and the sense of joy could be felt running throughout the congregation.

She had done it. The girl who had begged her father in high school to let her become a doctor because she wanted "to change the world" actually had. It's doubtful that even the runaway imagination of a teenager could have dreamed how completely Nafis would fulfill this fantasy, by orchestrating an international agreement that would change the lives of millions of women around the globe.

By the closing bell of ICPD, however, its secretary-general was giddy with delight, as her speechwriter Alex Marshall remembered. "Right at the end of that conference, when everything had gone well, and it was a huge success, she actually kissed me. I don't think she had ever even touched me before, in all the years that I'd known her. She was not the sort of person you'd go kissing, or who kisses you . . . she just doesn't do it. But she did that day, with a big grin on her face. And you suddenly saw a different Nafis."

Mona Daoud | Cairo, Egypt

When the Cairo conference took place in 1994, Mona Daoud was only thirteen years old. Nonetheless, she still remembers the dialogue it created in her country, and without realizing it at the time, she would become a part of that dialogue years later when the fledgling journalist took an interest in the sex education workshops being offered for adolescents. At ICPD, these services for youth had fomented a vitriolic feud between liberals and conservatives; fast forward a decade, and the government of one of the most fervently Islamic nations on the planet would be bringing teenagers together to discuss . . . sex. Mona certainly did not want to miss out on *this* conversation.

She recounts these stories to me as she sits in my hotel room, staring out at the Nile. The twenty-four-year-old would look at home in any city in the United States, with her curly dark hair cropped short, and dressed in jeans and a white T-shirt with a striped un-ironed oxford shirt hanging loosely over the top. Only her exotic features would give pause, a chubby pink-cheeked face housing lazy black eyes and full lips, which frequently curve into a smile. But those eyes repeatedly express anxiety when we talk about the issues facing her country—a concern unusual in someone so young.

The sex-talk sessions she attended were sponsored by the Egyptian Family Planning Association (EFPA), an organization that had been one of the ringleaders in the progressive movement at ICPD. Enter the young journalist, who had already been writing about sex education until her research had thoroughly depressed her, mainly due to the conclusion that, overall, Egyptian society rejected the notion of sex ed in schools. Ironically Mona first learned of the new youth movement through the BBC. It published a series titled "Learning the Facts of Life in Egypt," talking about the activities in Menoufeya, an agricultural region north of Cairo (coincidentally the birthplace of Anwar Sadat and Hosni Mubarak). Excited to see this group in action, Mona accepted their invitation to attend a conference and visit their youth center. "When I met these young people, I had been doing research throughout Cairo, dealing with officials, adults who were supposed to be, you know, more understanding . . . but it was a terrible situation. And when I found these people in Menoufeya, talking freely about sex education, I was impressed—I mean Menoufeya is one of the places in Egypt which is supposed to be very regressive. I was even more impressed when I saw how their facility is organized, with a medical center, a library for family planning, the youth themselves—who are very active and very productive, and Mr. Abdel Raouf, the social worker who ran the center.

"This gentleman spends his whole life going around trying to fix social problems that are related to families . . . and I remember something that he said that affected me so much: he's spending his whole life trying to introduce people to family planning and then one day, on a Friday, after spending all this time and effort, he hears a sheikh saying in Friday prayers that family planning is harmful and just forbidden by religion. In Egypt, of course, the minute people hear something is forbidden by religion, this pretty much seals the deal. So this social worker went and spoke to him. Then Mr. Raouf realized that what the sheik meant when he said "family planning" was really tubal ligation, and he tried to explain that family planning is not necessarily this type of permanent contraception . . . he tried to illustrate things with religion, because unfortunately you can't talk to people from a separate perspective, they will never listen to you. They will only listen if you try to support whatever it is you are saying with religion."

Mona reported how at one community meeting a sheik provided reassurance to the mothers in the room on proper handling of their daughters. "Not all women are to be circumcised," he said, "only women whose clitoris is more than two centimeters." Upon hearing this news, one mother confided that she was now so worried that she must take her six daughters to the doctor to have him measure each one's clitoris.

In addition Mona witnessed an educational session sponsored by the Egyptian Family Planning Association, one intensive training course for the adolescent peer educators and their parents. "What really unsettled me was how the women were so passionately defending female genital mutilation, they call it a term in Arabic which means "cleanliness." So the idea which they associate with female genital mutilation is that it's important for the cleanliness and health of a woman, and it hit me how completely ignorant and uneducated they are—yet completely confident. That's a very dangerous combination. To make it even worse is the ingredient of religion coming into it, because across history religion tends to give people the right to do pretty much anything. You just try to connect with religion in any way, and there you go: a divine way to violate people's rights."

In order to affect change, the journalist decided to appeal to a different audience with her writing. "I thought by talking to people who are educated, the class that can actually do something in the future, that it would be productive to get them to be more active." Thus Mona began submitting her articles to *Campus*, one of the rare uncensored publications in Egypt. Their tagline pretty much sums up the magazine's editorial viewpoint: "The Voice Of Our Generation." Written in English, it's full of colorful ads and graphics for products directed to a hip college-aged crowd, promoting "flashy, fun-related things because we are trying to open the eyes of youths."

Mona studied her audience with the stealth of a big game hunter stalking her prey. She sat in a coffee shop (where *Campus* is distributed) and observed readers scanning the pages. She noticed how they would frequently flip straight to the VIP section with photos of celebrities at parties, and they would momentarily freeze at any copy containing the word "sex." So it should come as no surprise that her next article's headline read—you guessed it—SEX EDUCATION 101, and not to take any chances, the S-word was adorned in red type three-inches tall.

On the page her narrative voice features a cynical, humorous take on dealing with the status quo, as in one section where she portrays her visit to two sheiks in the Fatwa section of Al-Azhar University—just as Nafis had done years before her—to ask their advice on how a mother should discuss you-know-what with her children. In *Campus*, Mona describes the holy men's reaction to her query:

"What is this crisis! Your mother wants your siblings to receive sex education? Teach them religion! Teach them prayer! Teach them obedience to God!" he then looked me up and down. I was in baggy jeans, long sleeved very loose cotton shirt, and the scarf I got as a present from Dar Al Ifta.

"Teach them how to dress conservatively!" I think I saw a hint of a sarcastic smirk. I refrained from informing him that this was as conservative as it gets.

Another sheik intervenes. "The mother just wants her children to know what they will be going through."

"Is it in the school syllabus?" The first sheik asked, his eyebrow arched as if he had something very wise to say.

"Yes, but now they are asking more questions," I answered.

"Of course it is impermissible!"

"Why?" I asked.

The two sheikhs looked at each other taken by surprise.

"Because . . . because . . . it arouses their instincts!"

"Aren't those instincts already there? Shouldn't they learn how to deal with this?"

"No! Teach them prayer. Keep them in the dark about it, they do not need to know this."

The other more tolerant sheikh intervened. "Take your sister and explain things to her carefully, as for your brother, do you have any authority over him?"

"Yes," I said.

"Yell at him. The next time he asks any questions, yell at him and tell him to shut up!"

Mona's mission is emblematic of a new advocacy in Egypt, of note particularly because of the participation of women and youth. Their message is woven throughout a vast network of popular arts and media making its way into the minds of millions, and depending on your point of view, this message is either the gospel or propaganda.

Other individuals discussed with me their methods of disseminating the ideas they surely believe are the gospel. Amani El-Sayad is the director for women's programs for Egyptian Radio, the official national station. Each morning for sixty years they have been presenting *Illa Rabbabitir Buit*, a very famous show geared to women, and it has proven particularly important as it reaches rural housewives, most of whom do not even leave their homes, let alone their villages. This show's message links the issues of population with development, examining topics such as unemployment and overcrowded public transportation.

El-Sayad talks about the changes they made with their programming after ICPD, which prompted the creation of the National Population Council and the National Council for Women. "Also, we do not forget the role of Cairo Demographic Center. It's an academic situation established and supported by UNFPA in Egypt; there are a lot of studies: masters' theses, PhD dissertations, and all of these studies resulted in a wealth of academic knowledge. We were always there to bring the results of the research to our audience."

Another change that came about as a result of the Cairo Conference was the media's realization that not only had their audience increased, but so had the scope of the issues. "For example, the reproductive health of young people was not an issue before, or females' circumcision. There are some new issues. And old issues which were there, but we shied away from talking about them. Of course we know female circumcision has been around for ages, but talking about it is new. So we started to realize that it is possible to talk about these things in a dignified, respectable way."

One of the challenges they faced was how to bring this information to a radio audience, and they have explored a variety of formats to make it entertaining: talk shows, music, songs, reporting examples from the community, and women telling their own stories of what has happened to them. They know when they've hit a nerve by the letters and phone calls to the station asking where to go for services.

Another artist, Said El Abasiry, has several different talents, as he's a poet, scriptwriter, and director. Like many Egyptians, El Abasiry was stunned by the coverage of female genital mutilation at ICPD, because even though he is a native, "This was something that was never talked about, even at home, with the family. They never talked about this." He was asked by the UN to write a play that would dramatize the issue, but first El Abasiry felt he needed to educate himself on a topic he knew nothing about. And so he set out on a journey of research and reading until he came to a conclusion: "I discovered that this is something that came from Africa, and it has nothing to do with religion because in Egypt it is equally practiced and celebrated by Christians and Muslims alike. So, it has nothing to do with Islam per se, and the doctors told me that it is not even taught in medical schools, so there is no health basis for it." Now that El Abasiry was fully convinced, he felt he was ready to convince others, and so he created his first theatrical production, *Warda and the Rabbits*.

In this drama the playwright used every production technique at his disposal to entertain, engage, and enlighten the audience—the choice of cast, costumes, set, and most of all songs to stir emotions. Geared to families, the character of Warda is a magical little girl, so sweet and lovely that she is the type of daughter every parent hopes to have. They fall in love with her by the end of the show, and when the play concludes with the scene of her circumcision, and her piercing screams, the audience is devastated. Even after the curtain falls, the pathos continues. The director decided that when the cast comes out to take a bow, the character playing Warda should not return to the stage, leaving the audience to head home wondering: *What happened to the heroine?* This situation mimics real life, because these little girls simply disappear from the community one day as they recover from their mutilation—this practice that is never talked about in society. And millions of them never return, since one fourth of them will die from complications.

Mona Daoud, just at the beginning of her career, is already studying the rhetorical tools at her disposal. She hopes to put her degree in English literature from Alexandria University to good use by writing books, and to someday follow her passion for film and create screenplays. But like most activists she struggles with her limitations to affect change, and she is further influenced by the impatience of youth as she questions the long term: "So this is how we do things. I'm enjoying my work okay for the time being . . . I could see myself doing it three or four more years. But it will have to be taken to another level eventually, a higher one. I wish I could say I'm 100 percent satisfied, but I'm not, because . . . you know, I'm writing in an English magazine that is distributed in cafés and coffee shops. I'm just wondering where the next news is coming from, while the majority of the population is living in brick self-made homes. Things like that, that disparity, make me wonder, but changes are actually going on, and I try to think to myself: *If you change one person's life that is good. That's productive.*

13 BEIJING

Once again, the location of the conference was significant. Nafis joined the sisterhood as they landed in the volcanic center of a controversy raging around the rights of Chinese women to control what went on in their own wombs. As news leaked out from beneath the Red Curtain—details of population quotas and targets, extortion rackets by enforcers of government policies, mandatory abortions, forced sterilizations, girl babies abandoned, and even outright infanticide—the cry over human rights abuses rocked the global community. Worse still, Dr. Sadik would later be accused of being a collaborator in all these abuses, a situation that would produce a crisis at UNFPA.

But before this debacle occurred, Nafis and the liberals were still sailing on the wind of their triumph in Cairo. This success had a downside, however, as it prompted right-wing groups to target their nemesis, as Nafis learned from intercepted communications: "Some of their faxes would say that they'd been outwitted by me in Cairo, partly because I had gotten so many NGOs to come to the conference. This was true, since we had found funding to bring these organizations from developing countries for the first time. Then from the close of ICPD onward, these anti-abortion groups started to register for the next conference, so they had a lot of people with debuts in

Beijing. They initiated this big drive to get themselves registered by the Economic and Social Council, which accredits NGOs in the UN."

The creation of new right-wing NGOs was just a fraction of the frenetic activity that grew out of ICPD. From the community level to the global level, new ideas rippled out to create a paradigm shift, and countless individuals weighed in on what they believed to be the lasting legacy of that September week. In Egypt Amani El Sayad, the radio programmer, talked about how she had become much more aware of the interconnectedness of issues as a result of the conference; she then brought this complexity into the works she presented on the air. As a result talk shows wouldn't merely address the problems of illiteracy amongst women; rather, they would look at how illiteracy affects motherhood, that a mother who couldn't read or write would have more children, and she would have more problems raising those children.

On a national level, governments changed their practices in many countries to empower women, giving them the legal right to inheritance, offering increased access to health care, and promoting a reduction in maternal mortality; a handful of African countries that had practiced female genital mutilation outlawed it. The movement also encouraged governments to create population policy divisions to specifically define a strategy for the country's growth according to its needs; then the conference gave them the tools to monitor it. Alfonso Lopez Juarez from Mexfam recalled: "The document of Cairo, the Program of Action that was a product of Nafis's team, is listened to now like the Bible for the development of the world."

International partnerships formed to assist each other with implementing the new policies that had been formulated. Steve Sinding felt one of ICPD's most important legacies was South to South mentoring, where developing nations with successful family planning policies (Indonesia, Thailand, Bangladesh, Kenya, Mexico, and Zimbabwe) mentored other nations to design and put into practice their own programs.

Stafford Mousky noted that the creation of a realistic budget was ICPD's most pragmatic accomplishment. "Part of this success was to see that the number didn't get so big that it would scare everybody off. Because the number that had come out of the Earth Summit in Rio had been so big, like $625 billion, that everyone just ran in every direction they could. By comparison, $17 billion divided between developing countries sounded more palatable, a figure derived through work by Sadik and others. Then the head of the IMF said I think that's a perfectly reasonable sort of thing, so it was given credibility by various parties including the World Bank." In fact, the World Bank became the single biggest financier of population and reproductive health activities worldwide, with annual lending doubling from US$300 million to US$600 million.

Even the feud between the Vatican delegation and UNFPA seemed to subside when they came back from Egypt. Nafis noted that when she returned to the States, participants at all kinds of events would congratulate her on the triumph of ICPD. "On one of these occasions, the Holy See's New York representative was there, and he said, 'Oh, we also joined the consensus, and we want to congratulate you, too,' and he put his arm around me. I was just teasing him, and I said, 'Monsignor, in the United Nations, that's called sexual harassment.' He said, 'Oh, you are very naughty.' But, you know, actually we have quite a good relationship with the Vatican members here. We joke a lot, and I tease them often. Because on most things, really we agree. I agree on their concern about value systems, and their concern about conflict, and the poor, and all that, and they make very, very good statements on debt cancellation for the poor countries. They are really strong on the need for the poor countries to have a place in the decision making.

"You know I have a tendency of saying things in a very strong way, whatever it is that I'm talking about, and many times they agree. They'll quote me and say, 'Well as Dr. Sadik says . . . and we agree with what she has to say.' Sometimes they tell me, 'We will convert you to our side,' and I say, 'I think before that, I will convert you to mine,'" and she laughs heartily at this notion, her Radha eyes twinkling.

While opinions on family planning were still far from unified, one thing everyone could agree on was that the ICPD debate had created a dialogue that still reverberated a year later. One observer, Dianne Dillon-Ridgley, who had accompanied Bella Abzug to the Women's Caucus, even compared the fomenting of ideas in Cairo to the Renaissance: "You know the Renaissance was a huge shift in society. I think the people who came along in the first fifty years of that era—by and large we don't even know their names right now, and certainly they didn't call it the Renaissance, but they could see the future, and they saw it early. I feel like that's where we are, but the major change hasn't happened yet, we are still on the assent to the shift. But Nafis is one of the leaders in that—Nafis, Bella, me perhaps, many of us have contributed to the groundwork that's going to shift, happen in a way that is an earthquake, that allows the society—not to fall in—but rather opens it up for the Phoenix's rise. But ICPD is still an essential moment when there was a global collective that made a huge shift mentally. It's the opening of the box, and the truth has been set free. It may be defused for a while, but it will come together again, and it will be sharper."

As the secretary-general of the conference, Nafis had earned much praise, and on occasion it came from surprising sources, such as the comments from the abortion foes who begrudgingly acknowledged that she had outsmarted them. Others held appraising views that sprang from a more positive light, including Congresswoman Carolyn Maloney: "In my view, Cairo was one of the most important international victories for women and reproductive rights. And the lion's share of the credit for that victory must be given to Nafis for having the leadership skills and the chutzpah to ensure that the Cairo document was a shared vision of governments and civil society, that put the rights and well-being of women firmly in the center."

Fellow Pakistani and UN officer Shahida Azfar had long marveled at Nafis's ability to remain a "complete person" in spite of the demands of her work. When discussing her colleague, Azfar first noted Dr. Sadik's accomplishments at ICPD: "It linked all the things together: that women's empowerment is the cornerstone of—not just population—but it's the cornerstone of development, and development in turn has a fundamental effect on the population norms of the small family. But the strategy emerged with a very holistic paradigm. And that is what people are still quoting. The holistic paradigm of development was actually crafted by Dr. Nafis Sadik, in my view, because she pulled the different elements together and made empowerment of women the cornerstone of development. And I think that still is the paradigm. At Beijing, in fact, we were mainly trying to protect that the Women's Conference did not reverse the gains made at ICPD."

Yet in spite of the gains made in Cairo, the centuries of mistreatment of women had not come to an abrupt halt in the year since the hammering of a gavel had closed the International Conference on Population and Development. While she had seen much good come from its consensus, Egyptian radio programmer Amani El Sayad admitted: "The problem is that I myself get very frustrated and very unhappy because what we advise on the radio is not being followed, the behavior of people is not changing at the pace that I would like to see. For example, every morning I see the porter of my building, and his wife is very tired, having more children, and that same wife listens to our show and she approves of what we are saying, but she doesn't do anything different because she is worried that if she becomes a burden on her husband, then her husband will go and marry someone else. Or she is worried about the religious issues. As everybody knows about these concepts and ideas, the rich families or the educated families are now behaving in the right way, but the majority of the Egyptian population—it seems that there is something missing, that this is not enough. I mean, it's not enough to convince people, because of the linkages between all of these problems. The woman has to have children, because the children are working and they make income. So all of these things are not left to the woman's decision to change her behavior; a lot of other things need to be done. For example, laws to prevent child labor." Which meant that the Crusaders still had a lifetime of work ahead of them, and they knew this as they packed their bags for Beijing.

In 1995 their squadron of planes flew into Beijing Capital International Airport, their destination the UN Fourth World Conference on Women, a summit meeting with the goal to empower females globally. When the representatives landed, they strode across the tarmac with more of a swagger than they'd had while deplaning in Cairo, because they had seen what their wit, hard work, and galvanized community could accomplish. They converged on the capital city with a determination to stop the type of mistreatment that China's population policies had engendered.

But one fact that made the agenda of the Women's Caucus even more complicated was that the same policies they decried had, in twenty years, reduced China's numbers by 250 million—a size equal to the entire United States. As one Chinese official noted, their government felt the one-child policy represented a noble offering by their citizenry. "We had made a pretty big sacrifice for the benefit of the whole world population." Yet while the world population felt relieved by this sacrifice, it was China's methods they questioned, especially since the Asian giant had joined 179 other governments at ICPD to embrace family planning initiatives supporting the wishes of the individual, versus "narrowly defined demographic goals and targets."

For hundreds of years the West has regarded China as a mysterious force to be dominated. Even Napoleon warned not to wake "the sleeping dragon," because once roused "he will shake the world." However, by 1994, as diplomats were gathering for the International

Conference on Population and Development, the sleeping dragon was awake and shaking the world in a way that only a billion people can. China had exploded to become the planet's most populous nation, the land where one-fifth of all humans resided, and befitting its size, President Jiang Zemin sent a delegation seventy members strong to participate in the dialogue taking place in Cairo. With a population of 1.2 billion, China depended on abortion as a mainstay in its struggle to curb runaway growth; this fact made the country a natural adversary of the tiny Vatican, where fewer than a thousand people lived—mostly celibate males—all of whom vehemently opposed abortion. The Holy See, still a powerful contender in the chess game to control human life, realized the need to adjust their strategy. Yet one ploy remained the same. As the *National Catholic Reporter* stated, "In a highly unusual diplomatic move, the Holy See . . . sought to bar four abortion rights Catholic groups from attending the September 1995 Fourth World Conference on Women in Beijing, China." This request at the PrepCom was met by "stunned silence."

Yet as it turned out, other factors would aid the Vatican. The leadership of the Women's Conference was again female since Boutros-Ghali appointed a Tanzanian woman, Gertrude Mongella, as the secretary-general. She was a wife, a mother, a teacher, and a politician who had filled a number of cabinet and diplomatic posts. In the midst of her UN assignment she would celebrate her fiftieth birthday in Beijing. And interestingly enough, Mongella was a Catholic, having attended "a school run by Maryknoll nuns whose intention was to educate a generation of women to be able to participate in the development of their country when it gained independence from Great Britain." In this she and Nafis shared a similar upbringing.

Dr. Sadik noted a distinct change in the Catholic Church's approach when they arrived in Beijing. "The Vatican took a much lower profile in this next conference, because they had really lost in Cairo. You see, I think they felt quite embarrassed with the fact that some of their own supporters deserted them." In a clever move, Pope

John Paul II selected an American woman to lead the Vatican's delegation to Beijing: Mary Ann Glendon, a Harvard law professor.

Veterans of past Women's Conferences remembered that some countries had shown up at these summits with *no* females on their delegations. "They said there is a real difference between the conference *of* women and a conference *on* women." Mongella also emphasized that the Beijing Conference was "about women, not for women only." Evidently, what we have here is a rare debate over a diplomatic *preposition*.

Whether the conference was of, on, about, or for women, one thing was certain: in the twenty years that had elapsed since the first such UN gathering, the world community had evolved a very different perspective on the importance of these summit meetings. Or as Alex Marshall remembered, "In 1975, the attention was, wink, wink, there are all those girls going off down there. I remember one Australian paper had the headliner, 'Sheila's off to Mexico Gabfest.' That was '75, and that's Australia, but it's so typical of the way that it was kind of dismissed, you know. However, by '95, you couldn't dismiss it. Not only could you not dismiss it, it was clearly very powerful."

As the delegates entered Beijing, everyone had an opinion on the Chinese one-child policy, but few really understood it. Of course, this confusion was exacerbated by the general mystery of China itself, understandable since the Communist Party had kept the culture closed off from the outside world for nearly thirty years. The sheer landmass of China presented another factor influencing the confusion; in 1995 the nation remained largely undeveloped, and the regulations promulgated by party officials in Beijing were not necessarily the practices carried out nine hundred miles away in the provincial hinterlands of Mongolia.

On top of it, one could get whiplash from trying to follow the trajectory of national family planning dictates. Mao Zedong had forbidden birth control to enter his utopian kingdom, proclaiming in

1949, "Even if China's population multiplies many times, she is fully capable of finding a solution; the solution is production." With that he set out to convert the rural farmlands to steel mills. It seems that runaway population growth plus a drastic reduction of food supply equals disaster, as 30 million people starved to death—a lesson that should have caught the notice of other world leaders. Later Communist Party leader Deng Xiaoping's population policy took China on a 180-degree turn, as he launched a plan to limit growth. These measures were successful, but the damage had been done, and even with the reduced birthrate, the phenomenon demographers call "residual growth" continued, meaning even with a reduced birthrate it would be decades before the net number of mouths to feed dropped. By 1979 the country had adopted the radical one-child policy, meaning couples from China's ethnic Han majority could have only one baby. But enforcement of the measure varied depending on where you lived, your ethnic makeup, and whether your parents were themselves the only child in their family. Still, for the greater part of the citizenry, they looked at a future dramatically different than their past, a shift from a rural economy, where more babies meant more wealth via cheap labor, to a more urbanized, developed society, where unchecked growth meant the steady degradation of their quality of life, and where families lived with a dictum that the number of offspring, once prolific, had now shrunk to a single baby.

Here the Asian preference for boys that had caused Nafis so much ire began to rear its ugly head in myriad ways. If the parents could only have one child, they wanted that child to have a penis—a situation that inspired the destruction of an untold number of female fetuses and newborns. The government realized the long-range effects of this behavior: boys would outnumber girls by millions, making for a completely disproportionate, unmarriageable population. As a result, in the year before the Sisterhood invaded their country, the Chinese government had outlawed prenatal sex screenings to stop abortions based on gender.

However, not only were abortions legal, but reports of them being forced on pregnant women who did not have a birthing permit were common. In years to come bureaucrats doled out heavy fines to violators, and even wilder tales abounded as officials struggled to enforce their policies: taking sledgehammers to the homes of offenders, forcibly terminating babies in their seventh month, sterilizing men and women against their will, even torturing the relatives of women pregnant with a third child until they turned themselves in and submitted to abortions.

The central government condemned these outlaw enforcement tactics as illegal, attributing them to local family planning officials who were not privy to the humane practices the Chinese had adopted in Cairo—which forbade coercion, quotas, and targets of any kind. And yet these local bureaucrats were in danger of losing their jobs if they did not meet their population targets.

During the Reagan era the United States had already been demanding that UNFPA withdraw from China; the agency's continued work there made them accessories to these human rights abuses, or so went Reagan's argument. Continued negative media coverage in the press only served to fuel the fire. Huang Baoshan, deputy director of China's State Family Planning Commission, recalled that friends from all over the world would email him after having read the *New York Times*. The outcry over these articles detailing the Chinese tactics to control population put them under tremendous pressure. "The journalists in China were also pissed off," he recalled, by what they felt was misrepresentation.

Into this turmoil entered Nafis Sadik. "I think 1984 was quite a turning point for UNFPA. The U.S.'s position changed, and in '85 they wanted us to move out of China. They said, if we didn't have a mission in China, then they would finance us. We said, 'We cannot just pack up and leave.' Our program is approved by the United Nations executive board; only they can tell us to do or not to do something."

Reagan, the anti-Communist, anti-abortion president, would naturally be opposed to Chinese policies. Interestingly he didn't favor economic sanctions to protest their human rights abuses. Rather he continued trade negotiations with the country, which left the United States with a $6 billion deficit. At the same time he used the lure of U.S. funding as leverage for UNFPA to cut ties to China, and when the agency refused, he stopped all American contributions to them. Nafis did not kowtow to Reagan's pressure, instead choosing to cope with the reduced funding and staying the course of her mission in China to wake the sleeping dragon.

For over two decades she met with Chinese leaders Deng Xiao Ping, Li Peng, Jiang Zemin, all the health ministers, and the family planning minister, Madame Peng Peyoun. Nafis felt she had a successful relationship with these officials, because "China is a country which remembers all its friends, so they are always very hospitable and very courteous and nice to me. But we had a period in which I was quite upset with them, around 1991, where we were negotiating the program because I found that many of the provincial laws and regulations were very coercive. They said a woman must be sterilized if she has a third child, things like that. So, we were negotiating the program, but the Chinese used to feel that UNFPA was being pressured by the Americans to change China's policy. And it took me a while to convince them that, you know, it had nothing to do with the Americans. I said, 'The Americans have been pressuring us since 1985, but we've maintained a mission here in China because I believed our presence was helpful, and I believed that your approach was not coercive at the national level, but now I find all these provincial rules and regulations that have been drafted *after* the national policy.'"

Part of this surge of activity in the provinces grew out of Madame Peng Peyoun's realization that she could not bring the population down below replacement level; in spite of all her efforts it hovered around 2.4 percent. She determined that many laws were in conflict with her mandate, such as the pronatalist movement in the rural areas that encouraged people to have children. As Siri Tellier, the head of UNFPA's office in Beijing recounts, "So that's when it became the local party officials who were responsible for enforcing regulations, not the family planning folks, and that meant that since they were quite removed from the capital, they start implementing all kinds of measures because they just want to get their promotion. And that's what you see reported in the newspaper articles, that's the outcome. It's a local official who is saying 'I didn't get my promotion,' and so he cracks down by hook or by crook."

Other fine points of the Chinese one-child policy contained economic penalties, such as free schooling for the first child but increased taxes for each additional sibling to cover the cost of services for health and education. In other words, you can have as many babies as you want, but there's a literal price to be paid for that. Nafis didn't have a problem with these tactics. "That kind of thing was different to forcing a woman to have an abortion or to have a sterilization, which we are against.

"I remember one discussion with China when I was saying, 'Do you see this law? Look at what it says: a woman will be sterilized.' So, you know, they really didn't understand what I was talking about, so they said, 'Oh, we should have said a man or woman will be sterilized?' I said, 'No, I'm not telling you to sterilize the man *or* the woman; I'm telling you that *no one* should be sterilized against their will.'

"With all this discussion, finally we agreed on our strategy, which was that in counties where UNFPA was present, no one could be coerced. China promised they would suspend the policy. They realized that it was the view of UNFPA, and my own view, that this was the approach that had to be followed, and because they had great confidence in UNFPA, that what we recommended for them was in their own best interest, they agreed. As I always said to them, 'China is such an important, powerful, and big country, you cannot be condemned or held up or censored by all the other countries. In many nations, when they talk about a successful program and China is mentioned, they always say, 'Oh, well, we can't follow Chinese policy, because we are democratic.' I pointed out that this is a negative view of China, when, in fact, they could present a positive view. And I was telling them, 'Your one-child policy has had nothing to do with the decline in the birthrate. The reason your birthrate is declining is because you have educated your girls, and you have women who are working everywhere. You have good health care, and you have good access to family planning, and women use these services, because you hear women themselves saying that they don't want so many children. They don't want one child, which is what you are trying to advocate, but with two children, or three children, you will get to the same number eventually. So, having one child is going to reduce your population, but it's not going to get to the same number you want.'

"When we first started to implement our plan, we set up many demographic research centers as well and trained thousands of demographers in the U.S. Before that, I think there were only one or two demographers in the whole of China. All the others had been imprisoned; demography was a discipline that nobody went into because the Chinese used to say that they wanted this large population, they had all this food, and they could look after people, people were their biggest asset, and all that. Then the demographers who used to say, 'Our population is going to be a huge problem,' were dishonored. So there were no demographers under Mao."

UNFPA trained all the Chinese demographers, then they set up these demographic centers in their universities. Before the entrance of UNFPA, there was no reliable data about China's population, a void made all the more dangerous considering the impact of the nation's gigantic size. After the training of demographers and the meticulous execution of consecutive ten-year censuses, the whole world community had access to this data. This would provide the benchmark upon which the assessment could be measured.

Next came the programs themselves, as Nafis recalled: "I think that we showed the Chinese that the way to have a successful plan of action is not to tell people what to do, but to inform their citizens, to educate them and to provide good services, and to follow up. So that quality of care was very important along with a well-trained staff. Also, we showed them the benefit of a more integrated approach. We had some programs in which we did literacy education for women and vocational training and then provided some credit to set up their own businesses—showing how all that worked together with education and family planning services.

"One of the research projects which we financed was an alternative to the one-child policy, basically that if you had two children, or you spaced your children better, the end result would be the same. And I believe firmly that if the U.S. hadn't started condemning China in the way that they did publically, they would have changed their policies. China is a very proud nation, and they say, 'Who are these other countries to pass judgment and condemn us?' They became very, very angry and hostile. And so any suggestion they suspected to be at the insistence of the U.S. was just unacceptable to them. I used to jokingly say to the U.S., 'By this time, the Chinese would have changed their policy if it hadn't been for you shouting from the House steps.' Because there is such a thing as engagement, and the engagement which the U.S. themselves talks about, is to have a dialogue. And you can't have a dialogue if you are not there, or if you antagonize them. You have to build some confidence that what you are saying is in their interest. I said, 'There is no country that wants more to progress and become modern than China. Everything they do is to bring their country into the twentieth century, and now into the twenty-first century, as quickly as possible. They really want good for their population, regardless of what everyone else might think. In the '80s, everyone—wherever you went—had these tape recorders on. They were learning English because they had been told that it was the language of technology and the future. And so the whole nation was on the march. Learning. It was quite an impressive sight. They're a very diligent and hardworking people.

"We sent them on some study tours to look at family planning approaches elsewhere. We helped with the first proper census in China; there were several million enumerators, and it was a major event. The UN participated in it, and on the first day of the census, Mr. Salas was there, and accepted the first count. Because it was such a significant event in the world's eyes, everyone was covering it, and every donor wanted to be involved in it. I mean, China is such a huge country, one which is so focused on its own future, and its own progress, that it's a pleasure to have a mission in China. They argue a lot about what they want, and why they want it, and all that. But in the beginning years, it was very impressive to deal with them because it was so contrary to most other countries, where in fact you always had to be careful that the money was actually going to be used in the best possible way. In China, you could be sure, at least in all the early programs, that it was going to be used in what they considered the most effective way for their country.

"You know, several thousand people went for training, not just with our agency, but with many others, and the Chinese were very happy to send people for training everywhere. They took tours to see programs, and they would come back and say, 'This one we liked, and this we want, and this one we didn't like because we have better facilities.' They were willing to share their own experiences. At that time they had these 'barefoot doctors,' which were everywhere—now, of course, they've replaced them—but at the time they had these health workers, paramedicals, not fully trained doctors, but trained enough to look after the common health issues for the rural population. So, this was to get everybody access to some kind of basic services. And they started out simple, very pragmatic, with what they could afford, and sent these people out everywhere in the country, focusing on how to deal with simple things, maternal health and child health. They also had many initiatives to improve the status of girls, and that was one of the Communist views, that girls and women were as good as men. So women had access to all jobs and were employed everywhere. They were in factories, they were in the party, they were heads of industrial organizations, of factories. In the '80s as part of the Communist philosophy, women and men were equal. And at that time they were treated equally, and they had many important party jobs everywhere—not just in Beijing, but in local communities wherever we visited. And we visited a lot of places.

"It's been reported many times on the status of girls, that girls were not often sent to school, or if there was a selection, the boys went on further than girls. However, China has changed the education for girls, and now they're as educated as boys. All girls have access; education levels in China are very high. Literacy is high for girls and boys. The Communist regime, which continues, still has many programs to improve the status of girls. One was, of course, compulsory education. Second was that women workers were given preference for housing. This is again to increase the status of women. A woman worker, especially if she was an only child, was given many preferences. This is again to increase her status. They had many educational programs on the value of the girl child. All in an effort to change this attitude towards girls. And to some extent it's been successful, but we're talking about a tens-of-thousands-of-years-old engrained attitude. It's going to take a long time to change. And now, or course, they find such a shortage of women, so there's a bride shortage, as they call it, resulting in girls are being abducted. So suddenly the value of girls is going up.

"But, you know, I noticed how in the '90s, that there were less women at the top than there used to be in the '80s. Because as far as economic areas, such as access to credit and loans, there is less available now for women because of investment from the outside. The foreign investors in China, they always look at men as partners .... it's more an injection of the outside world, in which the prevailing environment is a male environment."

Stirling Scruggs was UNFPA's representative to China from 1990 to

1993, and he fought in the trenches over some of the nation's policies, a position that put him in the crosshairs on several occasions. "At one meeting Nafis and I attended, the Chinese accused us of being lackeys of the West, of the Americans, and the Americans were accusing us of being a part of China's one-child policy. We were being accused by people who were opposed to us, of being the instrument of coercion in China and forcing people to have abortions and sterilizations, which of course was not true. The truth is that UNFPA worked hard to convince China to discard the one-child policy. UNFPA supports human rights, especially women's rights everywhere in the world. There was always a battle with both sides—convincing China that our mandate was based on human rights, and telling the U.S. that the best place to fight abuse is on the ground in the country. Nafis was not one to beat around the bush; the big issue at that time was sterilization of the mentally retarded, and she came to China to discuss it."

The agency found this practice of sterilizing the mentally retarded particularly unacceptable. Stirling had visited the "villages of cretins," as the Chinese called them, and wrote a report, which cited iodine deficiency as the culprit. He offered to bring in a team of experts from the World Health Organization to work on the problem. "There was one particular woman in the Ministry of Health who was very stubborn about wanting to have high-quality people, and I kept saying, 'But that's a bad interpretation of eugenics, and you can't do that. You just can't decide who lives and who dies because of them having some sort of ailment. Particularly in this case, because most retardation is not hereditary, it's environmental.' And we went over this many, many times. When it came time for Nafis to visit, I'd set up a meeting with the minister of health, and it was cancelled, and this deputy said, 'Dr. Sadik shouldn't see him. He's very busy.' And so I went through a back channel and got through to someone else, and they set up a banquet. This deputy came to see me and said, 'Dr. Sadik can't talk about our sterilization policy tonight at the dinner.'

It turned out this official was doing some of this on her own in the provinces without the ministry involved. So I told Nafis about all of this, and we went to the banquet, and everything was very nice, and she greeted everyone. We sat down.

"The minister welcomed her, and Nafis said, thank you. And then she said, 'You must stop sterilizing women and men and retarded people,' and then went into her well-practiced harangue. This woman deputy minister was glaring at me the whole time, and I was glaring right back at her, because I had already told Nafis about everything, and she said, 'Well, they can't do that.'

"We went to see President Jiang Zemin the next day at Zhongnanhai, where all the senior party people stay. Here we are, with the flags flying and so forth, and Nafis sat there. She started off by thanking the president for seeing her and telling him what a beautiful country China was, what a rich history, and you've done so much for the culture of the world—that sort of thing.

"And then she said, 'You've done so much since the revolution to support women's and children's health, but you can't go forward with something like the one-child policy. Even if you do everything you can to protect people, there's going to be abuse, and you can't continue the sterilization on the mentally retarded. You're too great a country to do something like that. You care too much about people; I know because I can see it in your other policies.' This translator was sitting behind her, and I could see these big bullets of perspiration drip down his forehead. I could understand Chinese fairly well, so I knew he was straightforward in his translation, and he said everything she said. Jiang Zemin didn't lose a breath. He replied, 'I thank you for your concern' then he goes into a spiel about how many people there are in China, and how much land they have. Nafis didn't give an inch, she persisted as usual."

Stirling was present when a reporter interviewed Nafis, and she said she supported what China had done to improve women's and children's health since the revolution. However, she was quoted in newspapers the next day—by the government-controlled Chinese media—as having said she supported the one-child policy. "I called the newspaper," Stirling recalled. "I did all I could to control the damage and demanded a clarification. But the very next day, that article was read verbatim by a senator in a session at the Australian Senate, and he embarked on a crusade to do us in. 'No funding for UNFPA!' and so forth. And it was used in the U.S., too. That article circulated around the world."

At one point in 1993 UNFPA—caught in a squeeze play between the Chinese and the Americans—nearly threw in the towel. The agency, which had been defunded for twelve years by the United States, was under constant attack from the Reagan and Bush administrations, which accused them of supporting the coercive tactics used in China, and Nafis was the point person for this attitude as she recalled. "I remember some congressman ringing me up saying, 'Lady, we want to help you, so why don't you just get out of China?' So I said, 'Congressman, why don't *you* get out of China? You could also not have a trade agreement. I mean, you spent $10 billion there. We only spent $10 million.'"

When Bill Clinton came to power that January, he immediately sought to remedy the situation by refunding UNFPA, but the media's continued reports of human rights' abuses incited dissent in Congress. Nafis was quoted in the *New York Times* as saying, "The Chinese might just get fed up with everybody and say, 'We're doing very well, thank you, and goodbye.'" She attributed altruistic motives for this possible end to their relationship, noting that the Chinese, "also don't want to be seen as jeopardizing resources to us from other donors."

This was a most generous assessment on the executive director's part, especially considering that at one point in the 1990s the Chinese were so suspicious of UNFPA that they had bugged their offices in Beijing.

In spite of the wiretapping, misinformation, and political posturing, through time the UN's diplomatic dialogue would make an impact. The Crusaders continued to repeat their argument that by empowering individual choice the Chinese could receive better results than with their current one-child policy. Nafis convinced the government to at least experiment, to let UNFPA have a finite region where they could implement the Program of Action to which China had committed in Cairo. "What we will show you is that by respecting the rights of individuals to make their own choices, you stabilize population." Now with the demographic teams up and running, it would be easy enough to calculate the results.

In 1998 the government gave Dr. Sadik thirty-two counties for a control group; the UNFPA team went to work implementing their time-tested formula, and women were allowed a choice of birth control methods. The government also lifted the quotas and allowed couples a choice of how many children they chose to have. The first measurable result was that the rate of abortion dropped by two-thirds. The birthrate under the one-child policy was 1.8 percent; for the overall population numbers to remain at the status quo, the birthrate must remain under 2.1 percent, which in the UNFPA-controlled region, it did. The experiment was later expanded to offer the women of eight hundred additional counties in China the option to control their own fertility. Years after the ICPD consensus, Nafis continued to push daily for its implementation.

Ten years after Cairo, diplomat Siri Tellier, a leading expert on China's population policy, still wondered at Dr. Sadik's ability to negotiate the Program of Action. "She was able to get the damned thing through and get the feminists on her side and get the environmentalists on her side, to get *everybody* on her side, get everybody to sign, get everybody to adopt by consensus—the Vatican, the U.S., China, the Muslim countries, the Latin American countries. I don't remember what happened at the Mexico City conference, whether there was anybody who didn't sign, but in Bucharest the Vatican and China didn't sign for completely opposite reasons. But in Cairo everybody agreed. You know, if you look through my papers today, I will be quoting ICPD in various places. Really my platform from being here in China is ICPD, and people will go around chanting it almost, because it's so technically sound, as well as ethically sound. But how she did it exactly? I still don't know."

Preparations for the Beijing Conference had actually begun two years before 1995, when the SG had asked Nafis for a recommendation on a worthy diplomat to run the summit meeting, although he knew he wanted an African this time around. The conference dealt with themes of violence against women and the rights of women within marriage to avoid physical abuse, including rape. After Gertrude Mongella was named to lead the Beijing Conference, Nafis invited her to speak at ICPD and participate in the preparations. But after Cairo, when the time came to switch focus to Beijing's agenda, Nafis remembered that her colleague was under tremendous pressure from the Catholic Church to avoid the topics of reproductive health and abortion. "Gertrude, in fact, came to see me many times, and once suggested to me that I should say that reproductive health had been dealt with, and therefore shouldn't be dealt with in the Women's Conference, and that abortion should not be a topic discussed there. And I said, 'There is no way that those issues should not or could not be addressed, even if they'd been addressed in another conference, because a lot of it has to do with violence against women and the status of women in the societies.'"

One of the themes UNFPA continued from ICPD was the focus on adolescent health. They organized panels and discussion groups, bringing to Beijing young journalists eighteen to twenty-four years old, who went back to their own countries and reported on the stories that would be of interest to their peers.

The major headliner in Beijing, of course, would be a bit more established than these ingénues. The honorary head of the U.S.

delegation, First Lady Hillary Clinton, arrived at the conference hall to great fanfare, wearing a pink suit, her shoulder-length blonde hair styled into a smooth wave framing her face. In her address Clinton touched on many of the human rights abuses for which the Chinese had been excoriated in recent years; her comments clearly disparaging the Chinese were not well received, considered improper behavior for a guest in their country. Once again Senator Tim Wirth headed the U.S. delegation, joined by Chairs Madeleine Albright and Donna Shalala; they also brought a large contingent of NGOs. And indeed at this conference the nongovernmental organizations continued to play a major part in the dialogue on women's issues, arriving from six continents. However, unlike the convenient, adjacent layout at ICPD, the Chinese Organizing Committee (COC) moved the NGO Forum to a small town thirty-five miles from Beijing, thereby sequestering them from the location of the actual deliberations. In March, before the August 30 opening, the officials cited "structural defects" of the original location (the Beijing Workers' Stadium), but the media rumor mill cited the fact that the move was announced immediately following an incident where Prime Minister Li Ping had been heckled for human rights abuses at another conference. No amount of protest could budge the NGO Forum banishment to the periphery. Indeed, the Chinese continued to add ring after ring of bureaucratic hoops for participants to clear: special applications (complete with a $50 fee) sent to Beijing, which had to be confirmed before one could apply for a visa. "As soon as the forms began arriving, the COC changed the hotel form and demanded that everyone send new ones." In July the COC announced participants needed special conference visas. Of the 35,000 who had originally registered, only about 23,000 of the Sisterhood succeeded in clearing the hoops, plus 1,500 of their male cohorts. As one attendee, Jo Freeman, opined: "By the time Forum participants arrived in Beijing, they were exhausted by the hassle, time, and anxiety consumed just to get there. And there was more to come."

Part of the entertainment at the NGO forum consisted of Catholics for Free Choice circulating a petition requesting an evaluation of the Holy See's UN member status, citing their "undue pressure" on women's issues at past conferences and questioning the legitimacy of the Roman Catholic Church to be represented at the UN as a state. One Canadian activist even said the Vatican's effort was "frightening and intimidating to women, especially those from Catholic countries." One hundred and fifteen additional NGOs signed the petition to remove the Holy See from UN proceedings, including the National Coalition of American Nuns of the United States. At the end of the Beijing Conference the pope's spokesman Joaquin Navarro-Valls announced that the Holy See's delegation had not spoken for the few hundred citizens of Vatican City, but rather for "the 900 million Catholics around the world."

Abortion had been the lightning rod that magnetized the crowd in Cairo into two polar extremes, and a climate of propaganda swirled around the globe surrounding its discussion. In Beijing the propaganda centered around gender, with the scuttlebutt being that the UN was promoting four categories: men, women, gays, and lesbians. As Nafis remembered: "This was just manufactured by someone. It was not on the table; this was not a discussion at the conference itself; rather it came from, again, this discussion on the family. The family is the basic unit of society, and the conservative countries were saying there is only one type of family—husband, wife, and children—that's the unit, and no other type of family exists, meaning like gays and lesbians and so on. But you know this was not the discussion; nonetheless, it became the rallying cry for the conservatives against the conference."

As part of this dialogue, the Vatican's representatives "bracketed all references to gender, insisting that this term sanctioned homosexuality. Underlying the Vatican's objection was an insistence on a fixed nature of men as active and women as passive, seen as God-given and not as socially constructed," according to the *National Catholic Reporter.*

In addition the Holy See demanded a more positive portrayal of motherhood in the conference's 149-page Platform of Action. As Betty Freidan noted, "The Vatican wants to change the word 'woman' wherever possible to 'mother.' To *define* women as mothers in the face of the reality of an eighty-year life span in which motherhood can occupy only a few years would be a paradox indeed."

However, overall the Fourth World Conference on Women was able to build on the ground covered the previous year, and it made advances in their rights, addressing violence, rape, and incest. The *Christian Science Monitor* conveyed, "Mid-way through what some-times seemed like endless round-the-clock negotiations, a working session finally agreed to recognize that the human rights of women include the right to exercise control over their own sexuality—free of coercion, discrimination, and violence." The testimony was poignant, especially the tales of faithful African wives infected with HIV by philandering husbands.

Beyond the narratives, the chilling facts created a more prominent discussion at this conference, noting the effects of the AIDS virus on women's health: that females are biologically twice as likely to contract HIV through unprotected heterosexual intercourse than men. And they frequently have no control over whether or not their partner chooses to use a condom. As a result the Beijing accord demanded that all women's rights should supersede national traditions.

Others reported that "UN Secretary-General Boutros Boutros-Ghali lauded the 'growing influence, passion and intellectual conviction of the women's movement,'" and political scientist Elaine Wolfson, head of the Global Alliance for Women's Health, noted the maturing of the feminist movement. "What were perceived as radical ideas in Western countries, and a form of cultural imperialism elsewhere, twenty years ago, are mainstream today." Or as one NGO participant from India noted: "In Cairo, we had to scramble and lobby intensively for governments just to understand what we were talking about. In Beijing the vast majority of governments have gotten the point."

It was quite late in the evening when Nafis spoke to the assembly, yet a large crowd of people still remained. Like Hillary Clinton had earlier, the UN leader did not shy away from the controversy, and her remarks addressed the decade-old criticism that she supported the abuses doled out as a result of China's one-child policy. "No one has the right to impose reproductive decisions on women."

She continued, discussing how so-called value systems were frequently used to discriminate against women, and her words were quoted around the world, modified into a mantra, immortalized on posters for posterity:

> We must be courageous in speaking out
> on the issues that concern us.
> We must not bend under the spurious arguments
> invoking culture or traditional values.
> No value worth the name supports
> the oppression and enslavement of women.
> The function of culture and tradition
> is to provide a framework for human well being.
> If they are used against us,
> we will reject them, and move on.
> We will not allow ourselves to be silenced.·

Her status as a celebrity survived intact after her triumphant role in Cairo, and she had especially become an icon in all the Muslim countries, which were delighted to see one of their own perform such a starring role on the world stage—ironic, considering all the grief she'd encountered at the hands of the sheiks before the conference had even begun, and the nonstop questions from reporters about how she reconciled her feminist positions with Islam.

She had become the hero for women as well. Richard Snyder

commented, "She had transcended just being executive director, the first woman head of any UN organization, to become someone who was truly a person of the world, and the person who was so noble that she took on the cause of women everywhere.",

Nafis was respected for her more prosaic contributions to her gender as well. She was noted to have the best record in the UN for hiring women professionals into the system. No queen bee, she used her position to help the Sisterhood, not sting them.

Nafis had already served as a mentor to females entering the diplomatic corps, but after her performance in Cairo she became a legend. As a young woman working in the Arab Bureau in the 1980s, Thoraya Obaid recalled seeing her first glimpse of the leader at a summit meeting. "I'd already heard a lot about her; then I finally saw her as she flashed through the crowd in her sari. At this conference in the United Arab Emirates the UNFPA staff had asked for my assistance translating the final report of the meeting into Arabic, and I had stayed up all night working with them. Although I'd never reported this to anyone, later my boss got a letter from Dr. Nafis Sadik thanking me for my support to her team, and asking him to charge the cost of my participation to UNFPA. So I think in that sense she did touch my life, as being so fair and generous about recognizing young people coming into the world of professionalism.

"Before I'd even seen her, though, I'd heard that she was tough, oh, you can't stand in front of Dr. Sadik. But the real change came in 1994 with the Cairo Conference at ICPD. At this time she took another stature. She was larger than human size. Because she was in front of all this wave of attacks, she was defending the positions very strongly. And she was doing it as a Muslim woman, she was doing it as a UN leader, and as a gynecologist who has seen women suffer, and so that gave her a different image, at least to me. I think people talk about her as being strong and aggressive and a fighter, and that's what she is, she's a fighter. I really don't think that if she had not been that strong, the agenda would have held as hard as it did.

But it did hold because she was willing to fight the battle." Nafis was a soldier in a sari.

One of the keys to UNFPA's work lay in their access to parliamentarians, because no other outside organization had the opportunity to influence national legislation in the way they did. Nafis was especially prized for her power to sway parliamentarians and create equality for women, to get the lawmakers motivated to look after the interests of women and girls in reproductive rights. But ever the pragmatist, she was aware of the delicate balance required in these negotiations, a belief she voiced in a speech: "I do not see empowerment of women as a zero-sum game in which women's gains are men's losses. Rather I see women's empowerment as the rising tide which will raise ships." Men, as Nafis saw it, were not the enemy. Rather, men needed to be co-opted to become partners in the crusade.

Those colleagues who were close to Nafis Sadik realized that the years of stress and life on the road had taken their toll. After her bypass surgery she hadn't slowed down, yet her heart ailment reoccurred shortly before she visited Stirling Scruggs in China for a long mission. During this trip they sailed down the Yangtze River with Madame Peng Peyoun and visited the Three Gorges. Stirling, the Tennessean and ever the southern gentleman, knew better than to make a fuss over his boss. Instead he quietly brought along a young doctor who carried a case full of emergency drugs for heart failure and an oxygen bottle. Nafis thought he was just another member of the entourage lugging around a big briefcase. When the group stopped to visit a Buddhist site that required them to all hike up a mountain, she uncharacteristically chose to wait down below. "So the doctor stayed down there, too, and he sat on a bench several feet from her. There was a nice little garden, and at one point, he told me that she came over and sat down and said, 'Why aren't you hiking with the others? You're a young man, and you look strong.' And he complained that he had hurt his foot, and she said, 'Well, you should get that looked at,' and he said, 'Yes, ma'am, I will.' She never caught on to the whole thing that he was there to watch out for her."

Their fearless leader, ever the idiosyncratic individual, continued to defy classification or even predictability. Australian ambassador Penny Wensley noted in a tribute that everyone used "warrior words" to describe Nafis. Alex Marshall presented a variation on this theme. "Every now and then you see a flash of Nafis as a different sort of person, who is not the professional, but you can imagine her in another life being a jockey, for example. Really driving, you know. Or a soldier—in fact, I've seen her with soldiers, and she has almost a fellow feeling. I don't know what it is, but she has a nineteenth-century quality about her, the sort of girl who used to run off and dress up in a hussar's uniform and join the army. Maybe I'm too imaginative, but there is that flavor about her. She can do anything that a man can do, and probably better. She doesn't make a big thing out of it, but every so often you see that little flash." Nafis, the soldier in a sari.

Wang Lijuan | Beijing, China

The young woman sitting next to me in the office of the China Population Communication Center in Beijing is no stranger to the ambivalence many women possess surrounding babies . . . or certainly the decision to have one of their own. In our conversation we agree that it's not that the infant itself presents a dilemma; it's the notion that we must trade so much in return for motherhood, choices that most men will never face—like forfeiting our careers, travel, freedom.

Lijuan continues: "My husband and I have discussed whether we should have a kid or how many we should have. We finally agreed that if you want to have a complete life maybe you should have a child. You know we have many friends who do not want to have a baby at all because they are very busy. We do feel our work is more important and we want to devote ourselves to a kind of mission. We know having a baby is very costly and then we will have a lot of trouble taking care of one child. So I think that life pressure is very heavy for young people today, particularly young adults in urban areas. If you talk with them you will understand that they have various demands, from work, from competition.

"I think China got this term 'dink' from the United States, meaning 'double income no kids.' We say 'they're a dink family.' But I've decided I don't want to be a dink family." She notes that having children is an expensive proposition in both time and money, which "makes becoming parents a difficult choice, because we do want to enjoy our life. This is our generation's thinking."

Wang Lijuan is an attractive twenty-eight-year-old with a round face as pale and serene as the moon, except the smooth surface is interrupted by her prominent cheek bones and sensuous lips. Her dark hair is styled in a modern layered haircut with feathered bangs combed to either side of her broad forehead, framing wide-set eyes that project an intelligent, knowing expression. When she says her dad always wanted a son—instead of the two daughters he sired—I see tears pool in those brown eyes.

But she insists that this penchant for boys is a thing of the past in China, at least amongst urbanites. I ask if she has a preference for a girl or a boy when she starts her family. "Not at all. Actually my mother prefers me to have a girl, because she thinks girls are easier to raise. And since my mother is living with us and will be the one caring for our baby while we're at work, she has a vested interest!"

Lijuan grew up in a small village called Zhumadian in China's Henan Province where her high school sat across the street from a local blood bank, a fact that would come to have a profound influence on her. While the first mention of AIDS was being made at the Women's Conference in Beijing, Lijuan and her friends knew nothing about the disease. Some of her poorer classmates would quietly visit the clinic and sell their blood to help support their family. Fortunately Lijuan's parents eschewed this practice, which they thought brought hardship on a household—far-reaching bad luck beyond any physical ramifications from having blood drawn. "Traditionally, in the Chinese mind, blood is very valuable, and if you just lose some drops people will think, 'Oh, that's very bad for your house, you will get diseases, you will be poor.'"

Back in high school she watched the clinic mobbed daily by impoverished farmers who would pool their money and hire a truck to transport them into Zhumadian for the express purpose of selling their lifeblood. Men, women, teenagers—many falsified the donor record books documenting their schedule of bloodletting so that they could donate more frequently. While the officials mandated testing for anemia and hepatitis, before 1995 they did not require screening for HIV, because that would be to admit the virus was present in China—a situation the government not only denied but had taken aggressive action to prevent. Tragically this action would morph into the deaths of untold thousands.

In 1985, as news of the existence of AIDS filtered underneath the Red Curtain, China took action to protect its one billion citizens. The government prohibited the import of any blood or plasma products. And yet since a population this size required eight hundred tons of blood annually for its residents' health, the supply had to be refurbished from some source. Enter a class of entrepreneurs who saw in this life-or-death equation the opportunity for profits; sadly this group of profiteers contained members of the government ministry charged with overseeing the collection and distribution of plasma throughout the nation. The workers who operated the commercial blood banks became known as "bloodheads."

Official and unofficial clinics sprang up throughout the countryside, with more than two hundred official stations in Henan Province alone . . . and an untold number of illegal ones. They were located mainly in rural areas where they would take advantage of the extreme poverty of the farmers. In time this new source of revenue became the primary income for this group. As one critic noted, "Perhaps most fatal, however, was the method of collecting blood plasma and returning the remaining red blood cells to the peasant blood-sellers. In order to separate out the plasma, the bloodheads would take blood from several donors of the same blood type and spin it in a centrifuge. Then they would reinject what remained back into the donors, putting all of them at risk for HIV." The lab workers proudly advertised this practice as a health measure that helped prevent anemia and created a situation where "healthy individuals could donate twice in one day." In Tianjin there were even ghoulish reports of a group that kidnapped children, took their blood, and sold it to state-owned plasma banks.

Yet what the bloodheads didn't know initially was that some of their donors were HIV positive. The practice of reinjecting them from the shared pool of blood, along with unsafe methods of collection such as reusing needles, began to spread HIV at an alarming rate. By 2003 the World Health Organization estimated one million people in Henan Province alone were carrying the AIDS virus. In Houyang village 80 percent of the residents tested HIV positive.

The long-term ramifications of this epidemic, especially in a nation devoted to the one-child policy, would prove to be devastating. The younger generation found themselves in the hell of nursing both parents, as their elders withered to skeletons and died of AIDS, leaving their offspring orphaned . . . with no siblings. Eventually the government took action to end the unsafe blood collection methods and put into place policies to deal with the AIDS pandemic these practices had engendered.

By the time Lijuan entered her career in Beijing, she had seen close at hand the dangers of HIV. Today, although in a monogamous relationship, she insists her partner use condoms for reasons beyond their contraceptive properties; the prophylactics also protect her from STDs. "I trust my husband but I still understand there are some possibilities, so we just choose to use condoms," she says, delicately skirting the issue of infidelity. This decision provides Lijuan with "peacefulness."

The young woman preaches what she practices. While the farmers in her village were being infected with HIV, she didn't even know the disease existed. But today she has a great deal of knowledge as part of her professional duties to promote public awareness, particularly among young people. For this reason Lijuan organized a project at the university, soliciting celebrities to speak to the students and distributing six hundred thousand free condoms that she managed to have donated from a manufacturer. "I wanted to promote awareness so basically the young people know that even at Beijing's best university it's okay to talk about the condom." One of her other projects is a survey of middle school students, and in this study Lijuan learned that thirty members of the control group were already sexually active.

She showed me a photo that had appeared on the front page of the *Beijing Morning News*; in it teens are learning how to apply condoms. They can practice slipping one over a stainless-steel penis designed for demonstration, and I smiled thinking some things had come a long way in the fifty years since Nafis taught the Pakistani soldiers how to apply a condom as she slid one over a pencil.

Lijuan actually met Nafis Sadik when the doctor visited Beijing on a mission to discuss with government officials ways to prevent the spread of HIV and to consult on their family planning policies. "UNFPA's role is very important, I think particularly in changing the minds of policymakers in China. Dr. Sadik's program eliminated the quotas, and this is a huge liberation, a very visible role of UNFPA." Lijuan feels that her country has made great progress, and she sees the national commitment to supplying women with access to birth control as empowering them. "You understand, if a woman keeps on giving birth to children, she will lose a lot of opportunities. I say this is true feminism. I feel a woman should be independent, particularly economically, and should realize her value—not only through giving birth to children—but also through all the things she can do well. Let me explain: I think a woman should not only be valued through her reproductive capacity, but also through her talents—all kinds of talents which she can contribute to society. I mean she is more than someone who will belong only to one family, but rather a person who can contribute to the world at large."

14   BACK HOME

To breed or not to breed: that is the question. But it is a question that females have seldom bothered to ask throughout history, because they had no control over the answer. In the 1940s two women set out to change that: Margaret Sanger and Katherine McCormick. Sanger, who watched her mother die young after she gave birth to eleven babies, went on to become a nurse in New York City. There she witnessed the horror of her patients dying from childbirth and self-induced abortions (the same type of nightmare Nafis Sadik encountered at Baltimore's City Hospital). Since becoming a young woman, Sanger had dreamed of creating an easy-to-use birth control pill that would end this suffering; when Katherine McCormick inherited $15 million, she joined with Sanger to provide the financial backing for the drug's research and development—a collaboration that eventually led to the oral contraceptives on the market today.

Also in the 1940s another young woman had dreams of making her mark on history. When Nafis announced she intended to go to medical school, her relatives had marveled that any female would eschew the practice that had existed since time immemorial: that of marrying, then staying at home and nurturing a family. Her husband's and children's achievements were *her* achievements. Their failings were also hers, especially in Muslim culture where "Amma" was responsible for the misdeeds of her young.

Turn the calendar forward two decades, and we find women taking advantage of a handy little creation called the Pill, oral contraceptives that allowed them to prevent pregnancies without any sacrifice (or consent) from their partner. This innovation, released in 1960, launched a paradigm shift that changed history . . . and there was no going back. Now that females were capable of controlling their own fertility, they were also capable of taking charge of their own destiny—a reality that some opponents continue to fight with every weapon at their disposal because they are loathe to surrender their power over the "weaker sex."

Also in the 1960s, while Nafis was creating one of the globe's first family planning agencies, she found herself in the ironic position of being mother to five children. She became an early practitioner of the juggling act millions of modern women currently perform on a daily basis: that of simultaneously holding down a career and raising a family. And just like every other aspect of her life, in this area Nafis had to do it better than anyone else, in spite of her enormous professional demands. And even though she now traveled hundreds of thousands of miles each year, a practice that would find her sleeping more nights in hotel beds and airline seats than in her own midtown apartment, Mrs. Sadik remained the lady of the house.

From the get-go Nafis knew she didn't want to be a single career woman, because she adamantly wanted to have children. "I knew I didn't want to be alone," she said, but she admits if she'd lived in the United States during her childbearing years she would have had only one baby because "it's so difficult here," meaning the lack of support for working mothers. Having grown up with such a happy family life on the subcontinent, she wanted to duplicate that experience. Yet unlike most women of her generation, she didn't view this desire as a reason to abandon her career aspirations. It's doubtful, however, that as a teenager plotting "to change the world" the young Nafis could have imagined the level of responsibility she would undertake both at home and at work simultaneously. Her son Omar found his mother rose to the occasion in this regard. "There is nobody smarter than my mother and there is just nobody that I know who is responsible like my mother."

Her old friend Goga Mahmoud Saeed observed Nafis close at hand for decades and analyzed her methods for success. "She's committed to everything—to family and to work and to friends—and to little things like knitting. She sees all the latest movies, listens to all sorts of music: pop, classical, Pakistani, Indian. I think she is sincerely committed to it all, and if you do that then you channel your commitments and your passion. Only then can you find the time, but if you are not committed to one of those things, then that is the area which lags behind. And Nafis is interested in everything. You know, like you say 'don't miss out on life'? That is not something you worry about with her."

Probably Nafis's most defining characteristic, however, lies in her phenomenal self-discipline. And in an unlikely turn of events, the lack of this attribute in one of her children created a gulf between them that would tragically destroy their relationship.

Goga Saeed observed another trait of Nafis's: "I think she gives everyone total respect—her children total respect and her husband total respect. Even if they are doing something which she wouldn't do. She says everyone in the world is different. Nobody is like another person, so one should not be judgmental. She never judges anyone and that is why nobody gets rubbed the wrong way, and that's why her friends and family rally 'round her, because they feel respected and secure. She always sees everything from another person's perspective, their point of view, and she gives everyone their due." Not coincidentally, the same traits which have made her a renowned diplomat.

The respect Nafis paid to Azhar formed an integral part of their marriage, and the inner workings of this union have long been a source of curiosity to onlookers, because so many facets of its success fly in the face of probability. Inside observers offer illumination on how this relationship functions: "People say that behind every great man there is a woman. But behind Nafis Sadik there is also a man. And that man is Azhar Sadik. Azhar has been supportive of her completely, in Nafis's desire to move forward, to do well, and I think she draws tremendous strength from that. Her family life is complete. She is fully satisfied with her environment—socially, professionally, and as a human person. I think she just gains that inner confidence from the world that surrounds her, and she then plays it back. That cycle is the one that drives Nafis."

Another friend opines: "Possibly the greatest reason for Nafis Sadik's public success is due to her husband." His choice to give up his career and follow his wife's was extremely rare for a Pakistani man.

As one relative reflected: "It was an amazing thing to do, but I think he realized that her work was ultimately going to be more important than what he was doing . . . she is going to reach out and help so many people."

Thus Azhar made the big decision to sell the house in Karachi and relocate to New York. And even when Caltex announced they were moving their offices to Houston, Azhar chose to remain in New York City rather than uproot the family once again. As a result of this situation, now out of a job, he pursued other business options. While he chose to lease their residence, he took full advantage of the downturn in the local real estate market and invested in rental property. There were, of course, other adjustments. Azhar missed his family, his cronies, his school chums and colleagues in Pakistan, the easy life with servants, and a high standard of living for the middle class.

The Sadik home was now reduced to one domestic, Amosh, who had been part of the household in Pakistan since he ran away from home at twelve and was discovered on the streets by Nafis's uncle, who brought him home to live with the family. Amosh began helping out around the house at that point and then emigrated with the clan to New York, where he served them as chief cook, cleaner, and driver—a situation met with glee by the children after the Shake-and-Bake era under Wafa's domain. The loyal servant told the siblings to remember that he had been with their parents long before they were born, and he would be there long after they were gone.

When Azhar—who by his own admission had previously been unable to boil water—arrived in Manhattan, he decided he would learn how to cook so he would not starve when their lone domestic went back to Pakistan for a holiday. Azhar watched Amosh in the kitchen carelessly tossing random ingredients and spices into a pot. Yet somehow Mr. Sadik managed to transcribe these actions into meticulous recipes, and he measured everything with precision. His wife found no end of amusement at her husband's finicky methods. "And he used to cook like this: five little bowls, with each spice separate. 'Why put each spice separate?' I asked. 'Just put them all in the same bowl.' 'No, just leave me be,' he'd insist. Everything has to be done just so, the onions have to be cut fine and even, all exactly the same. I say 'Hum, hum, hum' then I'll offer to help and start cutting something. He'll say to me, 'What are you doing? Don't do it like that.' Such contrasting personalities! He thinks I'm so careless, so sloppy. He'll have the whole kitchen laid out meticulously with utensils, as if he's in the operating room. One day a friend of mine and I, we were in hysterics at this display, and Azhar was getting really angry. 'Laugh, laugh as much as you like, but when you eat it, you will see how good it is!'"

Yet he found appetizing trade-offs in the Big Apple: "I think New York grows on you. The city grows on you. Nowhere in the world can you walk down the stairs of your apartment building, and you will get Bloomingdales, you will get the finest cuisine that there is, and it's open all night long. You name it—museums, ferries, trains, busses—everything is here. You may have some of these things in any one place, but you will never have all of them as you do in New York City."

The Sadiks took full advantage of these opportunities, too,

attending embassy parties, the theater, and sporting events on a regular basis. In keeping with their Pakistani heritage, they loved going to the track and betting on the ponies. In fact they both were obsessive sports fans, following tennis, golf, football, basketball, and baseball, watching games on TV and attending them at the stadiums around the city's five boroughs. As the couple had aged, they transitioned from playing golf and tennis, and their respective athletics of cricket and badminton, to the world of spectator sports. But their passion remained the same; they knew all the players, the stats, the dramas. "What Nafis doesn't know she learns from me," Azhar boasts. "She says, 'Where do you read all this rubbish?' I say, you know, in the *New York Post*, the evening rag which I buy for the sports, but you and the girls all read for the gossip."

However, like most married couples, Nafis and Azhar had their issues. For one, Nafis being a Yankees fan and Azhar following the underdog, the Mets. An old friend, Akhtar Isphahani, told a story that illustrated another source of friction. "One day I met them for lunch, and when I walked in, Nafis looked at my shoes and immediately said, 'Oh, those are nice, I'd like a pair. Please get me one sometime when you are out.' Azhar said, 'Nafis, you have seventy-five pairs of unworn shoes. Where are you going to put them? There is no room in the apartment.'" The truth was that her infamous shopping hobby and her collection of saris had filled up every square inch of closet space at home, including her husband's.

Nafis realized from the very beginning of their acquaintance that in many ways she and Azhar were poles apart. "We're totally different personalities in a way, I would say we're basically opposite to each other. I'm extremely outgoing and I like people around, and Azhar is shy. When I go to a place I ring up all my acquaintances, because I always keep up with everyone. He has few friends, but they're very close, and that's it. He thinks about all the things that could go wrong, and I think when things go wrong we'll have enough time to ponder. I say, 'Well, let's think that everything's going to be fine.' We are totally different personalities, and yet I think a good combination."

Azhar has his own theories on married life. "Over the years, it's difficult, two people having professions. I think we worked hard at smoothing out the edges. Of course, don't let anyone fool you into believing that everything is always perfect. It isn't. Nothing is always perfect. If it were, life would be very dull.

"Throughout the years together your thinking changes, your priorities change. A thing that might irk you at a certain stage of your life, you wonder why it ever hurt you. And something that was of no consequence now becomes an important matter, so it's an evolutionary thing. And we've got to evolve; otherwise, life can be very difficult indeed."

One battle to which the man of the house finally surrendered was correcting the volume of people who addressed *him* as Dr. Sadik. "Talking about a man's world, everyone—including my doorman—cannot conceive of the fact that I am not a doctor—that Nafis is the M.D., so they call me the doctor. You know I tried my best, I tried very hard to say that I am not Dr. Sadik, but eventually I have given up. Now yours truly is a doctor."

He also found his place at the company picnic quite out of the ordinary, providing some situations bordering on the comical. At the various embassy and United Nations functions, the other diplomats wanted to talk shop with his wife. "Meanwhile I am standing there like an idiot with the women, and the men's wives are used to this—they are used to talking about their babies, their grandchildren, what they did while shopping, and etc. . . . so who do you think is the odd man out?" Azhar's acceptance of this state of affairs was not without a struggle on his part. "You have to develop a mechanism to try and overcome these situations, and if you don't, god help you."

The oft-cited difference in their personalities provides a primary reason the marriage has lasted over fifty years. While Nafis stood in the limelight for all those decades, she did not have to compete with a partner who sought equal billing. As her sister-in-law, Salma Shoaib, observed, "I think that she would have needed to have that kind of husband, to tell you the truth. I can't see her married to a very dominant man, someone who was on equal or higher status with her. I just can't see that. Because I think she's a person who needs prominence, you know, and Azhar is a shy, more retiring person, who I think was quite happy to take a back seat to her. That's my impression. And it's worked. It's been a very long relationship, and it seems to be imminently successful." Yet his strength of character has prevented him from feeling overshadowed.

One thing everyone agrees on is the couple's commitment to friendship, their equal loyalty to both the commoner and the prince. As their son noted: "They have more friends than anyone that I know, and many of them they have known for the last fifty years and longer."

Indeed, in the various address books Nafis owns—each one organized by city—the ink on many a name has faded with time. She has been pals with Goga Saeed since the two met in 1958 on Goga's wedding day. Later, when her friend got divorced, Nafis helped the newly single woman through the transition and encouraged her to stay on in New York. "She told me don't cook food at your house. Come and eat with me at my place every day. I didn't do that every day, but very often I just walked over because I didn't live too far away. When her son and daughters married, we did their weddings together. And we would drive all the way to Secaucus to the sales at the outlet mall. I mean, she'd do all the things that many housewives do, but she'd have to cram them all into one day. Then she would say, 'I'll go with you to the bridge club and play, but I have this engagement in the evening, so she would leave the house in the morning dressed for a dinner party."

Nafis was still deeply imbedded in her culture, as her sister-in-law noted. "There is a fairly large Pakistani contingent in New York, and this small contingent is constantly having parties. It's really the same life, just transported from one country to another country. They live the same life here that they would live back in Pakistan, and so they socialize . . . one person has a dinner, and a second person has a dinner, and a third person has a dinner, and then they go the rounds again. And Nafis, by the way, loves parties. I think it's a family thing because Nighat loves parties as well. But if there's an event at 8:00, Nafis would come off a plane from China, and after traveling twenty-five hours, she'd go straight to that party rather than miss it."

By all accounts Mohammad Shoaib was the person who most influenced Nafis to become a successful career woman. He started her on this path from the time she toddled through the library pulling tomes off the shelf, and her father refused to punish her "love of books." When she entered the professional arena, she still relied on her father, not only as a role model but also as a source of wisdom in his capacity as a respected statesman and economist. When he died of a heart attack immediately after retiring from the World Bank in 1976, Nafis was forty-seven years old. "We got so many letters from people all over the world, people we had never known, who told us how he had helped them."

After her mother's early death, elder daughter Nafis had stepped in to fill the void and served as matriarch to the clan. Now with their father gone as well, she became the official head of the family. The siblings all called her "Apa," meaning "eldest sister," and in her culture this designation carried considerable weight, a position of respect. Or as her nephew noted: "In Pakistani families when you are asking someone for their hand in marriage, you would normally ask their father. I think in our family you would go and ask Nafis for permission."

Mohammed's emphasis on education paid off for his other progeny as well. Two of his sons, Hassan and the youngest, Tariq, followed their father's example in the world of high finance, studying in England and becoming chartered accountants. The other two brothers,

Iqbal and Kemal, became successful engineers. But in 1987 Nafis would lose Icky, her childhood partner in crime, when he died from a heart attack at fifty-six. In fact, the history of heart disease and hypertension in the family saw three of the siblings undergo bypass surgery within a few years of each other. Even more shocking than Icky's early death was the loss of the beloved baby of the family, Tariq (the uncle who had taken Nafis's brood to see *Hair* when they passed through London). He died from an asthma attack before his fortieth birthday.

That left Hassan, who had married the lovely green-eyed Salma and moved to Bronxville, New York, close to Apa. Kemal, after years of living in London, returned to Karachi and became a professional bridge player who competes internationally. Those boyhood years in Britain, bilking the upper crust at cards, had paid off in more ways than one.

Chicky had fulfilled her fantasy of being a grande dame of society. She married and gave birth to a daughter, Nyla. But the marriage was not to last. Her next husband, Naseen, a cousin of Azhar's, turned out to be a very conservative gentleman who forbade his wife to smoke, work, or drive. Naseen was a *zaminar*, a very, very wealthy landowner in Pakistan, which might initially seem an enormous asset, until one realizes he does not go to the office, as Chicky recalled. "You know, having a man in the house all the time can be a bit unnerving. But then he took up golf, which took up a lot of time, so I was very happy with the golf. For four or five hours he'd be at the golf club in Karachi, so that gave me an afternoon to myself." This situation worked well until he died of kidney failure, leaving behind a very wealthy, gorgeous widow.

Even though the two lived fourteen thousand miles apart, Nyla, Chicky's only child, would grow very close to Nafis and called her "Khalajan," meaning "dearest aunt." Nyla was born a year after Omar, and the cousins of the international clan reunited each year when the Sadiks would return to Pakistan over the summer holidays. Nyla remembered her aunt's arrival: "She'd come visit us, and she'd get protocol in Pakistan, but I didn't think anything of it somehow because she was always so low-key about it. We'd have to give identification cards beforehand when we were going to come and get her at the airport. My mother, myself, my cousins, we would all go to the VIP lounge and wait for her, and she would meet us there. The luggage would be collected and one of the UN cars would come to pick her up, and we'd go home. It was quite unnerving sometimes, because there would be all these sirens behind us, and the police van. I'd say 'Khala, this is so embarrassing, you know. Can't you stop this from happening?' But she was never into any of this. Anybody living in Pakistan is very into it, and they'd say, yeah, we want this protocol. Get the van to follow us and get the sirens going. But she said, no, no, please don't have this—she used to be embarrassed too, actually."

The relatives traveled west across the pond to visit the Sadik household as well, escaping steamy Karachi to frequently stay in New York for the whole summer. As the nieces and nephews grew older, these trips took on different functions. Nyla fondly remembers how she journeyed to New York before her marriage, and Khalajan took the young bride-to-be trousseau shopping, an opportunity to practice the aunt's favorite workout routine, as they traipsed from Bergdorf's to Saks. "But at the last minute, I backed out of that marriage, which turned out to be a good thing. Fortunately, I've always been pretty close to my aunt—she's my mother's only sister—so I was able to confide in her and discuss anything."

Then again, there was a flip side to this intimacy. "I mean if she didn't like what anyone was doing, she would tell you. You didn't have to wonder about it with my aunt. She'd let you know if she was irritated with you."

Other members of the clan remarked on the matriarch's devotion to the younger generation. As Faizan, Kemal's son, remembered, "We moved to England in 1974, and as a result we didn't really see much of each other for the next several years. I do remember fleeting visits where she would arrive on a Thursday night, stay for dinner, and that car would always be waiting to whisk her off somewhere—she'd be running here, there, and everywhere. Then in 1989, I went to college in New York. I lived on campus, but obviously her flat was there, and for the next several years I saw her a hell of a lot, even though she was still traveling five or six days a week. This era was when I really got to know her properly. Up until then our image of Auntie Nafis was . . . well, being a bit of a scary character actually, because she has so much power. But you know, when I saw a lot of her I realized she's the total opposite—she's a very, very soft and kind person.

"One time I broke my foot playing soccer. I know this sounds like a minor injury, but it was pretty horrific—the bone came out and everything—and I was in hospital for a week. I remember she came to see me three or four times while I was there, and then the day I was coming out she arrived and said, 'No, you are coming back to our place. I have to look after you.'

"Another thing that actually astonishes me most about her is that despite how much she does in her professional life, she has so much time for her family and her friends. She has not let that side of her life slide at all, quite the opposite, in fact."

While in 1975 Dr. Sadik, as UNFPA's technical adviser, oversaw the agency's 1,200 projects in ninety-two countries, similar to most mothers she still had a few niggling concerns demanding her attention back home. Like the fact her daughters were warning her that Omar, who was attending high school in Tarrytown, was illiterate. This news prompted the Sadiks to transfer their only son to a school in the city, and they soon relocated there as well.

Evidently moving to Manhattan was the right decision for Omar because the young man made the most of his formative years there, attending the United Nations high school in the daytime and permitting his big sisters to sneak him into the Big Apple's hot discotheques, like Regine's and Studio 54, at night. This in the heady days when the clubs were hopping with regulars like Mick Jagger and Andy Warhol.

"You know, in Manhattan children tend to grow up a little faster than in the suburbs," Omar deduced. He also appreciated the brushes with celebrity on the home front and our Leo-in-the-limelight's passion for entertaining. "Every week there was a dinner party at our house, and you could have an Indian movie actress walk in, you could have Kofi Annan walk in, you could have Al Gore walk in, the next prime minister of Pakistan—I mean literarily that spectrum of people. They always took the time to speak to you, and in that five or ten minutes you could feel you learned something from them."

In Omar's junior year of high school he spent a month abroad in Jamaica, and the poverty there offered an eye-opening lesson to the youngster. Still, the high life in Manhattan appealed to him, and in an argument familiar to Nafis, her son quizzed her on why she didn't go into private practice, where she could have made much more money than her position at the UN. "Later in life I understood all the concepts about her work, but not initially when I was a teenager," he admitted. That's why I asked her, 'Why didn't you just continue practicing medicine, all these doctors make so much money.' Meaning that then you'd get a lot of money, right? Meaning that then I'd have access to a lot more money, right? Boy, did I get it. Oh man, she was furious. She said, 'I can't believe you said that.' I don't remember the exact words, it was so many years ago, but she was very upset that I would even think that, given the context of what she does, money should have been my primary concern. But I didn't understand that at the time because I was growing up American, and growing up American meant getting a first-rate job and making money. But she was serving a greater good. So my comment was merely about status, that's all."

Omar's mother felt quite disappointed, as if she realized the ideals with which she had been raised in the old country were not passing along to her children. "You know, unfortunately we are losing that value system in our societies. Like when we were young, we wanted to become somebody. Never did it occur to me, I mean personally, that I wanted to be rich. However, now you see so many young people—and ask them what do they want? Just to be rich. Not to achieve something personally. And, I think it's a different mindset and in a sense more materialistic. And then people are not valued for what they contribute to a family, a society . . . because it's not necessarily only money that you contribute. You also contribute love and wisdom and compassion or support. You just spend the time listening to people. You know there are so many other things that you can contribute in a family, or a society, for which people can be valued. Kindness, to be courteous, to be helpful when somebody needs help . . . all that. These are not values that are so much appreciated today. Instead of appearing as normal caring acts, I've noticed how these situations are seen as people imposing on you. Like I remember whenever anyone needed some advice or medical attention, I was always ready to go. If any of my family members became ill, I would always go to visit them. And my children used to say, 'Oh, they're taking advantage of you.' I said, no, nobody's taking advantage of me, because I *want* to do it. It's only taking advantage if I don't want to do it, and then I'm being pressured to do it against my will." Here we see Nafis fired up again on her main mantra of human rights, the lightning rod that has made her the champion of choice: the notion that everyone must have free will to control his or her own destiny.

"But I think all these things are changing in our societies also. Like, you know when I was growing up in a big family, people never lacked a home. Even if they didn't have any money, they would just come and live in someone's house. And we had people living in our home for many years, and then they would go to someone else's home, and nobody ever said, 'What is so and so doing here?' The point being, they knew they wouldn't be on the street. But, I don't think that assurance will exist anymore."

Azhar also fretted over some of the cultural differences the couple encountered in the States, especially the future the next generation would face. He observed the incredibly long hours of the American workers around him, professionals like his nieces and nephews who had Ivy League résumés. "For instance, take lawyers and investment bankers; they have no life, they earn a lot of money, but they get home when it's dark and the children have already gone to sleep, having been with the nanny all day long. I think that everyone must question themselves and ask, 'Is this the life that I want to lead?'"

During their transition to culture stateside, other things had changed in society as well. Of Omar's five close friends at the UN school, all their mothers worked, a fact that was the opposite to the siblings' experience in Pakistan. Even though his mother may have been returning from a summit meeting with the president of Cameroon the day before, when she was in town she came to her son's plays and soccer matches just like the other moms. She never forgot anyone's birthday, although the remembrance may have been in the form of a long-distance phone call from a Sydney boardroom.

In the tradition of his grandfather, Omar went on to study economics and business at Boston University, and while at school he used to call his father, the up-and-coming chef, for advice on cooking. Their son would become an investment banker, and later transitioned to international finance, then settled in a stately six-bedroom home in Chappaqua, New York. "I'm married, four kids, ages twelve to seven. So population planning didn't work at my house, but we had twins, so they were not quite planned."

The outcome of the Sadiks' decision to relocate to the United States in order to provide their children with access to topnotch colleges proved ironic at best—especially considering their family's generations-old commitment to providing girls with an excellent education. And it was even more ironic considering girls' access to education was one of the primary planks in Nafis's human rights' platform. Azhar, too, felt one's schooling was of the utmost importance. "I think anything else can be taken away from you, but nobody can take your mind. Nobody can take your education away from you." So the

Sadik girls had access, they had opportunities, they had encouragement . . . but they had little interest. After their mother had risked the ire of her relatives to go to medical school, it must have struck her as a very odd decision for her daughters to be so blasé about higher learning or a professional path, but they swear she never tried to pressure them into any decision. In fact, all her children have gone on record as testifying that Mummy remained amazingly nonjudgmental and open-minded about the choices they made as adults.

When the clan moved across the planet and colonized Tarrytown, Wafa had risen to the occasion to take over as domestic goddess and run the household while her adopted mother ran programs for the women of the world. While Nafis was away, her eldest looked after the other four children, and she was like a mother figure to the youngest, Omar, in much the same type of relationship Nafis had had with her baby brother, Tariq. The ambitious Wafa also babysat for the neighbors to earn extra cash. After graduation from high school, she took a job as a cashier at Barker's, a local department store, and within a week the management had promoted her. The same take-charge attitude that she had displayed on the home front was now being rewarded—and perhaps better appreciated—at work.

Interestingly Wafa's boyfriend, Nadoo, the one Azhar and the servants had chased from the Karachi house like a burglar, the one Wafa had been pining for since she arrived in the States, followed her to New York, where he planned to attend college. He rented a place in Queens, and the two picked up where they had left off, but they soon found it quite problematic to travel the long distance between their homes to visit.

Even though Wafa was nineteen, she had no aspirations to attend college but was eager to work. "So I told Bhabhiji, 'What do you think if Nadoo and I get married? And she said, 'No. How can you get married? He doesn't even have a job. How will he support you?' I said, 'We'll do something. He'll work and he'll study and I'll work, and we'll manage somehow.' She wasn't too sure about that. The only thing going for him was the fact that she knew his family, because his cousin was married to Bhabhiji's brother Kemal."

When Nafis traveled to Pakistan for a holiday, an entourage from Nadoo's family came to pay their respects and make the formal marriage proposal on his behalf, asking for Wafa's hand. For whatever reason, the matriarch said yes.

In the Shoaib family tradition they threw a three-day wedding at the Tarrytown home, borrowing Christmas lights from all the neighbors to decorate the trees. Those same neighbors watched in awe as night after night girls were dancing on the lawn and guests showed up unannounced to take part in the festivities. This proved a challenge for the hosts, who were expecting twenty-five people, when a hundred showed up, as Nafis remembered. "So Amosh said, 'You know, I haven't cooked food for all these people!' and I said, 'Well, whatever it is, we have to feed them.' So he had food frozen, and he was thawing it out as best he could, and guests would come back to the table and say, 'Hum, this curry was not there before.' I'd say, 'Oh, you just didn't see it.' I don't know how, but Amosh managed to feed a hundred people—I mean, nobody left hungry, and everyone was praising the food."

Good at her word, Wafa moved into the city with her new husband and took a job working at a shop called Chor Bazaar, named for the thieves' market in Mumbai. The boutique's owners were an Indian man and his French wife. "It was fascinating because I remember when I walked by, I looked at the window and said, these clothes are so familiar, and yet so different. The fabric was from Afghanistan and India, and the designs were all European."

Wafa became the conduit, dealing with the cadre of textile manufacturers overseas, the designers, and tailors. She also dealt with the boutique's celebrity clientele. "The kind of people I met in the shop, I would never meet in my lifetime. Jackie Onassis came in many times . . .

we had a rapport, we used to talk to each other. She had this habit of trying on everything, and then she used to stay back and help me put it away. I mean she was very sweet. I used to see her daughter going to school every day, passing by, because it was on the corner of 61st and Lexington, two blocks away from Bloomingdale's. And Dustin Hoffman used to come in a lot, because he was our neighbor. Sonny and Cher, when they still were together, used to come. Diana Ross.

"And these are people you spoke to. They spoke to you, and there were so many other artists, writers, and we were on a first-name basis, and we were friends. They didn't act like big actors, or artists, they were human beings. We met each other, we spoke to each other, we shared the same food. I mean, we'd be eating samosas, and they would come in and eat samosas with us."

Eventually Wafa and her husband would return to Pakistan, where they would raise their family. She continued her go-get-'em approach and as an entrepreneur started several ventures, including a children's fair and a coffee shop.

In the family drama Wafa's younger sister Ghazala reminds one of Beth from *Little Women*. While the older girls experimented with varying degrees of rebellion, she was quiet, shy, and retiring; her life revolved simply around home. Ghazala never worked or ventured out to university, but she later married and returned to Pakistan, where she excelled at the domestic arts.

Ambereen, the girl who had dreamed of moving to Paris just for the autonomy of riding the Metro alone, was thrilled with the independence she was able to garner in Tarrytown for the first time. Like Wafa, she also worked at Barker's, but once they learned Ambereen could add and subtract, the owners took her out of menswear and stationed her up front as a cashier. Yet because this was not Paris, she didn't ride the Metro to work; rather, without her mother's knowledge, she hitchhiked.

She and a friend also took the bus into the city, wandered around the Village, and read the *Voice*—all the while thinking they were very hip. Ambereen attended Richmond College in England for a couple of years, where she majored in psychology. Then on one of her holidays back to Pakistan she met a young oncologist, and the two were married in Manhattan.

As luck would have it, just before the nuptial marathon a friend sublet a huge apartment directly below the Sadiks' midtown abode. This arrangement allowed for plenty of space for out-of-town guests and several days of singing and dancing for dozens of people. The bride's parents took all the furniture out of the living room to make way for the nightly festivities and rented a hall fronting the UN for the reception.

After her marriage Ambereen settled in suburban New York, and today she's the business manager for her husband's medical practice. She also gave birth to two children, and as had been the tradition for generations in her family, she moved back home when her due date drew near, so her mother could attend her.

By all accounts from friends and relatives, Mehreen was clearly the most beautiful and the brightest of the four girls, and coincidentally the one who looked the most like her mother. Her relationship with her siblings, however, was not exactly rosy. Ambereen said that while they were growing up her older sister thought that she was the hippest and coolest of the bunch, and therefore couldn't be bothered with housework.

Family friends had their own views on Mehreen: "She was a very rebellious child and as a teenager wanted to do things which nobody else was doing at that moment, like smoking. In those days, the young girls never smoked, and if they did, they certainly didn't do it in front of the elders. But Mehreen would smoke. She wouldn't care, she'd be wanting to show that she was her own person. You know it must have been very difficult to live with somebody like Nafis, especially if you were intelligent."

Evidently Mehreen objected a great deal to the fact that her mother was out working, and this in a time and place, Karachi in the 1960s, when no other mothers in their social circle worked outside the home. Zeenat Haroon Rashid, a chum since the young Nafis's first days in Karachi and another charter member of the Intellectual Society, has remained a friend for decades, observing at close range the dynamics in both families as they raised their daughters together. "Mehreen didn't have her mother sitting at home, waiting for her to come in, putting meals in front of her, concerned about what she did or didn't do. She would have liked that type of a life. She didn't have it. I am sure Nafis didn't give the same attention—say, that I was giving my daughter or somebody else was giving—because we had nothing else to do except be housewives. That was Mehreen's main complaint." She concluded, "Some people with famous parents measure themselves against them and fall short."

When it came time for Nafis and the children to make the big move to New York for Mummy's job at the UN, Mehreen went, but much like her Auntie Chicky had before her, she longed for a love she had left behind. Reluctantly her mother granted permission for her daughter's return to Pakistan to stay with Azhar. Upon her return, the sixteen-year-old girl announced she wanted to marry her beloved. Immediately.

The prospective groom was not the source of her father's objections; evidently Azhar approved of the young man who had a promising future and hailed from a good family. It was the insistence of Mehreen that the marriage had to happen at once. Azhar, at his wits end, didn't know what to do with this girl. He didn't tell Nafis—who was charged with starting a new job at the United Nations and finding a home for the family in New York after the first one had burned to the ground before their eyes.

Rather, he permitted Mehreen to marry, and Nafis didn't find out about it until she landed in Pakistan for home leave. When she arrived, Azhar said to their headstrong daughter, "Tell your mother what you've done." After six months Mehreen left her husband and joined Nafis, Wafa, Ghazala, Ambereen, Omar, and Amosh in the grand adventure in Tarrytown. The cause of the sudden marriage and the cause of the sudden divorce remain unknown.

As an adolescent Mehreen had begun drinking with friends in Pakistan, and this habit would later develop into a problem that would define the girl for the rest of her life. As one could expect, this habit did not go over well with her mother, the devout teetotaler. A friend affirmed of Nafis: "She really despises drink, she says it's a weakness and one doesn't need it." The doctor and diplomat, whose life grew out of a sense of duty and an ironclad will to serve it, must have been hard-pressed—no matter how open-minded—to watch her elder daughter squander her brains, looks, and privilege.

By the time Mehreen joined the family in New York, she already had a serious problem with drinking and drugs. Then in 1984, the year after her younger sister's wedding and Nafis's heart surgery, Mehreen married suddenly for a second time. Even those closest to her were shocked, as family friend Marina Fareed remembered: "One day Nafis rang up and said, 'Well, I called to inform you that Mehreen got married yesterday.'" The bride did follow some traditions though; at the ceremony Mehreen wore her mother's exquisite shell pink wedding gown and dupatta, the garments that had been sent from Pakistan and arrived on a silver tray at her mother's doorstep as a gift from her father.

Mehreen's groom was a tall, handsome man who passed himself off as a wealthy landowner, and in 1986 they had a son, Ali. Then she fulfilled her long-held dream of returning to Pakistan, and they settled in Lahore. But matrimonial happiness was not in the stars for her, and the reality of her unfortunate circumstances emerged—mainly that her husband was a wheeler-dealer who had no steady source of income. At one point Nafis was not able to get in touch with Mehreen for several weeks and had to send some friends out to find her daughter and see if she was all right. They discovered that the couple had moved to a village and were too poor to have a phone installed. The Sadiks sent some money to help with bills and enough for Mehreen to bring her toddler to the United States to visit his grandparents.

When Mehreen left Pakistan, she had planned to return to her husband, but the marriage quickly unraveled after her departure, and she never saw him again. Now, thirty-two years old and twice divorced, she and her child moved in permanently with her parents in Manhattan. Still, Mehreen glowed at all the parties held at the house, and amongst her large circle of devoted friends the woman was known as a delightful raconteur with a sparkling wit. She was as outgoing as her mother, as charming, as lovely . . . but was in one regard the exact opposite of her mother. "Azhar simply said that the problem with Mehreen is she's not disciplined, and this lack of discipline was just getting her nowhere. And Nafis is about discipline every minute of her life."

After years of struggle, the Sadiks' daughter entered rehab, but this attempt was not successful. Her counselors advised that she should attend a longer therapy program in Tampa, and so her parents sent her south to Florida and paid for her treatment. This stay evolved into their daughter living in Tampa permanently, with them buying her an apartment.

To provide him with some stability, Mehreen felt that it was best for her son, Ali, to stay in Manhattan with Nafis and Azhar. He resided with his grandparents in the same midtown flat where they had lived for years, and he attended the UN school as his Uncle Omar had done before him. And as far as Mehreen's relationship with her mother, for a long period they eventually stopped speaking altogether. Or as one friend noted, "Actually, one doesn't even question Nafis very much about her daughter, because this is a crucifix that she must bear."

Parents throughout history have asked why one child falters while the others in the family thrive. And for all her worldly wisdom, Nafis admits she does not have an explanation. "We have all wondered about this, but I don't think there's any answer to it. If we knew the answer, then we would be able to solve so many other people's problems. I think the reason is in somebody's makeup. It's not to do with the environment, because the environment would have affected everyone in some way or the other. In fact, the environment affected the other children in a way in which they felt like they were not getting their share of attention; rather, we were always focused on Mehreen, because she was always in difficulty."

Sevdie Ahmeti | Pristina, Kosovo

When the war was over and the families returned home from hiding in the mountains, each day the children went to gather water from the well, until one morning they began to scream, "There's something down there!" When the parents came running, they peered into the dark hole and could see a woman's long hair floating on the water.

Today, six years later, we stand at the site of this well, and it's difficult to imagine the tragedy that occurred here. On a sunny summer afternoon the trees, lush and green, dot the countryside, adding color to the gently rolling hills covered by grassy meadows and wheat fields. The modest farm next door boasts a haystack and a few dozen chickens clucking as they roam free throughout the yard. Even the old well itself seems serene now, literally bursting with vitality, because the watery grave was filled in with dirt when the bodies of the mother and her three daughters were removed, and today a healthy green tree, fertilized by their spirit, grows from the spot. The rubble of a bombed-out house is the only clue to this bucolic landscape's past as a rape camp, where the Serbian Army kept female prisoners, drowning eight of their victims in the three wells here in the village of Qirez.

But while the peaceful setting may belie its sinister past, one woman will never let the world forget what took place in Qirez and hundreds of other villages like it throughout Kosovo. Her name is

Sevdie Ahmeti, and while she tells me these stories in her precise English, delivered in a deep resonant voice, she maintains a grim poise, her patrician features stoically calm, an appearance she had plenty of time to perfect during the war, when she and a million other Kosovars lived under siege. While nearly half of them fled the region, she determined to stay and help the most vulnerable victims of war, founding the Centre for Protection of Women and Children.

Sevdie began by gathering the community together in Pristina, the capital of Kosovo, and telling them that they must help each other during this push toward "ethnic cleansing," an effort by Serbian forces to rid the region of ethnic Albanians, who are largely Muslim. Across the road from the rape camp Sevdie points to the ruins of a mosque, where witnesses claim the Serbs locked 1,500 people inside before blowing it up. The wreckage sits there today as a legacy to the region's horrifying history.

While she struggled to help in the liberation of Kosovo, Sevdie resented the media portrayal of her countrywomen, and how they were used as pawns in a political game, even during the recovery effort after the war. "Everybody knows of an apartheid in South Africa, but nobody knows that we also had an apartheid here. We didn't have a different color, we were white the same as the others. Instead, it was our culture that segregated us. It was our language and our names. This is what really happened here in Kosovo.

"Women are instrumentalized by the perpetrators, because they want to intimidate the population that is not wanted. Actually any war is made for the land, for the soil, for the minerals, for the richness, and not for any other purpose, and of course they have to make their strategies in targeting women and then attack in order to make people move or 'ethnically cleanse' the region that holds interest for those behind the war.

"We were those who had to wear a scarf on our head and were presented to the world as 'poor women, poor things,' which is not true.

We don't differ from anybody else." Sevdie herself does not wear a headscarf, nor do the vast majority of the Muslim females in Kosovo. Rather her short white hair shines for all to see, and she wears jeans and a jacket, making her stand out in the crowd. Most who don't know her believe that she's a foreigner, but this distinctive appearance became a real liability when she was on the run from the Serbs.

"I come from Jokova. That is a place in the western part of Kosovo which has paid the highest price during the war. It has the highest number of people gone missing—1,600 or more, the highest number of people killed, the highest number of buried women, and the highest number of people that have been jailed or have been kept in Serbian prisons. In my family alone, I had ten people killed, eight people gone missing."

Before the invasion Sevdie had been an academic, educated locally and in London at King's College. She worked as a professor at the University of Pristina until the Serbs shut down the school; her specialty was bibliographic research, studying what foreigners wrote about the Albanians. She learned that in Yugoslavia the image portrayed of her fellow countrywomen was that they had the nation's highest birth rate "and reproduced like mice."

As she watched the mistreatment of her fellow Kosovars, she became increasingly active writing political commentary until she was dismissed from her job at the university. Along with a friend she started the Center for the Protection of Women and Children in 1993 to provide services in the war-torn country. She saw this group had special needs in addition to their basic human requirements for food and shelter. The center did everything from providing its clients with sanitary pads for their periods to delivering their babies to listening to their nightmarish stories of surviving the rape camps. "I would take accounts of women and disseminate them in English all over the world through a list of 1,300 email addresses. I had a website that was created for me by a network of the first independent female journalists from Kosovo. Also, I kept a diary of the conflict;

I called it my 'chronicle of war.' Every day I noted what I saw, what I read, what I heard, what I witnessed. That was on a daily basis . . . actually I never slacked." Her goal was to inform the outside world of the human rights violations happening in her country, in hopes that NATO forces would intervene. To this end she posted on the Internet her daily chronicles of the killings and abuses she witnessed around her. Later the Sorbonne published Sevdie's record as *Diary of a Woman from Kosovo*.

As could have been predicted, these activities put her life in danger, and yet she remained in the country. Sevdie's conflict with the Serbian military who controlled the region came to a head when she tried to photograph the invaders as they prepared to attack students; she had hoped that she could smuggle the picture out to European news agencies. "I remember that day, October 1, 1997. Serb police forces took me into the street, and they wanted to shoot me on the spot. Then they entered into the center, bringing some alleged witnesses to intimidate me, asking why I was making a picture. They accused me of being 'enemy number one of the state.'" But thinking quickly, after snapping the shot, Sevdie had handed the camera off to a nurse in her office and told her to hide it; the police did not think to look under the filing cabinets. Yet this victory would be short-lived because Serbian retribution was on its way to the humanitarian activist.

"I will never know who those criminals were, those perpetrators," she said grimly. "There were four masked men. We were taken with only whatever we had with us, and we were brutalized actually, all of us.

"I was with my older sister, her husband, and my husband. By the end of the ordeal all of us were blood-stained, and the police ordered us to leave the country before nine o'clock that evening. If we didn't, they threatened to kill us. So, this would be our deportation, but we had no place to go. On top of it, I knew if I traveled openly, then I would be shot."

Instead of leaving Kosovo, Sevdie chose to go into hiding, feeling it best for her family's safety to separate from them. "I lived alone in a barn for ten days with a cow as a roommate. That was my dining room, my sitting room, my sleeping room, my restroom. And I would get just a piece of bread once a day, a small piece of bread. Any move of the cow would shake me up—keep me in anxiety, thinking, oh someone is coming."

She stayed in hiding for three months until contacts helped her to reunite with her husband; they constantly changed the rendezvous point so their whereabouts couldn't be traced, until they settled on the fourth meeting site at an apartment complex. But this location wasn't without danger either, as the conspirators worried about hiding Sevdie, a wanted woman whose gleaming white hair made her a highly visible bull's eye. "The women helping me came and said, 'Please, we are afraid. Can we dye your hair? Because, if they find you here, they will kill us all.'"

I ask why Sevdie, a married woman, a mother of two, and a grandmother, didn't escape across the border to safety in Macedonia as so many others had done. Her disdainful expression telegraphs her opinion of this notion. "How could someone claiming that she is a human rights activist leave the country to save her own skin? That wouldn't be fair. For the price of being killed you have to be there with people to witness. To morally support these people, to say that you are not alone—I am with you. Whatever happens to you will happen to me, too. But, believe me, it was very hard, and I was quite traumatized by it all. The way I looked, my best friend didn't even recognize me right after the war, like a concentration camp survivor. But then again, everybody looked like that."

When the activist returned home, she found her house had been looted. It sat empty, but at least the culprits had been interrupted before they could reenact the same fate they had delivered to so many others in the region—including her sister: burning the structure to the ground. Her luck may have merely hinged on a matter of seconds, as she found a full can of gasoline sitting next to her front door.

In spite of the danger, Sevdie decided she would return to her work with the center. Her enemies had planned for this eventuality, though, and had stripped her home and office of any evidence of their criminal activity, material that could be used to prosecute them in the future. Yet in place of all they took, they left her something in return. Sevdie discovered that her enemies had rigged her office computer with two bombs, and had she switched it on, it would have blown her to bits.

"You see, in this way, I believe in God, and if God wants you to live, then you live. I knew my mission then: the first thing to do was to help the war-raped women, to advocate for them . . . to restart the work of the center."

When NATO forces liberated Kosovo and The Hague tribunal began to prosecute the Serbs for war crimes, Sevdie and her colleagues agitated to make rape a war crime, and indeed they were successful in this goal. But one day she returned to her office to find there were more problems with her computer. She had previously had her office de-mined, but this time someone had stolen the computer hard drives altogether, which had stored all the stories she'd recorded from the rape victims. At the same time, the thieves left all the monitors and keyboards, so Sevdie knew the robbery was not motivated by money. The perpetrators wanted to be sure they could not be prosecuted, and they knew that she—as a journalist, an academic, and a specialist in documentation—had been amassing a large body of evidence.

"The Center for Protection of Women and Children had our witnesses in The Hague testify against the former president of Serbia and Yugoslavia, Milosevic, who was the commander-in-chief of the forces that perpetrated this crime against us and used rape as a tool in the conflict, a weapon. We became the agency of documentation of war rape, cooperating very closely with the ICTY," she says, referencing the International Criminal Tribunal, a body of the United Nations established to prosecute serious crimes committed during the wars in the former Yugoslavia. "The center worked documenting crime, presenting data, and supporting the victims, the survivors. We continued in that. But there was another job to do," she said. "To develop campaigns. You have these Hague Tribunal investigators here. But you have to also develop campaigns to have the international prosecutor change the indictment against Milosevic, actually add systematized rape as a war crime, because that had been excluded up until then. And we did it.

"After the fighting ended, we worked to deal with many other problems affecting groups of women who became victims of domestic violence and of sexual trafficking." When the husbands who had served in the Kosovo Liberation Army returned to a destroyed village, with no job or hope for economic recovery, thousands also rejoined a traumatized wife who had been raped by the enemy and, in an untold number of cases, given birth to a baby resulting from rape. As horrible as this reality was, it was not as unbearable as the hell the sex slaves continued to live with on a daily basis; their captors still kept them confined in forced prostitution long after the fighting had ended.

One day Sevdie received word that "Mrs. Nafis Sadik is coming. She is the under secretary of the United Nations and the head of UNFPA. I was asked to join Mrs. Sadik and accompany her in travels around Kosovo. It was right after the war, the fall of 1999, and very cold. It was not only dark because of the weather; it was dark because we didn't have electricity.

"We visited areas that were very cold, muddy . . . places destroyed where you could see tracks of old crimes that were committed in Kosovo. We met with Mrs. Sadik at the UNFPA facilities and then with their vehicles started to go into the field. We visited Mitroviza, and that was my first time to cross the bridge and see this area since the cease fire. It was very sad when I saw the house of my first cousin burnt and leveled to the ground, because I knew where it had been. You could certainly define which were the houses of Albanians, because those were the houses set ablaze . . . just for the purpose of not having the families there. We drove through the region to give Mrs. Sadik a view of what had taken place. We stopped somewhere to talk about the situation and evaluate, and she was very interested to learn what had happened in Kosovo."

In order to best illustrate the confrontation, Sevdie invited Nafis to visit Qirez, "where you will see tracks of the crimes against women and girls. She accepted and we went to the village. When we went to the water well, it had just been drained and closed off. This was where a mother and her three daughters were drowned after they had been systematically raped," she said, describing the scene where the children had discovered the bodies after the water table had receded to expose their heads. The victims had been murdered in the village schoolhouse, and everyone around could hear their screaming. "And there were two other water wells, also drained, because they contained corpses. In one was a young woman, twenty-one years old, war-raped, then drowned there, and the third one held three women, ages fifty to sixty.

"So Mrs. Sadik saw all this, she heard stories from the people living there, because their houses had been used for rape camps. It was also their barn that was actually used as a center for rape and set ablaze afterwards. Of course Serb forces were so well equipped with the knowledge of how to conduct a war, because they had a big history of it—they had made a war in Slovenia, they had made one in Croatia. They better learned how to make one in Bosnia. By the time they arrived here, they were perfect in conducting the war in Kosovo and losing the tracks of their crimes. We worked to document the hardships, but it was not easy. For example, all victims of war rape cannot identify the perpetrators because they don't know their names. Those men were imported from Serbia; they were new faces. Those that were wearing bandanas over their faces—they were local Serbs. They would have been recognized, and if that happened the criminals knew they had to kill their victims so they couldn't testify against them. The best thing during the invasion was to pretend you hadn't recognized anyone, otherwise you'd definitely get killed, so those who were murdered must have known one of their captors, and as a result they were thrown down the well.

"No, the Serbs had learned their lessons well, and we were totally controlled in this perfectly conducted war against our population. And, against women. Because there was a war against women here, starting from 1987 until 1999."

When I arrived in Kosovo six years later, the gruesome tales of the war against women continued to circulate, as did the humanitarian organizations' efforts to deal with the aftermath. Rachel Hand, who worked in the UNFPA office in Kosovo, tells me of some of the agency's ongoing work years after the war has ended. The sexual trafficking in the region reached epidemic proportions during the conflict, and the UN operatives were asking the question of what the captors did with the babies of their sex slaves, since surely they didn't bother to provide them with any type of contraception. They were horrified by the answer to their inquiry: the infants were being killed, and their organs harvested to be sold on the black market. The United Nations investigation into these atrocities was handicapped by the extreme secrecy surrounding the crimes, and the UN's lack of financial resources as they attempted to break the trafficking rings by posing as clients in the bidding for the organs.

It was difficult to believe human beings were capable of such barbaric actions, but then again the documented acts of this war were so shockingly cruel that they defied comprehension. I thought of the line from Robert Burns's dirge: "Man's inhumanity to man/ Makes countless thousands mourn!" This trip had shown me that an even greater source of grief was man's inhumanity to women and children.

(*top*) Nafis (*center*) at family picnic in 1987. (*From left*) Niece Nyla, nephew Salman, daughters Mehreen and Ambereen.

(*bottom*) Nafis with Archbishop Desmond Tutu at a meeting of the High Level Group on the UN Alliance of Civilizations, 2002.

The Sadiks at Nafis and Azhar's fiftieth anniversary party. (*From left*) Omar, Azhar, Ambereen, her husband Khalid, Nafis, Omar's wife Ayiesha, and grandson Ali.

15   ON THE GROUND

An angry Nafis Sadik shouted, "There is still a war going on against women in this country!" She had arrived in Kosovo that winter with a military escort to see the situation on the ground for herself, and found that it was even worse than she'd feared. While aid money poured into the region, rebuilding factories and paving roads, she discovered the primary maternity hospital in Pristina had been wrecked by bombing . . . and remained that way. "There were no elevators working, and they had a strange concept of having the maternity delivery rooms on the top floor, and so these poor pregnant women were trudging up the stairs to go to the floor where the obstetrical cases were kept." Besides mothers going into labor, also navigating the five flights of stairs were postpartum patients, women recovering from C-section incisions, and staff carrying patients on stretchers. "And the hospital had no washing machines, no dryers, so you know there was no clean linen," Nafis continued. Anyone familiar with childbirth can imagine the conditions, with the sheets caked in the blood and afterbirth of countless deliveries, a situation ripe for infection.

In November 1999 snow already covered the ground in Central Europe, and the other health centers the UNFPA entourage visited were in no better shape. "Bombing had shattered all the windows, and they hadn't yet replaced the glass, or even covered them up with cardboard. There were no blankets in the wards, and the place was absolutely freezing since it was winter; so patients would come, but wouldn't stay there. The delivery rooms were so cold that if the woman did deliver there, she would just go home immediately. Incubators were not working, and if they were working, you couldn't keep newborn babies warm with the windows open. The thing was really—in the middle of Europe to see these places which were much worse than any developing country—it was quite a shock."

Dr. Sadik was disgusted that the most elemental measures to take care of the female survivors' needs had been overlooked by the government and NGO groups involved in the recovery effort—this after these women had been through hell during twelve years of war. In addition to the frustration of seeing women's health fall to the bottom of the priority list, she watched the aid money funneled into other projects like paving the way for the military. "To me, that was the least important thing. Troops can march on nonvulcanized roads."

She immediately circumvented the bureaucratic strictures that prevented UNFPA from buying equipment because "with new washing machines we could do more good for the health of women than anything else, so I said just go ahead with the purchase, and I think they were so pleased with the idea."

The report she wrote following her visit instructed UN workers to take care of these commonsense principles first, such as putting cardboard in the windows until they could replace the glass; fixing the plumbing to create access to running water; buying some generators to supply power to the hospitals; providing some simple heaters to keep the patients warm; and fixing at least one elevator in the maternity hospital!

Her anger was fueled by conversations with the local women, hearing their tales of beatings, torture, repeated rapes, and the pregnant women being confronted by Serbian soldiers: "You want to see what sex your baby is?" Then they would slit open her belly with a bayonet and rip the infant out of the mother's womb to offer her a look.

Accompanying Dr. Sadik on the Kosovo trip was Corrie Shanahan, a young woman from Ireland who was a junior member of the UNFPA staff. She had never traveled with her director on mission before and found the whole experience illuminating, watching Nafis in action in the meetings with the fledgling Kosovar government and officials from the European Union, NATO, and other UN agencies. Corrie noted that her boss did not hesitate to call the men—and they were all men—on comments they made that she found specious. "It was always certainly exciting, because you never knew what she was going to say next. She would come out with outrageous things."

In addition, Corrie marveled at Nafis's stamina as she powered through the week of meetings and tours, a pace that left her junior exec exhausted. "And this schedule that we had—she just kept going and was always *on*. Because when she's talking to people, she has to be on, and be on her message, be engaging and charismatic . . . and often we'd get to a place where she would be meeting with somebody, and I would kind of be slumped in the corner, and I'd be trying to keep notes on what was happening. And she would just be blooming—and you know the woman was then seventy years old! I remember thinking, 'How does she do it?' I was trying to learn, I was trying to see how does one do this?

"It was very impressive to see how she worked, and also her follow-up. And this was something I was learning with her, is how you follow up. For example, she said to one of the gentlemen—I forget which organization, but he was a German national. He made some reference to his government being very interested in the work that UNFPA was doing. She said, 'Well, I'll be sure to send you some information and follow up with you.' And it's something I made a note of, but she actually reminded me before I had gotten back to it a week later. 'Don't forget to contact—and she even remembered the guy's name—from that dinner. And that was the sort of thing that was just incredibly impressive. It was like she had this planet of a brain going on, constantly taking over and remembering everything.

"And we had some extraordinary moments, like when she met Sevdie Ahmeti, who had been part of the feminist movement in Kosovo and had set up a reproductive health center for women in Pristina. She'd had a rather ghastly time of it during the war and had come to Washington looking for support. She'd done some work with the Refugee Women and Children's Commission. And when Dr. Sadik met this woman, I remember that moment quite distinctly. We were in this small little office that they had, very sort of nondescript, poor furniture, and there's no electricity. It was about 6:00 in the evening, and it was already dark because it was November, and they have these candles lit. All the staff had come to meet Dr. Sadik, who swung in wearing her sari, with all her bracelets, and she sits down and starts listening to them tell about how appalling the situation was for women. Basically, this point was part of the whole reason we were there. That the war wasn't over for the women yet. The women were still feeling all the aftereffects of the war, on lots of levels, like the fact the women had been malnourished while they were fleeing the fighting, and a lot of them had had miscarriages, which hadn't been attended to. They had had premature babies, and so on. There was a huge aftermath of problems.

"And this woman, Sevdie . . . it was fascinating . . . she spoke terrific English, and sat and told us all about this, and Dr. Sadik asked her questions and probed, and said how is this? And what is that? And what did you do then? Really listened, incredibly attentively. We must have been there about an hour and a half. And what struck me most was the woman was also asking Dr. Sadik's advice. What do you think we should do? Is there any point in writing to Congress? Should we go to the States? I'll never forget Dr. Sadik's response. 'You must maintain, you must keep going. This is extremely important, you need to go to the States. You have to get visibility as an NGO. You must continue to do this work, it's not enough that you stay here and slog away. You've got to fight and get some prominence for this, because if you don't, it is all going to go under.' So she's giving the woman practical advice for her organization, for herself as an activist, and as a woman. And it was just very powerful. When we left, Sevdie had tears in her eyes, and she was saying thank you so much for coming. This means so much to us.

"She also invited Sadik and me to come visit some sites where bodies of women had been found after the war, and where some horrible atrocities had been committed. And I was thinking about our atrocious schedule that was already jam-packed. Oh, my God, how are we going to fit this in? But Sadik said we would go, and we did go. That was another thing that I found: her commitment, and I think this is an element of professionalism. She would always say, 'Yes, I can do that' or 'I'm not sure if I can. We'll have to get back to you.' But once she committed to something, she did it.

"And, in fact, we made a trip with a number of journalists, foreign and local Kosovar press, up to a couple of towns to see some clinics and to see a women's employment project that we were supporting, which actually was a sewing project where they were making sheets, which we were then going to use in the maternity clinics as bedding. It was very interesting and welcome. And it's kind of this incongruous scene, this woman floating in with the Armani sunglasses, the sari, the jewelry, and these women who have lost everything and who are completely destitute, and who don't really know who she is. And yet she—I don't know exactly how she does it—but you don't get that sense of visiting royalty. That's what it feels like initially as we all swan in, and there's an entourage, and there's me and there's the local representative, and there's a translator and a bunch of other people and you feel a bit sort of . . . you know, you cringe slightly as you all parade into this poor little room with all these women sitting behind sewing machines, working away.

"And yet, within minutes, through this translator Sadik is asking questions. 'What are the women doing? How many women are there? What do they get paid? How does that compare? What has happened to them? Why are they here?' There are young women and older women, but again, it was this extraordinary moment where they relaxed. They no longer felt they were being 'presented' in front of a visiting dignitary who is going to give the center—or so they hoped—lots of money. But they started responding to the translator, asking Dr. Sadik questions.

"And it was absolutely heartbreaking. You have these seventeen-year-old girls . . . I remember one; she had lost her father, her brothers, her mother had died, and she kept talking. Evidently, one of her brothers was still in jail in Serbia, and she's asking how were these women ever going to get their relatives back, and she was so upset. Somebody else was muttering on the side, 'Well, they're never coming back.' Then an older lady was saying she's got four kids, and her husband had been killed. It was just ghastly. And yet, it was never maudlin. I don't know quite how to describe it without being cliché about it. You did feel you were having kind of an interchange of equals, even though one person was about to leave and get in a Jeep and be driven back to her hotel, and the other person was going to be sitting at her sewing machine. I think the answer is that Dr. Sadik doesn't get emotional; she remains very concrete. She just asks them what happened. And I think people who don't get listened to very often really appreciate that, because it is so often the case with women—not just women in this type of trauma situation, but women in general—they don't get heard out. And Sadik does listen very actively and asks a lot of intelligent questions."

This mission marked the first occasion for Corrie to be in a region immediately following its destruction by combat, and it was a sobering experience. "The Serbs had come in and basically orchestrated a sort of reign of terror; they had been terrorizing villages, particularly villages that were suspected of being a stronghold for the Kosovo Liberation Army, the KLA. One of the reasons the Serbs attacked women and either raped them or murdered them was not because the women were particularly active in the KLA, but because it was humiliation for the men, and it was a way of getting at them. This was one of the biggest problems that we had, was the systematic rape of Kosovo women by Serbs in order to humiliate the Kosovo community as a whole. It's a tool of war in societies where a woman's honor is ruined if she's raped, and where her family can reject her or not take her back, where her husband will no longer be married to her. It's a very effective way of completely humiliating a population and breaking their morale."

This opinion was reinforced by the father of a thirteen-year-old rape victim in Kukes. "I have given her to the KLA so she can do to the Serbs what they have done to us," Haxhi Lokaj said of his daughter, who has been sent to fight with the rebels of the Kosovo Liberation Army. "She will probably be killed, but that would be for the best," the forty-year-old father said with more resignation than sorrow. "She would have no future anyway after what they did to her."

UN refugee interviewer Dominque Serrano-Fitamant reported on some of her interviews with victims and discussed how the most beautiful women were singled out for the rape camps. "According to accounts, Serb soldiers target young women, taking groups of five to thirty to unknown places by truck or locking them up in houses where the soldiers live. Some have not yet reappeared. Any resistance is met with threats of being burned alive. Kosovo men who try to interfere were immediately killed, and one woman was beaten to death in front of the house where her daughters were being tortured."

Another international organization, Human Rights Watch, began investigating the use of rape and other forms of sexual violence by all sides in the conflict in 1998 and continued to document rape accounts throughout the refugee crisis in 1999. The research found that rape and other forms of sexual violence were used in Kosovo in 1999 as weapons of war and instruments of systematic "ethnic cleansing." Rapes were not rare and isolated acts committed by individual Serbian or Yugoslav forces, but rather were used deliberately as an instrument to terrorize the civilian population, extort money from families, and push people to flee their homes. Rape furthered the goal of forcing ethnic Albanians from Kosovo.

Corrie shared her boss's anger over the lack of funding devoted to women's health care, and when asked to explain this dilemma, she stressed that donors wanted to fund projects that were highly visible. "You can't put a plaque on a woman who has had decent postnatal care."

During her speech at the Beijing Conference in 1995, Hillary Clinton had said: "Even now, in the late twentieth century, the rape of women continues to be used as an instrument of armed conflict. Women and children make up a large majority of the world's refugees. And when women are excluded from the political process, they become even more vulnerable to abuse." That same year a treaty ended the conflict in Bosnia, a war that proved to be a precursor to the invasion of Kosovo.

Perhaps it is no coincidence given Hillary Clinton's sentiments on the importance of women in politics that U.S. secretary of state Madeleine Albright emerged as a major player in negotiations, pushing for airstrikes against Serbia and warning that she did not want to see a repeat of the aggression Serbs had perpetrated in Bosnia. On February 13, 1999, President Bill Clinton broadcast his intention to send four thousand U.S. peacekeepers to Kosovo after a cease-fire and a Serb withdrawal had been won. Today, when entering Pristina on Bill Clinton Boulevard, one can see a multistory portrait of him painted on the side of a building, as the Kosovars regard him as their savior.

Nearly thirty years prior to this trip to Kosovo, Nafis had been sent to Yugoslavia as one of her first assignments at UNFPA. In exchange for a contribution to the fledgling fund, she agreed to organize a family planning program in Kosovo to provide the region's females with access to contraceptives. Before this, the Yugoslavs, like most former Soviet countries, had relied exclusively on abortion for birth control, which Nafis felt was unwise because beyond the emotional distress it caused, this practice subjected a woman to as many as fifteen abortions in her lifetime, surgeries performed under anesthesia and frequently not under the most stringent medical conditions. Nafis's goal was to provide access to contraceptives to lessen the need for abortion.

When UNFPA returned to Kosovo in 1999 to cope during the aftermath of the war, they felt the most humane thing to do was to provide rape victims with the morning-after pill, which must be taken within seventy-two hours of intercourse to prevent fertilization. A right-to-life group called Population Research Institute sent out press releases and posted on their website an article titled: "Milosevic and the 'UN Butchers': UNFPA's 'Reproductive Health' Campaign Dubbed 'White Plague' by Kosovars." The article goes on to say basically that UNFPA is in cahoots with war criminal Milosevic, and they've agreed to carry on his campaign to reduce the number of ethnic Albanians.

Please cue the trumpeters, as we witness the arrival of the men in robes. The Vatican publicly chastised UNFPA for distributing the morning-after pill to rape victims, claiming that this action was tantamount to promoting abortion; the drug was "not permitted by Catholic morality because it is abortive." Or as Lina Petri, a Vatican spokeswoman said of the issue: "A murder does not become less grave because of the circumstances in which it takes place."

Dr. Sadik was quoted in newspapers around the world as saying that the Vatican's position "shows an insensitivity to the suffering of the women of Kosovo. The women of Kukes need our support and care, not condemnation."

To demonstrate the dire situation, one NGO reported that "women in the camps were suicidal at the prospect of bearing their Serb rapists' babies and would opt for this rather than giving birth."

By the time Nafis Sadik visited Kosovo in 1999 she had worked in the family planning arena for thirty-three years; she'd been at UNFPA for twenty-eight years, where she'd acted as director for twelve of those. She was also serving on the UN Executive Board, which oversaw all the secretariat's agencies, and she'd reached the rank of undersecretary-general, a select group of senior officials chosen by the SG. In addition, she was appointed to the Blue Ribbon Panel designated with the task of examining global challenges. No longer the lone decorative she-wolf howling to blank stares at the conference table, Nafis was now one of the most powerful and outspoken members of the UN system. But at seventy, she had already overstayed her expiration date at the agency by ten years, which enforced mandatory retirement at sixty.

When her term had expired in 1996, Secretary-General Boutros Boutros-Ghali exercised his prerogative to extend her mandate with a political appointment. Within months of this decision, his own second term was denied, forcing him out of his position.

But before he left office, Boutros-Ghali had made his mark on the UN system because he felt he should do everything in his power to encourage women's presence in the institution. He had a greater agenda beyond creating gender equality in this diplomatic body, especially by ensuring Nafis's position of power, as he noted: "If you want to fight Islamic fundamentalism, the best way is to contribute to the emancipation of women in the Muslim world."

When Perez de Cuellar promoted Nafis to head UNFPA upon Salas's death, she became the first woman in history to reach that rank in the UN system. Within a decade, that situation would change dramatically, as nearly the entire humanitarian side of the United Nations would be headed by women: Nafis at UNFPA, Catherine Bertini at the World Food Program, Mary Robinson at Human Rights, Carol Bellamy at UNICEF, Sadako Ogata at Refugees, and Gro Brundtland at WHO. At a summit meeting where the women leaders were all present, Brundtland remembered how a moderator asked them to expound on the reasons they had risen to such professional heights in the formerly male-dominated world of international diplomacy. "Catherine Bertini said at this point, 'My father allowed me to compete.' She expressed that as an important part of why she had the courage, the independence, the urge and drive to become a leader. And then the moderator started asking all the others about this, what has the role of your father been? I remember all of us came out and said yes, our father had played an important role in our lives in inspiring us with the willingness to believe that we could do it, we could make it, we could do the things that boys did. Nafis said that without her father supporting her to become a doctor—and, of course, this was in a time in Pakistan when that was not an obvious thing—to the contrary—it would have never happened."

When Carol Bellamy arrived as head of UNICEF, there were three women in positions of power, and Nafis, as the only other colleague stationed in New York, became a role model for her. Bellamy began to study her methods. "God she was tough, but tough as only she can be because she does it so beautifully, wonderfully, and yet sharp and clear; she drew lines in the sand, but did it thoughtfully. She cared about her issues. And Nafis traveled, got out there. Went out and saw stuff." Dr. Sadik observed the situation on the ground.

Twice a year when the secretariat convened the heads of all the agencies for a meeting, the women leaders would go off alone for dinner, forming a sort of old-girls' network. Carol Bellamy remembered the routine at these gatherings: "The dinner conversation would range from very substantive broad discussions around key global issues, to some individual workings on deal making, to talking about some piece of clothing that Gro bought. It was a wonderful combination of the most extraordinary things that women can bring to the table, which are good management, vision, and a knowledge of where to go shopping."

It did not escape the old-girls' network that a disparity existed between their function on the humanitarian side of affairs—the nurturing role women have traditionally played, a role that is needed for succor, yes—but that has never been seen as essential to the power structure that runs the world and decides history. These latter positions were still filled by men on the political and peacekeeping side of the ledger. And this dichotomy set the stage for a drama that was soon to dominate the UN when Kofi Annan took over as the SG and announced plans to reform the gargantuan bureaucracy.

Enter stage right one James Gustave Speth, executive director of the United Nations Development Program, an agency tasked with providing people with income-earning opportunities to eradicate poverty. Gus Speth presented a plan to the new secretary-general that UNDP, which had at one point been the big brother agency over the infant UNFPA, should resume that role. And that UNDP should also take over control of the much larger UNICEF. This move would simplify matters within the UN system, with fewer voices to be heard at the Executive Board meetings . . . and coincidentally would mean two fewer she-wolves howling at the conference table.

Enter stage left Nafis Sadik and Carol Bellamy, who do not think the usurpation of their power is such a good idea. Nor do they agree that folding these organizations with very different agendas into one entity is the way to go. As Bellamy remembers: "I thought, what could be worse than the present faceless UN than an even more faceless UN, and so I was looking for allies in this fight." And she found one who was not afraid to speak her mind in these debates. "Nafis would make the blood rise in Gus Speth's face."

Shaukat Fareed described how at one point these reform meetings became so contentious that anyone who was not at the level of undersecretary-general was asked to leave the room. Nafis, her icy-blue Radha eyes now drilling holes into her opponent, was nonetheless still the woman of science. She used her tried-and-true method of suspending emotion, saving any hanky-wringing testimonials about the hallowed work of UNFPA, and instead brought in data to support her argument by presenting the board with statistics that showed UNDP to be the worst-run agency in the secretariat. "She showed that to put all these initiatives within a very broad, generic concept of development, to be managed by an organization which can't do its own work, was counter-productive." At some point during this discussion Gus Speth began to cry. "It was said later that Nafis was the only man in the room."

Dr. Sadik became more and more outspoken as she aged, feeling she had the power to say things others were afraid to say. Corrie Shanahan remembers one incident where her boss's frankness really stood out, when Nafis was being interviewed for a PBS documentary on John Paul II. "I remember in this interview that she really went into detail about her sense that it would have been so much better had the pope spent more time working on issues of poverty and being a force for good, rather than being such a negative force. And I remember in the car on the way back from this interview, she was sort of musing about her comments. She would never really ask you, 'Do you think I went too far?' She just said, 'I wonder, did I go too far?' And of course, I wasn't going to say, 'Yeah, that was a real disaster, I can't believe you said all those horrible things about the pope.'"

Shanahan also noted that her colleagues would ask if Dr. Sadik shouted at her, as her boss had a reputation for doing with others. "I've never found this about her at all." Interestingly this phenomenon of the frightful Nafis Sadik seemed to always be reported by men, never by women, so one wonders if the actions or the perception changed based on the gender of the recipient. The young UNFPA staffer did have an opinion on what caused this abrasive attitude from her boss though: "One of the things with Nafis is that because she's completely fearless and very strong willed, I think she hates cowardice in other people. I think it is sometimes an internal issue that if people are afraid to stand up to her, or afraid to stick to their guns about what they believe should be done—or shouldn't be done—she smells this fear, and she can't stand it, and I think she can be harsh. It brings out the bully in her.

"People used to say, 'Oh God, did she shout?' I'd say, she didn't shout, of course she didn't shout. Why would she shout? And I think it's to do with just not showing fear . . . basically, you being prepared and not wasting her time. You must not waste her time, you know.

"You get this sense that she has this kind of mission. She has to save the world . . . particularly she has to save the women of the world, and she has to hurry up and get it done."

Alex Marshall agreed that the key to Nafis's success was her courage. "She's completely fearless. She just told the pope what she thought—but then again she's done that with mullahs and dictators and presidents and prime ministers—anybody who will stand within three feet of her, she'll tell them what she thinks. And she has learned to do it in such a way where she doesn't create offense.

"Nafis's technique works because she knows two things: she knows how these societies work, and she knows how these guys think. She's a power player herself, and she's been around power players all her life. So, she appeals to the things that appeal to them. Do you want your country to work? Then here's a way to do it. Half your labor force is sitting at home, prevented from going outside because they all say they can't. If you look at what they're doing, they're doing seven or eight different things, and really contributing to household economies. But if you let them loose, what could they do? If you empower them, if you educate them, if you ensure that they are only pregnant when they want to be, what can women not do? And, you know, presidents and prime ministers listen to that. Nobody has told them that before in many cases. To talk to these leaders this way sounds easy, but believe me, it's not."

Alex told a story of one of their missions to visit the minister of health in Sri Lanka, a country that is successful in many issues of concern to UNFPA, except for one big problem brought about by the fact that many of the women go overseas to work and leave their children home alone with their father. "Nafis told the minister of health in this meeting, 'Do you know what's going on?' He said, no.

She said, 'Incest is a problem in your country.' And he sort of looks around, looks at the ceiling, then looks at the floor, then says, 'Oh.' Head waggle, you know—a wonderful Sri Lankan way of saying, yes, no, or bugger off—it can mean anything, so he does this and doesn't look her in the eye. She said, yes, and then tells him a story, and you can watch him not wanting to hear it, but he has to be polite. She just put it to him in really straight terms and says, 'You're a medical man. You understand these issues and there is something you can do about this.'"

Dr. Sadik's advocacy evolved throughout her thirty years at the UN, and she developed a special passion for issues she found to be particularly heartbreaking, namely female genital mutilation, obstetric fistula, and child marriage—all situations where cultures doomed the girl child to a needless life of woe. When the director would give speeches about these concerns, frequently her voice would break. "In fact, it got so that one person from another agency, who was not a fan of hers—a woman, of course—would nudge me and say, 'Can she do that on cue?' Which I don't think is the case . . . that's just part of Nafis."

"There are some terrible, horrendous stories in Africa," Dr. Sadik recounted, discussing the problem of fistula. "I saw a girl once who had lain in bed for many years, because they told her that if she lay in bed and put her legs together, this condition would heal. And her legs were all wasted, and she couldn't even walk. Then you saw these young girls wandering around the hospital, hoping that someone would pick them up and do some surgery and repair them. There were not enough beds, so they were just sleeping wherever they could find a spot, and they were being shooed away. I mean, it was quite a horrible site.

"When I visited Nigeria I gave a speech on television there, saying that the president should tell all these old men that they should not marry young girls, because some of these old men had several wives, and the older they got, the younger the wife became. These sixty-five-year-old men were marrying twelve-year-old girls, and those were the girls that were getting these fistulas. The whole thing has to be condemned, especially with these children who had not fully developed. I think people were quite shocked when I said this. And I met the president the next day, and he said, 'Oh, well you've gotten me into a lot of trouble now.' Then his wife happened to be there also, and she said, 'No, she's right. We must condemn these practices.' In fact, the president said he agreed with us."

On another UNFPA mission with Jurgen Sackowski, Alex Marshall watched his supervisor tell a group of Arab men that they were all in favor of early marriage for their daughters. "Why? You want to avoid that your daughters have premarital sex. The consequence is all the girls marry too early, none of them has a job, none of them ever gets independent, because they have never been given the chance. They will get married at seventeen, they will have their babies between eighteen and twenty-three, by which time they have four children. They won't go to college. Therefore, you guys, you are doing it all wrong, even though you are supposedly doing it on good morality."

The problem of female genital mutilation proved to be even more complex. After meeting with UNFPA, the parliament of Senegal banned FGM, and President Diouf signed it into law. They were stunned when a women's NGO protested, wanting to know why their government was submitting to pressure from Western countries to outlaw their cultural traditions. On the other hand, in Uganda a seventy-year-old chief from the Sabini tribe put into place a new tradition that celebrated the girls initiation into womanhood by giving them gifts but eliminated their circumcision.

UNFPA was in the business of changing public policy, and in this regard they experimented with initiatives ranging from telenovas to timekeeping—which is how Dr. Sadik came to be known as the Clock Lady. Not because she had an obsession with time, but because she distributed a tool called the Population Clock, a computerized timepiece developed for UNFPA by Sony as the number of beings on earth approached the five billion mark. The device could be set for the growth rate of each country and would calculate how many persons were being added each second. Nafis would present it to heads of state at the beginning of a meeting and at the end of two hours she could point to how many more mouths they had to feed. "It was a great advocacy tool because I remember I presented it to King Hussein of Jordan, and then the next day I had appointments scheduled with other people, but he called me to have another meeting with him, because he said he couldn't sleep the whole night. He kept watching that clock and thinking, 'I will have so many more people to look after tomorrow than I had yesterday.'"

Of course, one of the most important tools of persuasion is the media, and just as the Cairo conference inspired an onslaught of output from radio to theater, so UNFPA worked with scriptwriters in other countries from Mexico to India to incorporate their pro-family-planning message into soap operas and other forms of entertainment. The same individual who is illiterate or who might switch off a boring documentary will stay engrossed by the dramatic adventures of their favorite TV characters. They'll stay tuned as the high school dropout wends her way through life struggling to feed her twelve children, while her educated sister jets around the globe as an attorney.

For her own participation with the media, Nafis was known by her staff to be short on patience for the enterprise. Stirling Scruggs, UNFPA's director of communication, said she would fume: "'Why do reporters ask the same questions all the time?' We'd say, 'Nafis, that's your job, to answer them.'"

Another staffer, Christian Del Sol, described an incident where UNFPA was filming four public service announcements, and the final one required them to deliver the executive director to a sound stage in New York's Chelsea district. "Alex Marshall was supposed to go, but he couldn't make it so he asked me to go with the driver and pick up Sadik at her apartment in the morning. I get there, and she's waiting in the lobby. She sees me, she says, 'Hello,' then looks over my shoulder and says, 'Where's Alex? Why isn't he here?' I said, 'I can't answer that.' On the way down to Chelsea, I tried to give her a couple of jokes, but she wasn't laughing at all, she was thinking of something else, and I thought her mood was going to ruin the whole thing. We walk in, and she's really focused on something quite different than what she's supposed to be there for, and she has to have a good presence on screen. I open up the door of the sound stage, look inside, and I see all these punks with green hair, blue hair, shaved heads, shorts, combat boots, twenty earrings on their lips, nose, ears, and eyebrows.

"Oh great, we've got the crew from MTV, and they're going to be filming Dr. Sadik! And I say, oh my God—it's not going to work out. She's already unhappy Alex isn't here. We're not communicating very well. She's not finding my jokes funny, and here I'm throwing her into this weird situation. But I remembered that Stirling had said that she loves cashews. So, she walks in. She looks at me and said, 'I'm fine.' I say, 'Okay, I'll be back, I'm going to get you something to munch on.' I'm running for the cashews, and I'm thinking as I'm outside, something bad's going to happen. She's not going to like these people. But when I came back five minutes later, she's sitting in a chair in the middle of the sound stage, being prepped by some makeup artists. And all the punks were sitting in a semi-circle around her while she's telling stories, like a grandma. And they're all very silent, listening to her with their eyes wide open."

The media played another unintended part in Nafis's life. Since she refused to talk about her career at home, when she appeared on the BBC's *Hard Copy* and *The Today Show* in the United States, her family was surprised to learn about the many facets of her work at the UN and that her responsibilities had grown exponentially since she'd joined the agency.

As Nafis watched her tenure at the United Nations Population Fund draw to a close, she chose to pursue another opportunity to make an impact on global well-being. The World Health Organization would be hiring a new president, and she tossed her hat into the ring and began to actively campaign for the position. The competition was steep, and there were several candidates for the job, including her Cairo counterpart, Gro Harlem Brundtland, former prime minister of Norway, who was herself a physician. WHO was a much larger organization than UNFPA, with a mandate to look after all health concerns worldwide.

Unlike most other appointments in the UN system, which are at the pleasure of the secretary-general, the WHO position was determined by an election consisting of thirty-two voters; in the end, Dr. Brundtland received the nod. Opinions on this outcome, including Nafis's decision to run, ran the gamut of possibilities. Even though he supported her, Boutros-Ghali felt the Pakistani had little chance merely because she hailed from a poor country, and it's considered politically advantageous to have someone from a wealthy nation like Norway in the top spot, making it easier for her to rely on her countrymen for donations. Conversely, other spectators felt this is exactly the reason Dr. Sadik *should* have landed the job of running WHO — an organization designed to provide health care for developing countries. And who was more qualified to administer that than a doctor who had practiced medicine in the region herself? And yet other wags considered she must have been out of her mind to think that at seventy she would be seriously considered for a post as demanding as president of a large international organization.

Some colleagues at UNFPA admitted they were glad their boss hadn't gotten the job because they needed her at the fund. She would now be working with them for one more year, through the millennium. As Nafis told her staff wryly upon learning the news: "I guess you're stuck with me."

On November 12, 1999, just before Nafis and Corrie Shanahan were ready to depart from Kosovo, a World Food Program plane bringing supplies into Pristina crashed on a foggy night, killing all twenty-four UN staff aboard. The accident brought about the closure of the airport, and now the dilemma became how to get out of the region. The women were driven to an American Air Force base being used by K-For, where they waited for a military helicopter that would deliver them to Macedonia.

As they sat in the Jeep on this misty morning, they studied the scene around them, watching grunts trudge through the mire, scraping their combat boots each time they entered the Admin building. There was no sign of a helicopter yet, but Nafis instructed Corrie to pass forward to the front seat her green galoshes with the little heels, so that the director could slip them over her shoes. Corrie said, as she handed the boots to her boss, "God, I don't know how we're going to get through all that, it's just a sea of mud."

Nafis replied nonchalantly, "Oh, well, they'll probably carry me."

"Good for you, but what about *me*? I don't see them carrying me."

Nafis glanced in the backseat. "No, I don't either."

Suddenly they hear the thundering of the chopper, and naturally it's lowering into the muck at the far opposite corner of the landing field. The executive director began to shriek at the pilot, "What are you doing over there, you fool!" Corrie wondered if they'd actually make it out of Kosovo alive.

The pair climbed out of the Jeep and waded across the field under their own steam, Nafis's green galoshes burying ankle deep in the mud. The wind from the blades ferociously whipped about the black cape which covered her sari, sending the cloak sailing out behind her. With one hand she held the fur-trimmed hood close about her face, and extended the other to the Ukrainian crew, who pulled her up into the waiting helicopter.

Jintana Dahkling | Bangkok, Thailand

The Thai woman stretches out her palm and as I carefully count the baht into it, I glance up into her almond-shaped eyes, magnified by gold wire-rimmed glasses. She certainly doesn't look like a prostitute, I decide. Other elements offer more confusion: her tiny, childlike body, which she claims is continuously shrinking due to her disease; her conservative outfit, a dark skirt topped by a long-sleeved blouse buttoned up to the neck. No, you might peg her for a librarian, or perhaps a school teacher like her sister, but certainly not a former hooker. I'm shocked when she tells me she's only forty-one. True, her tobacco-colored skin is still taut; rather it's more the world-weary countenance, the lifeless, suspicious expression in those magnified eyes that ages her. Also in this face, other things besides her expression vie for one's attention: a broad nose; a mole on her eyebrow; a broken incisor—which occasionally peeks from behind the pink lipstick. The lady's black hair is combed back carefully from her smooth forehead, secured into a netted bun that's garnished by a purple flower. I note with curiosity that throughout our conversation, she holds her purse strap firmly on her shoulder, as if someone might try to steal it. This defensive posture offers the only hint of her former life as a prostitute.

A pseudonym has been used to protect this woman's privacy.

Jintana Dahkling doesn't look like the type of person you would ever suspect of having HIV either, but she has survived with the virus for nearly twenty years. Today she no longer plies her trade in a Japanese brothel run by the Yakuza; instead she works as a guest speaker, going out and talking to youth groups as part of a program that UNFPA funds. We are meeting in the conference room of a modern high-rise at the Planned Parenthood Association of Thailand, and a translator is helping us with our conversation. I want to tell my new acquaintance that it's okay to put her purse down and relax, but I resist this urge because I don't want to offend her.

Jintana begins to tell me her story, how she hailed from a family with several daughters in rural Thailand, until she left home at twenty when she learned two very important things simultaneously: one, when she found out that her mother could no longer afford to support the young woman while she finished school. And two, that her baby sister had fantasies of going to college to become a teacher. After much thought and discussing the situation with her mother, Jintana determined she would sacrifice herself in order to fund her sister's dream; she then bade her family farewell and moved to Rayong Province to start working in the world's oldest profession.

Unfortunately she soon realized the income she earned wasn't sufficient to cover a college education, and this is when a woman she met in the business advised her that she could make a lot more money working in Japan. When Jintana discussed this option with her family, the little sister said, "If you are going to go there to become a prostitute, I will not use any of your money." To make her feel better, the older sister lied, saying she would be going abroad to look for an ordinary job.

Once Jintana arrived in Japan alone, her connections led her to a prostitution ring run by organized crime, and they hired her on. Her family didn't even know she'd left the country, because she didn't want to discuss the situation with them any further. Soon the young woman realized that her goal of earning money for her sister's education was within reach because with the higher income she earned in the Japanese sex trade, enhanced by the exchange rate to Thai baht, prostitution was a much more lucrative proposition in this foreign land.

One thing was similar to Thailand, though: some of Jintana's clients insisted on wearing condoms, and others adamantly refused; but whatever their preference, she knew she had to abide by their choice if she wanted to keep working in the brothel. And although prostitution was lucrative, it was still illegal in Japan, which meant there were no government regulations covering the sex workers' health. Still, her boss sent the girls to the clinic to be tested for STDs on a routine basis.

The young woman had only been in the land of the rising sun for a few months when her test results showed her to be HIV positive. There was no way to know when, where, or from whom she had contracted the virus, and not knowing whom to trust, she told a fellow sex worker. Terrified, this comrade counseled that she had heard rumors that the Yakuza would kill you if you had HIV. Needless to say, the virus was very bad for their business, and they didn't want word to get out that their girls carried deadly diseases that could kill the clientele. They were especially concerned the clinic might inform the police about a Thai woman who was infected, and they suspected her of working in the sex trade. No, if one of their girls had HIV, she was no longer of any use to them.

Instead of waiting around to find out if this rumor was true, Jintana flew back to Thailand and had herself tested again to make sure she was HIV positive. The doctor confirmed the diagnosis, and his first advice to her was not to commit suicide. Instead, he sent her to a social worker, who in turn placed Jintana, now twenty-two, in an emergency shelter, where she would live for the next seven years.

Thailand's royal family covers the cost of an antiviral drug, GPO-VIR S30, which Jintana has been taking since she learned she was infected. During one of the checkups for her medication, she met a man she would later marry. This apparent bright light in her future was soon extinguished when the bride learned her new husband wanted her to return to prostitution to support him, and when she refused, he became violent. She was forced to flee again, to escape this desperate situation.

Finally at one point she traveled back to her hometown and visited her mother—a reunion she'd been dreading. "Mom," Jintana said, "would you still love me, even if you knew something horrible about me?"

Her mother immediately asked, "Have you got AIDS?" They both hugged and cried, and her mother said, "You know no matter what happens to you, you are still my daughter." She tried living at home with her family but worried about the social stigma of having the neighbors realize their daughter was infected with this modern-day plague—this in a time when the media publicized a famous case in Thailand of a man who had received HIV through a blood transfusion, and as a result both he and his wife were fired from their jobs. As her health and appearance deteriorated with the ravages of the disease, she feared she would not be able to keep its existence a secret.

Jintana's paranoia grew out of a general trend in the country as a response to the AIDS epidemic's spread during this era. As one NGO reported: "The prevalence among sex workers also increased, with studies in Chang Mai suggesting that 44% of sex workers were infected with HIV. The rising level of infection among sex workers led to subsequent waves of the epidemic among the male clients of sex workers, their wives and partners, and their children."

Finally Jintana made the choice to return to living in the shelter in Bangkok, where she would be around others in her same predicament. She managed to support herself through the small sums her sister would bring when she came to visit, and by stowing away the funds the shelter gave her for travel money when it was time to visit the hospital for checkups.

But fate was to have yet another turn in store for her: at the shelter she met and fell in love with a man who shared her dilemma. "My boyfriend told me through a period in his past—through being drunk all the time—he didn't use protection, so he got HIV from a lady." Now at least Jintana had a kindred spirit who shared her life.

The couple moved out together to live with his elderly mother, a stroke victim whom they continue to care for today. For spending money, they run a business on weekends, traveling to parks in Bangkok where they rent mats to people wanting to relax on the grass in the sunshine. "But my husband's health is not so good as mine," she remarks, and here a note of worry crosses her face, "because he smoked a lot and has asthma now on top of the HIV." Even though the drugs she takes have side effects, she has not as yet developed the symptoms of AIDS, and Jintana feels it's important to maintain a positive outlook and avoid stress to keep the disease at bay. She works with Planned Parenthood, traveling around Bangkok, a city whose name is synonymous with the sex trade, and speaks to youth. "The advice I give them is not to go sell yourself like I did."

As the danger of the AIDS epidemic became apparent to Nafis Sadik, she rallied more and more of UNFPA's resources to influence governments and work with NGOs around the world to create advocacy programs, and Thailand's battle against the spread of HIV is one of the true success stories in this deadly war. In 1991 Prime Minister Anand Panyarachun took action to slow the meteoric spread of the epidemic at a time "where you were damned if you do or damned if you don't. HIV/AIDS was something that was convenient for us to gloss over, to pretend that it did not exist." The Thai leader's agenda was compounded by Asia's cultural reluctance to admit the existence of a problem so firmly rooted in extramarital sex.

The data looked extremely dismal: 143,000 new infections in 1991 alone, with projections that in the next twenty years, 10 percent of Thais would die from AIDS. The prime minister took several important steps to avert this disaster: increasing the budget for prevention twentyfold to $44 million and adding a massive public education campaign that featured messages every hour on the country's radio and television stations.

Cabinet member and AIDS activist Mechai Viravaidya even opened a restaurant called Cabbages and Condoms in Bangkok, where their tongue-in-cheek approach includes prophylactic décor and a free foil-wrapped package included in each dinner check.

But probably the new regime's most important steps required every school to teach AIDS education classes, and the "100 percent condom program," which enforced condom use in all commercial sex establishments. Brothels that failed to comply could be closed. If such a program had been in place when Jintana Dahkling left home to fund her little sister's education, the talks she gives to youngsters could have told a very different story.

When we end our session, the translator tells me that Jintana wants to know how much money I intend to give her for today. I respond that as a journalist I never pay for interviews. The woman studies this news with a forlorn look on her face and then tells us she doesn't have enough cash for her bus trip home. I pull my wallet out of my purse and remove a stack of crisp bills with the king's face etched on them. Into Jintana's outstretched palm I count out enough baht for taxi fare.

16 ONWARD

Nafis Sadik had learned to cope with the wranglings over donor funding, the political battles, and the moral dilemmas that all accompanied her advocacy for women's health. In spite of the challenges from the Vatican, and the flip-flopping of the Americans, she knew that UNFPA was making a major contribution. The Crusaders were fighting the good fight and were winning, and she could retire satisfied with that knowledge. No one, however, predicted the ongoing level of devastation wrought by the emergence of a microscopic organism that would affect every level of society. Around the time Dr. Sadik took over after Rafael Salas's death in 1987, scientists and forward-thinking policymakers were moving beyond the rumors, fears, and search for blame that surrounded AIDS, to cope with the picture they faced before them: a deadly disease transmitted by sexual contact. There was no vaccine, and there was no cure. In the bitterest of ironies, the spread of this virus would make the director's work harder and easier at the same time.

Most high-level political appointments in the UN are for ten years maximum, but Nafis had been director for twelve. Other than her brief retirement in 1963, an experiment that had ended after a few weeks with her wholesale rejection of the boredom provided by a life of leisure, Nafis had been working nonstop all her life. Her parents started her studies with Teacher before the youngster even enrolled in elementary school, and then after graduating from high school early, she went straight to medical school; then came her internship and residency, followed by forty-six years of stressful high-profile careers in medicine and politics that had her "crisscrossing the world like a super-charged hornet." Yes, she still had energy, but as a septuagenarian she was looking forward to indolent days with her grandchildren, playing bridge, afternoon coffee, dinner parties, film premieres, idle gossip and chitchat, and, of course, her patented shop-aerobics workout routine.

This delicious fantasy percolated as the millennium approached, a symbolic time of change the world over and the year that would see Nafis hand over the reins of power to her successor. Although Kofi Annan had told Nafis she could stay on as director as long as she liked, she deemed it was time to hand over UNFPA to someone else. She cast about for someone she felt she could trust to continue with the same vision she and Salas had shared for the first thirty years of the fund's life. The organization that had started in the kitchen offices with six stalwart pioneers—one per continent—now had a staff of 1,018 worldwide, working in 110 field offices. Their budget of $366 million per year covered programs in 142 countries.

The usual international suspects queued up to compete for the executive director's job, and as could have been predicted, the unspoken preference would be for a female. Stafford Mousky commented on the field: "There were a number of candidates, mostly women, and one male from Bangladesh who I thought was quite, quite good—but he would have had to undergo a sex change operation."

A frontrunner emerged from outside the UNFPA coterie, a Saudi woman named Thoraya Obaid, who was a Muslim and a mother of two daughters, and who currently worked in Beirut as deputy executive secretary for the Economic and Social Commission, an organization known in UN-ese as ECOSOC. She had encountered Dr. Sadik at a few conferences down through the years, and on one such occasion Nafis had said to Thoraya, "I want to see you." Quite reminiscent of how Raphael Salas had recruited Nafis thirty years prior, Nafis was now wooing this woman. "I always ask about you," the director said, "I've followed your career and always thought that I wanted you to work for UNFPA. But every time I ask they tell me you won't leave the region because of your children." The boss told Thoraya to bring her CV, and she would set up some interviews with the agency's staff immediately. These appointments were just formalities because Nafis knew she was going to hire this woman.

"At noon," Thoraya remembered, "she asked me 'How are the interviews going, how are you doing?' I said that the interviews were still in progress, but so far they had been positive."

"Do you want the job?"

"Dr. Sadik, I still have two more interviews this afternoon . . . "

"Thoraya, do you want the job?"

"Yes, I do, but I'd rather wait till I'm finished before . . . ."

"I make the decisions here."

Thoraya remembered other parts of their discussion, as well: "She asked me, 'Do you have the passion? Because this job, if you don't have the passion for it, you can't do it. And I told her 'Yes, I have it, but I have a different passion than you do, and I express my passion differently than you do." She wanted to be sure that I had the correct emotional commitment, and she said, 'If you are working in our area, it's not just a bureaucratic job, it's much more than that because you are dealing with women dying, human lives, HIV/AIDS, you name it. And it's not something that you can just accept and walk away from.'" Thoraya agreed to take on the mission and the mantle of responsibility; she moved to New York and began working on the transition, preparing for Nafis to pass her the baton.

The new director acknowledged that everyone felt Dr. Sadik was much tougher than she was; by comparison Dr. Obaid was considered by everyone to be so much more quiet and gentle. Thoraya tells of her dealings with UNDP and states that even though she is slow to anger, the agency's continued pattern of leaving her out of decision making had her dander up. She had repeatedly written polite notes about the situation to Mark Malloch Brown, until one day the latest offense pushed her over the edge. "So I told Mark, 'Do you want me to continue to deal with you this way, or do you want me to do a Nafis Sadik on you?' He said, 'Oh no, Thoraya, please don't!'"

The Saudi diplomat felt there were two sides to her mentor, though. "She has a heart like a bird," she insisted and went on to tell how the boss had broken down crying during a staff debriefing after she'd visited the Fistula Hospital in Ethiopia. "When I went to Ethiopia and saw the hospital, I realized yes, she was correct in crying over these girls who were totally destroyed for a while, but after the surgery they can get their life back to a certain extent. But her reaction to this fistula situation showed these two sides of Nafis Sadik—the very strong and the very passionate, and they feed each other." Aware of her deep emotional commitment to this issue, Thoraya asked the now retired director if she would like to continue to help UNFPA by being their special envoy on fistula, to which Nafis said yes. One strike against retirement and the bridge playing has just been crossed off the list.

Thoraya noted the larger institutional changes Dr. Sadik had made during her three decades at UNFPA, the primary one being to decentralize authority. "So at the field level, the reps are really in a sense—not autonomous—but they have so much authority to make decisions at the local level, because you can't have an organization working in a country and coming to headquarters for every top-down decision, big and small. That change really made the difference in terms of allowing the representatives to move quickly and to respond to crises, to make decisions on money, on women, on certain rules."

Besides Thoraya, another of Nafis's important hires was Dr. Andrew Arkutu, whom she had recruited as well. He had previously been working at WHO in Tanzania, until 1980, when he moved to New York to join the technical branch of UNFPA, making him the third doctor to join the fund (Nafis being the first). He admits it was a tough transition from being a clinician to becoming a bureaucrat, and he later served in Swaziland, Zimbabwe, Nigeria, then came back to Tanzania again. Arkutu also endorsed Nafis's management philosophy, because he felt there are two types of people in an organization like UNFPA: "There are some people who could not survive a day out in the jungle."

He recalled that the boss formulated a rule that any staffer who aspired to go to a senior position must spend some time in the field, and here we see the importance of the leader's early days in the field herself. Thus she formulated her policy of rotation, because she felt people at HQ had no idea what happens on the ground. Of course, this system was not without its critics—some of whom referred to the regional directors as "country dictators." Needless to say, those ensconced in the art deco Manhattan office on the nineteenth floor of the Daily News Building, the employees who took the elevator down to the lobby at night, walked across the polished marble floor adorned by a gigantic sculpture of a globe, exited the revolving door into the crisp autumn night, and then hailed a cab to take them off to the theater in one of the world's most luxurious cosmopolitan cities, had a very different reality than did the staff sweating in the jungle as they treated the poor, sick, and dying.

Another legacy for which Dr. Sadik received considerable credit was being the first leader in the UN system to achieve gender equality with her hires. By the time she left office she had an equal number of males and females working in the fund. "That's a major contribution, and whenever we have to discuss issues across the street with the secretary-general, or the reports of the General Assembly on the situation of women in the UN Secretariat, UNFPA is always being singled out as the one agency that has consciously worked to reach a gender parity," Obaid said with pride.

The whole crew turned out for Nafis's black-tie farewell gala at the Waldorf Astoria, where tributes flowed like wine.

As with any good melodrama, the rivals meet again at the end of the play. And so it came to be that in 2000, the year of her retirement, Nafis Sadik and John Paul II would encounter each other again in Rome. The meeting of the UN's Inter-Agency Coordinating Committee prompted the occasion, and Secretary-General Kofi Annan and the twenty-two heads of the Secretariat were present. The pope had invited them to the Vatican and received the diplomats in a grand audience hall where they sat in chairs lining the perimeter of the room. John Paul, frail with the advanced stages of Parkinson's disease, entered and gingerly walked to his throne at the front. He delivered a flattering speech to the assembly about the important contributions of their international body, and afterward the UN representatives walked up one by one to shake the Holy Father's hand.

Shaukat Fareed was present that day and remembered his colleagues' reaction surrounding their meeting with the pontiff. "Everybody was very worried that Nafis was going to embarrass the whole system by challenging the pope on issues once again. So, jokingly or otherwise, we all pleaded with her to leave the pope alone and not rile him too much." Shaukat was two spots back from Nafis and watched anxiously as she strode up in her sari to greet John Paul, her brown bare arms gleaming.

It had been six years since the two met, and the pontiff, now eighty, didn't place Nafis at first. Since she was wearing a sari, he assumed she was from India, and when she corrected him, telling him that she was Pakistani, the pope recognized her. But in the way of professional diplomats, instead of dissolving into a finger-pointing brawl, the two merely shook hands and smiled. Nafis returned to her seat gracefully, catching Shaukat's eye as he passed by on his turn to approach the throne.

Her colleagues' fear that Dr. Sadik would confront John Paul was well founded, since they knew she wasn't exactly shy to express her opinion. However, Nafis realized after her last conversation in Rome with the pontiff that nothing she could say would change his mind. She would have been correct in this assumption, as an article in the *New Scientist* would later confirm, detailing how the Vatican's position on condom use remained astoundingly intransigent:

> The Catholic Church is spreading the claim that condoms have holes in them that allow HIV through. This information is discouraging people in developing countries from using condoms, greatly increasing their chances of contracting the virus.
>
> It is no secret that under Pope John Paul II the church has opposed any means of birth control other than the rhythm method. In developing countries the church often tries to use its influence to block both sex education and access to contraceptives. In Kenya, where around a third of people are Catholic and a fifth HIV-positive, it has publicly burned condoms.
>
> Now a team from the respected BBC television series *Panorama* has discovered that the church is going even further. While making a program on the effects of the pope's policies, the team visited Kenya, Nicaragua and the Philippines. They repeatedly heard the line that condoms have holes in them that allow HIV through, they told *New Scientist*.
>
> When the team investigated, they were shocked to discover that this claim came directly from the Catholic church. "Latex rubber from which condoms are made does have pores through which viral sized particles can squeeze through during intercourse. These facts must be brought to the attention of our people whenever the condom is being discussed," states a pamphlet on AIDS put out by Catholic bishops in Kenya.
>
> That is not the scientific consensus. In 2000, experts assessed all the available evidence on condoms for the U.S. National Institutes of Health and concluded that intact latex condoms (those that do

not leak water) are "essentially impermeable" to even the smallest sexually transmitted virus, hepatitis B.

Yet the claim that condoms have virus-sized holes is being promoted at the highest level. When asked if it was true, the president of the Pontifical Council for the Family at the Vatican, Cardinal Alfonso Trujillo, said: "Yes, yes, because this is something that the scientific community accepts." When told that the World Health Organization, for one, most emphatically does not accept this claim, his response was: "Well, they are wrong."

Perhaps this type of blatant propaganda was too much for Nafis—one of the taunts that prompted her to climb back into the ring. She delivered her response via a speech:

> Incidentally, I still find this fear of women today. It has led to many abuses, such as telling people not to use condoms on the grounds that the HIV virus can pass through latex. Of course this is nonsense, and puts women at risk of pregnancy as well as infection. The fear that women might misuse contraception is apparently greater than the fear that they might die of HIV/AIDS.

Or maybe her decision to return to work stemmed from a similar allergic reaction to retirement as she'd had in 1963, and she felt listless once out of the limelight. Or perhaps it was the princely salary the UN offered Nafis to lure her back: a dollar per year. But more likely she felt she couldn't sail off into her golden years while women were needlessly dying. "The Vatican keeps saying that having access to condoms promotes immoral behavior. What they don't say is not having access to condoms promotes HIV in innocent people. I mean that's what is happening."

In 2002 she accepted an invitation from Kofi Annan to become his special envoy on HIV/AIDS for Asia, a position that would see her back in the international terminal of JFK en route to Thailand, Malaysia, Korea, Vietnam, China, India—especially the last two locations. Being the world's most populous nations, they also happened to have the largest number of HIV cases in Asia. Strike two against retirement.

The territory assigned to Nafis was a natural fit, of course. Being Asian herself, she understood the cultural bias against admitting that your citizenry was having sex outside of marriage, or acknowledging that you had a large industry of sex workers transmitting disease; and she knew all too well the prejudice against anything that smacked of homosexual behavior or intravenous drug use—all of which were forbidden in traditional societies. The most popular method for coping with the spread of the virus was denial, which was quite effective in saving face, but completely ineffectual in saving lives.

Dr. Peter Piot, head of UNAIDS, welcomed the opportunity to work with someone of Dr. Sadik's experience to cope with this dilemma. "Nafis and I discussed how we're going to move the AIDS agenda in Asia and in the Pacific considering all this denial. And wherever we go, we hear 'All our Asian values protect us. We are not like those Africans or those homosexuals.'"

Beyond her practical knowledge, Peter appreciated her spirit. "What I like about her also is that we laugh a lot. That's also nice. Because the kind of topics we are dealing with—family planning, contraception, women's position, reproductive health, AIDS—it could all be very depressive when you're working there full-time. What you see is misery and denial and the bigotry and so on. It's not the most noble side of humanity that we are confronted with. Particularly, I'm not talking about people who have it, but the way that society reacts to the program. So I find these good qualities, her energy, her positive spirit. 'If it doesn't work today, I'll come back tomorrow and try again, and never give up.' She is truly one of the great international figures of our time, not only in health, but how she has mobilized everyone from parliamentarians to women's groups, and put the difficult issues out there where nobody wants to have them. That requires stamina—guts—in addition to having the credibility."

Dr. Sadik's advocacy also connected the spread of the AIDS

epidemic with the startling data showing it was becoming increasingly a disease affecting heterosexual women, who were biologically more predisposed to contract the disease than men—a situation exacerbated by the female's low status in many parts of the world, which made them incapable of demanding their partners wear a condom. With a wink and a nod it was accepted in many Asian cultures that husbands would have many extramarital sexual relationships—the result being faithful wives dying of AIDS, children growing up as AIDS orphans, and innocent babies doomed from birth by inheriting a deadly virus. The doctor lobbied to add HIV prevention and treatment programs to every country's reproductive health care plan. "HIV is a good entry point to push reproductive rights. They can't say that women *want* to get AIDS. I mean that would be a bit excessive even for the fanatics."

Nafis was back on the circuit again, meeting with heads of state, speaking at conferences, devising strategy. As one of the world's leading experts on women's health, she lent that credibility to how the spread of HIV was becoming increasingly a women's health issue. Her old chum Werner Fornos heard her give a talk in China and later made a point of complimenting the diplomat on her message. "Why you haven't been listening to me all these years," she responded with a twinkle in the Radha eyes. "All my speeches have been good."

Joel Rehnstrom, part of the UNAIDS team in China, watched the special envoy in action when she visited Beijing. "I remembered very well in her speech when she spoke about AIDS and the challenge that it poses to many countries and the particular statement she made about China, making the point that no matter how old and unique the Chinese civilization may be, there is nothing special that would protect China from HIV and AIDS. I could see how the hair started standing out on people in the room. It was a very good statement."

Reflecting the rate of China's growing epidemic, Rehnstrom noted that they had seen a 30 percent increase in reported HIV cases each year since 1999. "The government senior officials, such as the minister of health at the time, were still uncertain about a number of aspects related to the HIV problem. I think there was already a recognition, but they were not really sure about how serious the problem was, or how the government should tackle the issue. Nafis gave examples of already successful approaches, projects and initiatives in prevention, which had been carried out in the far western region of Xinjiang," Rehnstrom said, referring to a province on the border of Pakistan and Afghanistan that serves as a drug trafficking route between opium producers and the heroin markets of Central Asia, Russia, and Europe. "That was a very good way to convince the policymakers that AIDS was a problem within their borders. But Nafis also showed them AIDS was being tackled in successful ways that could be replicated elsewhere in China."

Dr. Sadik's core team still continued just the way it had when she sat at the helm of UNFPA in the big corner office. Alex Marshall still wrote her speeches—now for free—and her devoted secretary Sheila Murdock still catered to her boss's needs. Marshall watched Nafis address the Special Session of the United Nations General Assembly on HIV and AIDS, where she delivered her message: "If you want to defeat AIDS, the only way to do it is to prevent it, because there isn't a cure. And if you want to prevent it, you have to start with women, because more and more it's a woman's disease. It is not women who infect men. It's men who infect women, and that's happening more and more. You have to allow women to protect themselves."

Marshall felt the whole issue boiled down to "change or die. That's what it is. It really is. You know, these guys talk about cultural survival and all that. But cultures aren't there to survive. You go to a village in Laserta, and there is nobody there but old people and kids because all the adults have died. What's cultural about that?"

Always the woman of science, when Dr. Sadik gave the memorial Raphael Salas Lecture, she now expanded her signature no-nonsense approach to deal with HIV:

I would stress the necessity of approaching the pandemic as a medical emergency, rather than a moral crisis. HIV/AIDS is a sexually transmitted disease. It takes root among people who have several sexual partners; among men who have sex with men; among sex workers and their clients; among intravenous drug users and among people who combine these behaviors.

These are people whose habits are not acceptable to mainstream society. But members of high-risk groups are not separate from mainstream society; on the contrary. They are fathers, husbands, daughters, sons. They live among us: they bring their infections home. In a survey of HIV-positive wives in India, 90 percent claimed to have had no sexual partners but their husbands.

I think a useful parallel is the hospital emergency room. Hospital emergency teams take no notice of patients' social status, sexual habits or source of income. They take bullets out of drug dealers; they treat prostitutes for sexually transmitted diseases; they don't ask what a man was doing when he had a heart attack, or who he was doing it with. Why should HIV/AIDS prevention be any different?

Nafis went on to discuss her views on "abstinence," the current popular buzzword in HIV prevention circles:

Young people especially must have the information and the services to enable them to make their own decisions. I am greatly in favor of abstinence: it is part of responsible sexual behavior. But as a professional in public health, I must point out that promoting abstinence only, with no backup information on contraception, is unrealistic at best. At worst it is a threat to young people's lives and health. Promoting abstinence is an excellent strategy; promoting ignorance is foolish, and can be fatal.

Just as Dr. Sadik's previous speech had been her volley in the political dialogue with the Vatican, so this Salas Lecture served as her response to the policies of the U.S. president. The year 2001 saw the swearing in of conservative Republican candidate George W. Bush, whose very first act in office was to issue an executive order to reinstate the Global Gag Rule from the Reagan years. One of Clinton's first acts had been to repeal it, and now in a symbolic gesture lost on no one, Bush's first order of business was to make sure the word "abortion" was not mentioned by any agency that received U.S. aid. This policy ping-pong match would have been hilarious had not the consequences been so dire.

Bush's other agenda played well with his evangelical supporters; he cancelled the $34 million in funding that a bipartisan Congress had approved for UNFPA. The agency's spokesman, Stirling Scruggs, said this funding cut translated into "about 2 million unwanted pregnancies, 800,000 preventable abortions, 4,700 maternal deaths, 77,000 child deaths, and an untold number of preventable cases of HIV."

While the GOP retained some pro-choice members, by 2004 no-choice politicians dominated the party. Six Republican congressional representatives—Chris Smith, Mike Pence, Todd Akin, Steve King, Jo Ann Davis, and Joseph Pitts—joined in Bush's crusade to prohibit abortion worldwide. As the government of Uruguay debated whether or not to legalize abortion, these U.S. representatives (four of whom served on the International Relations Committee) took it upon themselves to send a fax on official U.S. congressional letterhead advising their fellow lawmakers that they should not afford the women of Uruguay the same legal right to abortion that American women currently held. Rather they should save our sisters to the south, advising that the bill they are considering "would legalize the violent murder of unborn children and the exploitation of women through abortion up to the 12th week of pregnancy."

Their letter continues with this testimonial warning of the American experience: "Our courts unilaterally legalized abortion and presented abortion to women as a solution. Abortion is not a solution. Because of that misguided action our country has wiped out generations of children and sentenced generations of women to pain and suffering. Please do not be part of that same mistake in Uruguay."

When this letter arrived in Montevideo, the government's lower house had already approved the measure that would have decriminalized abortion; a 1983 law on the books put women who had undergone illegal abortions in prison for up to nine months. But as one activist said of her nation, "A poor country like Uruguay cannot afford to ignore the wishes of the United States government." Instead, their Senate voted 17-13 against the measure, and as of this writing abortion remains illegal in this South American country.

When George W. Bush canceled UNFPA's aid he cited the same rationale his ideological mentor, Ronald Reagan, had used before him: the agency was complicit in forced abortions in China. Bush ignored the advice of his own secretary of state, Colin Powell, who testified to Congress that the U.S. should maintain their funding because UNFPA "provides critical population assistance to developing countries." Instead of heeding his own cabinet, the president listened to the accusations of the Population Research Institute, the same group that had accused UNFPA of being tools of Milosovic's ethnic cleansing campaign in Kosovo.

While Bush may have repeated the maneuvers of past Republican administrations on abortion, his approach to AIDS programs was innovatively his own. The ABCs of the president's program were abstinence, be faithful, and use a condom. "Abstinence" asks young adults to refrain from sex until marriage, a solution touted as the most effective way to avoid HIV infection. "Be faithful" asks people in relationships to be true to their partners and claims that fidelity in relationships reduces exposure to HIV. And lastly, if you absolutely must have sex, please use a condom.

To encourage the first two options—"abstinence" and "be faithful"—over condoms, the U.S. government donation required that one-third of the total $15 billion allocated for HIV prevention must be reserved for programs that promote abstinence. The nearly universal reaction of experts in the field of public health to this approach—from Dr. Nafis Sadik at the United Nations to Dr. Gro Brundtland at

WHO to Dr. David Satcher, the U.S. surgeon general—was that teaching teenagers the value of abstinence was to be applauded. But you could not rely on that measure alone to solve the problem; beyond the lecture full-fledged sex education and services were needed—especially for the rare instance when the little darlings decide to disobey their elders and do as they please.

By the fifteen-year anniversary of ICPD the world had seen dramatic changes for the better, particularly in the goal of reducing population growth rates. Yet here is where the bitter irony comes in. Critics of population policies have pointed out that the alarm sounded in Paul Ehrlich's *Population Bomb*, as well as the numbers prophesied by the UN and even those forecast by Nafis Sadik's Population Clock, had all been wrong. Those dire consequences never came true, did they? By far, the primary reason for worldwide population decline over projected levels was that organizations—among them UNFPA—helped governments take action to give their citizenry access to contraceptives. That's the good news. The sad news is that AIDS had taken the lives of 25 million people during this era, especially in sub-Saharan Africa, where it was the leading cause of death, a fact that canceled out what would have been a much greater increase in numbers on the continent.

The corollary to this equation is that funding that had been earmarked for the reproductive health initiatives by donors during the consensus at ICPD now evaporated, with much of the monies being redirected to deal with the HIV/AIDS epidemic. For instance, in sub-Saharan Africa the developing countries in 2009 spent 86 percent of their population activities budget on HIV. Overall, Steve Sinding, who now worked for the Guttmacher Institute, said that the family planning budget agreed to in Cairo had dropped drastically: "In constant dollars, this amounts to a reduction from $842 million to $718 million between 1995 and 2007. The combination of massive shifts in 'population' funding to HIV/AIDS and inattention to family planning within the health budgets of many developing countries have led to a decline in the availability of both contraceptives and the information and services that support their delivery. UNFPA executive director Thoraya Obaid and other leaders in the field have decried the fall in attention to family planning and the adverse health consequences of high levels of unmet need and unwanted pregnancies that attend it."

Needless to say, Nafis viewed this reality darkly. "On the issue of funding, unless the donor community comes up with the resources, all the goals are not going to be met. I think we have made a lot of progress, but I think we could have made a lot more progress if countries like the U.S. didn't go back and forth. Secondly, it would be a tremendous help if donors sustained their financial support, because I think you need that commitment to upscale programs. Donors have this habit of going from one issue to another. And currently, I think the AIDS issue takes up a lot of money. Although I think AIDS is important, if donors had supported reproductive health and rights, a lot of the AIDS issues would have also been addressed, especially those to do with the vulnerability of women, empowerment of women, developing the health sector, and the reproductive health services."

And yet along with the Bush funding cuts came an unforeseen stroke of luck that in the long run benefited UNFPA. Countries around the globe chose to make a statement by increasing their contributions to the organization; in 2001—the year of the cuts—UNFPA had 92 donors. By 2003, they had 147 donors, with many nations in Europe especially increasing their financial commitment. While the globe's wealthiest superpower gave nothing to the cause, even war-torn Somalia donated a small sum as a gesture of goodwill, and the Afghani ambassador walked into the UNFPA offices, rode the elevator up to the nineteenth floor, and handed the director a crisp one hundred dollar bill.

It wasn't just the needs of the United Nations that had dragged Nafis back from her languid dream of life on the retirement beach. A few of her former admirers approached the diplomat asking if she would be so kind as to serve on their board of directors. The offers wafted onto her desk from the four corners of the globe: the Netherlands, Germany, Britain, Switzerland, Pakistan, Canada, and the United States. Why yes, she wanted to be of service and agreed to be on the board of . . . fourteen organizations. The focus of their various missions ran the gamut of Nafis's professional experience: Harvard Medical School, the World Bank, the National Academy of Sciences, the Asia Society, the Center for Reproductive Law, and the UN Foundation, among others. At one juncture she even ventured to Singapore with Hillary Clinton, Henry Kissinger, and Mohammed Ali to represent New York City as a contender to host the 2012 Summer Olympics. Strike three against retirement—and you're out.

Azhar Sadik watched all this with a mix of mild amusement and resignation—no doubt feeling a twinge of déjà vu from the 1963 prequel. He also awoke to the dulcet sounds of their home fax machine whirring at all hours of the night, as documents poured in from other time zones. Nafis was busier now than ever before, and when his wife first had a pacemaker installed and then underwent an angioplasty to relieve a blocked artery the year after her retirement, Azhar quietly suggested maybe she should take it easy. "But I have realized that this is her get up, that she wouldn't want things any other way."

That same year, post–heart procedure, in one month her professional commitments led her to Brazil, Switzerland, and South Africa. Feeling overwhelmed at the frantic pace, Nafis vowed that she would stop committing to things and instead refer all requests to her secretary. "From now on, I'm just going to tell Sheila to deal with all this. I am not going to answer anybody. She tells them: 'It's just impossible.' And she's very sweet and polite. I get irritable and sound actually rude and brusque. Declining invitations—that's not my forte. I always say yes in the end, which my husband gets very irritated about sometimes."

Ted Turner also wooed the doctor to be on his Stop Nuclear Threat

Initiative Board along with Senator Sam Nunn. They had previously worked together on the UN Foundation Board Turner had created when he vowed to give $1 billion to the UN, in part to cover the back dues the U.S. government had refused to pay. He was after Nafis for the Nuclear Threat Initiative partly because of her sex, since he wanted gender parity on the board.

For over twenty years Ted Turner has also been a long-standing supporter of Dr. Sadik's work at UNFPA. "From what I know, I think that we have not been successful as yet in getting family planning widely enough accepted to halt the population explosion. We're still adding a billion people about every 10 years. It's slowing a little bit, but the problem is we have a higher and higher base of human beings. There is nothing more important long-term, intermediate, and even short term for the future of humanity than to stabilize the population as quickly as possible. And the UNFPA is the world's leading international organization with that."

As far as Nafis's contribution to the Nuclear Threat Initiative, Turner commented, "I think that she's got a tremendous background in international affairs and while weapons of mass destruction, nuclear, biological and chemical are not directly part of the population, they are very closely related, because nothing would reduce the population faster than an all-out nuclear war. There's still a chance that there could be a miscalculation, or terrorists could get their hands on weapons of mass destruction. If they got their hands on the smallpox vaccine and let that go, we'd lose close to 2 billion people within a year on the planet. Humanity is highly at risk at the current time, and obviously she's well equipped with her terrific education and her background to deal with all of the problems that face the human condition. The UN is attempting, with limited resources, to bring progress in these areas.

"The fact that she's Pakistani is a positive. Not only do we want to have gender diversity, but we also want to have cultural diversity and in order to do that, you have to have representation from the subcontinent."

The media mogul sought out Dr. Sadik because she played a part in some of his other political theories as well. "Since half the people in the world are women, women should be well represented. They ought to have proportionate representation to the percentage of the population that they comprise. And I think that their outlook and perspective in many ways is superior to men in a lot of areas. I've been saying for years that I really think that it would be a very positive move for mankind to bar men from serving in any kind of public office anywhere in the world for a hundred years, and let women run the world for a hundred years. Men can still be in business and in the military and everything else, but government officials of all levels would be comprised 100% of women.

"Men have had control of the world for the last 30,000 years, and they've made a real mess of it. Most of the wars were started by men. I guarantee that if women were running the world—the political part of the world—that the incidence of wars, of landmines and bombs, of nuclear, chemical, and biological weapons would go down dramatically. And very quickly, because there would be more emphasis on children's health, there would be more emphasis on education, there would be more emphasis on equality, there would be more emphasis on equity. The women would not tolerate the terrible inequities that we have in the world. I think that estrogen is a more powerful and benign chemical than testosterone. And I am deadly serious about that. I am deadly serious. I really mean it. It would absolutely change the whole way that humanity was progressing in the future.

"Women are much more nurturing, just by their very nature. And men are much more combative, because it's in our culture. Boys are brought up to be aggressive, but it's also, I think, a good bit of it is males are more combative and more competitive than females because it's in our genes. That's certainly true in a lot of animals. You know deer, the males have horns; the females don't have horns. They couldn't care less about fighting. The males are constantly fighting."

While Ted Turner is a big fan of the world's women, conversely—in spite of what some might assume of a leader who has spent her life promoting the status of females—Nafis is a great admirer of men. She also has some choice words to say about her fellow feminists who differ in this regard. "Some feminists, of course, project this image of hating men—which is, I think, quite ridiculous. Why would you hate men? I mean, what you're asking for is equality and equal opportunities. And that's not against men, it's *for* women."

While Nafis may have seen countless horror stories in her professional life, tales of what women had suffered at the hands of men, in her own life she had good reason to praise their contributions. Many of the colleagues who joined her mission to boost the status of females were men. In fact, in the beginning they were all men, and they had dedicated their lives—sometimes risked their lives—to promote the betterment of women.

On her personal history Nafis had acknowledged time and time again that she could never have achieved the things she had without the support of her father. When she married, she chose a man who likewise respected her ambitions to have a career and contributed his encouragement.

After her retirement Nafis still traveled around the globe as the SG's envoy, but not to the extent she had when she worked full-time. She spent more time at home now, and Saturday afternoon would find her and Azhar with their feet up watching football, or baseball, or tennis . . . or even golf. When Azhar's health began to fail, she fussed over him using her medical knowledge as well as her wifely concern.

On May 6, 2004, the couple celebrated their golden wedding anniversary at a party in New York City. It was arranged by daughter Ambereen and son Omar, who gave a speech about the gift of continuity his parents had given the children:

Stability and loyalty are themes that stand out with Mummy and Dad. They have lived in the same address for thirty years, worked at the same job for thirty-five years and have kept close friendships lasting a lifetime. They are so loyal that they even drove their green Mercedes for over fifteen years.

With Nafis and Azhar it's never about wanting something that they DO NOT have. It's always about enjoying and celebrating what they DO HAVE. I guess that helps explain how they have reached this incredible point in their lives today.

There were seventy loved ones present, including, as Omar noted, the many friends the Sadiks had known for thirty or forty years. At one point in the evening their grandson, Ali, who was normally reserved, stood up to give a tribute. "Well, everyone is saying how long they've known my grandparents. I've known them the shortest amount of time, obviously, but I think maybe I know them the best. And I hope that they'll be around to celebrate my fiftieth as I'm here to celebrate theirs."

Ali still lived with his grandparents as he prepared to graduate from high school, and he had become incredibly close to his grandfather, as the two spent a great deal of time together while Nafis was on the road; the two men looked after each other. However, his grandmother did accompany Ali when he went to visit universities, planning ahead for the future. In the end he decided he wanted to stay close to home, so he would have to choose a college in the New York metropolitan area.

In 2001 Kofi Annan named Nafis Sadik a United Nations laureate for her lifetime contributions to the organization. In Dr. Sadik's case, because of the work she did, her achievements were known not only to her employer but to the world at large. In a tribute to her, the secretary-general said: "Millions of women and girls around the world—and men, too, I should stress—owe Dr. Sadik a great debt of gratitude for her contributions."

When Nafis came to UNFPA, research done by USAID showed that

10 percent of women in the developing world used contraception. By the time she left it was 60 percent; the numbers had grown from 50 million users to 525 million, or ten times as many. The results of those statistics have changed the history of the planet as well. The average family size in 1970 was six children; in 2000 it was three—or cut in half. Infant mortality in many countries had dropped to one-fifth of what it had been at the time Nafis joined the UN. Maternal mortality for years had remained stubbornly high, in spite of the work the Crusaders had done; among other reasons, the complications of childbirth must be dealt with in a well-equipped hospital setting, and the funding and time to make those changes had not yet materialized. Pregnancy remained a risky business. However, new data show that, globally, maternal mortality rates have decreased 34 percent since 1990. And by 2011, twenty-two nations had passed legislation outlawing female genital mutilation.

When UNFPA first started, in many countries in Africa and Latin America family planning was *illegal*. Critics didn't want to touch the issue for fear of repercussions. But they also hesitated because they felt it would take too long to see any results—a situation most politicians consider professional suicide. The reality was that the dramatic change took place in thirty years, and by the end of that time span every country in the world had a family planning program. Some countries started their plan of action early and took advantage of the resulting smaller families and slower population growth to invest in development. Among them are the economic success stories of the 1980s and 90s. Their experience makes clear the connection between population and ending poverty.

Certainly neither Nafis nor UNFPA made these contributions alone; the Crusaders were assisted in their struggle by men and women who worked for governments around the globe and by thousands of advocacy groups and NGOs ranging in size from international behemoths like Planned Parenthood to tiny grassroots community organizations operating on a shoestring budget. The price tag for this achievement was around $15 billion dollars—or the cost of a couple of months of George Bush's invasion of Iraq.

UNFPA is regarded by Kofi Annan as one of the great success stories of the United Nations. The organization was able to bring respectability to the concept of family planning and meet with decision makers at the highest level of government to persuade them that their agenda was a serious political policy issue.

But while Nafis feels the movement has made tremendous progress, she sees future steps needed to continue this progress. To begin with, she wants to see the global community spend more time empowering females from birth until they're adults, because putting efforts into this development phase would be much more effective than trying to correct the damage afterward. "A lot of harm is done to their psyche already when girls are taught to be subservient, when they're not taught—like boys are—that they should be independent and be able to look after for themselves."

She would also like to see all the women's and development organizations formulate a common strategy of basic goals that must be pursued. At the top of this list would be the education of mothers on how to raise their daughters. "I would tell mothers that they should treat their boys and girls equally, because that's where it starts, I think, mothers treating their boys differently to girls. They should not pull the girls out of school to help them with the housework, and not teach girls that all they have to do is serve—cook, clean, and sew. Boys can also learn to be independent. In fact, myself, I was surprised with my own son, because I remember when he was fourteen I bought him a pair of jeans, and I said, 'Oh, give them to me, I'll take the hem up.' But he said, 'It's okay, I'll do it myself.' I was quite shocked, and I said, 'Do you know how to do that?'"

She feels society should also be doing more to address male behavior and male responsibility by teaching boys the proper way to treat girls. "To change a relationship, you have to address both men and women. In addition, I think you have to identify leaders in all societies, and that has to be done at the local level. A lot more work at community and local levels needs to be done by women's organization and women's groups to add male membership into their organizations. You go to a women's conference, and there are only women addressing women. And everybody agrees, so you are really not changing anything. Instead you really need to branch out to other disciplines, other groups, mainstream your work to development organizations—don't remain separate women's organizations."

The steps to make change are simple: first, speak out and get the issue on the table. "Now how to actually make the change happen is the next step. And to do that, we know you have to engage those who make policies and those who have the power, but we haven't made that transition, that next step. Many women's organizations and women leaders themselves don't want to have men at their meetings. They say, "No, why should we?" To really make change, however, you need men, because mostly they are the ones in positions of power and authority, from the family to all levels." Nafis admits that her mother was also an important influence on her life, but her father was the one with authority over the household.

"I'm struck that there are now men who support the equality and rights of women. And so, therefore, we need to find them and to nurture them, and make them our allies—not alienate them, because sometimes the rhetoric alienates those who are supporting you."

While Nafis was at UNFPA they launched a male participation program to understand male behavior and study how to involve more men in their agenda. "You need to understand how societies think in order to make change," she said.

Even though she's officially the representative for Asia, donning her hat as special envoy on HIV/AIDS, Dr. Sadik also visits Africa on occasion, where the data show approximately 50 percent of all new HIV cases are in young people, between the ages of fifteen to twenty-four, but many younger than that. "The girls are liable in some countries to have a rate of infection two or three times higher than boys, their cohorts, which means that girls are not getting infected from their peers, boys in the same age group. Rather they're being infected by older men. So, this means sexual violence or rape; however it's happening, it's really on the increase. One of the myths going around in Africa is that if a man who's infected with HIV or other sexually transmitted diseases, if he has sexual relations with a virgin girl, he'll be cured."

She has encouraged the secretary-general that as an African man he should speak up about male behavior. "Kofi is, in fact, very conscious of this issue, and he is quite courageous. He did include in a speech in Addis Ababa that men have to take responsibility for their own behavior and they shouldn't think of their power and status only in the way they treat or mistreat women. But I think more African leaders have to speak out about it, because the behavior at the top is emulated by people below. At the local levels, what tribal leaders and religious leaders do has an influence on the behavior and attitude of many other people."

The Sadiks had long discussed returning to live in their homeland. They bought a plot of land in Karachi, and in 1997 Azhar hired an architect to design a new house for them; he had intended to start construction the next year, but as they saw the political situation in the country continue to deteriorate, they held off. Azhar said, "I was very strong in my mind some years ago to return, but gradually a couple of things have happened. One is that I am so angry with the mullahs, the extreme right-wing conservatives in Pakistan—so angry—that is one thing that really disturbs me. The second reason we decided against going back is that all my children are here.

"But that's not to say that I don't miss home. My daughters and Nafis often say that if you miss it so much, why don't you just go there for a holiday? I used to go, but I have not been very well of late . . . it's difficult."

In the past, with all her UN commitments, Nafis could only squeeze in short visits to Pakistan, and she had looked forward to the time when they could go for an extended period, maybe even rent a house in Karachi, and spend some time with her family. But now with Azhar ailing she would have to make the trip alone; she'd stay for a couple of weeks, usually in December when the weather was cooler. Chicky laughed and rolled her eyes at the prelude to her sister's visit. "Before she even comes, people are calling me and taking dates for her—dinner, lunch, tea. I say, no, no I'm keeping one day free so we can relax. And when she comes, they persist, and she gives away the day. I say to her, 'Why do you do it?' Nafis just enjoys meeting people, that's all."

Her old friend Akhtar Isphani, who still lives in Karachi, has known Nafis since 1956. "When she became—what was it?—deputy secretary-general, we started calling her General Sadik. Funny thing is, she has remained noncontroversial in every single changing government, because I think people have recognized that she is one of the biggest patriots that this benighted country has ever had. This is where she came from, this is what gave her the opportunity, and therefore, she will never run it down. Nafis has a great dislike of Pakistanis working in the States who run down their country."

What some of her fellow countrymen deem even more remarkable is that the diplomat is so well respected in India, a nation noted for not having the best relations with Pakistan. But then, after all, she lived in India for the first eighteen years of her life. Today the High Commissioner's home in Delhi, where the young Nafis was sequestered during Partitioning and delivered her first baby, is still the location of the Pakistani embassy, but now the walls of the estate are topped by razor wire and fronted by sandbags stacked several layers deep. Today she occasionally passes through security, returning on official business.

After fifty years Nafis returned to visit Loretto College, the convent she'd attended in Calcutta, the school where the sisters had brought in special science teachers to prepare the girl for her future in medicine. She was surprised to find that all the teachers today were lay people; there were no nuns in their black habits as she remembered from childhood. "There was only one nun left, and she's really old and lives in a room upstairs."

The Indian government had a special surprise for Dr. Sadik, however. They had located her ancestral family estate, the whitewashed brick structure with the broad, shady veranda rimming the upper story, the place where Nafis's baby picture had hung on the door of Mohammed Abdulla 's study. When the officials escorted her back to Jaunpaur, it was a nostalgic visit. "You know, I had this vision of our grandfather's home as having this huge entrance area in the courtyard, and my recollections were always that he had his arms outstretched for me to run to him. Of course, when I went there it's much smaller than I remembered," she laughs. "But this was where my mother used to come back to have her deliveries, at my grandparent's home. Actually, I was born there . . . in that house."

EPILOGUE

In 2011 Nafis lost her husband of fifty-seven years when Azhar passed away. At eighty-two, she continues to circle the globe as UN Secretary-General Ban Ki-Moon's special envoy on HIV/AIDS for Asia, and she remains a champion of choice.

ACKNOWLEDGMENTS

Many midwives helped to deliver this book into being. First off, I'd like to express my gratitude to Nafis Sadik for making herself available for countless hours of interviews and follow-up questions and for connecting me with her friends, colleagues, and family; I would like to offer special thanks to Nighat Qureshi for her hospitality in welcoming me to Karachi. Likewise, my gratitude extends to everyone in this book who took the time to meet with me; these were minutes sacrificed from hectic lives, stolen during airport layovers, between meetings, after school, and while awaiting surgery. The conversations were conducted in hospital, hotel, and living rooms, offices, pubs, conference halls, lobbies, coffee shops, churchyards, and thatched huts. The generosity I encountered around the globe, in a post–September 11 era of paranoia, went a long way toward healing my worldview. And thank you, Charu Mitra, for the loan.

Without the assistance of the United Nations staff to provide information, arrange meetings, help me find sources, and navigate the minefield of security, this project would have been impossible. At the top of this list is Stirling Scruggs, who handled my endless requests with his droll wit and southern charm. Also I would like to single out Abubakar Dungus and Sheila Murdock at UNFPA who with good cheer fielded infinite emails. (I shudder to think how I would have managed the logistics of this endeavor in a time before the Internet).

My appreciation goes to a host of professional colleagues who shepherded my writing from laptop to bookstore: editors Kristen Elias Rowley and Ladette Randolph at the University of Nebraska Press, and my agents Susanna Lea and Mark Kessler—all of whom possessed the patience of saints as the years dragged on. Also a shout out to Kelly Harrison, my meticulous indexer; Veronica Oliva, permissions editor extraordinaire; and publicity guru Karin McKie.

My research assistants worked long hours, their diligence driven merely by a desire to contribute to a project they believed in, and for this I am truly humbled. My eternal thanks go to Lakshmikanthan Anandavalli, who worked with me for years without pay and was no doubt sent to me by my own personal goddess. I'd also like to thank Robin Somers, Shannon Bowman-Sarkisian, Tim Heath, and Nikolina Kulidzan for their skills in unearthing obscure information, ranging from Queen Mary photos to CNN footage to the Sind Club's history.

I relied on some collaborators who provided me with knowledgeable details to aid in description: Pamela Michael on the Taj Mahal; Kelly Stuart on Beethoven's Symphony No. 9; Amy Funge on the birthing process. Others aided me with their expertise as well: Camille Charpentier and Nancy Calef transcribing thousands of pages of interviews, Christina Delfico consulting on recording techniques, Annika Dalen translating in Buenos Aires.

Lastly, a huge hug to the coterie who kept me propped up during the darkest days—and there were many—as I struggled to finish this book: Susan and Don Vollmer, Sabrina Bryant, Katie Sigler, Scott Sublett, Camille and Russ Charpentier, Marty Courson, Elaine and Paul Gormsen, Jacqueline Harmon Butler, Suzanne LaFetra, Maureen Wheeler, Arturo Mendoza, Alison White, Sally and Frank Ashton, Jane Fazzari, Rick Perez, Baris Ozer, Carolyn Blackman, Suzanne Austin, and J.C.

I couldn't have done it without you.

NOTES AND SOURCES

The majority of information included in this biography comes from personal interviews I conducted with sources, and unless otherwise stated, the conversations were recorded between 2001 and 2006.

CHAPTER 1. BIRTH

Interviews conducted with Nafis Shoaib Sadik provide the stories for the siege at the High Commissioner's home in Delhi, Mohammad Shoaib's role in Partitioning, and the family's escape to Bombay. These interviews also contribute to the history of the Shoaib family and are supplemented by a conversation with her brother Kemal Shoaib. The stories of Nafis and Shamsa Riaz-Ahmad as teenagers, and later attending Calcutta Medical College, are based on interviews with them and are supplemented by articles: Qutubuddin Aziz, "Jinnah's Concern for Economy in the Government's Spending" (http://m-a-jinnah.blogspot .ca/), and Kaleem Omar, "The Quaid Was a Colossus" (Worldnews.com).

Background on Partitioning itself comes from an interview with Azhar Sadik and from the texts *India: A History* by John Keay (Atlantic Monthly Press, 2000); *India Britannica* by Geoffrey Moorhouse (Harper & Row, 1983); and *A Concise History of India* by Francis Watson (Scribner, 1975). Other accounts of current events during this period come from interviews with Azhar and articles found in the *London Times*, *Life*, and *Time* from August to October 1947.

Zadia Birru | Addis Ababa, Ethiopia

This vignette is based on interviews conducted with Drs. Catherine Hamlin and Mulu Muleta and anonymous patients at the Fistula Hospital in Addis Ababa, Ethiopia, during October 2005. Facts on fistula were supplied by UNFPA's "Campaign to End Fistula, Report of the Africa Regional Fistula Meeting in 2004," as well as reports from the Hamlin Fistula Relief and Aid Fund and the Population Reference Bureau.

CHAPTER 2. WELCOMING THE GIRLS

The history of the Shoaib family came from interviews with four of the siblings, Nafis, Nighat (Chicky), Kemal, and Hassan, and with their childhood friends Hashmat Shahabuddin Husain, Shamsa Riaz-Ahmad, and Iran Rahim. Information on the influence of birth order on personality development was taken from Robert Needleman's "Firstborns: The Family Pioneers" (Drspock .com). *KiteLife Magazine* supplied background information on kite fighting.

Nargis Ansari | Bhanwargarh, India

An interview with Nargis Ansari provided the basis for her story. Information on the Doosra Dashak program came from interviews with director Charu Mitra and her students, as well as their website. "Girl Child: Overview" (Indian NGOS.com) provided more background on the situation of girls in India.

CHAPTER 3. AZHAR

Azhar Sadik told me his personal history, aided by interviews with Nafis, Nighat Qureshi, and Jamsheed Rahim. Events surrounding Partitioning were reported in the *London Times* from August to October 1947. I also consulted "Lord Mountbatten and the Perils of Adrenalin" in *Eminent Churchillians* by Andrew Roberts (Simon & Schuster, 1995) and the following works: "India and Partition," a lecture by Nandini Gooptu on the University of Oxford website (http://www.sant.ox.ac.uk/events/lecturesarchive/gooptu.html), and "History of Pakistan" by Arsalan Malik (http://www.angelfire.com/al/badela/time line4.html#4). Information on Azhar's regiment came from John Gaylor, *Sons of John Company: Indian and Pakistan Armies, 1903–1991* (Spellmount, 1992).

Chanti Prattipati | Berkeley, United States

The tragic tale of Chanti Prattipati was re-created after her death, based foremost on my interview in June 2009 with the only eyewitness to the case, Marcia Poole, who also provided me with her letter to the Berkeley chief of police dated November 26, 1999. Information on the investigation of Prattipati's death and the subsequent trial of Lakireddy Bali Reddy, his two sons Vijay and Prasad, and Venkateswara Vemireddy came from a variety of sources: a large number of pieces found on the Indian website Rediff.com; articles in the *San Francisco Chronicle, SF Weekly, San Francisco Examiner, Oakland Tribune, Los Angeles Times Magazine, San Jose Mercury News, Berkeley Daily Planet, Daily Californian, Fresno Bee, Washington Post,* and *Telegraph* (Calcutta). One of the teenage journalists who originally broke the story in the *Berkeley High School Jacket,* Megan Greenwell, also corresponded with me about the case. Other sources on the trial included Newsmakingnews; Alliance of South Asians Taking Action; Women Against Sexual Slavery; and court documents for Jane Doe v. Reddy.

Sources on the overall problem of sexual trafficking included Human Rights Tribune, Human Rights Center, Population Issues, UNFPA, and David Batstone writing in *USF Magazine.*

CHAPTER 4. KARACHI

My re-creation of the colorful life in Karachi during Pakistan's early days came from interviews with Nafis and Azhar Sadik and the Shoaib siblings, Nighat, Hassan, and Kemal. Their friends also spoke at length of this era: Hashmat Shahabuddin Husain, Akhtar Isphahani, Shamsa Riaz-Ahmad, Iran and Jamsheed Rahim, and the Haroon sisters, Zeenat Haroon Rashid and Laila Haroon Sarfaraz. Historical background came from publications *Dawn, Chowk, Newsweek, Time, Life, New Yorker, Nation, Times of India, Nazaria-i-Pakistan Trust,* and Wayne Ayres Wilcox's *Pakistan: The Consolidation of a Nation* (Columbia University Press, 1963).

Dora Chemenu | Manhea, Ghana

My profile of Dora Chemenu was based on an interview with her and various Manhean Peer Educators, held at the Manhea Church in October 2005, including Phyllis Kuledo and Charity Gyamera. Information on George Bush's ABC policy for HIV prevention is based on conversations with Andrew Arkutu and Virginia Ofosu-Amaah, director of the Africa Division at UNFPA headquarters.

CHAPTER 5. THE WEDDING

For the chapter on Nafis and Azhar's wedding I interviewed them, as well as their relatives, Nighat Qureshi and Chhaya Rashid. I also consulted Ruth Crane's *The Modern Woman* on WMAL-TV and newspaper stories from 1954 in the *Washington Post, Washington Daily News, Baltimore Sun Magazine,* and *Times of Karachi.*

Angela Karogo | Narok, Kenya

To write Angela's story I met with her and several other students at the Tasaru Girls' Rescue Centre in Narok, located in Kenya's Rift Valley. I also interviewed Agnes Pareiyo on new strategies to end female genital mutilation. Additional information on FGM came from Eve Ensler's VDay website (vday.org); background on the Masai Mara region came from *Kenyalogy.com*.

CHAPTER 6. DOCTOR'S ORDERS

To re-create Nafis and Azhar's life in 1950s Pakistan and the early days of Nafis's medical career, I interviewed the Sadiks, Nafis's siblings Nighat and Kemal, and friends Hashmat Shahabuddin Husain, Akhtar Isphahani, and Shamsa Riaz-Ahmad. Alex Marshall discussed how this era became the foundation for much of his boss's philosophy once she arrived at UNFPA.

Rubima Javed | Tetral, Pakistan

I spoke with numerous sources at the home of lady health worker Asiya Rajput in Tetral: Moizza Aziz, Shafaq Harif, Humaira Mushtap, Pamela Seqeira, Ghulam Shabbir, Abida Yasmin, and, of course, Rubima Javed herself. More background on UNFPA policies in Pakistan was provided by Dr. France Donnay.

CHAPTER 7. MOTHERS

This chapter on motherhood and the Sadiks' move to Canada was based on interviews with Nafis and Azhar, their son Omar, and Nafis's sibling Nighat. Alex Marshall talked about the evolution of Nafis's advocacy. Background information on Kingston came from Frommers.com, "Introduction to Kingston, Ontario," and the city's population in 1958 was provided by city official Jennifer Lindsey.

Natasha Bankov | St. Petersburg, Russia

I rode through the streets of Leninsky Prospect outside St. Petersburg with a team from Humanitarian Action as they picked up prostitutes as part of their HIV-prevention program. The interviews were conducted with anonymous sex workers and anonymous children at the Night Shelter in July 2005. I also spoke with representatives Sacha Tsekhanovich and Nikita Bulanin from Humanitarian Action about the NGO's mission.

CHAPTER 8. FAMILY PLANNING

Chapter 8 outlines the simultaneous rise of Nafis's career in family planning with the planning and sudden expansion of her own family. For my research on the

Sadik home life I talked to Nafis, Azhar, and their children, Wafa Sadik Hasan, Ambereen Sadik Dar, and Omar Sadik. I also interviewed the children's aunts and uncles, Hassan, Salma, and Kemal Shoaib, and Nighat Qureshi as well as family friends Hashmat Shahabuddin Husain, Akhtar Isphahani, Shamsa Riaz-Ahmad, Iran and Jamsheed Rahim, Zeenat Haroon Rashid, and Laila Haroon Sarfaraz. Shaukat Fareed and Shahida Azfar weighed in on the early years of family planning in Pakistan.

Vianca Ivonne Huerta Garcia | Mexico City, Mexico

At the Ayuda y Solidaridad con Los Niños I interviewed several resident girls who were living at the shelter because it was no longer safe for them to stay in their own homes. This vignette centers on Vianca, a brave incest survivor. In addition I spoke with the director, Mariamar Estrada, who provided an overview of the project.

CHAPTER 9. THE UN

The pivotal choice for the Sadiks was their decision that Nafis should accept a position at the United Nations and move the family to New York. To understand all the factors involved, including the political climate in Pakistan, I talked to Nafis, Azhar, their children, Wafa, Ambereen, and Omar, as well as Kemal Shoaib and their long-time friends Akhtar Isphahani, Iran and Jamsheed Rahim, and the Haroon sisters, Zeenat and Laila. For information on the creation of UNFPA and its early years, I turned to Alex Marshall, Shahida Azfar, and Shaukat Fareed. Other sources that provided background on this topic were the Rafael M. Salas Memorial Lecture and Steven Schindler's "Curbing Global Population Growth: Rockefeller's Population Council" found in *Casebook for The Foundation: A Great American Secret* (PublicAffairs, 2007). Details on the setting at Sofia University came from the university's website.

Ermelinda da Silva Ximenes | Tibar, East Timor

This portrait of midwives on motorbikes and their clients came from visiting East Timor, where I met with Ermelinda da Silva Ximenes and her family, the midwife Ofelia Soares Madeira, and UNFPA representative Cecilia da Silva. "Midwives Get Motorcycles to Save Mothers' Lives in Timor-Leste" from UNFPA, 2003 gave me more information on the program. Other documents provided additional material on the region: Tony Wheeler's *East Timor* (Lonely Planet, 2004) and Gordon L. Rottman's *World War II Pacific Island Guide: A Geo-Military Study* (Greenwood, 2002).

To understand the family planning movement in the 1980s and Nafis's rise to become the first female to head a United Nations agency required conversations with numerous colleagues: Shahida Azfar, France Donnay, Shaukat Fareed, Werner Fornos, Roushdi El Heneidi, Imelda Henken, Alex Marshall, Allan Rosenfield, Jurgen Sackowski, Stirling Scruggs, Jill Sheffield, Mari Simonen, Jyothi Singh, and Stafford Mousky. I also consulted Mousky's "UNFPA's Role in the Population Field" in *An Agenda for People: The UNFPA through Three Decades* (New York University Press, 2002). Other helpful policy documents included "USAID's Family Planning Guiding Principles and U.S. Legislative and Policy Requirements" found on the USAID website. To understand the rising fear of overpopulation I turned to Paul Ehrlich's *The Population Bomb* (Sierra Club–Ballantine Books, 1970).

I spoke with Nafis, Azhar, their children, and friends on the topic of the Sadiks' bi-continental marriage to see how the family coped with this situation.

Juliana Di Tullio | Buenos Aires, Argentina

The portrait of foreign relations ambassador Juliana Di Tullio grew out of a meeting at her office in Buenos Aires in November 2005. Other information on the Piqueteros movement, on Argentine feminismo, and on the role of women in national politics came from interviews with Cecilia Merchan and Estela Diaz.

CHAPTER 11. THE VATICAN

As we begin the run-up to the International Conference on Population and Development, the ongoing conflict between UNFPA and the Vatican takes center stage. My research on this topic led me to question participants Boutros Boutros-Ghali, Nicolaas Biegman, Abubukar Dungus, Shaukat Fareed, Werner Fornos, Adrienne Germain, Roushdi El Heneidi, Alfonzo Lopez Juarez, Alex Marshall, Federico Mayor, Stafford Mousky, Mary Robinson, Jurgen Sackowski, Stirling Scruggs, Jill Sheffield, and Richard Snyder, as well as Nafis.

To understand Pope John Paul II, Carl Bernstein and Marco Politi's biography *His Holiness: John Paul II and the Hidden History of Our Time* (Doubleday, 1996) proved an invaluable resource. Also, I referred to the PBS documentary from *Frontline*, "John Paul II: The Millennial Pope" and *Rome and the Vatican* (Ats Italia Editrice srl, 1998). I would like to note here that the Vatican refused all requests for interviews, so any viewpoints from them are taken from press coverage and official documents they have posted on the Holy See's website, e.g., "Letter of His Holiness John Paul II to the Secretary General of the International Conference on Population and Development." John Paul's conversation with Nafis is based on her recollection and accounts in *His Holiness*.

In 1994 the media played a major role in covering the dispute between the Vatican, UNFPA, and the Clinton administration; some of the sources to which I referred for coverage are the *New York Times*, *Montreal Gazette*, *New Orleans Times-Picayune*, *Buffalo News*, *Guardian* (London), and CNN.

Portions on oral contraceptives came from "The Pill," part of the PBS series *American Experience*.

Teresa Lanza | La Paz, Bolivia

To write the story of Teresa Lanza, an advocate for Catholics for the Right to Decide, I interviewed Lanza and Bertha Pooley in La Paz.

CHAPTER 12. CAIRO

The Cairo conference provides the climax to Nafis's career and therefore to the book. To write this complicated chapter I included information from all the sources listed in chapter 11. In addition I interviewed Gro Harlem Brundtland, Lady Lynda Chalker, Carolyn Maloney, Nils Daulaire, Dianne Dillon-Ridgley, France Donnay, Ishrat Husain, Mona Khalifa, Bertha Pooley, Nighat Qureshi, Fred Sai, Steve Sinding, Mari Simonen, Jyothi Singh, Ted Turner, and Tim Wirth. To obtain more background on female genital mutilation in Egypt, I talked to anonymous young women about their experience with FGM.

The statement from Joaquín Navarro-Valls that ICPD provided "the toughest days" of his career came from an interview with Gregory Burke in the September 2001 edition of *Ulisse* titled "The Pope's Voice." Other quotes are taken from September 1994 conference coverage from the *New York Times*, *New Yorker*, *New York Newsday*, *Los Angeles Times*, *Washington Post*, *Cleveland Plain Dealer*, *Wall Street Journal*, *Montreal Gazette*, *Houston Chronicle*, and *Christian Science Monitor*.

"Bella Abzug (1920–1988)" by Blanche Wiesen Cook (Jewish Virtual Library, http://www.jewishvirtuallibrary.org/jsource/biography/abzug.html) provided biographical details on Abzug. *The Vatican* by Peter Hebblethwaite (Vendome Press, 1980) gave details on the workings of this institution. *Opus Dei: The Truth behind the Myth* by Maggy Whitehouse (Hermes House, 2006) discussed the organization's practices, as did *Time* magazine (April 16, 2006).

More background reading on issues came from *Healing the Planet* by Paul and Anne Ehrlich (Addison-Wesley, 1991); "Pondering the Population Riddle,"

Rotarian, April 1994; *Family Planning in the Legacy of Islam* by Abdel Rahim Omran (Routledge, 1992); and *Creating a New Consensus on Population: The Politics of Reproductive Health, Reproductive Rights, and Women's Empowerment* by Jyoti Shankar Singh (Earthscan, 1998). Records on the outcome of ICPD came from United Nations Population Information Network and Nafis's initial address, "Statement of Secretary-General"; the Rafael M. Salas Memorial Lecture; and the Program of Action.

Theories on how females handle stress came from Shelley E. Taylor et al. "Biobehavioral Responses to Stress in Females: Tend-and-Befriend, not Fight-or-Flight" (*Psychological Review* 107, no. 3 [2000]). *Palestinefacts.org* was the source for information on Anwar Sadat. Scenes of ICPD came from the video *Voices from Cairo* (UNFPA, 1995).

Mona Daoud | Cairo, Egypt

In Cairo I interviewed numerous artists about how they use their work for advocacy, including journalist Mona Daoud, radio programmer Amani El-Sayad, and playwright Said El Abasiry.

CHAPTER 13. BEIJING

Information on the outcome of ICPD came from interviews with Nafis, Amani El-Sayad, Roushdi El Heneidi, Alfonso Lopez Juarez, Steve Sinding, Stafford Mousky, Dianne Dillon-Ridgley, Carolyn Maloney, Mona Halifax, Alex Marshall, and Stirling Scruggs. I relied heavily on Jyoti Singh's *Creating a New Consensus on Population: The Politics of Reproductive Health, Reproductive Rights, and Women's Empowerment* (Earthscan, 1998) to understand the Program of Action. Other data came from NGLS Roundup (United Nations Non-Governmental Liaison Service) and the FGM Prevalence Profile.

To research the Beijing Women's Conference I again spoke with Nafis, Stirling Scruggs, Catherine Bertini, Abubukar Dungus, Richard Snyder, and Jill Sheffield; in Beijing I interviewed Huang Baoshan, Siri Tellier, and Joel Rehnstrom. I turned to 1995 media coverage of the conference to find reactions, including several articles from the *National Catholic Reporter*, *Christian Science Monitor*, *Earth Times News*, *off our backs*, and Betty Freidan's commentary in *Newsweek*.

Background information on China's one-child policy came from Nafis, Huang Baoshan, Siri Tellier, and Stirling Scruggs, as well as "A Brief History of China's One-Child Policy," by Laura Fitzpatrick, *Time*, July 27, 2009; "Who Controls the Family?" *Washington Post*, August 27, 2005; "A UN Agency May Leave China over Coercive Pop Control" *New York Times*, May 15, 1993.

Other sources: the population of the Vatican came from their website (vaticanstate.va); on the U.S. relations with China, "Waking the Dragon: Why Americans Need to Pay Attention to This Developing Superpower," ABC News; biographical facts on Gertrude Mongella from the website Kituo Chakatiba, Eastern Africa Centre for Constitutional Development.

I quoted Nafis's speech "Why Gender Balance Matters" delivered March 14, 1995, to commemorate International Women's Day. An interview with Thoraya Obaid provided her perspective on Nafis.

Wang Lijuan | Beijing, China

My conversation with Wang Lijuan formed the basis for her vignette. Her first-hand account of the spread of HIV in Henan village was supplemented by newspaper accounts from Xinhua, United Press International, Agence France Presse, *China Daily*, *South China Morning Post* (Hong Kong), and Tom Kellogg writing for the website Human Rights in China (http://www.hrichina.org).

CHAPTER 14. BACK HOME

For the story of Nafis's home life, I interviewed her, Azhar, their children (Wafa, Ambereen, and Omar) and other relatives: Hassan, Salma, Kemal, and Faizan Shoaib; Nighat and Nyla Qureshi. I also spoke at length with long-time friends Goga Mahmoud Saeed, Marina and Shaukat Fareed, Akhtar Isphahani, Zeenat Haroon Rashid, and Laila Haroon Sarfaraz. Colleague Richard Snyder described the Sadiks' sports fanaticism. I quote the fiftieth wedding anniversary speech delivered by Omar Sadik.

The introductory portion on the origins of the birth control pill came from a University of Southern California website, The Birth of the Pill (http://www-scf.usc.edu/~nicoleg/history.htm).

Sevdie Ahmeti | Pristina, Kosovo

The tale of Sevdie Ahmeti originated from interviews with her and her colleagues at the Center for Protection of Women and Children in Pristina and from visiting the sites mentioned. The information on the harvesting of infants' organs came from a conversation with Rachel Hand.

CHAPTER 15. ON THE GROUND

Nafis described to me her visit to Kosovo, as did her colleague Corrie Shanahan, who accompanied her. Stirling Scruggs provided information on the accusations that UNFPA was complicit in the ethnic cleansing plan, and the article "Milosevic and the 'UN Butchers'" came from the Population Research Institute's website (http://pop.org/content/milosevic-and-un-butchers--unfpas-1515). Press coverage added accounts of the war and the Vatican's reaction to distribution of the morning-after pill, mainly from articles in 1999 published in the *Vancouver Sun*, *Toronto Star*, and *Guardian* (London). Statistics came from the UN Refugee Agency, and a timeline of the conflict came from "A Kosovo Chronology" created by PBS.

Accounts of the rising women's presence in senior management within the UN came from interviews with Nafis, Carol Bellamy, and Catherine Bertini. The feud between James Gustave Speth, Nafis Sadik, and Carol Bellamy was outlined in conversations with Nafis, Bellamy, and Shaukat Fareed. The anecdote on Nafis as the Clock Lady was told to me by Federico Mayor, as was the account of Pope John Paul's comments at the UNESCO celebration. Other anecdotes were recounted in conversations by the sources named within the text.

The portion on Nafis's run for WHO president came from interviews with her, Boutros Boutros-Ghali, and Gro Harlem Brundtland.

Jintana Dahkling | Bangkok, Thailand

The vignette of Jintana Dahkling came from my meeting with her at the Planned Parenthood office in Bangkok. Other information on Thailand's HIV-prevention program came from interviews with Nafis and Thai cabinet member Mechai Viravaidya; from an article by Ushani Agalawatta, "UN Fetes Thai AIDS Fight But Group Protests Latest Policy" (September 17, 2003, http://ipsnews.net/news.asp?idnews=20193) and from the website HIV and AIDS in Thailand (http://www.avert.org/thailand-aids-hiv.htm).

CHAPTER 16. ONWARD

To write about Nafis's retirement from the UN and the process to find a successor, I spoke with her, Stafford Mousky, Stirling Scruggs, Alex Marshall, and Thoraya Obaid. Obaid and Andrew Arkutu talked about Nafis's legacy within UNFPA. A video of Nafis's retirement party at the Waldorf Astoria provided scenes and tributes from attendees.

Nafis and Shaukat Fareed told stories of the final meeting with Pope John Paul II at the Vatican. The quotations concerning the Vatican's position on condom use are from Michael Le Page, "Catholic Church Claims Condoms Do Not Stop HIV," *New Scientist*, October 11, 2003. Nafis's reply is from the Rafael M. Salas Lecture.

I discussed Nafis's role as special envoy on HIV/AIDS for Asia with Peter Piot and Joel Rehnstrom. Other information on successful projects in China came from an article by Bates Gill and Song Gang, "HIV/AIDS in Xinjiang: A Growing Regional Challenge," *China and Eurasia Forum Quarterly* 4, no. 3 (2006).

The description of Nafis's post-retirement work came from Alex Marshall and Stirling Scruggs. Scruggs's response to Bush's decision to defund UNFPA was found in "Bush Refuses to Release Health Funds to U.N." from *Nation's Health*, September 2002. Additional facts on Bush's policies came from the International Women's Health Coalition and USAID websites and the *New York Times* article by Diana Jean Schemo, "Surgeon General Calls for Sex Education beyond Abstinence Courses," June 29, 2001. Quotes from the letter sent by six GOP congressional representatives to the government of Uruguay came from a copy of the letter itself. More information on this topic came from the website LifeNews.com.

Commentary on the aftermath of ICPD at its fifteen-year anniversary and its attendant budget crisis was based on information taken from the websites of USAID and the Guttmacher Institute; in addition I consulted a report presented by the Commission on Population and Development from the UN Economic and Social Council, "World population monitoring, focusing on the contribution of the Programme of Action of the International Conference on Population and Development to the internationally agreed development goals, including the Millennium Development Goals," March 30, 2009. The quote on UNFPA donors as of 2003 came from Thoraya Obaid. I interviewed Ted Turner to garner his views on Nafis and women in politics.

Nafis and Azhar discussed their lives after Nafis's retirement, and their son Omar contributed to the discussion of his parents' anniversary celebration and their legacy to family and friends. I describe Nafis's induction as a UN laureate, which I attended; the stats on how the world has changed during her time at the agency came from the UN. The cost of the Iraq War was listed in an article by John W. Schoen, "How Much Is the War in Iraq Costing Us?" from MSNBC, October 22, 2006. And the quote "The price tag for this achievement was around $15 billion dollars" came from Stafford Mousky.

And lastly, the final segment on Nafis and Azhar's life today came from interviews with them, Akhtar Isphahani, and Nighat Qureshi.

INDEX

childbirth (*continued*)
discussions of, 119; and mother-daughter connection, 122; as woman's job, 113

child marriage, 425–26

children: boys valued over girls, 111; raising with servant help, 108

China: amd abortion and gender bias, 354; abortion and Vatican, 352; abortion drop in, 365; AIDS rates in, 446; barefoot doctors in, 360; demographers and, 358; education fairness in, 361; HIV denial in, 376; HIV/AIDS growth in, 377; leaders Nafis worked with, 356; one-child policy of, 354, 364; population and power in, 351; population policies of, 353–55; population reduction in, 351; preference for male offspring in, 354; Program of Action implementation in, 365; rights abuses and Nafis, 346; State Family Planning Commission, 355; U.S. bullying and, 359; UNFPA policy in, 356–66

circumcision, 100. *See also* female genital mutilation

City Hospital (Johns Hopkins and University of Maryland), 88

Clarke, Arthur C., 228

Clavijo, Hernando, 324

cleaning: Sadiks learning how, 186

Clinton, Bill: calling Nafis, 271; and funding UNFPA, 364; Mexico City Gag Rule and, 310; and peacekeepers in Kosovo, 418; and Planned Parenthood funding, 310; Pope John Paul II disagreements and, 287; repeal of Mexico City Gag Rule by, 271

Clinton, Hillary: on rape as war instrument, 418; Women's Conference address, 367

Clock Lady sobriquet, 426

clothing: given by father, 94; Nafis complimenting men on, 190; wed-ding dress embroidery, 95; worn in remote villages, 155

CNN documentary on female genital mutilation, 328

communism: equality and, 360; Partition and, 62

complexion: light skin preference, 124

condoms: burning of by Catholics in Kenya, 443; demonstration by Nafis, 113; demonstrations of, 378; male reluctance to use, 215

Congo, Ernest Kombo, 265

contraception: army hospital and, 112; Catholics and, 290; condom demonstration by Nafis, 113; contractual agreement to use, 113; demonstrations of condoms in China, 378; development of birth control pill, 379; morning-after pill used in Kosovo, 419; Nafis's defense of, 308; population growth and access to, 321; unmet need for, 317. *See also* family planning

Convent of Jesus and Mary school, 144

courting of Nafis and Azhar, 73, 90

Creative Hands (Argentine NGO), 247

cricket: Azhar as team captain, 42

Crowded House, 228

Cuba: family planning success, 210

Dahkling, Jintana, 431–36

Daily Express: wedding coverage, 94

Daoud, Mona, 339–45

da Silva, Cecilia, 196

dating, Nafis and Azhar, 76

Daulaire, Nils, 305

Day of Five Billion (movie), 228

death threats on Nafis, 288

de Cuéllar, Javier Pérez, 225; promoting Nafis to head UNFPA, 420

delivery. *See* births

Del Sol, Christian, 427

desserts, Nafis's love of, 64

Gordon, Evelyn Peyton: wedding coverage, 97
Gore, Al: environment and population, 271; ICPD security and, 296; ICPD speech, 302; Vatican attacks on, 287
GPO-VIR S30, antiviral drug, 433
Grand Trunk Road, 104
Greenwell, Megan: on Prattipati death, 57
growth rate formulas, 210
Gyamera, Charity, 81

hair shearing, 22
hajib: described, 119
Hamlin, Catherine and Reginald, 18; surgery rates, 19
Hand, Rachel, 410
Haroon, Lady Nusrat Abdulla, 63
Haroon, Sir Abdullah, 63
Haroon Rashid, Zeenat, 146; friendship length with Nafis, 236; *Life* magazine photo, 63; on Mehreen Sadik's rebellion, 398; on Nafis's nature, 190; on Pakistan and Islamic theocracy, 171
Haroon Sharfaraz, Laila, 63, 146
Hauser, Phil, 168
heart bypass surgery, 217–19; walking and retail therapy after, 218
heart disease (Nafis), 372
Helm's Amendment, 205
Henken, Imelda: shopping with Nafis, 241
henna wedding ritual, 95
heroin addicts, Russian, 133
high school examinations: Nafis and top scores, 9
Hindu-Muslim tensions, 43
Hindus: conch salute to dawn, 3; exodus during Partition, 44; Harish eating meat, 130
HIV: Chinese denial over, 376; education, 78; GPO-VIR S30, antiviral

drug, 433; prostitution and murder, 433; rates in Russia, 135–36; rates in Uganda, 79; sexual abuse and, 79
homebuying in Tarrytown, 206–7
Honda motorbikes for midwives, 194
honeymoon, 97
honorary degrees joke, 221
horseback riding to hospital, 110
house fire in Queens, 182–84
housekeeper Rolene, 128
Houston Chronicle ICPD coverage, 307
Humanae Vitae (On Human Life), 262
Humanitarian Action, 133
Human Rights Watch: Kosovo, 417
human trafficking: in Berkeley, California, 56; Lakireddy Bali Reddy and, 58; poverty and migration, 59; UN Population fund estimates of, 59
Husain, Captain Noor, 74
husbands: sex and wives' health, 112; and pregnancy care of wives, 140
Hussein, bin Talal (King of Jordan), 427

Icky. *See* Shoaib, Iqbal
ICPD Cairo: abortion discussion at, 302; attire at, 300; body guards for Nafis at, 298; budget proposed, 348; Cheops Auditorium described, 299; contraception needs and population goals of, 318; death threats against homosexuals at, 297; death threats on dignitaries at, 298; family planning and, 320; feminist influence of, 313; funding, 334; Gro Brundtland speech, 301; Hosni Mubarak and security at, 295; media coverage of, 330; Nafis's attire at, 301; Nafis's nervousness at, 299; NGO alliances, 307; NGO Forum at, 299; note passing, 316; opening day dignitaries, 299; security at, 296; speeches at, 300–303; standing ovation for Nafis, 338;

income during Partition, 62; India, civil war (1947), 1; literacy rates, 62; population growth in twentieth century, 303; President (first), Mohammad Ali Jinnah, 10; protocol for Nafis in, 388; public health plans for, 153; social expectations for women, 115; Sunday workday, 171; truck art, 117; upper classes leaving, 171

Pakistani army: headquarters in Rawalpindi, 104; pay as civilian doctor for, 107

The Pakistani Fund, 238

Pakistani High Commissioner, home as refuge, 1

Pakistani Ministry of Health, reproductive health program, 118

Pakistan Military Academy: Azhar as instructor for, 108

Panyarachun, Anand, 435

Pareyio, Agnes, 101

Partition: army commissions and, 50; Communism threat during, 61; deadline for exodus, 50; deaths during, 13; Delhi, violence in, 1; effect on marriage proposals, 83; exodus because of, 44; Karachi, 60; massacres during, 44; military assets during, 42; Shoaib family, 60; socializing and, 65; train of corpses, 44

Patati, Laxmi, kidnapping attempt on, 54

Pathfinder International for reproductive health, 79

peer educators, 78

Peng, Li, 356

Peron, Eva: as symbol in Argentina, 245

persistence: lesson on (contraceptives), 112

Petri, Lina, 419

Peyoun, Peng, 356, 372

Philippines: birth control in, 262; demonstrations against Program of Action, 297

physical abuse: stabbing of American woman, 89; of young girls and marriage, 102

physiology work (in Canada), 129

Pile, Barbara, 329

Pindi. *See* Rawalpindi

Ping, Deng Xiao, 356

Piot, Peter, 445

plagiarism of medical school exam, 11

Planned Parenthood: Bill Clinton funding for IPPF, 310; Dr. Fred Sai, 309; international funding slashed by Reagan, 220; Prescott Bush as a founder of, 172; Yugoslavia, 200

Planning Commission of Pakistan, 149; job as deputy chief of health, 150

Politi, Marco: coverage of pope and Nafis, 274–75

Pontifical Academy of Sciences, 287

Poole, Marcia: and Berkeley kidnapping rescue, 53

Pope John Paul II, 251, 275–79; Bill Clinton disagreements and, 287; blaming women for male violence, 277; described before becoming pope, 286; Galileo pardon, 265; infallibility of and control of sex lives, 261; against liberation theology, 259; Nafis dressing for, 250; Nafis meeting, 442; Parkinson's symptoms, 275; refusal to lift ban on birth control, 256; Ronald Reagan and communist Poland, 259; traits in common with Nafis, 256; war against Nafis, 285; warnings of moral decline, 289

population, global estimations of, 321

The Population Bomb, 201, 451

Population Clock, 426

Population Conference: appointment as lead for Cairo (1994), 254; death threats to participants, 288; NGOs as muckrakers at, 273; Program of Action wording and Holy See

cident, 54; and human trafficking crimes, 58; and molestation of Indian girls, 55; sex slaves of, 55

Red Fort, 3

Rehnstrom, Joel, 446

Religious Right political strategy, 266

reproductive health: ABC plan, 79; as term for family planning, 219; definition in Program of Action, 324; vs. family planning term, 273

Republicans' views on abortion, 449

retirement from UNFPA, 438; UN mandatory age ignored, 420

Riaz-Ahmed, Shamsa, 9; cadavers and, 11; Karachi group, 64

right-to-life groups, 308

rituals: questioning of, 41

The Robe (play), 32

Robinson, Mary, 420

Rockefeller, John D.: hotel stay in Pakistan, 170; Population Council funding, 169

Rolene (housekeeper), 128

Rosenfeld, Dr. Isadore, 217; meeting, 89

Rotary Club, 307

Roving Pack of Debutantes, 65

Rowen, Hobart, 335

Russia, HIV rates, 135–36

Sackowski, Jurgen, 226, 230, 426; Nafis's negotiation skills, 260

Sadat, Anwar, 295

Sadik family: apartment fire in Queens, 182–84; Asghar's second marriage, 124; Azhar's half-siblings, 124; Azhar's young siblings, 143; baseball and, 384; boarding school, 49; boat trip to Washington DC, 84; children as exotic in America, 184; children on move to New York, 180; daughters and boyfriend troubles, 160; divorce (Azhar's parents), 48; Doreen (Azhar's mother), 48; education of,

48; family life in the United States, 380–90; fiftieth wedding anniversary, 456; finances, 49; financial status, 145; Ilmas (Azhar's sister), 48; living in Canada, 126–31; move back to Rawalpindi (1958), 138; move to Washington DC, 84–92; move to New York, 181; move to Ontario, Canada, 126; Nafis's wedding, 92–98; name ("truthful"), 48; negotiating careers, 178–80; similarities to Shoaib family environment, 144; Younis (Azhar's brother), 48

Sadik, Ambereen, 116, 396–97; on America vs. Pakistan, 191; on Azhar's siblings joining family, 143; birth of, 116; closeness to Ghazala, 144; on dating, 192; on western life and dating, 180

Sadik, Asghar (father-in-law), 47; second marriage, 124

Sadik, Azhar, 42; aide-de-camp for Khwaja Nazimuddin, 68; on American materialism, 392; army commission (early), 50; army promotions, 51; army training, 49; Caltex job in New York, 208; career vs. Nafis's, 179; childhood, 47; civilian life, 143; cooking, 383; courting Nafis, 73; dating Nafis in secret, 76; daughter and sibling of same age, 124; death of, 464; emotional support of Nafis, 382; family home (losing), 46; father's death and raising siblings, 143; food incident as soldier, 45; impressions of America, 92; joining Nafis in America, 207; marriage proposal, 83; meeting Nafis, 68; Prime Minister Liat Ali Khan's assassination and, 52; promotion to major, 108; social graces of, 68; on violence, 46; wedding, 92–98; wedding dress described, 94

Sadik, Doreen: as matchmaker, 141–42

Sinding, Steven (*continued*)
ICPD and feminists, 317; Nafis and
NGOs at ICPD, 312
Singh, Bhupinder, 47
Singh, Jyoti: as ICPD executive coordinator, 309
singing, Nafis at social gatherings, 35, 66
single mothers in Latin America, 278
skin color in Indian culture, 21
Slow Coach. *See* Shoaib, Iqbal
smoking: starting as young doctor, 90
Snyder, Richard, 288; on ICPD and
Benazir Bhutto, 297; on Nafis as person of the world, 370
SOB, on medical records, 88
soldiers: contraceptives and, 113; in a
sari, 111
Soviet Union, opportunity with new
nations, 270
Speidel, J. Joseph, 321
Speth, James "Gus" Gustave, 422
Sri Lanka, 424
sterilization: Chinese policy on, 357;
mentally handicapped people, 362;
program in Pakistan, 158
St. Petersburg: Neva drawbridge, 137
Sun Magazine, wedding coverage, 94
Sweden, declining aid for family planning, 169
swimming: learning at YMCA, 217; Nafis's fear of, 28

Taj Mahal as childbirth commemoration, 43
Tarrytown, 184; buying a home, 206–7;
rental house described, 185
Tasaru Girls' Rescue Center (Kenya),
100, 102
teaching: in Canada, 129; English, 7;
first aid in India, 7
teen parenting: Dora Chemenu (Ghana), 81
teetotaler Nafis, 140

Tellier, Siri, 357; on Nafis and Program
of Action, 365
Teltsch, Kathleen, 198
thawbs (Arab clothing), 300
Times of Karachi, wedding coverage, 94
Tomsic, Vida, 200
Toyber, Eileen, 151; population growth
calculations, 202
train travel: by Shoaib brothers, 106
trousseau, in news media, 93
truck art, 117
Tsekhanovich, Alexander, 135
tuberculosis and pregnancy, 139
Turner, Ted, 307; population documentaries and, 329; support of Nafis, 453;
UN foundation donation, 329
Tymieniecka, Dr. Anna-Teresa: on Karol Wojtyla (Pope John Paul), 286

Uganda: celebration vs. FGM, 426; HIV
rates, 79
uh Haq, Mahbub (economist), 153
UN: Administrative Committee for
Coordination, 201; appointment of
Nafis as first woman to head agency, 225; Chief Executives Board, 201;
Cuba and family planning success,
210; early frustrations with, 176; history in brief, 201; Kofi Annan's restructuring of, 422; lack of female
leaders (1970s), 188; Nafis as first
woman to head UNFPA, 420; protocol for Nafis in Pakistan, 388; Sec.
Gen. U-Thant and trust fund for
family planning, 172; secretary-general Javier Pérez de Cuéllar, 225; Vatican status within, 306; women leaders in, 420
UNDP as worst-run agency at UN, 423
UNFPA: Beijing office bugged, 364;
Catholic church and quiet collaboration with, 263; Catholics and conservative delegates to, 269; China's

one-child policy, 362, 364; Chinese-American tensions and, 364; consequences from George W. Bush's defunding UNFPA, 449; creation of, 173; demographers in China, 358; donor increase as backlash for Bush policies, 452; Doosra Dashak school, 38; in East Timor, 196; former Soviet nations invited to Cairo, 270; gender equity at, 238; George H. W. Bush's reluctance to help, 254; headed by Rafael Salas, 174; Kosovar needs, 412; Mexfam collaboration, 255; mission of, 187; Nafis's assignment in Yugoslavia, 200; Nafis's work style, 226–43; NGOs and the Vatican, 283; Pakistani Fund nickname, 238; policy in China, 356–66; population control, 205; population control recommendations, 211; PrepComs (preparatory committees), 264; PrepComs and NGOs, 270; Program of Action, 269; promotion of Nafis to head, 420; Rafael Salas on Nafis as his replacement, 223; Reagan slashing budget, 220; Reagan's request to leave China, 223; recruitment of Nafis, 177–78; replacements for Nafis, 438; restructuring within UN, 422; salary rank, 178; sexual harassment at, 240; spouses for policy change, 259; staff dedication to Nafis, 228; strategy used at Cairo conference, 253; teamwork of Rafael Salas and Nafis, 216; Thoraya Obaid as head of, 440; U.S. support of under Clinton, 310; Vatican disagreement over ethics, 274; women's choice, 215

UNICEF, 268; caving to Catholic pressures on birth control, 268

Union of Concerned Scientists, 307

United Kingdom: India-Pakistan separation and, 3

United States: bullying China over population policies, 359

UN Population Fund: Fistula Hospital funding, 19; Ronald Reagan's budget cuts to, 220

Urdu: plagiarism of medical school exam in, 11

Uruguay: abortion policy, 450

USAID: funding of Catholic Relief Services, 335; scholarship to John Hopkins University, 149

Varanasi, 5

The Vatican: alliance building at ICPD, 307; allied with Islamic extremists, 286; American response to disinformation campaign, 289; anti-family planning stance and unsafe abortion, 326; asking Egypt to block visa for pro-choice NGOs, 294; Catholics for the Right to Decide, 290; China and abortion policy, 352; common ground with Nafis, 348; condoms and AIDS belief, 274; cultural imperialism claims, 286; delegate Mary Ann Glendon, 353; described, 250–52; and family planning phrases in UNFPA documents, 264; frustrations over abortion, 323; furor over Nafis on papal succession, 272; Holy See in New York, 274; Jane Fonda on, 265; Lockerbie bombing and support for Libya, 307; losing opposition to ICPD, 336; losing position of, 326; morning-after pill and rape victims, 419; NGOs against policies of, 283; photographer, 251; policies against condom use, 282; Pontifical Academy of Sciences, 287; press release after Nafis's visit, 284; refusal to negotiate on family planning, 281; representative at ICPD, 305; Teresa Lanza on policies of, 294; thwarting

The Vatican (*continued*)
definitions of fertility regulation, 325; UN member status in question, 368; work with Islamic leaders against population control, 304

Vemireddy, Venkateswara: Bali Lakireddy Reddy and, 55

Vijay, Atiya: death (early), 125; marriage into Sadik family, 124

violence: madness of, 46

Viravaidya, Mechai, 436

Vitaliy (Russian driver), 134

walima (fruit and flower tossing), 96

war crimes: Serbian soldiers' violence against pregnant women, 412

Warda and the Rabbits, 344

Washington DC press, 93

water: boiling for births, 3

Wazirabad Station (Pakistan): train of corpses, 44

wedding: Afshan (gold dust) in hair, 95; fruit and flower tossing, 96; tradition with mirror, 96

wedding (Nafis and Azhar), 92–98; house described, 92; news media, 94; photos described, 93; preparations for, 92; press coverage of, 93

WEDO, 311

WHO: initial policies against family planning, 175; Nafis's application to lead, 429

Wilson, James, 42

Wirth, Tim, 308; bullet-proof vest, 296; on ICPD and right-wingers, 308; symposium for U.S. position on population, 310; Women's Conference, 367

Wittrin, Heino, 224

Wojtyla, Karol (Pope John Paul II), 251

Wolfson, Elaine, 369

Women's Conference (Beijing): anti-abortion groups early registration, 347; Nafis's speech, 370; secretary-general, 352; women as delegates to, 353

women's health: vs. birthing sons, 115; contraceptives in army hospital, 112; hierarchy of who eats, 114; in war and postwar conditions, 414; NGOs at Population Conference, 273

women's issues: obstetrics and poverty, 72; value only as breeders, 252

Women's National Guard (Pakistan): Zeenat Haroon (member of), 63

women's rights: All Pakistan Women's Association and, 63; women's solution to global issues, 319

Wonder, Stevie, 228

working with men, 237

work-life balance, 234

World Bank, Mohammad Shoaib at, 85

World Conference on Women, 351. *See also* Women's Conference

World Population Conference, Romania, 212

World Population Plan of Action, 212, 219

Ximenes, Ermelinda da Silva, 193–96

Xioping, Deng: population policy of, 354

Yugoslavia: Iqbal Akhund helping Nafis, 199; Nafis's assignment for UN-FPA, 200

Zedong, Mao, on population and production, 353

Zemin, Jiang, 260, 352, 356; Nafis talking to about one-child policy, 363